HONOR THE WARRIOR

THE UNITED STATES MARINE CORPS IN VIETNAM

William L. Myers

Lafayette, Louisiana

Jacket Design by Courtney Fuller
Format by Cathy Ledoux & Andre Andrepont
Printed in the United States of America
by Andrepont Printing, Inc., Opelousas, Louisiana

ISBN: 0-9674365-0-8

Published by Redoubt Press
183 Steiner Road #117
Lafayette, LA 70508-6000
email: redoubt@bellsouth.net

In memory of:
Allen, Robert W. Pfc. 2128153; 10/3/65; 17; Birmingham, Ala.
Anderson, Edward E. Pfc. 2144079; 10/17/66; 20; Opelousas, La.
Currin, Jerry W. LCpl. 2198925; 3/30/67; 21; Sanford, N.C.
Jordan, Allan H. 1stLt. 0100357; 4/6/68; 24; Lynnfield, Mass.
Legeaux, Merlin P. Cpl. 2144012; 10/5/66; 19; New Orleans, La.
Malbrough, Charles R. LCpl. 2053790; 7/19/66; 20; Sunset, La.
Naimo, Joseph P. Pfc. 2391007; 9/14/68; 19; Ft. Lauderdale, Fla.
Prather, Henry L. III Pfc. 2252700; 1/10/68; 20; Shreveport, La.
Romero, Ronald J. Cpl. 2172521; 3/21/68; 22; Youngsville, La.

And to the other 14,682 members of the United States Marine Corps who died in Vietnam.

But they shall not grow old

As we who are left grow old.

Age will not weary them nor the years condemn,

But at the going down of the sun and in the morning,

We will remember them.

Excerpt from *For The Fallen*
by Laurence Binyon

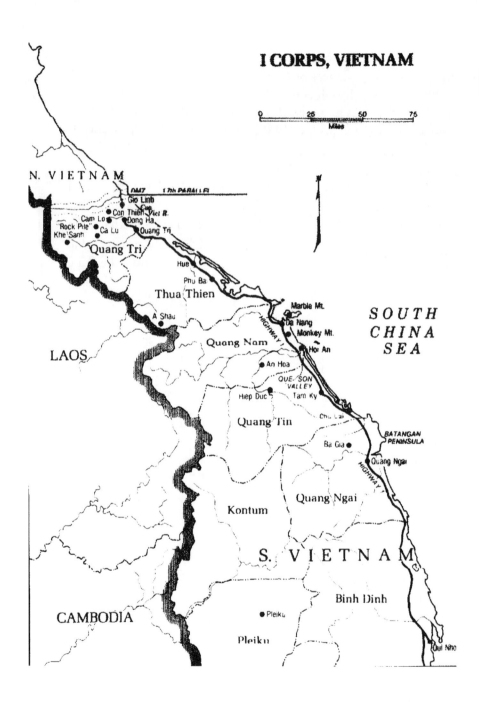

I CORPS, VIETNAM

0   25   50   75
Miles

N. VIETNAM

DMZ   17th PARALLEL

Gio Linh

Con Thien   Viet R.

Cam Lo   Dong Ha

"Rock Pile"   Ca Lu   Quang Tri

Khe Sanh

Quang Tri

Hue

Phu Bai

Thua Thien

A Shau

Marble Mt.

Da Nang

Monkey Mt.

LAOS

Quang Nam

Hoi An

SOUTH CHINA SEA

An Hoa

QUE SON VALLEY

Hiep Duc   Tam Ky

Quang Tin

Chu Lai

BATANGAN PENINSULA

Ba Gia

Quang Ngai

HIGHWAY 1

Kontum

Quang Ngai

S. VIETNAM

Binh Dinh

CAMBODIA

Pleiku

Pleiku

Qui Nhon

PREFACE

I decided to do this book in an attempt to comprehensibly describe the personal experiences of Marines in combat in Vietnam.

This work is largely a first person account. It does not deal with the big picture. I am not concerned about any great military strategy. Leave that to the generals and the powers that be. Let the historians attempt to straighten out the mess that these men made. My intention was to present a coherent and accurate account of the experiences of combat Marines through the eyes of those who experienced it.

Marines who fought in Vietnam made sacrifices and endured hardships as great as any in the history of our country. Their stories are a realistic and accurate account of what it was like to serve there. They fought well ... as well or better than during any other war Marines have participated in. It is so powerful a story, I let them speak for themselves.

These men returned from Vietnam to a largely ungrateful nation. It was not a popular war. Therefore, in this book, I chose not to honor the war but to honor the warrior.

In addition to the participants, many others made this book possible. I would like to express my thanks to Erika Blanchard, Charlene Rose, and Harry R. Smith of the Medals and Awards Branch in Clarendon, Virginia, and to Mrs. V. J. Smith of the Medals Branch after it moved to Quantico.

To the Honorable Chris John, Congressman from Louisiana and to George Neville, an old reconner.

To Bob Aquilina and Ms. Grambling of the Marine Corps Historical Center and to Ellen Guillemette, archivist at the Command Museum MCRD San Diego.

I am grateful to Betty Speyrer for encouraging me to begin this project and for providing early support.

Special thanks to my sister, Grace Myers, for being my editor and to my daughter, Rachel Graham, for help in the typing of this book.

And, to Maureen Kromis, my companion, who painstakingly served as my able research assistant and computer troubleshooter.

All were a tremendous help and have my undying gratitude.

CONTENTS

Preface

APPENDICES

* * * *

Shockwaves riveted across America on April 16, 1965 when *Life* magazine released an issue featuring the horrors of helicopter combat in Vietnam. It consisted of a fourteen page photographic essay by photographer Larry Burrows of Time, Inc. It was entitled *One Ride with Yankee Papa 13.*

The focus was on YP-13 an aircraft assigned to Helicopter Marine Medium Squadron-163. The squadron performed logistical and tactical work in support of the ARVN as part of a multi-squadron rotation called Operation Shufly. The assignment was to take the ARVN forces in I Corps where they had to go and to supply a large network of fortified outposts for our allies. The Squadron had arrived in Danang in February and had been in country almost six weeks.

On March 31, 1965, LtCol. Norm Ewers led HMM-163. He was the only combat veteran in the entire squadron. YP-13 was selected for the essay because of its unlucky number. Capt. Peter Vogel piloted it. The gunner was Pfc. Wayne Hoilen. The crewchief was Cpl. Jim Farley, 21, of Tuscon, Arizona who was spotlighted because of his all-American boy good looks. The photographer, Burrows, was along for the ride.

Ewers was in the lead helicopter with an ARVN intelligence officer. The seventeen planes from HMM-163 were to insert assault troops of the Fifth Vietnamese Airborne Battalion into a landing zone about ten miles from Tam Ky. As they approached the landing zone, things did not look right. Therefore, they switched to another zone about a mile away. From the beginning things did not go well.

On the third trip into this zone, 1stLt. Wendell Eliason in YP-8 was shot dead. Soon after Buck Crowdis in YP-16 took a round through the leg. In YP-13, the windshield and instrument panel were destroyed by gunfire and Vogel suffered a neck wound. YP-3 was shot down. Copilot Jim Magel and Gunner Billie Owens had to run through a hail of gunfire to YP-13. Pilot Dale Eddy was shot in the face. The bullet entered his right cheek and exited his back just below the neck and near the spine. He was temporarily paralyzed.

Farley dashed across the enemy line of fire to the aid of Eddy. Burrows who had many cameras dangling from his neck accompanied him. He climbed up the outside of YP-3 to the cockpit and attempted to pull the pilot out of the window. Unsuccessful in his rescue attempt and thinking that Eddy was dead he returned to YP-13. Maj. Bennie Mann and the crew of YP-2 later rescued Eddy. SSgt. Stan Novotny, Mann's crew chief, climbed the side of the helicopter and pulled Eddy out with one hand. He was aided in the rescue by 1stLt. Don Hamilton, Mann's co-pilot. At the time, they believed that they were recovering a body. Although temporarily paralyzed, Dale Eddy was fully conscious during the entire rescue.

The crew chief on Eddy's aircraft, Sgt. Cecil Garner, was rescued later after he was found in the grass conducting his own private war with the M-60 machine gun he removed from YP-3. He had been wounded in both legs. Magel and Owens were wounded in their dash to YP-13. Magel would die of his wounds on the flight back to Danang. Marine and Army casualties that day included two dead and seventeen wounded.

Upon there return to Danang, Burrows counted eleven bullet holes in the fuselage of YP-13. It had been the helicopter ride of his life.

If not for the essay in *Life,* this obscure incident would be just another war story. The magazine had an almost religious like following in those days.

The following excerpt is taken from the unpublished war memoir, *Life of Pops,* by John Hax. This memoir was written for his wife and grown daughters. It is reprinted with the permission of John Hax.

"In that minute or two, with his back
to the fire, he risked everything."

—Dale Eddy of Jim Farley
From *The Living and the Dead*
By Paul Hendrickson

1
3165

Our squadron had been in country about six weeks, and we had run many assault troop lifts. Almost always, these punches landed on air. The Viet Cong (VC) appeared to be well informed of every move of the South Viet Namese Army (RVN) and then managed to be long gone before we arrived. On this day Bruce Shirk gave the intelligence brief as usual, and from what he said we suspected that this one would be different. The neighborhood we were entering was most of the reason because it was a VC stronghold of long standing, and both our aircraft and the VNAF's (Viet Namese Air Force) had taken hits there. Just exactly what else was known about our strike zone to cause us to feel differently about that mission I can't remember, but I know that we did even before we climbed into our aircraft. I know, for example, that I didn't bring my camera that day.

I was flying co-pilot to Captain Marvin (Buck) Crowdis, an Okie ex-fighter pilot with a dry wit who could verbally slice you to ribbons in a slow drawl with a big smile on his face. He was a good guy and easy to get along with, but one never quite knew what was happening behind the iron smile. We were to lead one of the four divisions. Roberts was our crewchief, but I have forgotten who was gunner.

It was common on strikes for the co-pilot to carry an automatic weapon in the cockpit, in case someone should jump out of the weeds and start shooting while the gunner was looking elsewhere. The weapon of choice for most was the Armalite AR-15, predecessor to the M-16. I felt it was too bulky to have in the cockpit, so I carried an M-3 .45 cal. submachine gun, known colloquially as a grease gun, instead. I had never fired it on a mission.

If there was anything eventful about the flight to Tam Ky, I don't remember it. We were undoubtedly at 1500 ft. in a column of vees, each four-plane division in a loose cruise formation. What I do remember is the fact that we were all on edge. Buck was nervous about where we were going and it showed.

We landed at Tam Ky at the same place we usually did, a broad lawn surrounding the down-at-the-heels provincial capital, and loaded our troops. We dealt only with the elite regiments in I Corps, the Rangers, Airborne, and the Marines. Taking the standard ARVN infantry unit into an assault was a waste of time, as they would either shoot each other or run away or both. The bunch we had that day was an airborne battalion.

The heliborne assault was a relatively young concept at this time. The fundamental question of whether you landed your troops where the enemy was or where he wasn't hadn't been fully worked out yet. There was no question that today we were landing them where he was. For that reason, the troop commander was anxious to get as many troops in the zone on the first lift as he could. So we stuffed them aboard, trying to remain within our allowable take-off gross weight limit for that day's weather. As we sat there ready to lift, we watched the aircraft in front of us, Eliason/Wilson, struggle to clear the deck in a very obviously overloaded condition. They moved forward, but could not get enough height to clear a fence in front of them. At that point, Eliason moved the stick abruptly right and flew down the fence line a short distance and scratched enough altitude to get airborne by sort of flopping over it to his left side. It was a beautifully executed bit of improvisation that succeeded by a hair's breadth. We followed, not having anywhere near the trouble he had.

It was probably at about this time, or perhaps earlier, that the tactical FM radio frequency we were using for the day came alive with message traffic among the Army attack helicopters which had begun to fire on the landing zone. It was obvious that they had more live targets than they could handle, and that they were taking a lot of hits. One note here: the Marines had no doctrine for armed helicopters at the time, choosing to rely on jet attack aircraft for escort and zone prep. Well, we didn't have any of those at Danang: the only fixed wing aircraft at the base were Air Force and, for what reason I don't know, they seldom flew cover for us. So we relied on the Army, who had an aviation platoon which supported every mission we flew with armed UH-1 Bs. They did a fantastic job, never failing once to put their necks on the line when we needed them. Their call ID was Fang, and any former Fang who wants a free drink some day can look any of us up.

It was not planned that the Fangs do this particular job alone: some Seventh Fleet A-1 s (fixed-wing attack) had been assigned to the mission as well. Had they been there, it would have made a big difference. The one time we actually did get to work with A-1s (months later) we were most impressed, primarily by the amount and variety of ordnance they could hang under their wings. But they couldn't make it that day because they were north of the border retaliating for the VC blowing up our embassy in Saigon the day before. So the Fangs went in alone and found themselves over their heads. Two of their seven gunships were shot down. I ran into a former Fang pilot in the Sikorsky cafeteria about fifteen or twenty years ago (Oh, you were in Danang? When? Why so was I! What unit? etc. etc.), and he claimed that by the time our squadron approached the zone, they had expended all forward firing ammunition. Our guardian was a single undamaged gunship, flying sideways across the center of the zone so that his door gunner could lay suppressive fire. He just couldn't leave us to fly in there without support. As I said, we'll buy the drinks.

But now we're en-route from Tam Ky, and getting an increasingly desperate earful of this on our FM. You don't need to be told that funny things were starting to happen inside our heads and stomachs. Normally, pilot and co-pilot share the flying equally, but this time Buck never let go of the controls. The skipper then led us into the landing zone which, like 90% of our strike objectives, was a very large field with tree lines on at least three sides. I am disappointed to say this, but I remember nothing unusual about that first lift. Other guys in the flight saw the treelines on our right erupting in smoke and muzzle flashes, but I don't remember this. Maybe it's because I was looking out the left window, grease gun at the ready but with nothing to fire at. From radio traffic, I'm sure I knew that lead was flying in all directions, but I couldn't see it. I'm also sure I felt a bit exposed sitting that high off the ground in the middle of an open space in a crossfire (Climb into the cockpit of the one in the Smithsonian if you would like to imagine what that feels like). Our troops, meanwhile, were hopping out the other side of the aircraft and being cut down like wheat. We had VC on both sides of us, and the aircraft at the edges of our formation were evidently taking a lot of hits. Perhaps one reason we didn't is because, as division leader, our aircraft landed at the point of a V and was therefore in the center of the zone.

But our troops were discharged, and we all cleared the zone safely. When we got to the pick-up zone again, however, some aircraft were shot up too badly to continue. There were also wounded crew members, but I can't remember who or what aircraft left the party at this point. I believe Charlie Block was one of them, but I can't be sure. I can clearly remember Dennis McKinnon standing beside his aircraft with the cowling open, but I couldn't tell you today whether it was after the first or second lift.

Now there were fewer aircraft and still many troops to lift, so we again packed in all we could, lifted off, and headed for the LZ once again. I should remember what was going on in my head as we cruised back to that place because Buck was doing the flying, and I had little to do but think. But I don't. I must have been either doing the world's best job of blocking it all out or going quietly crazy, but I can't tell you which. I can tell you that Buck was in a high state of anxiety, giving orders to our gunners to keep VC heads down no matter what. Of course at this point many of the people on the ground were friendlies and it was the time to be extremely careful with suppressive fire, but I can't remember saying anything on that subject at this time.

It would have been hard to make myself heard, actually, because now the radio was alive with calls from the U.S. advisor with the ground troops asking for us to be careful when we landed, because his wounded were lying all over the place. He asked that we pick up some of these wounded after we offloaded our troops. He also asked that we somehow get the rest of his troops into the zone any way we could because he was pinned down and in deep trouble.

So in we went for the second time. This time, I remember being conscious of sitting high in the middle of a war. The wounded troops were staggering toward the aircraft, and the radio traffic among our own people was deafening. When our troops were clear we lifted, and that's when I heard a loud pop and felt something stinging my face. It was Buck who pointed to the hole in the Plexiglas right next to my head and then to my face, which was beginning to bleed. My left eye had been hit by something and was getting very uncomfortable. I should have been flying with my visor down, but never did because it was so full of scratches. I had escaped a bullet in the head by about two inches, but there I was thinking instead of the lecture I had coming to me at the end of the day on what visors were for. Buck saw that my face was bleeding and asked if I could continue. I could. Back we went to the loading zone.

Still fewer aircraft remained, but we could and did get the rest of the troops on board somehow because no one wanted to make a fourth trip. I think I was in good mental shape on the third lift because the thought of going back into that crossfire again was so ridiculous that a kind of fatalism set in. I didn't think we were going to get in and out alive, to be blunt, so I got resigned to it. I guess Buck was too, because he reached over with a big grin and tried to pick a piece of Plexiglas out of my face so he could scratch himself and get in line for a purple heart with me.

At this time, we were leading the whole show for some reason, which I can't remember. I think it was because the skipper's aircraft had picked up so many hits that he was delayed getting out of the loading zone. Anyway, I remember a lively conversation on the FM radio between him and Buck on the issue of where might be a good place to land the third lift, having found two bad places on the first two tries. I dimly remember having suggested a place, but whether that was where we went I can't say.

The sight of that place approaching with us the lead aircraft has to be the loneliest and the most vulnerable I have ever felt, just us in a Plexiglas cage heading for a spot between those smoking treelines. I remember a little thatchroofed house near where we were headed, off to the left. It might have been the landmark we used in identifying the zone. The next thing I remember is being on the ground. The picture in my mind has other aircraft unloading ahead of us, which doesn't compute with our being the lead, so I guess the skipper somehow got his division back into the lead on final approach. Anyway, there we were again, with the ground commander now pleading with us to make our door gunners lift their fire. His voice now sounded strained, as if he were wounded himself. He also again asked that we take wounded out with us. As we were waiting to lift, the aircraft in front of us took off and immediately turned two or three times around in a hover, at least once looking like it was heading directly for us. Finally it straightened, and flew off upwind. That was Eliason being killed and Don Wilson taking the controls. Now, when we lifted, is when my head went into overload. Something made me go slightly wild, I don't know what. Perhaps it was the chaotic jabber on the radio or the hits we were taking or watching Eliason/Wilson almost hit us or the confusion on the ground. Whatever it was, I did the helicopter pilot's version of the guy who stands up in his foxhole and sprays the enemy with his machine gun. I remember lifting in my seat harness and firing the grease gun at something, I think it was that little house. I was in a blind mixture of terror and total rage. What set me off? What had I seen? Who was I trading shots with? I have no idea. All I know is that the next thing I remember is our chopper being off the ground and my thirty round magazine being empty, my finger still squeezing hard on the trigger. That's when I felt the plane lurch up and bank to the left, and heard

Buck saying in a strained voice, "John, I'm hit." I looked to my right, and Buck's hands were off the controls. I got untangled from the grease gun and grabbed for the controls, and now the rage (or whatever) was totally gone and my head was clear. We had been lifting off when Buck was hit, and his motion of raising the collective must have continued without proper wrist motion on the throttle to compensate. The result was a co-lossal overboost (very high manifold pressure and very low RPMs) and I saw numbers on the instruments which were every bit as horrifying as what was going on outside. If that weren't enough, the same bullet that went through his leg had hit the center console* and knocked out the ASE, or automatic stabilization equipment. The aircraft had become sud-denly unstable, and when I got the controls we were wandering into a climbing left turn. Now the engine was starting to miss, so I lowered the collective, leveled out, added throttle, pointed the nose down (even though we were only a few feet off the ground) to get some airspeed, and started looking for a spot to land. This reaction was in fractions of a second, all from instinct (and training, long hours of it) because there was no time to think. The engine caught, smoothed out, and we roared across the paddy at about ten feet off the ground to get all the airspeed I could before climbing. Somewhere in there I punched in the ASE, and amaz-ingly it came on line. I can clearly remember the elation when it sunk in that I had a whole aircraft under me and we were getting out of there.

The rest of the flight followed, and I think I led the whole formation out of the zone. How does that compute with aircraft being in front of us in the zone? I don't know, but I can't remember following anyone. What about the drama with YP-3 and YP-13? I was aware of none of it, being involved with drama enough of my own at the time.

Now I had the choice of getting Buck to Tam Ky for a quick patch or flying all the way to Danang. I chose the latter because Buck was in pain and bleeding heavily, and I knew once I landed the aircraft it could not take off again: the engine overboost had been that bad. Luckily, the con-figuration of the UH-34D allowed the crew chief to reach up and ban-dage the leg, and I could see that the blood that was still coming out was not in arterial quantities. When I turned for Danang I think, again, the entire flight followed. I didn't baby the engine at that point - it was actu-ally running quite smoothly now - but I did expect it to quit without warning, so I cruised home at about 500 feet higher than I normally would have. My left eye hurt, but I was using it. While we cruised home,

I remember suggesting to Buck that we hire out as one three-eyed, three-legged pilot.

Approaching Danang, I again had a choice to either head for the small landing pad adjacent to our hospital or head for our main landing area. I chose the latter because the tower told me there was an ambulance there, and I didn't want to stack up the entire flight over the hospital pad (formation flight being the ultimate game of follow-the-leader). I passed up the runway, however, and shot a direct approach to our parking area adjacent to the ambulance. This is where I made a bit of a mistake: I landed with a little forward speed, forgetting that the brake pedals were on Buck's side. I had no choice but to force him to apply them or watch us taxi into some parked aircraft. I remember yelling at him until he did, but it was very painful for him, the pain continuing to the point where he was helped from the cockpit. His grimace was caught by a *NY Times* photographer in a picture which someone spotted much later in the *Sunday Times Magazine*.

The next thing I remember is filling out the yellow sheet, the paperwork a pilot must complete at mission completion to guide the crew chief's maintenance actions. Writing in the numbers I had seen on the manifold pressure gage and the tachometer meant simply that the engine could not be repaired or rebuilt, and it had to be scrapped. It was. There it sits today somewhere in engine heaven, wearing a big fat halo because it couldn't read the maintenance manual and didn't know it was supposed to come apart after 56" at 2300 RPM.

It was only when I got back to the compound to visit Buck in a tent hospital that I heard we had two dead. I had brought Buck all the Playboy magazines I could find because I knew he was bound for the Army hospital at Nha Trang, and found him talking to Dick Hendrix. Buck thanked me for getting his butt out of the zone. My eye? That was treated at the dispensary much later in the day, because there were more serious cases (20 wounded) to be tended to first, and I wore a patch for a few days. The last bits of Plexiglas were surgically removed on Okinawa months later. (The scars still amuse my ophthalmologist).

Winston Churchill has said, "There is nothing in life more exhilarating than to have been shot at without effect." I was in that state far into the night, and didn't go to bed until well after midnight despite being totally exhausted. I remember pestering Shirk for a while trying to figure what the day had meant in the larger picture, because by that time we knew that the ARVNs had somehow taken their objective, thanks to the USAF and some cluster bombs. Bruce couldn't help me then, and thirty four years later, I am really no wiser.

It was a tragic day: two men in there mid twenties had lost their chance to marry, have kids, grow old. I think the emotional impact on me was lessened by the fact I was not close to either of them. Try as I might, I had to concentrate very hard to keep their loss from being almost abstract, as it was with the death of Billy Reynolds three days earlier. It is still that way when I touch their names on The Wall. All that pain, and something has kept me from feeling all of it. I don't know if it is something I should be guilty about, or whether it is one more thing I have learned about being human.

But the rest of that day I still feel clearly. Although we never again were involved in anything that deadly, we were on several occasions briefed that we were going to be. The fact that it didn't turn out that way did not stop the same juices from flowing each of those times as I climbed into the cockpit. I cannot describe the feeling, nor can I say that I got less of it as the tour went on. I can say that we learned to cope with it. These mental adjustments held up nicely until the last days of the tour, when the notion that I might actually get home to my wife and kids crept in and upset everything. Others, in this war and in other ones, I think have said the same thing.

I would not have missed it for anything. That's the guilty truth plainly stated. The year 1965 I can remember almost day by day and some days, like March 31, can almost be remembered hour by hour. The years since I left the Marines have been very happy ones with Lizzy and the four girls, but there are some from which I can now remember nothing at all.

*The shot that got Buck hit the console near the top. Half an inch higher and it would have gotten me too. The UH-34D cockpit is not very big. A betting man might give long odds that two shots could go through the cockpit and not wound anyone seriously.

NOTES:
The two Marines killed that day were:
Eliason, Wendell T. 1stLt. 088405; 24; Escalon, California
Magel, James E. 1stLt. 087214; 25; Lemay, Missouri

The Billy Reynolds mentioned in the chapter was killed on 3/28/65: Reynolds, William D. Capt. 072705; 30; Ponca City, Oklahoma

For his actions that day, the Navy Cross was awarded to Maj. Bennie H. Mann, Jr.

The Silver Star was awarded to LtCol. Norman G. Ewers, Cpl. James C. Farley, Jr., Sgt. Cecil A. Garner, 1stLt. Don E. Hamilton, Cpl. Theodore W. Rostad and Capt. Peter J. Vogel.

Other Marines mentioned in this chapter are as follows:
Block, Charles H. Capt. 066065;
Crowdis, Marvin L. Capt. 068036; Oklahoma
Eddy, Dale D. 1stLt. 082011; 27; Columbus, Indiana
Hax, John H. 1stLt. 083360; 27; Waterbury, Connecticut
Hendricks, Dick D. Capt. 078609
Hoilien, Wayne L. Pfc. 2023063; 20; Viroqua, Wisconsin
Novotny, Stanley SSgt. 1424826;
Owen, Billie J. SSgt. 1442242;
Roberts, Donald R. LCpl. 2020763;
Shirk, Walter B. 1stLt. 086474;
Wilson, Donald R. 1stLt. 086993;

The following interview was taken from the video *Vietnams Helicopter Heroes*.

Jim Farley had the following comment about being featured in the Burrow essay:

"What was it about me? Larry said it was the All-American boy thing. I looked young. I looked naive. That was what he was looking for."

Here are his comments about going into the landing zone:

"As soon as we hit the zone, it was just like all hell broke loose. There was fire from everywhere. After a bunch of hollering and screaming and panic on some parts we got the troops out and headed back out of the zone. There was discussion about the zone being far too hot and we shouldn't go back. The Colonel merely said, 'We can't leave those men there to die. They need the other men. They need the full force and we are going to take it in', and that's what we did. We made three trips into that zone and the second and third, that would really pucker you up a bit. You knew exactly what you were running into."

His comments about the death of Jim Magel:

"Lieutenant Magel got hit in the leg just before he got in my plane and started going down. The pilot said 'we better get him' and I said 'Yes Sir!' and out the plane I went. When I reached Lieutenant Magel he was struggling to move. I reached under his arms to lift him up, and we were face to face as I was holding him up. As I turned toward the helicopter from our helicopter, I saw some North Vietnamese at the rear of our aircraft with Lieutenant Magel between me and the North Vietnamese. Larry Burrow's helped me push him up into the helicopter. I thought Lieutenant Magel just had a minor injury but then I looked down and I could see blood coming out of his mouth. At this point, I knew it was a chest wound, and I knew I was in trouble. I tried to locate the wound, but in the process he quit breathing. I am quite sure that he saved my life but lost his in the process."

Farley's comments about the impact of the article on the American people:

"Everyone—stateside—as soon as they saw it—was on the phone, and they were up in arms: 'We are not supposed to be doing this!'   Where as the photographer said, 'Hey people—there are things happening here— that you have never heard about—that the government isn't going to tell you about—things that they don't want you to know about. And here it is in graphic detail."

John Hax had the following comments about Stan Novotny:

The Stan Novotny story is a book in itself. He was tall with a handlebar mustache. Novotny had gotten into the crew chief business late as a staff sergeant, and was, therefore, constantly being instructed and corrected by mechanics far junior. In fact, he had been an object of ridicule until he demonstrated the existence of adrenaline by lifting Dale Eddy (no lightweight) from his seat with one hand and lowering him to Hamilton. The ridicule seems to have ended right about then. God bless him wherever he is—I know Dale agrees.

*   *   *   *

On October 27, 1965 Karl C. Lippard was a nineteen-year-old squad leader with I-3-9 in Quang Nam Province. On this day his unit was making a company sized sweep through the An Trach III area. Many years later he wrote a book about his Vietnam experiences and dedicated it to the United States Marine Squad Leader.

> "For some, walking point was punishment for falling asleep on watch or goofing off on a work detail. At point you were alone. You walked fifteen meters ahead of the rest of the squad. You looked for signs of a booby trap or an ambush. Often you were the one who tripped the booby trap or walked into the barrel of Charlie's rifle before the enemy opened up the ambush. In a 15-second fire fight, the life expectancy of the pointman was 0.8 seconds. Short-timers, men with just a few months left before they were to return home, avoided the point. So point fell to those less experienced or with less time in country. I was lucky. A great teacher showed me the signs to look for. Stones or sticks piled off the trail in a certain way indicated a booby trap. I felt good out in front. I trusted my instincts and I was slow and careful. I'd found several booby traps before and, more important, the others trusted me."

Pfc. Rick Eilert
L-3-26
From *For Self and Country*

Grateful acknowledgement is made to Karl C. Lippard for permission to reprint previously published material. The following excerpt is taken from *The Warriors* © 1983 by Karl C. Lippard by permission of Karl C. Lippard.

2
PROFILE OF A POINT MAN

A point man is one who takes the lead when a platoon or unit of men takes to the field on patrol. The job is dangerous. Usually it is given at random to several men. However, when in real danger, you do need your best man on point. The lives of you and your men depend on it.

The point man is the eyes and ears of all who follow. His job embodies a heavy trust in one's ability. Also, it is a thankless job, one that goes unnoticed to most. To me, he is the extremity of the commander's arm and, as such, his judgment, while on patrol, is vital. Accordingly, he must be trusted in all things. He locates the enemy in advance, covers your rear, sometimes in retreat. When asked, he will hold his position until death. When good, he dies young.

Such was the man, P.F.C. Stumpp. He stepped forward on my patrols as point and led the platoon on theirs. He was trustworthy and loyal to command. Most of all, I guess, he was loyal to me.

I remember one day he looked really down and I approached him on a subject of distraction. As we weren't close friends, I talked to him cheerfully, letting him come out with the problem. He did. It seemed his girlfriend had sent him a "Dear John" letter, found herself a draft dodger or something, and now was in love with someone else. The letter hurt Stumpp badly. Something like this could dull a man's edge and Stumpp was too good a man to lose.

I had the solution. "Just who to hell does she think she is?" I asked Stumpp, pretending to be seriously annoyed as I stomped around. "Just who to hell does she think she's talking to. Not everyone has the honor and privilege to date a Marine. Give me her address and I'll write her a letter right now!!"

Stumpp was noticeably moved and we sat down together and I wrote the finest "Dear Jane" letter ever written. He was killed a few days later.

It was one of those days, and we were on a company size sweep; Stumpp was on point. We had been getting a little H and F fire all morning. Some of that, "I don't give a shit who I hit" stuff. So everyone was a little jumpy. We came to a bamboo fence corner at a T-junction of a trail. We all stopped and were down on one knee, but exposed at the apex of the trail.

I was some 30 yards or so back to the rear near the company commander. I heard a shot come low through the trees and everyone crouched down a little more, all except Stumpp.

I yelled, "Stumpp, get your head down," and motioned him back away from the junction.

"Damn, that was close," he said.

"Get your God damn.. . " when a bullet hit him in the head. A large piece of skull and hair slowly sailed past to my right; he was gone. I removed my T-shirt and went to him. Someone wrapped his head in it and we hand carried his body back with us.

I cannot begin to tell you what this man meant to me, to all of us. On those many patrols you learn what a man is made of. P.F.C. Stumpp was the epitome of a Marine. Possessed of extreme courage and loyalty, he was one of those few men one could truly honor. His name will live on with the Marines who knew him, and his memory on my breath as long as I'm alive to tell it.

PFC Alma J. Stumpp wrote the following letters prior to his death on the 27th of October 1965.

Sept. 20th, 1965
"We are getting ready to move out again, we're going to the river now, where ever that is. There is a lot of action going on there and everybody wants to get in on it.

Would you please send me a few things that I can't buy here?
(1) Shick razor blades (injection)
(2) Shaving cream
(3) A couple of towels and face clothes
(4) Tooth brush and tooth paste
(5) Soap
(6) Foot powder

I could also use some saddle soap for my boots, a couple of tooth brushes and a small one inch paint brush to use to clean my rifle and a small wire brush if you can find one.

I have my pack all made up and ready to go, it is about twice my size but it's on a pack board so it's easy to carry.

When you send me those things put some fudge in too, you can send me candy anytime you want but when you send something send it airmail or it will take 6 to 8 weeks before it gets here.

Oct. 6, 1965:

"I'm fine and OK. We've had a lot of action. The other day they sent a 28 man patrol out of the PLT. They got ambushed and six got killed and as the rest got shot up except for two of them that played dead and got away. We lost our   ?   Commander, and PLT. Sergeant, the first squad leader, plus three other men. In the whole company there was 12 killed and 28 injured. But I got out of it without a scratch.

From what we hear over here the people back in the States are hanging Marines in California and New York and calling us Baby Killers. Well maybe we are baby killers but we have to be to stay alive. The people over here are so small that one that looks about as old as Timmy (our 6 year old nephew) is 14 or 15 years old and in the day he is just a damn kid that comes around looking for chow, by night he gets a rifle and comes back to kill you. If the people really knew how it was and not like they think they would never call us baby killers. It makes you hate anything that don't wear a green uniform. It makes you hate everyone when you see a kid that looks like he is 7 or 8 gun down one of your friends with an automatic rife.

October 27, 1965

"I hope that you are all doing better than I am. I'm alive but that is about the size of it.

Today and yesterday is the first time that I've been dry in a week. It has been raining for a week and I was wet all of the time.

We got fired on from our left flank every night and times they come pretty close. Me and two other men were up in the whole B.S. the other night when a sniper opened up on us. His first round came right between you and the next ones came in about three feet to our right. We could see the muzzle flash so we shot back. I guess that we must have got him because he did not fire again, or we ran him off. Then we got hit badly about half an hour later. About the same thing happens every night and they keep getting closer so maybe one of these night they will hit somebody.

Maybe we could make a best seller war story; but I don't know if many people would believe the truth about the war. It is a lot worse here than some people think it is so they would not believe it.

Tell Mandy (my dog) that she is lucky to even have a garage to sleep in because all I have most of the time is a foxhole and the edge of a rice paddy.

I have not got the package yet but I'm still waiting for it.

Love and see you soon

Alma."

NOTES:

The Marines mentioned in this excerpt were:

Lippard, Karl C LCpl 2024818; D-1-1; 19; Dallas, Texas

Stumpp, Alma J Pfc 2131646; D-1-1; 18; Afton, Wyoming

The ambush that Alma Stumpp writes about in his letter of October 6, 1965 probably occurred on 10/3/65 and resulted in the deaths of the following Marines:

Allen, Robert W. Pfc. 2128153; 17; Birmingham, Alabama

Ammerman, Roscoe SSgt. 583999; 37; Madison, Wisconsin

Bryant, Nelton R. Sgt. 1879467; 26; Tylertown, Mississippi

Ellwood, Eugene L. Cpl. 2061186; 19; Hamilton, Ohio

Fritts, Louie G. Pfc. 2128986; 19; Tacoma, Washington

Fulk, Michael R. Pfc. 2130894; 18; Oakley, Illinois

Hamilton, Paul Jr. Sgt. 1537785; 27; Saginaw, Michigan

Harvey, Larry D. Cpl. 2033936; 21; Oklahoma City, Oklahoma

Lampley, Leon P. Pfc. 2128489; 20; Hamilton, Ohio

Masny, Bernard J. Pfc. 2129582; 19; Chicago, Illinois

Nicholas, Reginald Sgt. 1463968; 29; Auburn, Maine

Simpson, Adam E. Jr. 1stLt. 090238; 26; Port Arthur, Texas

Thomas, James E. Pfc. 2124750; 19; Fort Worth, Texas

*   *   *   *

In September of 1965 a battalion from the Ninth Marines set up a command post on Hill 55 in Quang Nam Province southwest of Da Nang. They began patrolling the sector that surrounded the Hill. This patrolling continued during the following months with a large amount of casualties. Most of these were the result of booby-traps, mines and ambushes.

In the early spring of 1966 while patrolling an area north of Hill 55, a platoon walked into a large ambush and was almost completely annihilated. Two wounded Marines survived the slaughter by pretending to be dead as the enemy searched the bodies for weapons and ammunition. The Marines had established a pattern of repeatedly patrolling over the same ground. The Viet Cong had determined this pattern and prepared a devastating response.

On May 21, 1966 Company A, 1st Battalion, 9th Marines were on a counter guerilla operation in a little village north of Hill 55. This operation went smoothly. Later in the day, they were summoned to the aid of C-1-9, when it became engaged in a massive firefight across the river.

The third Platoon of A-1-9 was to be used as a blocking force and were lifted by helicopter to an assigned point. The rest of the company boarded two tanks and two amphibious tractors and moved to the aid of C-1-9. They proceeded due west to the river. Upon arrival they dismounted and formed a skirmish line with two platoons abreast and proceeded to move in a northerly direction.

A-1-9 immediately encountered a large group of the enemy moving almost leisurely south. This force was obviously out of ammunition and totally unaware of what they were about to encounter. The Marines poured a withering volume of fire into them and killed every Viet Cong soldier. It was a thrilling hard-nosed fight for the Marines in which they assaulted head on into the enemy and killed several in vicious hand-to-hand fighting. It was classic Marine "Hey diddle diddle right up the middle." The VC were slaughtered. During the course of the fight, Company A recovered M1917A4 machine guns lost in the previously described ambush.

As A-1-9 proceeded with their deadly work, they received a call for help from the badly wounded radioman from the third Platoon. The helicopters that were transporting the platoon had landed right in the middle of the Viet Cong regiment engaged with C-1-9. They fired directly into the 3rd Platoon as they tried to exit the helicopters. Six Marines were instantly killed and another 25 were wounded. Included among the wounded was the platoon commander, 2dLt. Simone J. Pace.

When the CO, Capt. Howard A. Christy, arrived only two pockets of men remained unhurt. Eleven were in one bomb crater and five were in another. They all fully expected to be killed. SSgt. Harry P.H. Chang attempted to maneuver the Marines but their machine guns jammed. There was little chance of gaining fire superiority. Additionally, whenever a head was raised above the edge of the hole the enemy who had fire superiority would rake it with fire. Neither group had a radio. With Pace and the radioman wounded all control had been lost. They were in deep trouble from the moment they landed.

Nevertheless, splendid leadership and courage was evident. In the crater that held the five Marines, Cpl. Charles D. Sadler, a machine gunner, took control. Expecting an assault, he ordered each man to count his ammunition and distribute the remaining rounds so that each Marine had an equal amount. He told each man to save one round to kill himself in the event that they were overrun. All would stand at the ready, back to back, and wait for the assault on their hole. They intended to die fighting.

When the helicopters landed all hell broke loose. One of the corpsmen, Shane Morris, ran from one wounded Marine to the next administering first aid. While working on a fifth Marine he was shot through the head. He had willingly sacrificed himself to provide aid to his fellow Marines. Morris was still alive when evacuated but it was assumed that he would die on the way to the hospital.

In the midst of this chaos a helicopter medevac team arrived on the scene. This crew was from VMO-2. Capt. James W. Rider piloted the helicopter. He flew into the bloody field seven times. Several times directly into enemy fire. The helicopter was hit by so many rounds on its first few entries into the zone that it had to be replaced. Just after the arrival of Capt. Christy, Rider and his crew returned for the sixth time and picked up the remaining wounded. They then returned for a seventh and final time to retrieve the bodies of the dead. Christy directed the remainder of his men to remain with their weapons and be prepared to defend against additional attack. He then assisted the corpsman and crew chief with the loading of the bodies onto the aircraft.

The preceding information was taken from an essay that appeared in the April 1994 issue of the *Marine Corps Gazette*. LtCol. Howard A. Christy, USMC (Ret.) wrote it. The title of the essay is *Patrolling Hill 55: Hard Lessons in Retrospect*.

Ernesto Gomez was awarded the Navy Cross for heroism on the morning of January 25, 1968. He was a crew chief on a CH-46 transport helicopter with HMM-262. They were on a medevac mission on Hill 881.

Gomez wrote the following poem about his last flight in Vietnam.

Fly-boy

You've been home now for thirty years,
   you wake you gasp you feel old fears.

It still seems just like yesterday,
   your wife will ask, "are you OK?"

You try to rest the sleep escapes,
   you're tired of seeing the same old tapes.

Your mind still sees those moments past,
   you pray this night will go by fast.

If I could just go back in time,
   I'd save your life or give up mine.

It was just moments of death and fear,
   yet I've relived it thirty years.

Ernesto "Gooie" Gomez

The following information was taken from the paperwork involved in the Silver Star recommendation for Captain James Wesley Rider 077451/ 7335 USMC. It includes the proposed citation and the signed statements of the witnesses to the action. No grammatical or spelling corrections have been made. The statements remain in their original form. It makes interesting reading.

3
JOHNNY RIFLE

The Proposed Citation

On the afternoon of 21 May 1966, while serving with Marine Observation Squadron Two in the vicinity of Da Nang, Republic of Viet Nam, Captain James W. Rider, USMC was the pilot of a medical evacuation mission in response to a request from the Third Platoon of Company "A" First Battalion, Ninth Marines, that was under heavy attack by a determined superior force of Insurgent Communist (Viet Cong) Forces. Upon arrival at the scene of action Captain Rider found that the Marine platoon had suffered heavy casualties and was still under fierce attack by the enemy. Initial radio communication had been established but the radio operator became incoherent as the intensity of the attack increased and he himself was wounded. Despite the fact that he had no assistance from the support unit or information as to the actual situation existing in the landing zone, Captain Rider elected to make an approach to the immediate vicinity of the wounded which he could observe from the air. The zone was under continuous fire from enemy automatic weapons, recoilless rifles, and mortars, as Captain Rider made the first of eight approaches and began his long afternoons task. As the huey touched down in the zone, the enemy fire was, directed at the helicopter. Since the wounded were helpless and their comrades were pinned down by fire Captain Rider skillfully air taxied his helicopter from one position to another amidst a withering hail of fire, while his crewmen left the aircraft to pick up the wounded.

During the first approach, Captain Rider's armored seat was hit by small arms fire and fragments sprayed his arm. Undaunted, Captain Rider completed four trips into this area under seemingly impossible conditions. At this point, he feared that some of the hits made on his aircraft were serious and, being short on fuel, decided to get a replacement aircraft. He was offered a relief crew at home field but decided to return because of his knowledge of the friendly and enemy situation. Captain Rider and his crew completed four more evacuation missions under the same conditions of hostile fire and limited assistance from ground units. Though not required to enter an unsecured zone nor attempt evacuation of casualties without reasonable communications with and assistance from the ground unit Captain Rider elected to do so through compassion for his fellow Marines. This mission covered a period of from three to four hours during which time Captain Rider successfully evacuated twelve wounded Marines and eleven killed in action. These accomplishments, under such conditions, could only serve to lift the morale of all the Marines who witnessed them. Captain Rider's courage, aeronautical skill and complete disregard for his own personal safety were in keeping with the highest traditions of the United States Naval Service.

Statement of Staff Sergeant Harry P. H. Chang, 1268032, USMC

On 21 May 1966 the 3d Platoon, Company A was helilifted to be utilized as a blocking force. When the choppers were preparing to land, we did not receive any rounds. As soon as the chopper landed, we started to receive heavy automatic fire and mortar rounds. The platoon was unable to move more than 20 to 30 meters at the most because of the heavy fire. We started to take casualties in the first minutes after we landed. An evacuation helicopter came in and started to evacuate the wounded. I saw someone jump from the helicopter and start to load the wounded aboard. The enemy fire started to pick up again and the helicopter lifted off the ground and flew away. The helicopter returned within minutes and started to load the wounded. Again, the enemy opened up with automatic fire. The one person who had jumped down to load the wounded aboard was looking all over the area for more casualties. As the helicopter started to take off, he started to run towards the helicopter and just barely made it when the helicopter was several feet off the deck. There was one instance when I had to wave off the medical evacuation helicopter due to heavy automatic fire. The ship flew off and returned in a few minutes and landed. The same person I had seen on most of the med evac's" jumped down again and started to load the KIA's on board. This one particular "med evac" ship made approximately 6 to 8 pickups. The ship didn't just load and take off. It would scoot around just off the ground hunting for Marines who needed help. The pilot showed exceptional skill.

The ship was under enemy fire throughout the evacuation and took many hits. The same marine repeatedly jumped from his helicopter and without regard for his own safety aided over 20 other Marines. I had the opportunity a few days later to meet this man, HM1 Mayton, and the pilot Captain Rider of VMO-2. The courageous acts that Captain Rider and HM1 Mayton did on this day should not go unnoticed.

Statement of Hospitalman First Class J.A.. Mayton 2973461 USN

At about 1415H on 21 May 1966, the med evac was called by "Sparrow Hawk" (I understand this was Major Gillis from Captain Rider's COMCON) that there was a med evac for us. We proceeded to the zone. Orbiting the zone, the ground radio stated that the Viet Cong had them all pinned down with many wounded or dead. They needed evacuation fast. "I probably have just 20 seconds left," the radioman said. Captain Rider upon ascertaining where the zone was made his approach and the escort gunship and Sparrow Hawk gave support. Entering the zone we received very intense fire. I saw several marines on the ground wounded and/or dead. On the first approach Corporal Abshire and I poured out the lead at Viet Cong positions. The first man I saw on the ground was dead, shot thru the head. The fire was so heavy that, after one man jumped aboard, we lifted out and headed for G-4. This man drew me a makeshift map on the stretcher of where the Viet Cong were located. We returned to the zone. On this touch down we took hits in the bird. One hit the armor and I heard the Captain say he was hit. A round also came within inches of Corporal Abshire. This load we picked up two more wounded, Corporal Abshire and myself getting out to retrieve them. The fire from the enemy was intense. We made two more pickups under heavy fire. Corporal Abshire fired the M-79, and knocked out a machine gun while going in. I shot at VC's and can only hope I got them. I really never knew nor do I care to; however, they weren't firing back after I started shooting. Corporal Abshire retrieved one marine who was hit again while Corporal Abshire was running back with him on his shoulders about 20 yards from the helo. I already had one head injury aboard from a trench by a small pond as well as one other guy. We took these to G-4. The next trip we took on more men which cleared the wounded in this particular zone. We made two more pickups for wounded after changing aircraft because of low fuel and battle damage. Corporal Abshire was really hustling to be a greenhorn at this stuff. He had just gotten his flight physical a week or so ago. We picked up five KIA and two WIA on another load, Corporal Abshire and me loading, The next load was for four KIA's at two different touch down spots. In over 900 hours of flying, I have never seen such skill and bravery at flying as Captain Rider and First Lieutenant Drury displayed. Several times, we (Corporal Abshire and myself) probably kept the pilot in hot water but they were there with all they had. The Captain received abrasions on his right shoulder from the right door's shattered armor plate, which saved his life I'm sure. Corporal Ashire had some very narrow escapes with hits close to him. The pilot, co-pilot and, crew chief displayed bravery above and beyond the call of duty in this afternoons work at the, inevitable risk of their lives.

Statement of Captain Howard C. Christy 069514, USMC

While serving as a helicopter aircraft commander with Marine Observation Squadron Two, 1st Marine Aircraft Wing, FMF, in the vicinity of Da. Nang Republic of Vietnam, Captain James W. Rider 0774519 USMC was piloting a medical evacuation helicopter on 21 May 1966. Responding to urgent calls for the medical evacuation of several Marines of Company A, 1st Battalion 9th Marines, he quickly flew to the location of the Third Platoon Company A which, upon being helilifted into a blocking position had been hard hit on all sides by intense mortar and automatic weapons fire from a company size Viet Cong force. As he maneuvered his aircraft to a landing he too came under intense automatic weapons fire and began taking hits. Observing the obviously desperate situation on the ground, Captain Rider, ignoring his own personal danger, landed his aircraft and began taking on wounded. He flew out, fully loaded, and then returned again and again, through the same intense fire to bring out 20 seriously wounded and 6 dead. He made a total of 8 trips, each time landing then moving over the ground from man to man, exhibiting superb aeronautical skill while bullets struck his aircraft, stopping long enough for his own crew to load on the casualties. He returned until there were no more casualties to pick up. He then returned one more time to make sure he hadn't left anyone who needed his help. I personally observed his last three trips into the embattled area. His devotion to the lives of others and his utter disregard for his own personal safety won the undying respect admiration and gratitude of the men of Company A who observed him and those whose lives he had such a large part of saving.

Statement of LCpl. Jerry W. Simon 2012697, USMC

On 21 May 1966, I Lance Corporal Jerry W. Simon saw many acts of bravery by the men who were working on the medical evacuation. While under very heavy enemy fire they landed their helicopters and then risking their own lives came out of the helicopter to carry wounded men aboard. On one occasion two men with a stretcher covered about 50 meters across a open rice paddy to get a wounded Marine. On another occasion a man jumped from the helicopter before it had even landed to aid a wounded Marine. All of these acts were done while under heavy enemy fire. Each time these men moved from their helicopters they were completely disregarding their own safety. The pilot made many trips. He would fly in and move around just above the deck under intense fire looking for Marines who needed help. The helicopter was hit several times. The pilot moved the helicopter around dikes and grave mounds in ways that didn't seem possible. The whole crew showed great courage, and didn't seem to care for there own safety in the many trips they made to pick up the casualties.

Statement of Corporal B.W. Abshire 1979928 USMC

On 21 May 1966, at about 1415 I was flying as crew chief in the medical evacuation aircraft. We were called by "Sparrow Hawk" to pickup an emergency medical evacuation in the area of Grid Square AT 9664. We had a lot of difficulty finding the exact zone. The unit on the ground was Third Platoon of Company "A", First Battalion, Ninth Marines, they were under heavy attack by a far superior force of Insurgent Communist (Viet Cong) Forces, in fact they were completely encircled. They were receiving intense enemy fire from automatic weapons, recoilless rifles, mortars, and small arms fire. We had a hard time locating the troops. The radio operator was incoherent in his broadcast and at one point, he said, "Come down and get us. Can't you see us? The man with me has been hit once) and he just got hit again." I didn't hear him any more after that.

At this time Captain Rider who was the pilot came over the ICS and told us, the crew that we were going in. On our first attempt, we were unable to pick any one up because of the intensity of the enemy fire. Captain Rider did a 360-degree turn and made another try. This time one Marine jumped up and ran to the aircraft he was hit in the back of the head by an enemy round. We took him to G-4 Naval Hospital and returned to the zone. The aircraft had already taken several hits from enemy fire. One round had hit the armor plating beside Captain Rider. As we set down in the zone the corpsman, Hospitalman J. A. Mayton and myself left the aircraft to help bring the wounded aboard the aircraft. Captain Rider and the co-pilot- First Lieutenant Drury gave us support- ing fire. The ground unit was so heavily engaged in fighting they could not assist in loading the wounded. This fact added to the time that the aircraft had to remain in the zone making it pretty rough. Hospitalman Mayton jumped from the aircraft and ran through enemy fire to bring the wounded to the aircraft many times. At one point, of the many times in the zone a mortar round landed about 20 to 30 feet from the aircraft. On the second trip we managed to get 4 WIA's from the zone. They were taken to G—4 Naval Hospital, on the third trip in the zone we managed to get two men out. On the fourth trip enemy fire was beginning to get hotter, we took a few hits in the right side, and one of the rounds hit the M-79 I was firing. Hospitalman Mayton, and myself again left the air- craft to get and help the wounded aboard. One man I was carrying was hit by an enemy round as I carried him to the aircraft. The pilot and Co- Pilot were still firing their side arms and rounds were hitting all around the corpsman who was carrying wounded to the aircraft. We took the wounded to the G-4 Naval-Hospital and returned to Marble Mountain to refuel, but our aircraft was found unsafe to continue, so we changed aircraft and returned to the zone taking 2 WIA's and 1 KIA out. When we returned to the zone, we were waved off by the survivors of the pla- toon. We went to the main body of the unit who were moving along the river. They were unaware that the Third Platoon had been hit so badly and they didn't know where they were. Captain Rider told the man in command the Third Platoon had been hit so badly and they didn't know where they were. Captain Rider told the man in command about the Third Platoon and a force began moving in their direction.

We took out some wounded from this zone. We returned to the Third Platoon and landed. Captain Rider ground taxied around looking for wounded. The only thing we could find was the dead and the few mem- bers of the Third Platoon who were unhurt. We took out four KIA's and took them to "C" Med. We made eight trips into the zone and managed to get out 12 WIA's and 11 KIA's.

I do not feel that we could have done it without the professional ability of the pilot, co-pilot and the corpsman. I have never in my life seen such bravery in the face of such enemy fire as I saw this day. On our last two trips into the zone the main body had reached the Third Platoon and a Captain walked around and directed Captain Rider who was ground taxiing to where wounded or dead were. We returned to Marble Mountain at this time and were relived by the night crew.

NOTES:

In the following commentary, Jim Rider explains how he got his nickname:

Cliff Reese, a pilot in our squadron, transferred in when he got out of the hospital after being hit by a small arms bullet at some high altitude (above 1500 feet AGL) where that was not supposed to happen. He was a good pilot but had never fired any ordnance, at least in the UH-1E.

On a mission one-day, Cliff was my copilot. I never was a gifted aviator as far as flight skills were concerned, but for some reason I could really shoot rockets well.

I had been a grunt enlisted man in Korea (E-2-1, 1953-54). Then I was a grunt officer after graduating from college (Cornell). Well, I was knocking the devil out of every thing I shot rockets at that day. Cliff's rockets were going acrobatic and performing interesting maneuvers after release. He dubbed me "Johnny Rifle" that day.

Shortly after that, we came into our ready room tent at MMAF. We had some old shot up wooden lockers in which we kept our flight gear. On each locker door there was a picture and a name. The pictures for the most part were perfect caricatures of the locker's owner. I remember they had a picture cut from a Captain Cornflakes cereal box for the CO. Mine was of some little guy with a coon skin hat and a rifle, and the name "Johnny Rifle" was underneath it. The name stuck.

All this handiwork was on the part of Lieutenants Steve Waltrip and Charlie Plunkett, who never had enough work to keep them busy when they weren't flying. They flew their butts off, which was a schedules officer's dream. I was the Schedules Officer (Assistant S-3. and later S-3 after Riley was killed). The only problem I ever had with them was keeping them off the schedule.

When I came home, we were entertaining Cliff Reese and some other visiting firemen at the club one night.

My wife asked, "Are those guys good friends of yours."

I said, "Yeah".

She said, "How come none of them know your name? They always call you Johnny."

The following Marines from the First Battalion, Ninth Marines were killed in action on May 21, 1966:

Company A

Griffin, Bruce F. Pfc. 2128862; 18; Goshen, Ohio

Maciminio, Antonio P. LCpl. 2068749; 20; Pawtuckett, Rhode Island

Manners, David P. Pfc. 2139979; 19; Durant, Oklahoma

Niemczuk, Peter R. Pfc. 2149975; 18; Chicago, Illinois

O'Neal, Marshal, Jr. Cpl. 2050020; 21; Essex, Missouri

Vines, Cleveland Cpl. 1630229; 26; Newport News, Virginia

Company C

Brophy, James J. Cpl. 2030014; 19; Jackson Heights, New York

Cloutier, Robert L. Pfc. 2192581; 18; Somerset, Wisconsin

Duff, Barry W. Cpl. 2098848; 21; Baltimore, Maryland

Goderre, John R. Pfc. 2114390; 20; Union, Maine

Schapanick, Chester Pfc. 2030576; 18; New York, New York

Mead, Peter F. HM3 9153852; 19; Paterson, New Jersey

The Navy Cross was awarded to Cpl. Bobby W. Abshire, Cpl. Barry W. Duff, HM1 James A. Mayton and Cpl. Charles D. Sadler for heroism that night. The award to Duff was posthumous.

In addition to James Rider the Silver Star was awarded to corpsman Lawrence C. Bollinger, Capt. Howard J. Christy, 1stLt. George M. Connell, 2dLt. Simone J. Pace, Pfc. Anthony Restivo, Jr., LCpl. Jerry W. Simon, HM3 Lawrence C. Bollinger, and HM3 Shane A. Morris.

This was Jim Rider's second Silver Star. He had previously earned one on March 10, 1966.

Rider's co-pilot was 1stLt. Richard L. Drury 088238 and the crewmembers of the escort gunship were:

Enockson, John O. 1stLt. 085563 pilot
Costa, A.D. 1stLt. 089104 co-pilot
Revier, C.W. SSgt. 1500038 crew chief
Pfeiffer, Frank L.1556335 aerial gunner
Gillis, James E. Capt. 058243. Executive Officer of VMO-1

We will now rejoin Jim Rider as he recalls the events that transpired on May 21, 1966:

The situation, as we understood it, was that A-1-9 made contact with an NVA force that had penetrated to a few miles of DaNang. I always thought they were NVA because we had just taken out a wounded NVA prisoner on the previous mission. A-1-9 was assaulting North with a small river on there left flank. One platoon had been lifted by the "Sparrowhawk" helicopters into an open rice paddy, to block the NVA force. As soon as the helicopters departed, the NVA opened up on the platoon.

The rest of the company pushed hard and fast to get to there beleaguered comrades. They pretty much ran out of ammunition on the way. But, the company commander, Hal Christy, kept them going. They were killing NVA with rifle butts, hand grenades and entrenching tools!

I heard a friend, John Martin, who was a FAC with ANGLICO on the air net. I could always recognize his dry, matter of fact tone of voice on the radio. In fact, I had heard him on the radio in practically every big battle we were in. John got his flight time with us at Pendleton and DaNang. He probably saw more ground combat and influenced the outcome of more fights than any other aviator in Vietnam. They would take his FAC team and send it to where the fighting was heaviest. John never received an award other than Air Medals although he was in some of the heaviest fighting of the war. We were never close friends but I always admired him.

In between med evac pick ups we landed to show him where the platoon was on the map. Those grunts were mad! We got them pointed in the right direction, and they drove on. There was a poor mangled dog in the landing zone. I told Doc Mayton to shoot him and put him out of his misery.

Shortly after that, we had to switch helicopters because ours was so shot up.

When we came back the company broke through to the rice paddy.

We had gotten a flight of H-34's to come in and take a lot of the wounded out.

I saw the company commander picking up wounded and dead Marines and carrying them in his arms to our helicopter. There was still a lot of shooting going on in the zone, but he carried those Marines to the helicopter oblivious to the bullets. I saw tears streaming down his face as he laid those "kids" on the bird. I had to pull my visor down so no one would see the tears on my face. (I am tearing up as I type this.)

They are very vivid memories!

While we were in the med evac zone Bob Abshire was firing an M-79 grenade launcher when a bullet hit it and split the stock. We hauled many Marines into Charlie Med. and the NSA hospital. When they unloaded the helicopters, we didn't notice that they were taking out all of their 782 gear, weapons etc. We discovered that our darn protective masks and the M-79 grenade launcher were missing when the night crew took over for us.

The next day I went to the hospitals and eventually to Hill 55 where we recovered our stuff. I met Hal there. He was a devout Mormon and a hard leader. There had been an investigation when some people in his company where blown away by a booby trap. In the testimony, one of his squad leaders said that the Captain had never been remiss in warning them about booby traps. He called Hal a "son of a bitch" because he used to physically shove them to keep them from bunching up!

Bob Abshire left the Marine Corps after about 10 years of service. By that time, he was a SSgt., and I think he had been awarded a Distinguished Flying Cross on his third tour in Viet Nam. On his first tour, he was a recon Marine. On the second tour, he was in VMO-2. On the third tour he was in an HML squadron.

After he left the Marine Corps, Bob went to work with the fire department in or near Ft. Worth or Arlington, Texas. Shortly after he joined the fire department, he received an award for reviving a little girl who had almost drowned in a swimming pool.

Bob usually called me on the anniversary of that med evac action. One Friday night he called me from the fire station and we talked for a long time.

On Sunday morning his wife called me and told me that Bob had gotten off work early Saturday morning. While driving home he stopped to help a stranded motorist. A drunk driver came over the top of a nearby hill, headed straight for them. Bob pushed the other guy out of the way and was struck and killed by the drunk driver.

The guy was always a hero.

Bob left a wife and little girl. We corresponded with his wife for a while. Then she must have moved without giving us a forwarding address.

The last I heard of Doc Mayton, he was the country & western DJ on Armed Forces radio of DaNang.

In the following commentary Howard Christy shares his recollection of the events that took place that night:

As the tragic melee ensued, a medevac crew of Marine Observation Squadron 2 flew in. The crew chief was James A. Mayton. Eyewitness accounts of Marines on the ground and the account of the medevac pilot described Jim's heroic efforts to carry on with the lifesaving work commenced by Larry Bollinger. His citation reads in part that "Petty Officer Mayton without hesitation leaped from the aircraft and with heavy fire hitting all around him raced back and forth carrying the wounded and dead to the aircraft. Again and again ... he exposed himself fearlessly to enemy fire in order to rescue the wounded Marines."

I assisted Jim in loading the six men who had died onto the helicopter. It was a gruesomely difficult task. The dead Marines, their bodies drained of blood, handled much like what might have been large sacks of potatoes that had been smashed by a sledgehammer. Like mush they flopped about heavily and awkwardly in the effort to half heave, half yank them up into the helicopter. The bodies filled the belly of the helicopter. Jim had no other place to sit than on top the mound of bodies.

As the helicopter noisily lifted away, our eyes met. On Mayton's face was an unforgettable look of shock and anguish. I will never forget the deep sadness he expressed. Mayton seemed to be trying to say how terribly sorry he was that he couldn't have saved them all.

The next day Jim Rider, the medevac crew pilot, came down to Hill 55 to ask if I might consider writing Petty Officer Mayton up for a decoration. I had already started to do so. Rider said that at each approach Mayton would jump the last several feet to the ground before the helicopter landed, run to a wounded Marine, carry out whatever medical aid that was necessary and then carry or drag him back to the helicopter. When the helicopter was loaded, he would signal to the pilot to go, then wrestle himself back aboard as the helicopter lifted off-all this to save as many precious seconds as possible. He was recommended for, and ultimately received, the Navy Cross.

But this is not all. There was still another heroic corpsman. Several Marine survivors of that bloody day at Le Son, again described with eyes wide with admiration that corpsman's heroism. As he went from man to man to give them lifesaving first aid he was shot down with a bullet through his head as he worked on his fifth and last wounded Marine. All presumed that he had probably died on the way to the hospital. Although his apparent sacrifice indicated the possibility of a Medal of Honor, he too was recommended for the Navy Cross. Presuming him dead, I did not follow up.

Now 32 years later and after returning from my trip to the Vietnam battlefields, and having been motivated by the sharing with those other Marines, I determined to look further into the matter. Recently, the lst Battalion 9th Marines Network, Inc., published its 1998 membership directory. Would it reveal a clue as to who that other corpsman was? Luckily, the name of Shane A. "Doc" Morris appears, along with his address and telephone number, as having been attached to A-1-9.

Matching the name with a brief Stars and Stripes fragment in my possession, but still not seeing any further connection, on 30 March 1998 I called Shane on the chance that he might know something about that other corpsman. The 1-9 Network also lists (in its honor roll) the name of a corpsman who, although not identified with any particular unit in 1-9, also died on May 21, 1966. I asked Shane if the man named in the honor role might be the one I was looking for. Shane stated that he knew of no other corpsman with his unit that day-nobody, that is, other than "Doc" Bollinger, whom he immediately named without any prompting from me.

Then Shane quietly and modestly said that he himself had been hit, not once but three times that day and that in the last instance he had been hit in the head, presumably by shrapnel from an exploding rocket or mortar round. The man, whom I believed to have heroically sacrificed his life 32 years ago, was quietly talking to me on the other end of the line.

And he has an incredible tale to tell. Let me share with you what he told me on the phone, and later in writing. I quote:

'At that time someone yelled Medic. I ran to his side and treated him the best I could. From then on it was one after another. I got hit the first time in the left arm and foot. I went down but got back up and went on to fallen comrades. The second time I got hit was in my right arm and knee. I lay there praying and heard other comrades calling for help. I got up and went about my business. This one fallen Marine was shot in the stomach bad. He looked me in the eyes and pleaded, "Doc, don't let me die," and I said don't worry but I knew it was hopeless. The VC were closing in and I heard a cry from another comrade. He was laying out in the open.... I crawled to rescue my comrade and as I did I got hit the third time. I knew I couldn't get up. I could feel warmth on the back of my neck and when I reached around to touch, it was blood. I lay there not knowing the outcome, if I would see my family or wife and my son born. When reinforcements arrived they were searching for the living. One man turned me over and said [I] was dead. With all I had I said no I am not.'

Shane remembers being flown to a field hospital, and vaguely remembers hearing someone say that he was to be evacuated to Clark Air Force Base, Philippines, but he soon passed out. He regained consciousness more than ten days later, but his doctors, nevertheless despairing for his life, flew him back to the States in order that he might at least die at home. However, he defied the odds and has survived, although he has suffered greatly from his wounds. He was transferred in critical condition to the Portsmouth Naval Hospital in June 1966. He remained there for many weeks, where his weight dropped from 143 to 93 pounds.

It was not until February 1967 that his condition was deemed safe enough to allow him to undergo surgery to remove the shrapnel that was lodged in his brain. However, it was to no avail since the shrapnel was so close to vital areas that removal posed too high a risk. To this day, he carries shrapnel in his brain, back, and one arm.

Shane was decorated, not with the Navy Cross but with the Silver Star on 28 October 1966, his twentieth birthday. Upon general recovery, he was medically retired from the Navy with 75 percent disability.

Shane carries ten scars from the multiple bullet and shrapnel wounds he absorbed in his head and body on May 21, 1966 at Le Son, when he repeatedly and willingly placed himself in harm's way for the sake of others.

Here was brotherhood of biblical proportions. The Lord speaks eloquently of such selfless service in the Book of John where He says "Greater love hath no man than this, that a man lay down his life for his friends."

Capt. Harold E. "Gus" Plum, 076530 and Jim Rider

Captain Francis J. West, Jr., a Marine reserve officer, was invited to apply for assignment to active duty during the summer of 1966 to research and write small unit action stories. Returning to active duty in May of 1966, he wrote the highly acclaimed *Small Unit Action in Vietnam: Summer 1966*. In the following excerpt, he describes the action for which Staff Sergeant Jimmie Earl Howard was awarded the Medal of Honor.

"Anytime, anywhere, no questions asked."

HM3 Bruce H. Norton
3rd Force Recon
From *Force Recon Diary, 1969-1970*

Small Unit Action in Vietnam: Summer 1966 was published by the government of the United States and is therefore in the public domain.

4
HOWARD'S HILL

Preface: The author was on another patrol the night of the Howard flight. He met with the men of Charlie Company, who relieved Howard's platoon, immediately upon their return and taped their comments and reactions. Then he went to the hospital at Chulai and interviewed Howard and his men, talking later with the pilots, the Special Forces officers, and Howard's company and battalion commanders. The pictures—the only ones taken on the hill during the fight—were provided by First Lieutenant Philip Freed, who was the Forward Air Controller with Charlie Company.

The Marine Corps has a tested tradition: it will never leave alone on the field of combat one of its fighting men. It will go to fantastic lengths and commit to battle scores of men to aid and protect a few. This is the story of a few such Marines, of the battle they fought, and the help they received from all the services, not just the Marine Corps.

Some 20 miles inland to the west of the marine base at Chulai runs a range of steep mountains and twisting valleys. In that bandits' lair, the Viet Cong and North Vietnamese could train and plan for attacks against the heavily populated seacoast hamlets, massing only when it was time to attack. In early June of 1966, the intelligence reports reaching III MAF headquarters indicated that a mixed force of Viet Cong and North Vietnamese was gathering by the thousands in those mountains. But the enemy leaders were not packing their troops into a few large, vulnerable assembly points; they kept their units widely dispersed, moving mainly in squads and platoons.

To frustrate that scheme and keep the enemy off balance, the Marines launched Operation KANSAS, an imaginative concept in strategy. Rather than send full infantry battalions to beat the bushes in search of small enemy bands, Lieutenant General Lewis W. Walt detailed the reconnaissance battalion of the 1st Marine Division to scout the mountains. The reconnaissance Marines would move in small teams of 8 to 20 men. If they located a large enemy concentration, Marine infantry would be flown in. If, as was expected, they saw only numerous small groups of Viet Cong and North Vietnamese, they were to smash them by calling in air and artillery strikes.

Lieutenant Colonel Arthur J. Sullivan had set high training standards for his battalion. Every man had received individual schooling in forward observer techniques and reconnaissance patrol procedures. He was confident his men could perform the mission successfully, despite the obvious hazards. "The Vietnam War," he said, "has given the small-unit leader—the corporal, the sergeant, the lieutenant—a chance to be independent. The senior officers just can't be out there looking over their shoulders. You have to have confidence in your junior officers and NCOs."

One such NCO was Staff Sergeant Jimmie Earl Howard, acting commander of the 1st Platoon, Charlie Company, 1st Reconnaissance Battalion. A tall, well-built man in his mid-thirties, Howard had been a star football player and later a coach at the San Diego Recruit Depot. Leadership came naturally to him. "Howard was a very personable fellow," his company commander, Captain Tim Geraghty said. "The men liked him. They liked to work for him." In Korea he had been wounded three times and awarded the Silver Star for bravery. In Vietnam he would receive a fourth Purple Heart and be recommended for the Medal of Honor.

As dusk fell on the evening of 13 June 1966, a flight of helicopters settled on the slope of Hill 488, 25 miles west of Chulai. Howard and his 17 men jumped out and climbed to a peak of nearly 1,500 feet and dominated the terrain for miles. Three narrow strips of level ground ran along the top for several hundred yards before falling abruptly away. Seen from the air, they roughly resembled the three blades on an airplane propeller. Howard chose the blade which pointed north for his command post and placed observation teams on the other two blades. It was an ideal vantage point.

The enemy knew it also. Their foxholes dotted the ground, each with a small shelter scooped out two feet under the surface. Howard permitted his men use of these one-man caves during the day to avoid the hot sun and enemy detection. There was no other cover or concealment to be found. There were no trees, only knee-high grass and small scrub growth.

In the surrounding valleys and villages, there were many enemy. For the next two days, Howard was constantly calling for fire missions, as members of the platoon saw small enemy groups almost every hour. Not all the requests for air and artillery strikes were honored. Sullivan was concerned lest the platoon's position, so salient and bare, be spotted by a suspicious enemy. Most of the firing at targets located by the platoon was done only when there was an observation plane circling in the vicinity to decoy enemy. After two days Sullivan and his executive officer Major Allan Harris, became alarmed at the risk involved in leaving the platoon stationary any longer. But the observation post was ideal; Howard had encountered no difficulty, and in any case, thought he had a secure escape route along a ridge to the east. So it was decided to leave the platoon on Nui Vu for one more day.

However, the enemy were well aware of the platoon's presence. (Sullivan has a theory that the Viet Cong and North Vietnamese, long harassed, disrupted, and punished by reconnaissance units in territory they claimed to control absolutely, had determined to eliminate one such unit, hoping thereby to demoralize the others. Looked at in hindsight, the ferocity and tenacity of the attack upon Nui Vu gives credence to the colonel's theory.) In any case, the North Vietnamese made their preparations well and did not tip their hand. On 15 June, they moved a fresh, well-equipped, highly trained battalion to the base of Nui Vu. In late afternoon hundreds of the enemy started to climb up the three blades, hoping to annihilate the dozen and a half Marines in one surprise attack.

The Army Special Forces frustrated that plan. Sergeant lst Class Donald Reed and Specialist 5th Class Hardey Drande were leading a platoon of CIDG (Civilian Irregular Defense Group) forces on patrol near Nui Vu that same afternoon. They saw elements of the North Vietnamese battalion moving towards the hill and radioed the news back to their base camp at Hoi An, several miles to the south. Howard's radio was purposely set on the same frequency and so he was alerted at the same time. Reed and Drande wanted to hit the enemy from the rear and disrupt them, but had to abandon the idea when they suddenly found themselves a very unpopular minority of two on the subject. Describing the reactions of the Special Forces NCOs later, Howard could not resist chuckling. "The language those sergeants used over the radio," he said, "when they realized they couldn't attack the PAVNs (Marine slang for the Peoples' Army of North Vietnam), well they sure didn't learn it at communications school." Even though the Special Forces were not able to provide the ground support they wished to, their warning alerted Howard and enabled him to develop a precise defensive plan before the attack was launched.

Acting on the report, Howard gathered his team, briefed them on the situation, selected an assembly, and instructed them to stay on full alert and to withdraw position at the first sign of an approaching enemy. The Corporals and Lance Corporals crept back to their teams and briefed them in the growing dusk. The Marines then settled down to watch and wait.

Lance Corporal Ricardo Binns had placed his observation team on the slope 40 meters forward of Howard's position. At approximately 2200, while the four Marines were lying in a shallow depression, discussing in whispers their sergeant's solemn warnings, Binns quite casually propped himself up on his elbows and placed his rifle butt in his shoulder. Without saying a word, he pointed the barrel at a bush and fired. The bush pitched backward and fell thrashing 12 feet away.

The other Marines jumped up. Each threw a grenade, before grabbing his rifle and scrambling up the hill. Behind them grenades burst and automatic weapons pounded away. The battle of Nui Vu was on.

The other outposts withdrew to the main position. The Marines commanded a tiny rock-strewn knoll. The rocks would provide some protection for the defenders. Placing his two radios behind a large boulder,

Howard set up a tight circular perimeter, not over 20 meters in diameter, and selected a firing position for each Marine.

The North Vietnamese, too, were setting up. They had made no audible noises while climbing. There was no talking, no clumsy movements. When Binns killed one of their scouts, they were less than 50 meters from the top.

The Marines were surrounded. From all sides the enemy threw grenades. Some bounced off the rocks; some rolled back down the slopes; some did not explode, but some landed right on Marines and did explode. The next day the platoon corpsman, Billie Don Holmes, recalled: "They were within twenty feet of us. Suddenly there were grenades all over. Then people started hollering. It seemed everyone got hit at the same time."

Holmes crawled forward to help. A grenade exploded between him and a wounded man. Holmes lost consciousness.

The battle was going well for the North Vietnamese. Four .50 caliber machine guns were firing in support of the assault units, their heavy explosive projectiles arcing in from the four points of the compass. Red tracer rounds from light machine guns streaked toward the Marine position, pointing the direction for reinforcements gathering in the valley. 60mm mortar shells smashed down and added rock splinters to the metal shrapnel whining through the air.

The North Vietnamese followed up the grenade shower with a full, well-coordinated assault, directed and controlled by shrill whistles and the clacking of bamboo sticks. From different directions, they rushed the position at the same time, firing automatic weapons, throwing grenades, and screaming. Howard later said he hadn't been sure how his troops would react. They were young and the situation looked hopeless. They had been shocked and confused by the ferocity of the attack and the screams of their own wounded.

But they reacted savagely. The first lines of enemy skirmishers were cut down seconds after they stood up and exposed themselves. The assault failed to gain momentum any place and the North Vietnamese in the rearward ranks had more sense than to copy the mistakes of the dead. Having failed in their swift charge, they went to earth and probed the perimeter, seeking a weak spot through which they could drive. To do this, small bands of the enemy tried to crawl quite close to a Marine, then overwhelm him with a burst of fire and several grenades.

But the Marines too used grenades and the American hand grenade contains twice the blast and shrapnel effect of Chinese Communist stick grenade. The Marines could throw farther and more accurately than the enemy. A Marine would listen for a movement, gauge the direction and distance, pull the pin, and throw. High pitched howls and excited jabberings mingled with the blasts. The North Vietnamese pulled back to regroup.

Howard had taken the PRC-25 radio from one of his communicators, Corporal Robert Lewis Martinez, and during the lull contacted Captain Geraghty and Lieutenant Colonel Sullivan. With his escape route cut off and his force facing overwhelming odds, Howard kept his message simple. "You've gotta get us out of here," he said. "There are too many of them for my people."

Sullivan tried. Because of his insistence upon detailed preplanning of extraction and fire support contingencies, he was a well-known figure at the Direct Air Support Center of the 1st Marine Division and when he called near midnight, he did not bandy words. He wanted flare ships, helicopters, and fixed wing aircraft dispatched immediately to Nui Vu.

Somehow, the response was delayed. And shortly after midnight, the enemy forces gathered and rushed forward in strength a second time. The Marines threw the last of their grenades and fired their rifles semi-automatically, relying on accuracy to suppress volume. It did and the enemy fell back, but by that time every Marine had been wounded.

The living took the ammunition of the dead and lay under a moonless sky, wondering about the next assault. Although he did not tell anyone, Howard doubted they could repel a massed charge by a determined enemy. From combat experiences, he knew too that the enemy, having been badly mauled twice, would listen for sounds which would indicate his force had been shattered or demoralized before surging forward again. Already up the slopes were floating the high, singsong taunts Marines had heard at other places in other wars. Voices, which screeched: "Marines-you die tonight!" and "Marines, you die in an hour."

Members of the platoon wanted to return the compliments. "Sure," said Howard, "go ahead and yell anything you want." And the Marines shouted back down the slopes all the curses and invectives they could remember from their collective repertoire. The North Vietnamese screamed back, giving Howard the opportunity to deliver a master stroke in psychological one-upmanship.

"All right," he shouted. "Ready? Now!"

And all the Marines laughed and laughed and laughed at the enemy.

The North Vietnamese did not mount a third major attack and at 0100 an Air Force flare ship, with the poetic call sign of "Smoky Gold," came on station overhead. Howard talked to the pilot through his radio and the plane dropped its first flare. The mountainside was lit up. The Marines looked down the slopes. Lance Corporal Ralph Glober Victor stared, then muttered: "Oh my God, look at them." The others weren't sure it wasn't a prayer. North Vietnamese reinforcements filled the valley. Twenty-year-old Private First Class Joseph Kosoglow described it vividly: "There were so many, it was just like an ant hill ripped apart. They were all over the place."

They shouldn't have been. Circling above the mountain were attack jets and armed helicopters. With growing frustration, they had talked to Howard but could not dive to the attack without light. Now they had light.

They swarmed in. The jets first concentrated on the valley floor and the approaches to Nui Vu, loosing rockets which hissed down and blanketed large areas. Then those fast, dangerous helicopters —the Hueys— scoured the slopes. At altitudes as low as 20 feet, they skimmed the brush, firing their machine guns in long, sweeping bursts. The Hueys pulled off to spot for the jets, and again the planes dipped down, releasing bombs and napalm. Then the Hueys scurried back to pick off stragglers, survey the damage, and direct another run. One of the platoon's communicators, Corporal Martinez, said it in two sentences: "The Hueys were all over the place. The jets blocked the Viet Cong off. "

Two Hueys stayed over Howard's position all night; when one helicopter had to return to home base and refuel, another would be sent out. The Huey pilots, Captain John M. Shields and Captain James M. Perryman Jr., performed dual roles—they were the Tactical Air Controllers' Airborne (TACAs) who directed the bomb runs of the jets and they themselves strafed the enemy. The North Vietnamese tried unsuccessfully to shoot the helicopters down and did hit two out of the four Hueys alternating on station.

By the light of the flares, the jet pilots could see the hill mass and distinguish prominent terrain features but could not spot Howard's perimeter. To mark specific targets for the jets, the TACAs directed "Smoky" to drop flares right on the ground as signal lights and then called the jets down to pulverize the spot. Howard identified his position by flicking a refiltered flashlight on and off, and, guiding on that mark, the Huey pilots strafed within 25 meters of the Marines.

Still on the perimeter itself, the fight continued. In the shifting light of the flares, the pilots were fearful of hitting the Marines and had to leave some space unexposed to fire in front of the Marines' lines. Into this space crawled the North Vietnamese.

For the Marines, it was a war of hide and seek. Having run out of grenades, they had to rely on cunning and marksmanship to beat the attackers. Howard had passed the word to fire only at an identified target—and then only one shot at a time. The enemy fired all automatic weapons; the Marines replied with single shots. The enemy hurled grenades; the Marines threw back rocks.

It was a good tactic. A Marine would hear a noise and toss a rock in that general direction. The North Vietnamese would think it was a grenade falling and dive for another position. The Marine would roll or crawl low to a spot from which he could sight in on the position, and wait. In a few seconds, the North Vietnamese would raise his head to see why the grenade had not exploded. The Marine would fire one round. The range was generally less than 30 feet.

The accuracy of this fire saved the life of Corpsman Holmes. When he regained consciousness after a grenade had knocked him out, he saw a North Vietnamese dragging away the dead Marine beside him. Then another enemy reached over and grasped him by the cartridge belt. The soldier tugged at him.

Lance Corporal Victor was lying on his stomach behind a rock. He had been hit twice by grenades since the first flare had gone off and could scarcely move. He saw an enemy soldier bending over a fallen Marine. He sighted in and fired. The man fell backward. He saw a second enemy tugging at another Marine's body. He sighted in again and fired.

Shot between the eyes, the North Vietnamese slumped dead across Billie Holmes' chest. He pushed the body away and crawled back to the Marines' lines. His left arm was lanced with shrapnel, and his face was swollen and his head ringing from the concussion of the grenade. For the rest of the night, he crawled from position to position, bandaging and encouraging the wounded, and between times firing at the enemy.

Occasionally the flares would flicker out and the planes would have to break off contact to avoid crashing. In those instances, artillery under the control of the Special Forces and manned by Vietnamese gun crews would fill in the gap and punish any enemy force gathering at the base of Nui Vu.

"Stiff Balls," Howard had radioed the Special Forces camp at Hoi An, three miles south. "If you can keep Charlie from sending another company up here, I'll keep these guys out of my position."

"Roger, Carnival Time." Captain Louis Maris, of the Army Special Forces, had replied, using Howard's own peculiar call sign. Both sides kept their parts of the bargain and the South Vietnamese crews who manned the 105mm howitzers threw in concentration after concentration of accurate artillery shells.

"Howard was talking on the radio. He was cool," Captain John Blair, the Special Forces commanding officer, recalled afterwards. "He stayed calm all the way through that night. But," he chuckled, "he never did get our call sign right!"

In the periods of darkness, each Marine fought alone. How some of them died no one knows. But the relieving force hours later found one Marine lying propped up against a rock. In front of him lay a dead enemy soldier. The muzzles of their weapons were touching each others' chests. Two Marine entrenching tools were recovered near a group of mangled North Vietnamese; both shovels were covered with blood. One Marine was crumpled beneath a dead enemy. Beside him lay another Vietnamese. The Marine was bandaged around the chest and head. His hand still clasped the hilt of a knife buried in the back of the soldier on top of him.

At 0300, a flight of H34 helicopters whirled over Nui Vu and came in to extract the platoon. So intense was the fire they met that they were unable to land and Howard was told he would have to fight on until dawn. Shortly thereafter, a ricochet struck Howard in the back. His voice over the radio faltered and died out. Those listening—the Special Forces personnel, the pilots, the high ranking officers of the 1st Marine Division at Chulai-all thought the end had come. Then Howard's voice came back strong. Fearing the drowsing effect morphine can have, he refused to let Holmes administer the drug to ease the pain. Unable to use his legs, he pulled himself from hole to hole encouraging his men and directing their fire. Wherever he went, he dragged their lifeline—the radio.

Binns, the man whose shot had triggered the battle, was doing likewise. Despite severe wounds, he crawled around the perimeter, urging his men to conserve their ammunition, gathering enemy weapons and grenades for the Marines' use, giving assistance wherever needed.

None of the Marines kept track of the time. "I'll tell you this," said Howard, "you know that movie—The Longest Day? Well, compared to our night on the hill, The Longest Day was just a twinkle in the eye." But the longest night did pass and dawn came. Howard heralded its arrival. At 0525 he shouted, "O.K., you people, reveille goes in 35 minutes." At exactly 0600, his voice pealed out, "Reveille, reveille." It was the start of another day and the perimeter had held.

On all sides of their position, the Marines saw enemy bodies and equipment. The North Vietnamese would normally have raked the battlefield clean, but so deadly was the Marine fire that they left unclaimed many of those who fell close to the perimeter.

The firing had slacked off. Although badly mauled themselves, the enemy still had the Marines ringed in and did not intend to leave. Nor did haste make them foolhardy. They knew what the jets, the Hueys, the artillery and the Marine sharpshooting would do to them on the bare slopes in daylight. They slipped into holes and waited, intending to attack with more troops the next night.

Bursts of fire from light machine guns chipped the rocks above the Marines' heads. Firing uphill from concealed foxholes, the enemy could cut down any Marine who raised up and silhouetted himself against the skyline. Two of the .50 caliber machine guns were still firing sporadically.

There came a lull in the firing. A Huey buzzed low over the hillcrest, while another gunship hovered to one side, ready to pounce if the enemy took the bait. No one fired. The pilot, Major William J. Goodsell, decided to mark the position for a medical evacuation by helicopter. His Huey fluttered slowly down and hovered. Howard thought the maneuver too risky and said so. But Goodsell had run the risk and come in anyway. He dropped a smoke grenade. Still no fire. He waved to the relieved Howard and skimmed north over the forward slope, only 10 feet above the ground.

The noise of machine guns drowned out the sound of the helicopter's engines. Tracers flew toward the Huey from all directions. The helicopter rocked and veered sharply to the right and zigzagged down the mountain. The copilot, First Lieutenant Stephen Butler, grabbed the stick and brought the crippled helicopter under control, crash landing in a rice paddy several miles to the east. The pilots were picked up by their wingman. But Major Goodsell, who had commanded Squadron VMO-6 for less than one week, died of gunshot wounds before they reached the hospital.

The medical pickup helicopter did not hesitate. It came in. Frantically, Howard waved it off. He was not going to see another shot down. The pilot saw Howard's signal and turned off, bullets clanging off the armor plating of the undercarriage. Howard would wait for the infantry.

In anger, the jets and the Hueys now attacked the enemy positions anew. Flying lower and lower, they crisscrossed the slopes, searching for the machine gun emplacements, offering themselves as targets, daring the enemy to shoot.

The enemy did. Another Huey was hit and crashed, its crew chief killed. The .50 calibers exposed their position and were silenced. Still the North Vietnamese held their ground. Perhaps the assault company, with all its automatic weapons and fresh young troops, had been ordered to wipe out the few Marines at any cost; perhaps the commanding officer had been killed and his subordinates were following dead orders; perhaps the enemy thought victory yet possible.

But then the Marine infantry came in. They had flown out at dawn but so intense was the enemy fire around Nui Vu, the helicopters had to circle for 45 minutes while jets and artillery blasted a secure landing zone. During that time, First Lieutenant Richard E. Moser, a H34 helicopter pilot, monitored Howard's frequency and later reported: "It was like something you'd read in a novel. His call sign was Carnival Time and he kept talking about these North Vietnamese down in holes in front of him. He'd say, 'you've gotta get this guy in the crater because he's hurting my boys.' He was really impressive. His whole concern was for his men."

On the southern slope of the mountain, helicopters finally dropped Charlie Company of the 5th Marines. The relief company climbed fast, ignoring sniper fire and wiping out small pockets of resistance. With the very first round they fired, the Marine 60mm mortar team knocked out the enemy mortar. Sergeant Frank Riojas, the weapons platoon commander, cut down a sniper at 500 yards with a tracer round from his M14. Marine machine gun sections were detached from the main body and sent up the steep fingers along the flanks of the hill to support by fire the company's movement. The North Vietnamese were now the hunted, as Marines scrambled around as well as up the slope, attempting to pinch off the enemy before they could flee.

The main column climbed straight upwards. While yet a quarter of a mile away, the point man saw recon's position on the plateau. The boulder which served as Howard's command post was the most prominent terrain feature on the peak. The platoon hurried forward. They had to step over enemy bodies to enter the perimeter. Howard's men had eight rounds of ammunition left.

"Get down," were Howard's first words of welcome. "There are snipers right in front of us." Another recon man shouted: "Hey, you got any cigarettes?" A cry went up along the line—not expressions of joy—but requests for cigarettes.

It was not that Howard's Marines were not glad to see other infantrymen; it was just that they had expected them. Staff Sergeant Richard Sullivan, who was with the first platoon to reach the recon Marines, said later: "One man told me he never expected to see the sun rise. But once it did, he knew we'd be coming."

The fight was not over. Before noon, in the hot daylight, despite artillery and planes firing in support, four more Marines would die.

At Howard's urging, Second Lieutenant Ronald Meyer quickly deployed his platoon along the crest. Meyer had graduated from the Naval Academy the previous June and intended to make the Marine Corps his career. He had spent a month with his bride before leaving for Vietnam. In the field he wore no shiny bars, and officers and men alike called him "Stump," because of his short, muscular physique.

Howard had assumed he was a corporal or a sergeant and was shouting orders to him. Respecting Howard's knowledge and performance, Meyer obeyed. He never did mention his rank. So Staff Sergeant Howard, waving off offers of aid, proceeded to direct the tactical maneuvers of the relieving company, determined to wipe out the small enemy band dug in not 20 meters downslope.

Meyer hollered for members of his platoon to pass him grenades. He would then lob them downslope toward the snipers' holes. By peering around the base of the boulder, Howard was able to direct his throws. "A little more to the right on the next one, buddy. About five yards farther. That's right. No, a little too strong." The grenades had little effect and the snipers kept firing. Meyer shouted he wanted air on the target. The word was passed back for the air liaison officer to come forward. The platoon waited.

Lance Corporal Terry Redic wanted to fire his rifle grenade at the snipers. A tested sharpshooter, he had several kills to his credit. In small fire fights he often disdained to duck, preferring to suppress hostile fire by his own rapid accurate shooting. Meyer's way seemed too slow. He raised up, knelt on one knee, and sighted downslope looking for a target. He never found one. The enemy shot first and killed him instantly.

Meyer swore vehemently. "Let's get that *****. You coming with me, Sotello?" "Yes, Stump." Lance Corporal David Sotello turned to get his rifle and some other men. Meyer didn't wait. He started forward with a grenade in each hand. "Keep your head down, buddy, they can shoot," yelled Howard.

Meyer crawled for several yards, then threw a grenade at a hole. It blasted an enemy soldier. He turned, looking upslope. Another sniper shot him in the back. Sotello heard the shot as he started to crawl down.

So did Hospitalman 3d Class John Markillie, the platoon corpsman. He crawled toward the fallen lieutenant. "For God's sake, keep your head down!" yelled Howard. Markillie reached his lieutenant. He sat up to examine the wound. A sniper shot him in the chest.

Another corpsman, Holloday, and a squad leader, Corporal Melville, crawled forward. They could not feel Meyer's pulse. Markillie was still breathing. Ignoring the sniper fire, they began dragging and pushing his body up the hill.

Melville was hit in the head. He rolled over. His helmet bounced off. He shook his head and continued to crawl. The round had gone in one side of the helmet and ripped out the other, just nicking the corporal above his left ear. Melville and Holloday dragged Markillie into the perimeter.

From Chulai, the battalion commander called his company commander, First Lieutenant Marshall "Buck" Darling. "Is the landing zone secure, Buck?" "Well," A pause. "... not spectacularly." Back at the base two noncommissioned officers were listening. "I wonder what he meant by that?" asked the junior sergeant. "What the hell do you think it means, stupid?" replied the older sergeant. "He's getting shot at."

Ignoring his own wounds, Corpsman Billie Holmes was busy supervising the corpsmen from Charlie Company as they administered to the wounded. With the fire fight still going on to the front, helicopter evacuation was not possible from within the perimeter. The wounded had to be taken rearward to the south slope. Holmes roved back and forth, making sure that all his buddies were accounted for and taken out.

The pilots had seen easier landing sites. "For the medical evacs," Moses said, "a pilot had to come in perpendicular to the ridge, then cock his bird around before he sat down. We could get both main mounts down—first—the—tail—well—sometimes we got it down. We were still taking fire."

Holmes reported that there was still one Marine, whom he had seen die, missing. Only after repeated assurances that they would not leave without the body were the infantry able to convince him and Howard that it was time they too left. They helped the Navy corpsman and the Marine sergeant to a waiting helicopter. Howard's job was done.

Another had yet to be finished. There was a dead Marine to be found somewhere on the field of battle. But before a search could be conducted, the last of the enemy force had to be destroyed.

First Lieutenant Phil Freed flopped down beside Melville. Freed was the forward air controller attached to Charlie Company that day. He had run the last quarter mile uphill when he heard Meyer needed air. With the rounds cracking near his head, he needed no briefing. He contacted two F8 Crusader jets circling overhead. "This is Cottage 14. Bring it on down on a dry run. This has to be real tight. Charley is dug in right on our lines." At the controls of the jets were First Lieutenants Richard W. Deilke and Edward H. Menzer.

"There were an awful lot of planes in the air," Menzer said. "We didn't think we'd be used so we called DASC (Direct Air Support Center) and asked for another mission. We got diverted to the FAC (Forward Air Controller), Cottage 14. He told us he had a machine gun nest right in front of him."

As they talked back and forth, Menzer thought he recognized Freed's voice. Later he learned he had indeed; Freed had flown jets with him in another squadron a year earlier.

Freed was lying in a pile of rocks on the military crest of the northern finger of the hill. Since he himself had flown the F-8 Crusader, Freed could talk to the pilots in a language they understood. Still, he was not certain they could help. He didn't know whether they could come that close and still not hit the Marine infantrymen. On their first run, he deliberately called the jets in wide so he could judge the technical skills and precision of the pilots. Rock steady.

He called for them to attack in earnest. When they heard the target was 20 meters from the FAC, it was the pilots' turn to be worried. "As long as you're flying parallel to the people, it's O.K.," Menzer said. "Because it's a good shooting bird. But even so, I was leery at first to fire with troops that near."

Unknown to them, the two pilots were about to fly one of the closest direct air support missions in the history of fixed-wing aviation. They approached from the northeast with the sun behind them, and cut across the ridgeline parallel to the friendly lines. They strafed without room for error. The gunsight reflector plate in an F8 Crusader jet looks like a bulls-eye with the rings marked in successive 10-mil increments. When the pilots in turn aligned their sights while 3,000 feet away, the target lay within the 10-mil ring and the Marine position was at the edge of the ring. The slightest variance of the controls would rake the Marine infantrymen with fire. In that fashion, each pilot made four strafing passes, skimming by 10 to 20 feet above the ridge. Freed feared they would both crash, so close did their wings dip to the crest of the hill. The impact of the cannon shells showered the infantrymen with dirt. They swore they could tell the color of the pilot's eyes. In eight attacks, the jet pilots fired 350 20mm explosive shells into an area 60 meters long and 10 to 20 meters wide. The hillside was gouged and torn, as if a bulldozer had churned back and forth across it.

Freed cautiously lifted his head. A round cracked by. One enemy had survived. Somebody shouted that the shot came from the position of the sniper who had killed Meyer. The lieutenant's body lay several yards downslope.

The F8 Crusaders had ample fuel left. Menzer called to say they could make dummy runs over the position if the Marines thought it would be useful. Freed asked them to try it.

The company commander, Buck Darling, watched the jets. As they passed, he noticed the firing stopped momentarily. The planes would be his cover. "I'm going to get Stump. Coming, Brown?" he asked the nearest Marine.

Lance Corporal James Brown was not a billboard Marine. His offbeat sense of humor often conflicted with his superiors' sense of duty. His squad leader later recalled with a grimace one fire fight when the enemy caught the squad in a cross fire. The rounds were passing high over the Marines' heads. While everyone else was returning fire, Brown strolled over to a Vietnamese tombstone, propped himself against it with one finger, crossed his legs and yelled: "You couldn't hit me if I was buried here!" His squad leader almost did the job for the enemy.

On the hill relieving the recon unit, however, Brown was all business. He emptied several rifle magazines and hurled grenade after grenade. When he ran out of grenades, he threw rocks to keep the snipers ducking. All the while he screamed and cursed, shouting every insult and blasphemy he could think of. Howard had been very impressed, both with Brown's actions and with his vocabulary.

He was not out of words when Darling asked him to go after Meyer's body. As they crawled over the crest, Brown tugged at his company commander's boot. "Don't sweat it, Lieutenant, they can only kill us." Darling did not reply. They reached Meyer's body and tried to pull it back while crawling on their stomachs. They lacked the strength.

"All right, let's carry him." said Darling. It was Brown's turn to be speechless. He knew what had happened to every Marine on the slope who had raised his head—and here was his officer suggesting they stand straight up! "We'll time our moves with the jets." When the jets passed low, they stumbled and scrambled forward a few yards with their burden, then flattened out as the jets pulled up. The sniper snapped shots at them after every pass. Bullets chipped the rocks around them. They had less than 30 feet to climb. It took over a dozen rushes. When they rolled over the crest they were exhausted. Only the enemy was left on the slope.

The infantry went after him. Corporal Samuel Roth led his eight man squad around the left side of the slope. On the right, Sergeant Riojas set a machine gun up on the crest to cover the squad. A burst of automatic fire struck the tripod of the machine gun. A strange duel developed. The sniper would fire at the machine gun. His low position enabled him to aim in exactly on the gun. The Marines would duck until he fired, then reach up and loose a burst downhill, forcing the sniper to duck.

With the firing, the sniper could not hear the squad crashing through the brush on his right side. Roth brought his men on line facing toward the sniper. With fixed bayonets they began walking forward. They could see no movement in the clumps of grass and torn earth.

There was a lull in the firing. The sniper heard the squad, turned and fired. Bullets whipped by the Marines. Roth's helmet spun off. He fell. The other Marines flopped to the ground. Roth was uninjured. The steel helmet had saved a second Marine's life within an hour. He was not even aware that his helmet had been shot off. "When I give the word, kneel and fire," he said. "Now!" The Marines rose and their rounds kicked up dust and clumps of earth in front of them. They missed the sniper. He had ducked into his hole. The Marines lay back down. Roth swore. "All right—put in fresh magazines and let's do it again." "Now!"

Just as the Marines rose, the sniper bobbed up like a duck in a shooting gallery. A bullet knocked him backwards against the side of his hole. Roth charged, the other Marines sprinting behind him. He drove forward with his bayonet. A grenade with the release pin intact rolled from the sniper's left hand. Roth jerked the blade back. The sniper slumped forward over his machine gun.

The hill was quiet. It was noon. Darling declared the objective secure. In the tall grass in front of Riojas' machine gun, the infantrymen found the body of the missing Marine. The Marines paused to search 39 enemy dead for documents, picked up 18 automatic weapons (most of them Chinese), climbed on board a flight of helicopters, and flew off the plateau.

The Marines lost 10 dead. Charley Company and the Huey Squadrons each lost two. Of the 18 Marines in the reconnaissance platoon, 6 were killed; the other 12 were wounded. Five members of Charlie Company were recommended for medals. Every Marine under Howard's command received the Purple Heart. Fifteen were recommended for the Silver Star; Binns and Holmes were nominated for the Navy Cross; Howard was recommended for the Medal of Honor.

If the action had centered around just one man, then it could be considered a unique incident of exceptional bravery on the part of an exceptional man. It is that. But perhaps it is something more. On June 14th, few would have noticed anything unique about the lst Reconnaissance Platoon of Charley Company. Just in reading the names of its dead, one has the feeling that here are the typical and the average, who, well-trained and well led, rose above normal expectations to perform an exemplary feat of arms: John Adams, Ignatius Carlisi, Thomas Glawe, James McKinney, Alcadio Mascarenas, Jerrald Thompson.

NOTES:
The Marines killed in action that night are listed as follows:
Adams, John T. LCpl. 2033889; 22; Covington, Oklahoma
Carlisi, Ignatius Pfc. 2170881; 20; New York, New York
Glawe, Thomas D. Pfc. 2130228; 18; Rockford, Illinois

Goodsell, William J. Maj. 055282; 37; Seattle, Washington
Mascarenas, Alcadio N. LCpl. 2129236; 22; Sapello, New Mexico
McKinney, James O. Pfc. 205546; 18; Monroe, Louisiana
Meyer, Ronald W. 2dLt. 091945; 23; Dubuque, Iowa
Redic, Terry P. LCpl. 2122764; 18; Anderson, Indiana
Thompson, Jerrald R. Cpl. 1892012; 24; Columbus, Ohio

I was unable to identify any helicopter crew chief being killed that night.

Every member of the recon patrol that survived the battle was wounded at least once with Howard being temporarily paralyzed from the waist down from shrapnel wounds.

Howard's patrol became the most decorated unit of the war in Vietnam. He was awarded the Medal of Honor for his gallant leadership. He had previously earned the Silver Star for bravery in the Korean War from August 12 to 15, 1952.

In addition to Howard's award, four members of the patrol earned the Navy Cross and thirteen the Silver Star. The Navy Cross was awarded to LCpl. John T. Adams, LCpl. Ricardo C. Binns, HM1 Billie D. Holmes and Cpl. Jerrald R. Thompson.

The Silver Star was awarded to Pfc. Charles W. Bosley, Pfc. Ignatius Carlisi, Pfc. Thomas D. Glawe, LCpl. Raymond S. Hildreth, Pfc. Joseph J. Kosoglow, LCpl. Robert Martinez, LCpl. Alcadio N. Mascarenas, Pfc. James O. McKinney, LCpl. Daniel K. Mulvihill, Pfc. Thomas G. Powles and LCpl. Ralph G. Victor.

In addition to the patrol members Maj. William J. Goodsell of VMO-6 was posthumously awarded the Navy Cross.

The Silver Star was also awarded to Capt. James M. Perryman and Capt. John M. Shields of HMM-362. A posthumous Silver Star was awarded to 2dLt. Ronald W. Meyer of C-1-5.

Perryman provides the following insight to what happened to Goodsell that night:

Mike Shields was my wingman throughout that night over Hill 488. We were a flight of two UH-lE Huey gunships providing close-in fire support to Howard.

Early the next morning I launched as wingman to Frank Goodsell back to the area to support with Howard's extraction. As the transport helos were finishing up Frank made a low pass over the top of the ridge to assess the situation; I was in tail chase right behind him. Although the Marines had done a great job of cleaning up, one of the VC/NVA hiding in a hole with an automatic weapon, sprayed the bottom of both our aircraft as we flew over.

In addition to shooting out the hydraulics, one round hit Frank in the femoral artery. Frank's copilot, Lieutenant Steve Butler, managed to land his helicopter on the valley floor below.

As the bullet spray had knocked out all my radios, I couldn't determine the exact problem with number one aircraft, but I followed him down, landing beside him.

The three other crewmen carried Frank to my helicopter and climbed aboard.

I flew back to the hospital at Marble Mountain/Danang but Goodsell, I'm certain, was dead on arrival. I do not remember another crewman being wounded, at least, not from our two aircraft.

Jim Perryman

✳   ✳   ✳   ✳

On July 15, 1966 Operation Hastings was launched with a morning troop lift utilizing thirty helicopters of MAG-16. All of the member squadrons provided aircraft. The initial lift of the 3rd Battalion, 4th Marines was into a hot landing zone.

During the first lift, three CH-46A's sustained strike damage. Two of these aircraft were from HMM-164 and the other was from HMM-265. Two other helicopters from HMM-164 received small arms and automatic weapons fire going into and out of the landing zone. One of these aircraft was forced to land in another zone but was later recovered.

The 2nd Battalion, 4th Marines was lifted into the second landing zone.

At 1815 a reaction force led by LtCol. Herbert Mendenhall was airlifted to the area of the downed helicopters. The mission of this reaction force was to provide security for the remains of the three CH-46A's that were previously shot down.

Aircraft number EP-171 of HMM-265 was part of this flight. This helicopter was hit by heavy enemy 12.7mm automatic weapon fire and subsequently crashed.

All survivors were extremely brave and calm under extremely hazardous conditions. Capt. Thomas C. McAllister, pilot, and his co-pilot 1stLt. George C. Richey performed in an outstanding manner while maneuvering the burning aircraft toward a landing site. Both pilots survived with minor burns.

Killed in the crash were twelve Marine passengers who were mostly from E-2-1 and crew chief Robert R. Telfer who had just turned 24 on the previous day.

The gunner, Sgt. Gary A. Lucus, valiantly tried to rescue Telfer and was severely burned. He was later taken to the United States Naval Hospital in Yokosuka, Japan. After regaining partial use of his hands he wrote a letter to Lt. Thomas McAllister. It was written on September 5, 1966, approximately two months after the crash. With the written permission of Gary Lucus that letter is reprinted here in its original form. No corrections have been made in spelling or grammatical form.

> "T.C.'s craft was in flames as it descended through about
> 800 feet. It rolled over and exploded on impact and there

was no doubt in my mind there would be no survivors."

John T. Maxwell
Bonnie Sue:
A Marine Corps Helicopter Squadron in Vietnam
By Marion F. Sturkey

5
THE CRASH OF EP-171

5 Sept, 66

Dear Capt. McAllister

It sure was good to hear that you and Lt. Richey got out and are in good shape and was also glad to get your letter.

As to my going to the states. Well I'll be leaving here in a week or so and as it stands I'll be going to either Camp Pendleton or San Diego.

The reason for my going to the states is because of my left hand. I have feeling in it, but it doesn't seem to want to do what I tell it. It is real stiff but the Dr. says it will come along in time. My skin graphs are doing wonderful and in a year or so they should be so smooth that no one will ever be able to tell I've had them. I have a few marks on my face, back, and legs, but they are all healed and all in all I feel like the luckiest guy in the world.

Well, I've spent the last week trying to remember just how everything happened back there and as near as I can recall, this is how it went:

We had just finished jettisoning fuel and I turned back on my gun when I heard Sgt. Telfer and his M60. He seemed to be firing straight down and a little aft. He fired about 100 to 150 rounds when I heard a "Wham" "Wham" (like some-one out on the stub wing with a ball bat) and the next instant fire was starting to sweep around the hatch and inside the aft of the plane. At first I thought it was the excess fuel (from when we jettisoned) burning but in a couple of seconds the entire upper section, around the engines, was on fire. This was when I told you we were on fire. I grabbed the fire extinguisher and Sgt. Telfer took it from me and started aft, at this time the smoke was starting to roll forward toward the cockpit. It seemed to hang from the ceiling and my eyes started to burn, Sgt. Telfer wasn't able to go all the way aft to use the extinguisher because the flames were about half way forward and the heat to intense.

I heard Lt. Richey tell you that he couldn't see and asked you to take it. I don't know what I was thinking about, but at the time I figured that maybe if I stood in the opening between the cockpit and the cabin, that I could keep some of the smoke out, so I unbuckled and tried to block the doorway. My eyes were burning from the smoke and when I looked aft I couldn't see anything.

The next thing I remember was that my knees seemed to be up in my stomach and I was rolling and bouncing around and dirt, sticks, and sand was being thrown into my face. I grabbed for something to hold on to and the next thing I remember was looking aft and I could see green bushes through the smoke and fire and I realized we were on the ground.

Before we hit I could feel the intense heat, but now I seemed cool and started to think how I was going to get out. I saw Sgt. Telfer Laying on the M60 and I grabbed him and told him to get out. He said his leg was caught so I crawled over him to see what was holding him.

His right leg, from above the knee, was on the outside of the plane and was pinned there. He hollered for me to pull him out but he wouldn't budge. He then told me to break it off, god how I tried to pull it out but it just had to much weight on it. While I was pulling on Sgt. Telfer I saw another man move, I told Sgt. Telfer I'd get this guy to help and I started for the man I saw moving. I had forgotten, until now, that I hadn't found a way out so I thought I'd try to open the hatch that was just aft of the 50 Cal. so that when someone was free I could shove them through it.

I pulled the cable and pushed on the hatch it didn't budge. I got excited and put my shoulder against it and tried to ram it open, it didn't open. I kept hitting it but I saw I was wasting my time so I started looking elsewhere. This is when I thought about you and Lt. Richey. I went forward and found that the co-pilots escape hatch was open so I went back to the man that was moving and found that the only thing he could move was one hand. I layed him over my shoulder and started forward when something seemed to knock us down. I fell with this guy on top of me and I rolled him over to find out that a round, from one of the troops, had cooked off and hit him in the side.

He stopped breathing and it scared the hell out of me. The only thing

I could think about was to drag Sgt. Telfer out and get away.

I grabbed Sgt. Telfer's flack jacket, through the arms, and started pulling with all I had, then all of a sudden his head dropped and he didn't seem to be helping me at all. I grabbed his head and lifted it up and I could see bleeding from the face. I grabbed the bottom of his flack jacket and started lifting when I saw a hole in the back of his flight suit. I tried to feel his temple for a heartbeat but I couldn't feel one. I tried to talk to him but he wouldn't answer, he was dead, I couldn't believe it. I couldn't move, I didn't want to move, I was scared to death. I sat there a moment or two and finally realized there was nothing I could do, I thought that maybe there was at least one person I could help so I went aft to check the closest man. He was still strapped in and leaning over. I grabbed his shoulders and pushed him back and I can still see his burning hair. His chinstrap was burnt into and his helmet fell on the deck. I remember squeezing up through the co-pilots escape hatch and rolling off onto the ground.

I didn't want to leave the plane but I guess the cookoffs kind of helped me make up my mind.

All in all I guess I was lucky because after about ten minutes in the brush some Marines found me and took me to a Battalion C.P. of some sort.

I stayed in the plane only 5 or 6 minutes after we hit and as far as I could tell everyone was still in their seats. I guess the smoke must have gotten to them because I didn't see any signs of panic.

Their are two men here in the hospital that were on the hill when we hit and they said that one man ran out of the back when we were about half way down and that another man jumped out just before we hit and the plane landed on him. They also said there was an explosion and screams just after we hit but I don't remember them, maybe I was knocked out. I don't know. I imagine this seems like a long letter but these are the things I remember and, in time, hope to forget. I haven't slept a nite since it happened because I keep thinking I could have helped someone besides myself.

Like I've said before, this seems as tho its kind of long and drawn out but its the first time I've tried to tell it to someone. I talked to Lt. Sturkey about it but never really in detail.

I hope you'll forgive my spelling and composition format because if I don't write fast I might not write it at all. I guess that is about it.

There are a lot of ifs and I'm going to try to forget everything. I called my wife just after I got here and the first thing she asked was, "how did you get burned". I told her that a barrel of cleaning solvent, in the armory, exploded. If she were to find out that I had my feet off the ground she'd worry herself sick.

Tell Capt. Harper and Lt. Carey that I'll get a letter to them in a day or so.

Capt. McAllister, I want you to know that without someone like yourself at the controls, I might not be here today. Thanks for bringing her down as soft as you did.

Hope to see you again in the future. Good luck and may God bless.

Respectfully
Sgt. G.A.. Lucus

P.S. I think it has helped me quite a bit to write this to you. Thanks again for listening.

Sgt. Gary Lucus was from Cody, Wyoming and was 25 years of age on July 15, 1966. He provided the following commentary on February 7, 1999 in an e-mail addressed to the author:

In a recent email, you mentioned numerous units that participated in "Operation Hastings". There is at least one you have not mentioned, 3/26 which was out of Hawaii, at that time. I know this because I was in the Yokosuka Naval Hospital with a few of those guys. We were all on the plastic surgery ward when some of them found out that the guy who was bandaged from head to toe (me) was one of the guys in the helicopter that crashed less than 300 meters from their position on 7-15-66.

This crash on 7-15-66 can be broken down into: The in-flight warning; being hit at 3500 feet and burning to the ground where we crashed; In the helicopter on the ground at the crash site; exiting the helicopter and finding friendly troops; the night in the field with a Chaplain and the emergency MedEvac up through 70 foot trees while taking small arms fire. I'm sure I will run things together, but I will try to keep things straight.

This account of the rescue attempt was related to me by a number of Marines in the Yokosuka Naval Hospital a couple of months after the crash. Although their position was taking small arms and incoming mortar fire, a bunch of Marines from 3/26 said they ran to our helicopter only seconds after it had crashed and got the pilots. They said they banged on the belly of the helicopter, the helicopter crash landed on the starboard side (right side), but they got no response from inside. They said they tried to get to the back ramp but could not get close because the fire and heat was too intense. After a few minutes of exposure to incoming small arms fire from the surrounding hills, coupled with the multitude of "cook offs" from inside the helicopter, one of the Marines shouted, "No one else could be alive inside, lets go!" They retreated to their positions, 300 meters away, and watched it burn. It burned for two days they told me.

During this time I was still inside the plane, on the ground, I didn't remember hearing anyone pounding on the aircraft. Everything was in "slow motion". The flames were everywhere but there was no sensation of the heat or even being hot.

My first concern was, I could finally breath, unlike when we were on our way down; the smoke had been so thick you could not see out of the portholes. The glass for the porthole windows had been removed on all helicopters to prevent the shrapnel effect in case they were hit by small arms fire. The air draft, while on our way down, was such that the thick black oil and hydraulic based fire was producing a toxic smoke that was being drawn forward through the helicopter and into the cockpit. Below the smoke was this searing, constant, unbearable heat that penetrated your skin like steam through your pores and straight to the bone. There was no place to go, no place to hide. I didn't want to breathe because the smoke clogged my throat and my lungs burned as if they were on fire. My brain was trying to refuse the intake of air, but my body needed to breathe. I felt I was dying!

In an attempt to see aft in the cabin I had to get almost on the floor. Although there was less smoke close to the floor there was more fumes, heat and fire. I could see the troops still strapped in the troop seats, their upper body's hidden by the dense smoke (I remember thinking that this might have been a sign that they were either new troops in the field or troops that were very well disciplined).

Sgt. Bob Telfer, the Crew Chief, and I attempted to extinguish the fire with small fire bottles, but it had no effect at all. We could not see where we were spraying and the flames were coming from all directions.

About this time, I heard the Lt. (over the headset) tell the Capt. to take the controls because he could not see. It was at this point I decided to stand in the cockpit entrance in an attempt to keep the smoke out of the cockpit so the pilots would have a better chance for clearer vision for landing.

I have heard how some people say their entire lives flash in front of them just before they thought they were about to die. I had a similar, but quite different experience. While I was standing in the cockpit entrance, eyes closed to prevent further pain from the midnight black smoke with soot particles as big as "BB's", my arms pressing against the bulkheads on either side in an effort to restrict the flow of smoke from entering the cockpit and the intense heat from the fire covering my entire body, I quite clearly remember feeling so very sorry for my three young sons. They would now grow up never knowing who I was or how much I loved them. I almost cried at thinking I might be giving up.

It was then that my knees buckled and everything went spinning around. I remember bouncing and banging around with dirt and sticks hitting all over my body and then nothing.

After what seemed to be a few short moments, I could see out the back of the helicopter. The flames distorted the view, but I knew we were on the ground and everything was going to be alright....I could finally breathe!

My letter in 1966 pretty much describes what happened next aboard the helicopter.

The following has only been related twice. The first time was in Yuma to the NIS/FBI interviewers and now this time. This is the first time I have written about it and I don't know if I can get it all out just right.

After unsuccessfully attempting to help either the crew chief or any of the troops I next thought of self survival. I made my way forward to the co-pilots escape hatch which was now at the top of the cockpit. The emergency exit side window was very small and I can remember the near panic I experienced as I wondered if I was going to be able to fit through it. I put my hands together over my head in a diving position and pushed off of the co-pilots, armored seat with my feet. I was able to get my shoulders up through the exit opening and laid my elbows on the outside of the plane to push my body up through the opening. The exterior of the helicopter was very hot and my forearms and elbows were burned through my flight suit. I put my hands on the side of the helicopter to push my lower body up through the opening and as I did I could hear the sound of meat frying in a very hot skillet. After a modest struggle, I finally got my buttocks up through the exit opening and it was then I realized the frying sound was that of my hands as I was pushing on the side of the helicopter. Upon realizing what was happening I quickly lifted my hands and instinctively looked at them. I could see the bones in my hands because the skin and muscle from fingers and the palms remained stuck to the side of the helicopter. There was no blood, just a dark red outline around what used to be hands and fingers. Pieces of skin hung from my fingers like spaghetti and the pain was all I could endure. I pushed backwards off of the side of the helicopter.

I rolled off the plane and landed on the ground expecting someone to be there to help. I knew the pilots were gone, but I did not know who took them or where they were. I lay there a minute until I realized that the only people who knew I was there and could see me was the bad guys. I noticed small arms rounds impacting the area all around me. I'm sure some were "cook offs" from inside the plane, but most were from the hills around the crash site. I remember thinking "out of the pan and into the fire, what an unlucky bastard, but at least I was alive"!

At that point my only thought was to get out of the clearing. I started crawling in a zigzag line as the small arms continued to impact around me, I got to my feet and started walking or stumbling in a zigzag manner until I got to the edge of the jungle. (I was unaware at this time that I had taken a hit in my left thigh). I crashed into the thicket for about 50 meters and fell to the ground from exhaustion. As I lay there looking up through the 60 to 70 foot trees, I began wondering what to do next. My imagination got the best of me. I started thinking about a Viet Cong (VC) patrol finding me and putting the muzzle of their rifles between my eyes. This terrible thought plus the thought of being a POW renewed my strength and I stood up to survey my situation.

I looked at my hands, which were now starting to ooze blood and were covered with dirt and grass. God, how they hurt. I could hardly close them. They seemed as though they were not a part of my body.

My next thought was of how I was going to protect myself. I reached for my .38 caliber pistol in my shoulder holster, but I could not unsnap the safety strap that held the pistol in the holster and as a result I could not remove the pistol. Oh God, what next?

The jungle started closing in, my head and body were aching. My helmet was squeezing my head. I tried to unbuckle the chinstrap on my flight helmet but I could not undo the snap. In a mild panic I pushed up on both sides of the helmet with my stub hands, the pain was intense and I wanted to cry out but knew I couldn't. I tucked my chin as I pushed and the helmet pushed off. I let it fall to the ground. As I looked at it lying on the ground, I was amazed. The thick plastic protective visor, which I had down the entire time, was warped and melted. The back left side had two small caliber ricochet holes in it and the top was cracked about 6 to 8 inches. It was all twisted out of shape and I could not believe I had just taken it off. Again I dropped to the ground and lay there listening. Listening for anything, but all I could hear were the rounds "cooking off" and grenade explosions from the crashed helicopter in the distance.

I knew any friendlies in the area would be on the high ground, so I decided to quietly move up this little ridge that I could see through the brush. I was trying to be very quiet but I was falling and stumbling. One side of me said to scream for help but the other side said to be aware of the bad guys. I decided to keep quiet.

I stumbled for a hundred meters or so and again fell from exhaustion. After a few minutes of rest, I started crawling although I was getting very tired and every inch of my body was in pain. All I knew was I had to keep moving upward because that seemed my only hope and I was not ready to die. I had realized in the helicopter that life was too precious to give up and I would not give in to the pain.

By this time, it had been about an hour since the crash and I was very upset that there were no friendlies to come to my aid. I pushed onward up the ridge very slowly wondering what I would do if I were not found. Suddenly I could faintly hear voices speaking English. One said, "Did you hear that?" and another said "no".

I stopped, my heart was filled with joy and I struggled to my knees to yell, "Here I am, come help". I opened my mouth to speak, but realized my mouth was already open and my tongue and lips were swollen and cracked so much I could not talk. I tried to wet my lips but there was no moisture. I could not breathe through my nose and the only opening in my face was a tiny air hole that I had been breathing through.

My heart fell and I lay back down on the ground. I didn't know what to do. As I lay there trying to think I started worrying about being shot by friendly troops. Why did this have to happen to me? It is going to be dark soon. What now?

The voices were quiet and I was afraid to move. I had to get those Marines to notice me without being shot by them. After a few scary minutes, as I lay there thinking of my options, I felt an intense pain in my left forearm. As I lay there I noticed the Velcro closure on the sleeve of my flight suit was very tight on my left arm because my entire forearm and wrist was extremely swollen. I felt I had to loosen the sleeve and relieve the pressure on my arm, but I didn't know how. I could not use my teeth because my tongue and lips were swollen shut, I didn't know if I could grab the Velcro flap with my hands and pull it to release the pressure because I could barely close my hands due to them being so swollen. After a few tries, I was able to grasp the Velcro flap between two fingers that were stuck together and what was left of the heel of my hand. I was afraid that the flap would be stuck very tightly so I held tight and jerked it.

The silence all around was broken by the sound of the Velcro separating. This is an unmistakable sound and one I will always be thankful for. This highly audible loud sound echoed over a 50-meter area and I heard a voice say, "Did you hear that? And a response was, "Yes I did. What was it"? I lay quite still, refastened the Velcro, and pulled it apart again. Again, the sound echoed. A voice immediately said, "Who goes there"! I could not talk so again I fastened the Velcro and pulled it apart. Again the same sound, but this time one of the voices said, "Look over there, is it one of those guys from the helicopter crash"?

As I rolled over I could barely see two Marines that were in a Listening Post just below the ridge line about 30 meters ahead. One of them said, "Hey, if you're from the crash stand up so we can see you." I struggled to my feet and as they saw me, they started screaming and yelling for a Corpsman. They ran down to where I was and laid me down and started pouring water all over my face and body. One of them became sick to his stomach from the smell of me and had to leave. He said he was going to show the Corpsman where I was.

The Corpsman arrived in a couple of minutes, gave me two morphine injections and helped me up the ridge to their command post. It was a small defensible area surrounded by dense vegetation and trees and was located in their area of responsibility. Everyone came to have a look; there was a Newsweek reporter and cameraman snapping pictures. They were all amazed that anyone could have gotten out of the helicopter alive, but admitted I would not make it through the night.

The Corpsman immediately injected me with the maximum dosage of morphine, assigned a Private to pour water into my mouth and began to treat me for shock. His next concern was to clean the burn areas he could see; face, arms, hands, back and legs This treatment they were administering to me was being done at the same time a Division of North Vietnamese Regulars was tying to over run our position.

The initial assault was repelled with no breaks in the defense. As everyone was sealing in their positions for a night assault that was sure to follow, the Corpsman asked the Chaplain if he would continue to administer a salt solution to me while he tended other Marines who had been wounded. All of the wounded Marines kept telling the Corpsman to leave them alone and spend his time making sure I was OK. I could not believe it when the Corpsman returned and relayed this story to the Chaplain. MARINES! What a group!!

As night fell I was put between two very large trees that had been knocked over during earlier bombing runs in the area. Lucky for me there was enough room for me to lay with the Chaplain having enough room to sit at my head. There he could administer a salt solution so I would not dehydrate.

For the next few minutes all was quiet and I could hear the Marines digging-in and trying to get a bite of cold rations while they had a little time before the next attack. The conversations were very quiet, almost muffled, and I could bear the prep-orders being given to the Night Reconnaissance Patrol Leaders, as they were getting ready to slip outside of our perimeter to check on "Charlie" to see what he had in mind for later that night.

About 2300 the Corpsman returned and told me he was giving me another morphine injection even though I didn't think I needed one. I told him I wanted to be alert and available if I was needed later that night. The Chaplain said I had already done my share and that I should try to rest. He then shoved the canteen back into my mouth in an effort to change the subject.

All was quite and my mind was racing. I had spent many nights in the "bush". In fact, I had done so twice on this tour. Once while flying we had engine problems and had to "put down" in the "badlands". The other time was earlier in July when we were distributing "Chou Hoi" pamphlets. We were dropping them out of the helicopter over selected villages. During this process some of the pamphlets were caught in the "blade wash" and were sucked back up and into the generator air intake screens. This blocked the cool air intake. This resulted in the generators overheating and eventually burning out. We had to put-down on the beach and were picked up the next day. We spent a very interesting night with six Army Special Forces Troops that had been in the field for three months. These guys were very strange. I had spent nights out on my previous two tours. Anyway, back to the night with the Chaplain. I had some idea what might be in store for this unit once "Charlie" decided to come back. This was the first time that North Vietnam Regulars had entered the war. This was to be their introduction to the American Fighting Man. The Marines were going to initiate them.

It must have been about 0230 when the serene silence was shattered by small arms fire as the Last of the Night Patrols came running back hollering that "Charlie" was on their heals. Our position started receiving incoming light mortars and selected small arms fire. The night sky was lit up with flares and you could hear the distant screams of the advancing North Vietnam Troops. The initial wave was repelled. A second wave advanced and was beaten back only a few feet from our perimeter. Then at about 0400 the third and largest wave hit and breached our defenses. "Gooks were in the wire" then "Gooks were through the wire" and rounds were going in all directions. As I lay between the fallen trees I could see figures jumping over them so fast that I could not make out if they were good guys or bad guys. All of my exposed body parts were wrapped with bandages. My hands were bandaged and my head was wrapped with only small peepholes for my mouth, nose and eyes.

The Chaplain had only been "In Country" for two weeks. This was more terrifying to him than he had ever imagined in his worst nightmare. The ground was shaking and dirt and rocks were flying everywhere. Mortars were impacting our defenses and exploding only a few feet away as small arm rounds slammed into the very trees that were protecting us. Ricochets were bouncing off every limb, rock and dirt pile. Both wounded Marines and North Vietnam soldiers were screaming for help. I lay there feeling as if I am breathing my last breaths.

In all of the excitement, I heard one of the most genuine soul searching conversations I have ever heard. The Chaplain had a serious dilemma facing him for the first time in his life. He had always been taught to turn the other cheek and live to fight another day. Well if he turned the other cheek today there might not be another day. This was the subject of his inner discussion. He was asking himself if a North Vietnamese Soldier would jump into our space would he be able to shoot him to protect himself and me?

He was recounting his reluctance to accept a .45 Caliber pistol that he had been issued. The Company Commander had ordered him to accept the pistol and carry it for personal protection while in the "bush". The CO had given it to him the day they left for the "bush" from the staging area at Da Nang airbase. The Chaplain was explaining that he had told the CO he had no need to take another human life. He felt that the situation would never arise. His mission was not one of taking lives. He was here to comfort the souls, listen to troops with personal stateside problems and give mass on Sundays.

As he talked to himself, he kept asking himself if he could actually pull the trigger? He thought on that question for a long while and then he removed the pistol from the holster and started to review all of the safety features aloud. He went over the assembly and disassembly of the pistol. He described the pistols action, the muzzle velocity, the projectile speed and the foot-pounds at impact. He understood the weapons use, but doubted if it was for his use. He inserted the magazine, removed it and reinserted it. He did this five or six times. Each time asking God what he should do! I could see him; because the flares were popping all around He would raise the pistol as if he was pointing it to shoot. He would point the pistol, hold it for a few seconds and say "click", and then lower it. As figures would jump over our position he would raise the pistol as if to engage a target. At first, his movements were quite slow, but after a few tries, he became very quick to raise the pistol and align the sights.

I startled him when I asked if he was practicing to be Wild Bill Hickcock? He, at first seemed very embarrassed but then quickly said, "I have a very important decision to make."

I immediately told him that someone had looked over me yesterday and I would be disappointed if nobody was looking over me today. He looked down at me and said, "Son, I promise to do the right thing!"

As daylight broke the shooting had stopped. "Charlie" had gotten through the wire but the cost far exceeded its value. They suffered over 225 KIA. The Marines had lost about 20 KIA and 40 wounded. I think the North Vietnamese Regular Army had gotten a little insight into the determination of the US Fighting Man and the Marines.

As I lay there having my morning salt solution, I asked the Chaplain if he would ever forget last night? He said he had dreaded having to experience a night lake that, but now that he had, he was a much wiser man. He said the counseling sessions with the troops would now have new meaning because life itself now had new meaning. He said that Sunday services would now take on an entirely new approach with an emphasis on having your inner house in order. He seemed like a much older man with a mission. I really liked him a lot.

As they carried me away for my trip up through the 80-foot trees for the MedEvac to "Charlie Med" I could see that the Chaplain had a whole new demeanor. Although he didn't have to fire his weapon, I think he would have. He seemed much relieved and more relaxed, older, stronger, wiser and more confident. I could also see that he was wearing his pistol just a little lower, stood a little taller and seemed to understand why he was there. I thanked him and was carried away.

A side note is that a corpsman exited the plane. He ran out of the rear ramp at 1,000 feet and one of the Marines exited at about 300 feet on the way down. The corpsman's family thought that they recognized him in a POW photograph in the mid seventies. They somehow traced him to be on my plane on 7/15/66. The Naval Investigative Service and the FBI located me in Yuma, Arizona in 1980. I was still on active duty. I retired in 1983. They interviewed me for 6 or 8 hours. They taped the entire interview and had me authenticate it the following day. Then in the early nineties the television show, *Unsolved Mysteries,* aired a reenactment of our flight. They were looking for anyone who may have information about the missing corpsman.

NOTES:
Government records indicate that there were 12 passengers aboard EP-171. All were killed. The following group of 8 Marines and 2 corpsmen were members of the first Platoon, E-2-1:
Case, Orson H. Cpl. 1894238; 25; Johnstown, New York
Chamaj, Andrew P. HM3 6979759; 24; Scenery Hill, Pennsylvania
Chambers, Paul R. Cpl. 2056522; 23, Scottsboro, Alabama
Cherrick, James W. Pfc. 2205708; 19, New York, New York
Cunnion, Michael A. Pfc. 2170734; 21, Mount Vernon, New York
Dennis, Mark V. HM3 7789145; 19; Miamisburg, Ohio
Gooden, Michael A.. Pfc. 2127938; 19; Bellflower, California
Schloemer, Carl W. Pfc. 2149732;19;Bellefontaine Neighbors, Missouri
Simmons, Herolin T. SSgt. 1900256; 24, Ahoskie, North Carolina

Stubstad, Gerald E. Pfc. 2179223; 20, Chicago, Illinois
    Also killed was the helicopter crew chief:
Telfer, Robert R. Sgt. 1877872; 24; Fonda, New York

The following were killed in helicopter crashes that day: Two of these four were aboard EP-171.
Cullers, Ronald K. 2dLt. 092158; 23; Shelbina, Missouri
Lilly, William J. Cpl. 2041198; 22; Rowayton, Connecticutt
Reid, James M. Cpl. 2050762; 20; Philadelphia, Pennsylvania
Morris, John N. HN 6834551; 22; Meldrim, Georgia

The following synopsis was taken from the P.O.W. NETWORK on the Internet:
    Hospitalman Mark Dennis was a Navy corpsman aboard a Chinook helicopter when it was shot down on July 15, 1966. All men on board were declared Killed in Action. Three and a half weeks later, a casket arrived in Ohio and was buried. In November 1970, an issue of Newsweek carried a photograph of an "unknown POW" which his brother felt was Mark Dennis. That, combined with an earlier report from the Navy, that "a couple of men could have gotten out of the helicopter" sparked Mark's brother to travel to Paris, Bangkok and Vietnam in search of the truth.
    The remains claimed to be those of Mark Dennis were exhumed and exhaustive tests made. The results proved to Mark's family beyond a shadow of a doubt that they did not bury Mark Dennis, but someone else, unknown to them. Mark's family continues to actively pursue answers to their question, "Where is Mark Dennis?"

Other Marines mentioned in this chapter are as follows:
Carey, Richard L. 2dLt. 089159
Harper, Richard O. Capt. 071918
Maxwell, John T. Capt. 072054
McAllister, Thomas C. Capt. 085394
Plante, Douglas E. Sgt. 2023006
Sturkey, Marion F. 1stLt. 091161; Plum Branch, South Carolina
Richey, George C. 1stLt. 088665

Gary Lucus is mistaken about the participation of 3-26 in Operation Hastings. The Marines were probably from 3-4. George Neville, a Silver

Star winner as a recon Marine in Vietnam, has done extensive research on Operation Hastings. Here are some of his findings: The battles that occurred on this operation took place between July 15 and July 25, 1966. After July 25 there were very few casualties. The NVA were not engaged after July 25. The brunt of the fighting was done by Companies E, F, G and H of 2-1, Companies E, G and H of 2-4, Companies I, K, L and M of 3-4 and Companies I, K, L and M of 3-5. There were no units from 3-26 in Vietnam at this time. In fact, 3-26 did not arrive in Vietnam for duty until December 11, 1966. Neville is currently writing a book about Operation Hastings.

John "Doc" McNiff, a corpsman with I-3-4 witnessed the crash of EP-171. His description of what he saw is as follows:

We were waiting for the resupply choppers to bring in reinforcements. We watched the approaching Sea Knight helicopters in a formation of three abreast and four or five rows deep. About a half mile in front of our position the choppers started to take heavy groundfire. We saw the tracers- white this time- going up at them, and the lead chopper flew directly into the tracers' path. It shuddered and wiggled and began to smoke as it lost altitude. It had been about 300 feet in the air when it was hit and so close to the LZ that the pilot didn't have a lot of room to maneuver. The rest of the formation broke and dispersed.

The pilot brought his wounded bird down quickly, intending to land on our plain. But when he saw all the Marines there, he pulled it up and got behind a small hill, using it to screen us from the crash. He was no more than 50 feet off the deck as he passed us, smoking heavily. I saw a hand pushing against one of the round windows, a Marine trying to get out. There was obviously panic inside the chopper. The ramp was partially down, and one Marine, on fire, jumped off the bird but was killed by the fall. Someone yelled to get down in the holes just as the chopper crashed and blew up. A rotor blade landed directly behind the hole I was in. Ammunition that the Marines had been carrying started to cook off and sent projectiles in all directions for about 15 minutes. Then it was quiet. I later learned that the pilot, co-pilot and crew chief escaped but all others on board were killed. Had the pilot set down in our position, surely many more men would have died. The image of that hand pushing against the porthole will be with me till I die.

LCpl. Paul Stenzel was a member of E-2-1 on July 15, 1966. Here is his recollection of the crash:

Near the end of June 1966, 2-1 had moved north to Dong Ha. Echo Company had been there since 22 June, providing security for Marine artillery. Operation Hastings kicked off on the morning of 15 July.

Later that evening, E Company, 2-1 was flown into LZ Crow. One helicopter, with part of the 1st platoon aboard, was shot down by the NVA. Thirteen were killed, including the platoon sergeant and seven men of the first squad.

A month before this happened; I was squad leader of the first squad. Then I was hospitalized with malaria. I often wondered, if I hadn't gotten malaria would I have been on that helicopter?

One thing that sticks in my mind is a strange incident involving Michael Gooden that took place one month before this happened. While in the Co Bi Tanh Tan area, a stray round had hit Gooden's helmet and ricocheted off. It left a good dent in the helmet, but he wasn't hurt. I remember we all told him how damn lucky he was. The round had come out of nowhere. We weren't engaged in any fighting at the time, but were moving into position to sweep through a hamlet. Michael Gooden was on that helicopter that was shot down.

Roy Lanham had just arrived in Vietnam and had only recently joined E-2-1. In the following, he recalls the incident:

Being new in the country, I was attached to the platoon leader and the radio operator instead of a permanent squad. On my first operation involving helicopter transport troops, I was told to wait near the back ramp of the chopper my group was boarding; because it was possible I would be shifted to another one in order to balance the weight in each one evenly. I was standing outside the tail of the CH-46 when the crew chief of that chopper pointed to another one. Being 19-years old and knowing—if only briefly—only those Marines on the chopper where I was waiting, I did not want to go. My heart sank, as I really wanted to board that first chopper. But I did as I was told.

All the choppers took off. When we had been in the air about 40 minutes, I was looking down toward the ground through a small round window when I saw a chopper's back end on fire. Then moments later I saw the chopper crash and burn into the side of a mountain. We tried to land nearby, but because of heavy small-arms fire in the area we could not, and so went back to Dong Ha Airport.

After landing, there was a head count to determine which chopper had gone down. It turned out it was the one I was supposed to go on with the platoon leader. All on board were killed.

Delano Cummings was a member of E-2-1 that day. Years later, he wrote a book about his Vietnam experiences. The following excerpt is taken from that book, *Moon Dash Warrior.*

It was hurry up and wait. All those Marines in one place ready to go and not a chopper in sight. We sat down and lay back on our packs, hot and miserable, waiting for the time to pass.

Around noon two CH-46 helicopters came in and took some of the Marines. The rest of us still waited. Someone said, "Maybe they called it off." Another Marine answered, "Bullshit." He cursed Vietnam and the Marine Corps some and then added, "We'll be going." Finally, someone yelled, "Saddle up! We're getting out!"

CH-46 choppers started coming in and someone else called out, "Line up! " After that I couldn't hear anything because of all the noise, but we were getting on 12 to 14 Marines at a time; when one chopper got enough Marines they started loading another. Platoons and even squads got separated. Sgt Plant shouted that we'd regroup when we got to the field, but Marines started changing places so they could go out with their friends.

Sources:

Background information and the Maxwell quote were taken from *Bonnie-Sue; A Marine Corps Helicopter Squadron in Vietnam* by Marion Sturkey.

The eyewitness account of John McNiff was taken from an article that appeared in the February 1998 issue of *Vietnam* magazine. The title of the article is *Operation Hastings: Costly Offensive in Helicopter Valley* by John "Doc" McNiff.

The comments of Roy Lanham and Paul Stenzel were taken from *We Remember: The Vietnam Stories of the Men of 2nd Battalion, 1st Marines* edited by David and Marian Novak.

Operation Prairie began on August 3, 1966. It was designed to monitor the activities of the NVA in Quang Tri Province. After more than seven weeks of sometimes-fierce combat and numerous casualties the Marines of the Third Battalion, Fourth Regiment squared off with a large NVA force on Nui Cay Tre Ridge. Arnaud de Borchgrave of Newsweek Magazine, John Schneider, a UPI photographer, and Derek Taylor, a British reporter, accompanied the Marines. These men were about to experience two days of fierce combat in the struggle for Hill 400.

As a young reporter, Arnaud de Borchgrave had parachuted into Dien Bien Phu in 1954. He was no stranger to combat but would be wounded on September 28 and evacuated by helicopter. Drawing from his experiences during the fight for Hill 400 he wrote one of the most vivid first person accounts of war ever put to pen and paper. His account of this battle first appeared in *Newsweek Magazine* on October 10, 1966. With the written permission of *Newsweek,* a transcript of that article is reprinted below:

"Randy Fassett and Buddy James saved our butts a lot.
They were a really good pair of Marines."

LCpl. James T. Bass
I-3-4

THE CRUCIAL TEST: Just south of the Demilitarized Zone (DMZ) that runs along the border between North and South Vietnam, U. S. Marines and North Vietnamese regulars are now locked in one of the most crucial campaigns of the Vietnam War. For more than a month, units of North Vietnam's crack 324B Division have been seeking to seize control of "the Rockpile" — a rugged 700-foot-highoutcropping which dominates the main valley approaches to northern South Vietnam. By last week the fight for the Rockpile had become the focal point of Operation Prairie, a Marine spoiling attack against North Vietnamese penetration from the DMZ. At stake in Operation Prairie is nothing less than a decisive test of whether the U. S. can defeat the North Vietnamese in their own backyard . . . . As a result, the fighting has grown so fierce that two weeks ago American casualties soared to a record 142 killed and 825 wounded. In the midst of the swirling battle last week was Newsweek Senior Editor Arnaud de Borchgrave, who was slightly wounded. Below is his report.

6
THE BATTLE FOR HILL 400

"I hope to occupy that hill by tonight," says Col. William Masterpool, the soft-spoken commander of the Third Battalion of the Fourth Marine Regiment. It is the morning of Sept. 27 and we are standing on the top of "Hill 363" (so designated because of its altitude in meters). The colonel is pointing to "Hill 400" — control of which is vital to control of the Rockpile itself.

Eight hundred yards of jungle separate us from the objective. Everyone already had a three-day beard. We are handed a C-ration pack and rationed to one canteen of water each. Here is the record of the next 31 hours:

0930 [Hours, September 27, 1966] As we thread our way along the ridgeline between the two hills, I notice a few bone fragments on the trail. Then dried, bloodstained Marine flak jackets and fatigues. "What's this?" I whisper to the man behind me. The answer chills me. This was where a Marine company took 60 percent casualties during an earlier operation.

0940 — We pass a skull on a stake at the side of the trail. A few yards further a crudely penned note on a branch says in English: "We come back kill marines." K for Kilo Company is ahead of us.

1005 — After an exhausting climb, we reach the top of Hill 400. Point man stumbles over bamboo pole. It triggers claymore mine 3 yards back of him as well as several grenades strung from branches. Four casualties. Suddenly, machine gun fire opens up. Impossible to see where it is coming from. Marines return fire forward and on both flanks. Shouts of "Corpsman (medic)!"

1020 — As I emerge in a small clearing, there's deafening explosion followed by shouts of "Incoming mortar!" I run a few feet, see old artillery hole and fall in. Five Marines land on top of me. Mortar shells impact all around us. I can't move and have trouble breathing. Mercifully, shelling stops after four minutes. One Marine is lying with his head half severed 3 feet from a hole he didn't quite make. Everyone seems to be shouting at once: "Quick! More ammo forward" "Corpsman!" and "John's got his foot blown off." "Where's Mathews?" someone calls — and is answered by "He's KIA (killed in action), sir."

1025 — Capt. "Jay-Jay" Carroll of Miami, commander of Kilo company, sees me without a helmet. He says he never wears one, unhooks his own from his belt and throws it to me. I also pick up a flak jacket from a KIA.

1030 — Casualties stagger back across small clearing where Marines have set up a 20-yard wide perimeter on both sides of trail. Marine gives me two hand grenades, saying "You may need these soon." Single rounds coming in from three sides of perimeter. Some Marines digging furiously while others provide covering fire. I peer over my hole and spot four NVAs crawling past no more than 50 feet below. I yell to Captain Carroll who is standing up ramrod straight under heavy fire a few feet away, giving orders to his radioman, Carroll pulls the pin from a grenade and hurls it over my head, throws three more before going back to his radio. I toss another one for good measure. A Marine shouts at me: "Release the spoon or the gooks may have time to toss it back."

1035 — The chaplain, Capt. Stanley J. Beach of Sass City, Mich., stumbles by with wounded man slung around his shoulders. Marine in nearby hole shouts to a buddy: "I got a feeling they don't like us."

"Personality conflict," says the other.

1040 — Lead squad falling back on perimeter. Carroll leads reinforcements forward — forward being less than 100 yards away. Two machine guns keep up intense fire. NVA now have us almost surrounded. I have a terrible feeling I will never see my family again.

1043 — First air strike. Two Phantoms scream in at treetop level, dropping napalm, then, on their second pass, 500 pound bombs. Fragments fly over our holes, thudding into trees. Two men get hit by shrapnel. "Not close enough," says Captain Carroll to the FAC (Forward Air Controller). I feel if it's any closer, we'll all get killed. But Carroll says the ordnance fell 200 meters away and he wants it 100 meters closer. Next strike comes in at 75 meters. This must be what an earthquake feels like.

1050 — Captain Carroll leads his men forward again. We have a whole company, but only a few men can go forward at a time single file. Almost sure death for the point man. No sooner out of the perimeter than NVA machine gun fire starts up again. NVA still clinging to our positions. The closer they stick, the safer they feel from air strikes. More bombs and napalm.

1105 — Second mortar attack. I crawl out of my hole to the rear of perimeter, hoping to be closer to the battalion CP (Command Post) if and when lull in fighting comes. I dive under thick tree trunk that was blown down by artillery. Nine more terrifying mortar explosions followed by the sickening cries of "Corpsman, over here." Chaplain Beach is still carrying wounded back to a bomb crater where we have requested a hoist lift by basket for the critical cases as soon as the choppers can make it in. Carroll says to one wounded man: "Nice going, Marine. Sure appreciate what you did up there. "

1115 — More air strikes, still just 100 meters away. I am going deaf. I can't hear what wounded Marine is asking me. Water, I think. He has a stomach wound so I just give him a few drops to wet his lips. Another Marine tells me NVA bodies are stacked up waist-deep on the trail, but no one can get near them because of automatic crossfire from both sides of jungle. He could see NVA dragging bodies away with vines tied to their ankles.

1130 — Grenade rolls down to where Derek Taylor, the correspondent for Britain's Guardian, is crouching. Taylor, quick as lightning, grabs it, throws it downhill and flips back into his hole. It explodes a second later and doesn't so much as scratch him.

1145 — Two MIA (missing in action) just outside the perimeter. Five volunteers go forward to look for them. One gets cut down by automatic fire. Carroll hurls a smoke bomb, tells FAC to drop ordnance 50 yards beyond where bomb lands, then takes cover. More air strikes.

1215 — Finally, thank the Lord, a brief respite. Just occasional incoming sniper rounds. Keeping my head down, I make my way back to the bomb crater where emergency cases are waiting in the broiling sun. My remaining canteen is shared among the wounded. Most of the men from Kilo company, who left Hill 363 before me, have not had food or water in 24 hours.

1310 — First chopper tries to hover overhead while basket is lowered. He is driven away by ground fire. On second try, pilot radios air too thin to hover and drops back into valley. On third try, one man is hoisted. Corpsman tells me he has about 30 minutes to live. Pilot radios he died in chopper on way to hospital at Dong Ha. Ten minutes later, two more are taken out. Rest must be carried back along trail to headquarters. NVA ground fire getting heavy.

1430 — Arrive at Colonel Masterpool's CP. Engineers are carving an LZ (landing zone) out of the jungle with twenty pound charges of high explosive. Every few minutes an engineer yells "Fire in the hole" and everyone scrambles for cover as another charge of TNT rattles your teeth and covers you in dust and tree bark. Colonel Masterpool is lying on the ground studying his map, quietly giving orders to artillery, air, and his company commanders. His calm voice restores my confidence, by now badly shaken. I catch his eye. "Do you think you've got a story yet?" he wisecracks.

1500 — Fierce fighting again at Kilo which is taking place on the lip of Hill 400. All hell seems to be breaking loose 200 yards away in straight line (about 400 yards by trail). Sniper rounds begin whistling across the CP. Once again the NVA appears to be working around our flanks. Marines spray bushes below the CP. Wounded still coming. After blasting some 250 pounds of TNT the LZ still looks depressingly small. I figure that it won't be completed before sundown and begin digging my own hole.

1630 — After 90 minutes of intermittent digging, my hole also looks depressingly small. I lie in it to try it out, but it's a foot and a half short and only 2 feet deep. Blisters on both hands are open and bleeding. Six feet from my hole, UPI photographer John Schneider has found an NVA hole with log roofing. I am envious.

1700 — Hungry, nothing to eat or- drink. Schneider shares his last sip of water with me. We agree mortar attack is coming as the enemy can pinpoint our position from all the LZ blasting that is still going on. Schneider goes forward and I crawl into my hole and wait. Sniper fire continues, punctuated with the chatter of Marine machine guns. Still rough at Kilo. Air strikes almost continuous. Word is that the fighting is still seesawing across 100 yards of terrain. Marine bodies are being laid out just behind our holes.

0220 [five hours before dawn on the morning of September 28] — Beautiful cloudless night but cold (low 50s). Smell from decomposing bodies makes me nauseated and I pull my poncho over my face. Now immune to sound of gunfire and confident will pull through and get out by chopper tomorrow. Then, I think that it won't be possible because there are too many wounded to go first.

0230 — Musings interrupted by first shattering mortar blast. It knocks me out of my hole. I quickly roll back in as second, third and fourth — all the way up to twelve — impact in CP area. Again heart-rending shouts of "Corpsman!" Twenty feet below my hole six Marines are wounded — six men of a seven-man squad knocked out of action.

0820 — Fourth mortar attack. I lose count of number of rounds. Fear is a hard thing to dominate. Wounded hobbling in from bushes. I figure it won't be long before my number comes up. Terry Sicilia of Pasco, Wash., bleeding and waiting for corpsman, tells me it's his third Purple Heart in six months. "I guess it's home for me."

0900 — Artillery now whistling in just ahead of us. One of our own 105-mm. shells falls short — smack into CP perimeter, 4 yards from Chaplain Beach's hole. Five more wounded. Beach's left leg shattered. He's also bleeding from the stomach. All he says is: "My God, I hope the choppers make it today." One Marine begins crying when his buddy dies. Artillery is instantly called off. Air strikes ordered instead. FAC reports enemy mortar position spotted. In minutes direct hits are reported.

1010 — Fifth mortar attack catches me some 50 yards from my hole. I zigzag back and literally throw myself into my hole. A Marine lands on top of me and is hit in the back with the third burst. I push the Marine off me and lift up the top of his fatigues. A piece of shrapnel is sticking out of his back. Someone says my arm is bleeding. I don't feel anything, but there are three small holes in a neat little row just below my elbow. Mortar fragments. My helmet, already peppered with dents when I got it from a KIA (I had returned my first one to Captain Carroll), now has a few more holes in it. James Bourgoin of Great Falls, Mont., is the wounded Marine next to me. He is 19. He tells me that he and the chaplain were going to have a long chat soon about a personal problem; his fiancee is Catholic and he is Protestant.

1045 — UPI's John Schneider brings good news from Kilo where he had gone for the third time (I would like to believe he doesn't know what fear means, but know I am wrong). The Marines have overrun several NVA machine gun nests and captured a Chinese gun mounted on wheels. Intelligence also reports we have forced the CP of the 42nd NVA Regiment off Hill 426 — the lip that protrudes from Hill 400.

1205 — LZ is getting bigger — 450 pounds of dynamite have gone into it by now. Chopper should be coming in soon. Barely have time to sigh in relief.

1210 — Sixth mortar attack. Back in my hole. It's now almost routine and I am no longer quite as scared. Nearest one this time landed 20 feet away. I am now convinced that one can survive anything but a direct mortar hit.

1355 — The worse yet. NVA have infiltrated back. Firing breaks out on all sides. "Quick! All ammo forward!" yells a sergeant. Kilo is being battered again. "All corpsmen to Kilo," comes another order. The ground-air liaison team at Kilo — three men — has just been wiped out by a mortar hit. Someone shouts, "We've run out of battle dressings." I hand over my first-aid kit.

1440 — "Every available man in the line," shouts a lieutenant. Grenades are issued to the correspondents. Another voice says: "We need more men to hump ammo over to Kilo." A wounded man tears off his WIA (wounded in action) tag and lifts two boxes of ammo in each hand. As he passes the CP on his way to Kilo, Colonel Masterpool calls out: "What's your name, son?" I can't hear the man's answer, but I see Colonel Masterpool pat him gently on the back. Several shrapnel casualties are now moving into the firing line.

1445 — Air strikes coming every 30 seconds. The ground trembles continuously. Once again, I feel the end is near — at least for me. I get an uncontrollable case of shakes. I wonder if I ever had what it takes to be a Marine and conclude that I never did and don't now.

1500 — Miraculously, the firing dies down. Choppers are ordered in — fast. They had been hovering one mountain range away. The first one is once again driven away by ground fire. Rocket-firing Hueys silence the fire. Then the choppers begin coming every two minutes, dumping ammo and water — the first water in 48 hours for most Marines — and taking out the casualties.

1600 — The KIA are now being loaded. The rotor downdraft blows the ponchos off the bodies. There is one man without a head.

1612 — Schneider and I jump into a chopper with two new casualties just up from Kilo. Schneider only leaving because he has run out of film. He plans to return tomorrow morning.

NOTES:

The following Marines were killed during the fighting for Hill 400:
Geary, John W. LCpl. 2126932; K-3-4; 22; Batavia, New York
Hall, Arvel H. Pfc. 2208909; K-3-4; 19; Columbus, Georgia
Hanson, James R. Pfc. 2192586; K-3-4; 20; Barnesville, Minnesota
Jordet, Ronald G. LCpl. 2156757; K-3-4; 21; Reedpoint, Montana
Keith, Archibald K. Pfc. 2241203; K-3-4; 23; Bainbridge, New York
Kinnear, Lawrence F. Pfc. 2136290; K-3-4; 18; Elkins Park, Penn.
Laws, Billy W. Pfc. 2156134; K-3-4; 23; Kansas City, Missouri
Mathews, Grover C. Jr. Cpl. 1955385; K-3-4; 26; Roseburg, Oregon
Najar, Miguel F. Pfc. 2233999; I-3-4; 20; Houston, Texas
Sprouse, Lonnie D. Sgt. 1597309; 27; Mableton, Georgia

Captain James J. Carroll was killed by friendly fire on Hill 400 during the October 5, 1966 assault on Hill 484. He did not participate in this assault but remained on Hill 400 to help direct artillery fire. He would later receive the Navy Cross posthumously. The name of the Marine artillery base at Cam Lo would later be changed to Camp Carroll in his honor.

Several Marines earned the Silver Star for their contributions to the success in taking Hill 400. They were SSgt. Robert Bergeron, LCpl. William R. Hutton, LCpl. Ronald G. Jordet, Cpl. Leonard C. Kasson, Pfc. Archibald K. Keith, Pfc. Billy W. Laws and 2dLt. Richard W. Mullen. The awards to Jordet, Keith and Laws were posthumous.

Kasson from Cincinnatus, New York was 20 at the time this battle took place. Here he gives this account of the action:
India Company had the point. We had been moving north along the mountaintops for several days. Some areas of ascent were so steep that we had to use ropes to climb them. As we approached the area called Hill 400, the ground was littered with numerous wires. They ran over the ground like multi-colored snakes. At first there were just a few. As we walked along they became so commonplace that we ignored them. We walked in column due to the dense underbrush of the jungle terrain as we gradually ascended a long flat area. A loud explosion sounded ahead of us.
Following the explosion, we began to be mortared. I remember jump-

ing into a shell crater with another Marine. We had just gotten into the hole when the radio operator, LCpl. Albert E. Huffer, and a couple other Marines jumped in. They told us that the C.O., Capt. Carroll, was taking this position as his command post. The mortars were still coming in.

At first, I didn't want to get out. The other Marine that jumped in with me left the hole. He was on his knees at its edge when more mortars hit. When he turned around, I saw he was covered in blood. I then jumped out, ran deeper into the jungle and found another ground depression. There, I hugged the dirt.

We later heard that the first explosion had killed about 8 to 12 guys at the point. The NVA had demolitions attached to the wires that we had learned to ignore. As the point got into the killing zone, they detonated them. I must admit—although we had checked out the wires when we first saw them, we later ignored them because they were just loose.

We lost the India Company point. Several other men were also lost during attempts to push forward. Kilo Company was then ordered to take the point. This was the second day. Cpl. Arthur J. Downey's squad attempted to cross the level terrain several times but was unsuccessful. They suffered numerous casualties.

During one of the assaults, a young Marine named Kinnear became so upset that he jumped up and yelled, "This is how you kill these bastards!"

He got off about two rounds before he was machine gunned down.

Eventually, it became my squad's turn to go up front. Our platoon leader, Lt. Mullen, told me that there was a gun emplacement to the left of the trail. He explained that the NVA had full field of fire coverage on the trail extending to the hill's descent into a ravine. It was then a steep climb to the top of Hill 400. Each assault up the hill was followed by air strikes of bombs and napalm, and 105 and 155 howitzer cannonades. Each time the NVA was back in place when troops tried to advance.

I recall a friend of mine nicknamed Rolli. He had been wounded by mortar fire and was lying near the edge of the front area. Doc Cook and another corpsman were working on him. Doc said he probably would have lived if we had been near a trauma unit, but not here in the bush. Rolli died.

Lt. Mullen said, "Kasson, I need a volunteer and you are it. We have tried squad assaults and bombed the hell out of them, but we can't get through. So, it's time for something different."

Mullen's plan was to send one man through the bush and off the trail with a couple of hand grenades. This Marine was to try to take out the first gun emplacement. His committee of one elected me. Mullen was the best platoon commander we had. He took good care of his men. If he had thought there were gooks in front of us, Mullen probably would have spent more U.S. tax dollars on reconnaissance by fire than there is money in the U.S. Treasury.

I was scared as hell, but I had to be a Marine. So, I said nothing and just did it. I stripped of my helmet, flak jacket, and top—left my rifle and ammo—and took two grenades. Through the bush I went. I felt like a herd of elephants as I crawled along.

When I was in range and could see the edge of the hole, I threw the grenades in. Then, I jumped up and ran like hell back to the lines.

As I got there, I tripped over a tree root on the trail and fell flat on my face right on top of another Marine knocking the wind out of myself. The other Marine was pissed! He had some bullshit thing to say about me watching where I was running.

Well, after this, I took my squad forward. When we got to the first gun emplacement that I had fragged no one was there. There were no bodies. This was not unusual for most of the time the NVA would drag there dead away.

We went down into the ravine and began to climb Hill 400. The point man, Kenneth Keith, and an automatic rifleman led us. Keith was in front.

We were about a quarter of the way up the hill when we were hit by machine gun fire coming from three different directions. One gun was at the top of the trail near the crest of the hill. There was another one to the left and one to the right further down the hill toward us. The field of fire covered the entire front of hill 400 from the top of the hill to the ravine below. It also covered the smaller hill that we had descended to get into the ravine.

Keith was hit by several rounds and went down. The Marine with the automatic rifle said he couldn't get to him. He thought that Keith was killed immediately. Two more of my men were hit behind me. We lay in the bottom of the ravine, where they couldn't hit us due to a natural depression in the terrain. We called in mortar support and were able to pull back to the front area where we had been the last few days.

Again we bombed and napalmed the hill. I felt like shit because Keith was still out there.

Lt. Mullen and J.J. Carroll then decided to send three volunteers up the hill after other squads had attempted to take the hill without success. This time before we *volunteers* went, Carroll had the hill bombed and napalmed. The bombs landed so close to our front that it singed the hair on our arms, and we could hardly breath.

Bill Hutton, a machine gunner and I went back down into the ravine, at the base of Hill 400. I had the machine gunner stay in the ravine. He now had a good field of fire up the hill for there was no vegetation left.

As we got about a quarter of the way up the hill, we found Keith. His body was black. It was in three separate pieces. We crawled along to the right, and Bill went toward the left. As we neared the crest of the hill, we saw a gun emplacement. I motioned to Bill to come over to where I was and to cover me as I cleared the hole for the other Marine to bring up our machine gun.

The gook in the hole was split down the back and laying across his gun. I tried to pull him off the gun. He was too heavy, and the hole had steep sides. I then stood up and pulled the body out of the hole. I was still holding on to it when another machine gun to my front opened up. It was so close that I could see the muzzle blast. I fell over backward pulling the gook on top of me. The hill had a reverse slope right at the edge of the hole with a big tree root partially exposed from the ground. I lay right in along that depression. The gooks started throwing grenades into the depression.

Bill had begun returning fire from his position off to the right. I was kicking grenades left and right further down the hill. One went off near the edge of the hole, and I was hit in the arm. I was scared shitless!

I put my rifle over the tree root, turned the selector switch to auto and let go. At the same time, I began throwing hand grenades back at Charlie. We didn't have much ammo between the two of us. Charlie was over the crest of the hill, which made our machine gun in the ravine useless.

Hutton and I began yelling for the machine gunner to move up, but he had already started. We used the dead gook for cover and got our gun in the hole but soon ran out of ammunition. At this time, one of the platoons with Lt. Mullen in the lead came charging up the hill. We fought with Charlie for about 20 or 30 minutes and when it was over we had secured hill 400.

After we took the hill, another company had moved up front to assault the next hill. I was sent back with my squad to Hill 400 to meet the press.

Later, one of the guys' folks from back home sent the newspaper article. It was from one of the southern states—probably North or South Carolina, or maybe Georgia. Bill, some others and I were mentioned in the article. The reporter who interviewed us back on hill 400 wrote it. Some one had some dead gooks piled up there, so we sat on them and ate chow. Sick—right, I know! I now wish we hadn't done those things.

I remember when they told us to go back to the front with the reporters. I got scared all over again. It then became our job to lay down a base of fire from Hill 400 for the company assaulting the next hill. We also had to retrieve the dead. The dead Marines were heavy. The sniper fire sucked, too!

One day we were firing mortars, M-79 grenade launchers and recoilless rifles over the top of the assaulting company onto the crest of Hill 484. We were running low on ammo. Willie Adams and I went over the reverse slope from the Rockpile to bring up M-79 rounds.

A hell of an explosion hit the top of 400. We were blown back down the hill.

Several rounds hit the top of the hill. Our own damn tanks fired these rounds! (They came from the Cam Lo area, which would later be named Camp Carroll.)

Willie and I went back up the hill. It was barren—like a tornado touched down! There were body parts all over, in the trees, sticking out of the ground. Everywhere you looked there was blood, flesh and bones. God! It sucked!

J.J. Carroll was still alive, with no legs, and nothing to even put a tourniquet on. He died quickly.

Albert Huffer, the radioman was standing next to J.J. when I left the hilltop. Al was now part of the radio. His torso was imbedded into the radio. It looked like he and it had been manufactured as one. Al had no extremities, no head! The only way you could recognize him was by the radio on his back.

After a few more days, we had pushed the NVA back across the DMZ. We walked off Mutters Ridge, past the Rockpile to Highway 1 and loaded on to six-bye's which took us back to Quang-Tri.

I served in Vietnam with some great guys and good Marines. Hell! They were all great guys. We were too young to be anything else but great guys.

Randy Jarrell from Odessa, Texas and I were very close. He was wounded on Hastings and got the Bronze Star. Randy was killed later in the war by a single piece of shrapnel to the temple.

Billy Turner was a good Marine. But, the morning we left for Operation Prairie, he told one of the guys that he was not going to go with us.

I went to talk with him. Billy said, "I'm not going to go back into the shit again!"

We had all been on Hastings. That was some of the most vicious fighting in all of Vietnam. Billy had done well on that one but he had had enough. There was no doubt he meant what he said.

He had that look about him that said, "I have made up my mind so don't fuck with me!"

I told the platoon commander, but Billy didn't come with us. We never saw him again. He was smarter than the rest of us.

Willie Adams was a black Marine from one of the southern states. We were together on the first two choppers that sat down on the LZ on Hastings. It was later called Helicopter Valley and for obvious reasons.

The damn choppers got hit and came down together. The blades broke off. One was jumping up and down on Willie's leg. I pulled him out. He wasn't hurt bad.

Those poor bastards trying to get off the two choppers were! One guy was sliced completely in half by the blades. The top part of him went into the treetops. The bottom part kept running on the ground until it fell over. The goddamned war sucked!

Kenneth A. Keith came from the same region as I did. Although the K-3-4 roster says Kenneth A., his Silver Star citation says Archibald K. I am not certain which is correct.

Keith was older and a college boy. I asked him why he didn't come in as an officer. Keith said he just wanted to do his time and get the hell out. He lasted about 2 weeks in Vietnam.

I still feel guilty Keith was killed. I've always felt that it should have been me. He volunteered to be my point and wasn't even in my squad. My guys all claimed they didn't know how to operate a shotgun. We always used one on the point. They were probably lying. I knew how to use it, but I was the squad leader. Leading your men from the point or tail end Charlie was not good policy. I still wish he wasn't killed. I do hope he was dead before the napalm struck.

Arthur Downey was the kind of Marine of which movies are made. He took his squad up Hill 400 several times. Downey loved to talk and in that way he was kind of like Bill Hutton. He had a comical homespun way about him. Must be that Boston flare. His Vietnam exploits were written up in Soldier of Fortune Magazine. I think it was maybe 1966 or 1967.

Jeremiah Purdie was our company Gunny. When I saw him at a 3-4 reunion in 1993 in D.C. he seemed like an O.K. guy. But, in Nam, Jeremiah was an arrogant ass. We always thought we would kill him before Charlie did. However, maybe that's how gunnies are in war.

There was a great machine gunner with us on Mutter's Ridge. His complete name I cannot recall. We called him Matt. He was an older guy in his thirties and a Corporal in weapons platoon. Matt was standing with us on Mutters Ridge as we were about to distribute cigarettes taken from the packs of dead Marines and given to us by Chaplain Stan Beach. A mortar round hit between us and shrapnel hit me. Although I was unconscious for a time I was not seriously injured. However, Matt was blown up. His head, one arm and one shoulder were gone. The body landed on top of a machine gun emplacement drenching those poor bastards in blood. It looked like someone had poured red paint all over them. This shit sucks!

I can still picture this stuff as if it happened yesterday. These memories are so vivid that I fear they will always be with me. War is stupid, governments are corrupt and life doesn't seem to get any better. Money, egos and lies rule!

I am against war. I would not do it again. I was lucky— I think— I did come back. But it has not been easy. I have to live with these memories. I do not understand why we do not learn, as a people, from our history.

Bill Hutton from Canoga Park, California was a nineteen-year-old Corporal during the battle for Hill 400. Here he reflects on his experiences:

Merlin Legaux was a roomy of mine in Okinawa. He was killed on the same day as J.J. Carroll. We had traveled to Vietnam on the same tugboat, the William Wiegel and were squad leaders at the same time.

I will never forget our liberty days in Okinawa. We all tried to get Merlin set up with a "short time". Merlin however, was dedicated to the girl he was engaged to in New Orleans and would not have anything to do with that. He was a fine person and a dedicated Marine.

I later learned that Merlin had earned the Silver Star on Operation Hastings. When I learned of his death I was devastated. We all wished that he had experienced a "good time" on Okinawa.

I was with Billy Laws when he died. He had a gut wound. I was with Billy and several others who had been wounded. His death was a complete shock because he seemed to be doing fine. Billy was talking and joking about going back to the states, etc. when all of a sudden, someone blew off some C4 to clear a Landing Zone. Billy Laws went into shock and died. It was as if Billy was stunned by the blast. The news of his death quickly went to the front. It was tragic.

J.J. Carroll was killed by friendly fire after we took Hill 400. He, Randy Jarrell and I had been firing M40 grenade launchers at another hill. The tanks were requested by J.J. to also give H&I fire on that hill. The tanks fired on our troops, killing J.J. and several others. I do not recall who else was there. I had left the position about ten minutes earlier. I was told that J.J. had both legs blown off and still got up on his stubs and tried to render aid to the other fallen Marines. If you could have seen J.J. on Hill 400 you would have been proud like the rest of us. What a LEADER!

LCpl. Richard G. Burgess was an automatic rifleman with L-3-4. He was wounded and captured on Operation Prairie. Here he shares his experiences:

On September 25, 1966 I was wounded in the right forearm by a round fired from an AK-47. The bullet followed the bone structure and shattered my elbow. Two other bullets struck my flak jacket and went around to my back and exited. Upon leaving, the bullets threw two pieces of the fiberglass panels into my back. These pieces caused some serious infection. When they were removed, I lost quite a bit of flesh. It took almost three months for the elbow to heal. There were many times that I thought that I might lose the arm. The infection was so severe that the fingers were black, blue and yellow. They were so swollen that I couldn't move the fingers at all. A Chinese doctor (about six feet two inches tall and speaking five languages) came along after about two months. He made a couple of incisions to drain the puss and infection and the healing began.

While a Prisoner of War I was first taken into Laos and then into North Vietnam. I was in solitary confinement for five years. Total solitary confinement for 27 months. Six months in hand cuffs. I was in a tiger cage for thirty days and in leg stocks for thirty days. I escaped twice and was placed on a salt and rice diet for over six months. My body weight dropped from over 230 pounds to about 65 or 70 pounds during the Tet Offensive. I could put both hands around my waist and still had about four inches of space between my thumbs—approximately a 22-inch waistline. At a camp called D-1, I spent eight days on my knees with my hands in the air for fourteen to sixteen hours a day for ripping the speaker off the wall and breaking the light bulb.

I was on the sixth flight out of Hanoi on March 25, 1973. Upon reaching the States, I was sent to Oak Knoll Naval Hospital for recuperation and debriefing procedures. I was retired as a Staff Sergeant on January 1, 1975.

In addition to James J. Carroll the following Marines were killed on October 5, 1966:
Bohn, David J. LCpl. 2156793; 19; North Delta, Utah
Davidson, Robert G. LCpl. 2212355; 19; Glen Burnie, Maryland
Huffer, Albert E. LCpl. 2128880; 20; Germantown, Ohio
Legaux, Merlin P. Cpl. 2144012; 19; New Orleans, Louisiana
Mitchell, Paul H. LCpl. 2103805; 20; Mentor, Ohio
Owens, David L. LCpl. 2117351; 19; Holyoke, Massachusetts
Smith, John R. LCpl. 2149469; 19; Decatur, Illinois
Thornton, Rodney G. Sgt. 1887836; 25; Salt Lake City, Utah
Vargas, Julio C. Cpl. Cpl. 2030433; 20; New York, New York
Vicich, Albert L. Cpl. 1980849; 22; Joliet, Illinois

Other Marines mentioned in this chapter were:
Adams, Willie F. Cpl. 2012494; K-3-4
Bass, James T. LCpl. 2061393; I-3-4; Americus, Georgia
Bourgoin, James C. Pfc. 2191124; H&S-3-4; 19; Great Falls, Montana
Burgess, Richard LCpl. 2054229; L-3-4: 20; Aloha, Washington
Downey, Arthur J. Cpl. 2083506; K-3-4
Fassett, Randolph D. Sgt. 1963302; I-3-4; 24; Sacramento, California
James, Buddy L. Sgt. 1579538; I-3-4
Jarrell, Randall LCpl. 2158256; K-3-4; 19; Odessa, Texas

Purdie, Jeremiah GySgt. 649210; K-3-4
Sicilia, Terry J. LCpl. 2143385; K-3-4; Pasco, Washington
Turner, Billy G. LCpl. 2039132; K-3-4

Bill Hutton

∗   ∗   ∗   ∗

On January 28, 1967 India Company, Third Battalion, Seventh Marines was inserted into the middle of the Viet Cong infested Duc Pho District. The battalion was the first American unit to enter this district that straddles Route One, named the "Street Without Joy" by the French during the war in French Indo-China in the early 1950's. They were a part of Operation Desoto that only lasted three days.

The Marines of India had landed with three meals in their packs and plenty of ammunition. Now after two days at Duc Pho just about everything was gone except the ammunition. On January 30, they were to assault the tiny fortified village of Hai Mon, which lay across about 800 yards of flooded rice paddies. The only way to get there was to march single file down a three-foot-wide dike leading straight to the village.

> We were nineteen. Pure testoterone. Crude. Primitive. We'd been trained to be violent, and violent we were. Violence was as common in the Marine Corps as green. Violence was considered to be an attribute. Disagreements were often dealt with immediately in a physical manner. Many a time I'd seen arguments turn to punches. Occasionally grudges would be held but more often than not end of fight meant end of discussion.

By Joe Holt
I-3-5
From The Becky
An unpublished short story

Here we join Pfc. Larry W. Callahan, a fire team leader in the first squad of the first platoon. Callahan wrote the following unpublished story. It is reprinted with his permission.

7
THE DAY ON THE DIKE

The day began as a typical Nam morning. We quickly felt the damp, cool air, which immediately aggravated aching bones. We started moving down the hill in columns by platoons; First Platoon's Commander was Staff Sergeant Holloway. Lieutenant Blakely, our former platoon leader, became India Company's XO.

I was a team leader in the first squad at that time. Our squad leader was a sergeant we called Wally; I remember that he was from Ohio and claimed to be part Sioux Indian. Eddie Sanders, we called him Sandy, came from El Paso, Texas. Sandy was another team leader. He only had thirty days left in country before his tour of duty was up. I can't remember the other team leader of our squad. My team members were Richard Garcia, Maldonado and a new Marine whose name I've forgotten. Some other squad members that I remember were Steve Wilhelmsen, Fowler, and Landro.

On Operation Arizona, while I was acting as squad leader, I had Maldonado walking point going up a mountain stream. A deadly snake struck him. We all thought for sure that he would not make it. About four weeks later he was back in the company AO.

As we walked, I noticed the lack of locals who were in the area the afternoon before. I gave the thought little mind; I just figured they were out in the rice paddies working. I am not actually sure which platoon took the point because my world existed around the squad and fire team. I believe third platoon led the way followed by second platoon, and then first platoon bringing up the rear. Our squad had just entered the main trail below the small hill that we slept on the night before. This trail ran along the base of the hill and straight across a huge rice paddy.

The Third Platoon moved along the wide dike, which crossed the middle of the huge rice paddy and headed in the direction of a village on the other side. About two thirds of the way, the men turned right along a smaller dike around the right side of the village. I guess they were setting up the right flank and acting as a covering force for the First Platoon. After the Third Platoon stopped, the First Platoon took the lead and continued down the main dike into the village. This main dike was wide enough to drive a jeep along the top. We were so spread out that half of our platoon was still coming off the hill by some village huts when the word came down the line for First Platoon to move up and take the lead.

As the platoons were moving into positions, all hell broke loose. Enemy small arms fire and automatic weapons firing could be heard from up front on both sides. Everyone hit the deck. Third Platoon and First Platoon were first to be hit hard.

Bill Moses was a squad leader that day and on point when we were hit. He was wounded by two rounds that hit so close together that we thought he had been hit by a 50cal. round.

I knew we were in a lot of trouble. Sandy spotted what he thought were VC to the rear of the trail, and he opened up on them with his automatic rifle. Wally started moving the squad into positions on either side of the trail to cover the main column.

Our squad was told to stay while Holloway took the rest of the platoon forward into the middle of the paddy. I was glad we got to stay put because the volume of firepower coming from the front stated that the big paddy was not the place to be. There was not enough room for Wally to place my fire team on line to be of any use except to act as a reserve team. I kept my team off the trail to the left and in a ditch.

Things quieted down at our location, but I could still hear exchanges of gunfire from the front. As good as things could be at the time, I sensed it was going to get worse.

Sure enough, Wally came to me and said, "Holloway needed the rest of the platoon to join up with them. Take your team up front and tell Holloway I'm staying here with the rest of the squad to cover the rear of the column."

It made sense to me. I knew my team was the odd team out because we had no field of fire, no room to move. We obviously were not doing any good where we were except staying out of harms way, which was about to change. I was very reluctant to leave this comfortable ditch. I had two eager Marines, Maldonado and Garcia, itching to get into the action. I had no other choices except to go and to do, so we went.

Running in spurts for about twenty yards, I ducked for cover in the same large ditch. Before I made it to the opening of the big paddy, I jumped for cover in the ditch one last time and landed next to one of our rocket team members. The other rocket team members were already up front and needed more rockets.

He was out of breath, exhausted—something that all of us would experience throughout that day. He begged me to carry his rockets up front for him. Since we were headed that way anyway, I bought off on his request, grabbed one rocket, and yelled for Garcia to pick up the other one.

While waiting for a lull in the enemy firing, I can remember thinking how crazy I must be knowing that I could be killed going out into all that openness with no place to hide or to take cover. Not a tree, a rock, a ditch—nothing but rice paddy and about fourteen inches of dike of which four inches were under dirty paddy water. The dike went straight for what seemed to be half a mile. There was a large paddy to the left side of the dike, probably four hundred yards across. Another small paddy lay to the right of the dike about a hundred yards across.

I yelled out an obscenity and took off running with my team behind me.

I passed Captain Clark, who was on the left side of the dike staring straight at me. Capt. Clark, not a very tall man, was standing up and yelling something at me. I had no idea what he said, I just wanted a place to hide, but there was no room on his side of the dike.

I finally stopped running and knelt down on the right side of the dike just past the captain.

Now I was getting to the exhaustion point like the rocket team member I was helping.

I could now hear other Marines yelling, "You're on the wrong side".

The reason I chose the right side of the dike was that there was no room on the left side of the dike. Marines were packed in like sardines; too close I thought.

Before I could answer the other Grunts as to why I was not on their side, I heard the crack and zing of a bullet whiz by my head. This was not unfamiliar to me; I had been in other firefights, but nothing like this one, nor would there be another one like this one. I knew then that I had messed up.

Up and running again, I jumped as far as I could to the other side of the dike landing next to Ron Moore, a machine gunner of first platoon. Ron and I spent practically the rest of the day right there.

Ron was a great guy normally always smiling and joking, but not that day. We conversed that day, but what about who knows. I do remember seeing some fear in his eyes that day. He had to have seen my fear, too.

We were still moving forward as best as we could by crawling over or behind the other Marines along the cover of the dike. Sometimes someone took a chance by getting up and running for a couple of feet. Marines would curse us and tell us to stay down when we did this because we would draw fire.

By now, we were exhausted. We probably only got as far from Ron's position as maybe thirty yards. I stopped and waited or rested while my team caught up.

About then the word came up from the rear of the line that Wally needed us back because they were taking fire. What a pickle I was in at the age of nineteen. I was exhausted and stuck in the middle of hell. Either way I went death was looking at us really close. I knew my team had to be exhausted, too, but Garcia and Maldonado wanted to continue. I had to rest for a moment. I decided that we had come too far to take the same risks in going back. Wally would have to do without us.

Reluctantly, I sent Garcia and Maldonado forward thinking I could follow with the other new team member shortly. That never happened. We were able to pass off our rockets to other Marines up the line to where they needed them.

Two Marines of the Third Platoon had been killed. They were passing their bodies down the line as we had done with the rockets. Marines had to drag them as far as they could down the line and hand them off to a couple of other Marines.

We were next in line. We crawled and pulled the Marines bodies all the way back to Ron's position along the dike.

Exhausted again, I had lost track of the time at this point. I did remember watching with Ron the F-4 Phantoms rolling in at tree top level on the tree line across the big paddy dropping their bombs. The impact of the bombs' hitting the earth just tore up everything hit. Trees, dirt knocked a hundred or even two hundred feet straight up in the air. What a sight that was, we were not thinking about how close they were to us.

They called it "danger close," which meant they were about two hundred and fifty yards away. It was still something to watch. Some of the shrapnel would come whooshing by, sometimes splashing in the paddy right to our front. Amazing that no one was hit by our own jet planes.

A terrible place to be that day - exposed to friendly fire as well as the enemies constant firing. I knew then that there couldn't be any enemy over there trying to hit our exposed left flank. There was obviously nothing left alive over there. However, we were too close to the enemy on our right front. Some places we were as close as fifty yards. We did engage our sixty and eighty-one mortars, but apparently not very successfully; the enemy kept returning fire.

About mid-afternoon a medivac chopper came in to pick up our wounded and our dead. I remember seeing Private Yost as he was trying to make it to the chopper. His head was bandaged, and he was dizzy and falling down as he tried to reach the helicopter. I knew he wouldn't make it by himself, and I couldn't stand to watch his ordeal. I ran to help him. Fortunately, the chopper picked up and hovered closer to us.

After getting Yost on board the chopper, I remember the door gunner with his arm-outstretched saying, "Come on and get in."

I could only reply "But I'm not wounded".

Amazing, I can remember what I said so long ago. I can only assume that it was due to the intensity of the situation. For some people I guess it had the opposite effect, and they just block memories out.

One of my biggest regrets that day was having to turn in my weapon. The word again came down the line for all jammed weapons to be turned in by passing them up toward the center to the company commander so they could be flown out on the next chopper. I guess they were afraid someone would leave his weapon behind. I looked at my weapon for the first time that day not having had the opportunity to even fire at the enemy yet.

Ron saw it and said, "Man, don't even shoot that thing around me. It will blow up for sure."

I'm sure this happened while dragging the dead Marine through the paddy.

I still did not want to just turn in my weapon, so I placed it on the dike, ducked and fired off a round. I figured the most that could happen was that I would lose a hand. Ron was really pissed.

I still had my hand, but my rifle was definitely jammed now. I gave in to Ron and sent my weapon up the line. He did loan me his forty-five pistol which I gave back later that night. I stayed there with Ron the rest of the day.

I must have dozed off, which seems hard to believe, but I can't remember much else except that it was getting dark and that we were finally moving off the dike. We were carrying wounded, and as I looked back, we were dropping everything we had on the enemy area. It was a joyous moment for me. I thought it was a beautiful sight. I have no idea how many enemies we killed that day. I hope a lot.

Everyone that early part of the night was scattered along the ditch below the hill as we moved back up. Maldonado found me and gave me the news about Garcia. He had already informed Capt. Clark.

My good buddy Steve Wilhelmsen, a new Marine named Stoedard, possibly, volunteered to go with Maldonado and me to retrieve Garcia.

Capt. Clark's radio operator, who I think was named Carvey, had been wounded early that morning, so Capt. Clark carried the radio and a 12 gauge shot gun with us.

I remember feeling more at ease with our Skipper along. I was sure he was just as scared as we were, but he never showed it. The Capt. never had a clue, but he would be my role model for a leader later in my life.

Someone gave me a M-2 Carbine to carry. Not a popular weapon since we were being shot at all day by the same kind of weapon. Nevertheless, I had a plan. If we were seen or challenged by the enemy, I would speak a little Vietnamese and fire the carbine hoping this would confuse the enemy long enough to get out of the area. Sounds like a dumb plan looking back, but at least I had a plan.

Capt. Clark, shot gun and radio in hand, stayed at the fork in the right dike that veered off from the main dike to cover us as we moved farther up to where Maldonado remembered last seeing Garcia. Steve and Maldonado climbed over the big dike and out into the paddy where Garcia had fallen while we covered them. They found him and dragged him to our position on the dike. He was very light and already stiff which helped us; we all grabbed him and ran back to Capt. Clark's location probably only fifty yards away. It was the end of the most terrible day of my life.

The next day Maldonado was medivaced for a wound in the arm. I had no fire team left. Staff Sergeant Holloway was killed, and his radio operator was wounded that day on the dike.

They assigned me to the platoon radio operator's job. I assumed I was assigned the job because that was where I was needed and not because I lost a man from my team.

Sergeant Russell Moses was wounded that day also, along with several of his squad members. He was the second or third squad leader up front with Holloway. There were several others whose names I can't remember, wounded that day from first, second and third platoons.

Both Doc Wilkinson and Doc Cash were our corpsman and they were kept busy trying to save as many Marines as possible.

Staff Sergeant Spahn came in from battalion headquarters to become our platoon sergeant.

Lt. Blakely, who missed the action that day because he was back at Chu Lai, came back to the platoon as our platoon leader until a new replacement could be found for him. Blakely was another Marine officer I would set my standards of leadership qualities by later in my life.

We rested most of the next day on that hill we previously left. Late that afternoon we left heading back to our battalion area. That put us arriving around midnight. This move turned into a company (minus) night patrol. Not since the DMZ had we moved at night as a company.

Notes:

The following Marines from I-3-7 were killed that day;
Esters, Charles Jr. Cpl. 2182370; 19; Orlando, Florida
Garcia, Richard Pfc, 2251755; 19; Galveston, Texas
Holloway, Paul D. SSgt. 1283040; 37; Orlando, Florida
Posey, Robert L. Jr. Sgt. 2047504; 22; Savage, Maryland
Rhodes, James R. LCpl. 2171969; 18; Brunswick, Georgia

Other Marines mentioned in the chapter are:
Blakely, George M. 2dLt. 24; Portland, Oregon
Carvey, Dave
Fowler, Henry Cpl.
Landro, Troy Pfc.
McGinley, John G. LCpl.
Moore, Ronald A. LCpl. 2241747; 20; Manhattan Beach, California
Moses, Russell W. Sgt.
Sanders, Edwin H. LCpl. El Paso, Texas
Spahn, Jordan A. SSgt.
Stanley, James R. Cpl.
Stoedard, Billy R. LCpl.
Wilhelmsen, Stephen W. Cpl.
Wilson, Lawrence E. 2dLt.
Yost, John R. Pfc.

The Silver Star was awarded to Capt. Read M. Clark and Pfc. Robert

P. Maldonado for heroism on 1/30/67. Another Marine from Winston-Salem, Sgt. Alphonso C. Dickey, a squad leader, received the Bronze Star.

The diminutive Clark was only 5' 7" tall and weighed 135 pounds. His commentary on the action that day is as follows:

I could see it coming. We came under some nice, casual, well-aimed sniper fire. It was about 1700, we were running out of ammunition and I was running out of ideas. Charlie was in a bind too. We had him so he couldn't get out of the hamlet either.

I do not know who nominated me for the Silver Star and I can't believe I got one. In my opinion, I rated a kick in the rump for getting that many people in trouble. But, that's the way these awards go.

We rejoin Larry Callahan for the following commentary:

By mid July 1967, I was returning from my second R&R after eleven months in country. I was getting short, meaning that I had only two months left of my tour of duty. There was an old saying that the guys that had only been in country three months or less and the guys who had only three months or less in country to do were the ones that bought it. I was determined to take as few risks as possible. I wanted to survive this place.

The first platoon was located at a new site called Hill 10 or St. Pete by some. I always called it "Pimple Hill" because that was about the size of it. It was just off the main road that went to Danang from the Dia Loc area where our battalion was located on Hill 37.

I guess we were there to help protect the road that was always being mined by the VC. Most of our missions were to guard the engineers as they swept the road for mines and booby traps.

I remember one day a busload of Vietnamese, waving and laughing, ran our roadblock and passed the Marine minesweeper. We thought they probably knew the road was not mined that night. They didn't. They hadn't gotten very far when they hit a large mine that blew the bus and all on board up. It took a couple of Sea Knight Helicopters to pick up all the pieces.

The jeep ride from battalion was a short one. I stepped off the jeep with a new set of jungle fatigues but still had not been re-issued my weapon. Just as I started walking up the hill, or bump of a hill, Stanley came running down saying I had to go out with them; Moore's gun team had been ambushed and needed help and we had to find them. Find them, I thought not. Looking for an ambush is a good way to run into the same ambush.

Stanley had someone with him. A fresh new face. I remember asking whom this was as if I was the boss. Stanley introduced our new Lieutenant, Larry Wilson. "Another fresh and eager face," I thought.

I now think we all started out that way, but eventually if you survive long enough, you lose that look.

Lt. Wilson turned out to be one of the best platoon leaders I knew if only for a short time.

I know I didn't impress Lt. Wilson that day, because I wasn't about to step out there in the boon docks after just arriving back in country. I was not prepared.

About that time McGinley, who was part of the gun team, came limping up the hill. Apparently, McGinley was able to escape the ambush with just the shirt on his back by running all the way back. Now Stan and the Lieutenant had a source of information if we could get him to calm down long enough to answer our questions. For a moment, I thought I could get him to lead us to the exact location of the gun team, but he was still too shaken up.

The first squad did get to the site, but it was too late to save Ron Moore and another team member named Stoker.

The other team member also managed to escape although he was wounded several times. He stumbled and crawled a good thousand meters to the main road. There a Marine jeep driver headed to Da Nang picked him up. I believe he recovered from his wounds.

There were all kinds of rumors about what happened that day. Some thought the team had fallen asleep; some thought they were cooling off in the river. Whatever happened, they were surprised and hit hard.

It wasn't until thirty years later that I found out that Sergeant Ron Moore, everyone's buddy, had posthumously received the Navy Cross for his gallant actions that day. It was believed that he held his position and while engaging the enemy covered the escape of the rest of the team. Ron was the last person to whom I felt close to killed during my tour.

The Marine killed with Moore on July 19, 1967 was Pvt. Kenneth G. Stoker, 19, from Alameda, California.

*   *   *   *

On February 3, 1967 the members of the Second Platoon, Company A, First Reconnaissance Battalion, First Marine Division were on an 11-man patrol deep in enemy controlled Quang Ngai Province. These Marines were based at Chu Lai.

LCpl. David Verheyn, 21, from Lenoxdale, Massachusetts was a team leader on this patrol. He had arrived in Vietnam in November and was a veteran of many such patrols.

In the following chapter Verheyn describes the events that took place on this day.

"Life is assimilating what is thrown at you according to the circumstances at the time."

1stLt. Ernest Spencer
D-1-26
From *Welcome to Vietnam, Macho Man*

8

THE LONGEST NIGHT

This was to be a difficult reconnaissance patrol deep behind enemy lines.

The patrol leader was Sgt. Robert Starbuck. He called a meeting for the Marines who were going. At first there were to be 13. He explained that this patrol would be different from previous ones. It would be in an open area. We would be weighed down because we would be required to wear helmets and flak jackets this time. We would also need to carry our entrenching tool for digging in and one day rations instead of cans. As usual we wore camouflage and painted up.

Starbuck explained what our positions would be—who would be with who and where.

We said, "Aw shit! We are fixing to get in some shit now!"

A Recon patrol is not supposed to be spotted. Our job was to go into this area before the infantry came in and determine how many men and what kind of equipment and movement was going on. Our job was strictly to observe. We were not supposed to engage in combat unless it was absolutely necessary. However, it seemed that we would run into trouble about seven out of ten times.

The patrol now made up of 11 Marines departed our base camp by helicopter at around 1330 on the third of February 1967.

The patrol leader was Sgt. Robert Starbuck. I had been on several recon patrols with him before and he definitely knew what he was doing—he was an excellent Marine and patrol leader—squared away—a professional—I have nothing but respect for that man—he was tops with me!

The assistant patrol leader was Cpl. Robert Shafer—another good Marine and also a veteran of many patrols.

This Recon patrol was heavily armed. In addition to weaponry and equipment, each member of the patrol carried a claymore. I was carrying an M-16, M-79 grenade launcher, hand grenades and a claymore mine.

We were inserted by helicopter at about 1500. Because of the presence of pangi sticks it could not land.. The pangi sticks were sharp spears that had been placed in the ground by the Viet Cong.

The pilot hovered about 15 feet above the ground. One by one, we made our way down a rope between the panji sticks.

This was the only time I had to rappel from a helicopter in Vietnam.

As soon as we landed and before the helicopter had a chance to get out of sight, the patrol made for a nearby hilltop. It was there that we hoped to spot any troop movement.

Little did we know at that time, the helicopter pilot had dropped us in the wrong location. The patrol was approximately four miles from where it was supposed to be. We had been dropped right in the enemy's front yard.

It was a fatal mistake by the pilot.

The hill was steep—a difficult climb of about a half-mile. It took the patrol about an hour to reach the top.

The peak was so pointed the patrol had difficulty spreading out.

Although we normally liked to set up in a circle-the-wagons type of defense at complete 360, the terrain prevented us from doing this.

On one side of the peak there was thick bush—a heavy impenetrable jungle. On the other side was a long sloping field.

Starbuck sent Pfc. Raymond Chaplin and me to the field side of the peak and told us to dig in. Like wearing the helmets and flak jackets, digging in was also unusual on a recon patrol.

In the foxhole next to us on the semi-bald side of the peak were Shafer and Robert Armitage. Armitage was on his first recon patrol.

The next hole was the machine gun nest. It was occupied by Ed Smith, the machine gunner, and Chuck Davis. Davis was a wild kid from Alabama.

Sgt. Starbuck set up his command post in the center on the thickly vegetated side. Along with him was LCpl. James Rowe, the patrol radioman. Klaus Urbaniak was probably with them. I had nicknamed Urbaniak "Snake" for he had a habit of continually flicking his tongue.

I am not sure if the command post was dug in. Later, I came upon Rowe laying above ground.

Boo Boo Smith—a southern black and a damn good Marine—and James O'Leary were in the last hole near the bush.

At that time, I was probably closer to O'Leary than anyone else on the patrol because we were both from Massachusetts.

All were veterans of many recon patrols except for Armitage.

By about 2100 we had finished setting up and had placed claymore mines around our perimeter. Each two-man foxhole had claymores out.

It was a perilous position that we occupied.

Before it had turned dark, I looked out over this beautiful field from our lofty position and pictured cattle grazing on a hillside pasture in Pennsylvania.

It had just turned dark, when it sounded like a thousand guns went off.

"Bwrooooom!" sounded constantly for about five to ten minutes.

Chaplin and I were relatively safe. The Viet Cong had attacked from the jungle side of the peak. We were on the bald side. We were the lucky ones. No one came up on us as we sat, unthreatened, in our hole for about an hour.

I began wondering why we had not been lifted out. Usually recon patrols were extracted as soon as contact was made.

As the firefight died down, I decided to find out what the hell was going on.

I told Chaplin to remain in the hole while I crawled to Starbucks command post.

Armitage and Shafer occupied the hole closest to mine. When I arrived I discovered that Shafer had already been killed.

Armitage was excited and somewhat panicky. I told him not to fire his rifle for any reason. The flash from the muzzle would pinpoint his location to the Viet Cong, and they would direct their fire to it.

I said, "Do not fire! Keep your ass down and your head down in that fox hole!"

I crawled about four feet from his foxhole.

The Viet Cong must have heard me or saw me moving. They began to direct their fire at me as I lay on the ground right next to Armitage's foxhole.

In pure panic, Armitage stood up and fired back! He took a round in the chest killing him instantly.

Then, a Chinese grenade hit me on my right ankle!

I just lay there, curled up and waited for it to go off.

Thank God it was one of those chicom's!

Chicom's did not explode as our grenades did. Our pineapples would throw shrapnel in a 360-degree area, whereas their grenades would only cover 180-degrees.

As the grenade exploded I expected to die.

I had a flashback to childhood—I was sitting at a little place called The Sons of Italy, a members club on the main drag of our little town—I had my bike and my Little League uniform on—I had just come back from a Little League game—as I did many, many times—I went in and bought a pizza for 75 cents—I sat there and ate my pizza—got on my bike and pedaled the 2 or 3 miles back to my house. –It just flashed back to me, sitting there with my pizza on my bike with my baseball uniform on. It was just like I was there!

When the grenade exploded I did not get the brunt of the blast because of where I was laying. I only got the side portion of it.

My flak jacket was torn up pretty good. I also got a lot of shrapnel in my butt and lower back. In the hospital they removed a large piece of L-shaped shrapnel that was about a half of an inch long. I later gave it to my son Ryan.

After I got hit with the grenade, I shouted out a moan because of the burning metal in my ass!

A gook came up to me. He ripped off my dog tags, searched me and took my Lenox High School ring. Why he didn't knife me or cut off my ears for souvenirs—I don't know. I'm sure he thought that I was dead. I did piss my pants at that time!

I continued to crawl all the while looking for Sgt. Starbuck and the command post.

I then ran into the radioman, Rowe. He was in bad shape. He had five bullet holes in him.

I saw O'Leary on the skyline. I saw him get shot—hit!

O'Leary was standing up and running on the hill. He was moving from position to position when he was hit. O'Leary was trying to help someone else out. He went down and landed inside a hole that was already up there. It didn't have anything to do with us.

I wrote O'Leary up for a Silver Star. I'm pretty sure he got one.

I spent the night with the radioman. The radio would not work. It would not transmit but we could hear the helicopter transmissions.

The pilots of the choppers were trying to get us out. We could see all of the helicopters in the distance searching for us but they were in the wrong location. They were at the position where we were supposed to be.

The cord from the radio to Rowe's ear had been shot off. We were trying to splice the wires together.

We could hear the pilots calling our call sign, "Crankcase! Crankcase!"

Rowe and I spent the whole night trying to splice these wires together so that we could transmit. We could not talk loud because the Vietnamese were only about ten feet away. We didn't move a muscle all night.

It was the longest night of my life.

I could hear the wounded Viet Cong moaning and groaning and dragging their bodies through the bush.

While I had been on the other side of the hill, Boo Boo Smith, O'Leary and Rowe had really done a number on the VC by setting off claymore mines and throwing grenades.

The Viet Cong must not have realized that we were recon or they would have totally annihilated us. The fact that we were wearing helmets and flak jackets led them to believe that we were part of a much larger infantry group. They probably thought that we were an advance squad and had a battalion of Marines at the bottom of that hill.

Throughout the night all of the patrol members who survived the initial Viet Cong assault had been cool and professional with the exception of the Armitage kid. He was a nervous wreck. It cost him his life.

When daybreak came, I told Rowe, "Hey, I gotta get out of here. We gotta get out of here."

I told myself, "I'm going to walk out on this hill which was only about—oh shit—10 feet away."

I got out a smoke grenade.

"If I make it, I make it. And, if I don't, I don't! I said. "I'll see you later Rowe."

And, that's what I did.

I decided to myself, "Somebody's got to do this. I'll either get myself waxed, or I'll get us the hell out of here."

So, I just walked to the top of that hill.

Being nervous, I pulled out a red smoke grenade instead of a yellow smoke. Red means enemy. But at that time I really didn't look at the color code.

I popped a smoke. That's when the pilots finally saw us. They saw the smoke, came over to investigate and saw us.

A little piper cub came over first.

I just stood on the hill.

There must not be any Viet Cong left looking at me. Otherwise, I would be dead. They must have retreated. We had done a number on them with the claymores.

I didn't do this to win any medal. I did it to get my ass off of this hill!

The helicopters and the Phantoms came in and circled the hill.

Then, I set off the remaining two claymore mines.

The patrol still did not have verbal communications with the air. When the pilots saw the exploding claymores and ammunition going off they thought that we were being attacked again. They thought that we were taking on fire.

The Phantoms came over the top of that hill and napalmed all around.

They just did a number on them!

If any Viet Cong—wounded or whatever—were left, they were then gone.

The time came for the helicopter to land on that hill.

It was then that I noted just how steep that peak really was. As I stood at the top an F-4 Phantom flew by. The pilot and I were at eye level. He gave me the thumbs up sign. I could clearly see his face!

I don't know the name of the helicopter pilot who came to rescue us.

But, it was a hell of a feat for him to land. The helicopter was rocking.

I directed him in as best as I could.

When he landed, Chaplin and I went around and got all the wounded and the KIA's aboard. Then, we got all of the weapons that were left.

Chaplin, like the good Marine he was, remained in his assigned position all through the night. He was unaware of all of the events that had taken place. Chaplin had not been wounded.

Although I had also been assigned to Chaplin's position, I had to find out what the hell was going on. If I had not moved and remained in the foxhole, I would not have gotten shot either.

Snake also was unwounded. He was just lucky. The brunt of the action had occurred at his location.

The Viet Cong had opened with a burst of fire. It is my theory that they had crawled right up to our position on that side of the hill where the radioman and the machine gunner were located. These guys were right in the Viet Cong's sights. They knew where Sgt. Starbuck and the command post were.

It was just like the fourth of July when the firing began. It was all at one time. It wasn't a pot shot here and a pot shot there. It was nothing but Bwroooomm!

Starbuck, Shafer and Ed Smith were killed within the first ten minutes—maybe five.

The enemy had crawled right up and sighted in—and boom! When they opened up it was unreal.

The Viet Cong unit was probably Battalion sized. The ones that actually hit us were about three squads—about 35-40 men. So few were sent because they had to quietly crawl up to our position.

After we were extracted, I was sent to Okinawa to recover from my wounds. My injuries were not severe enough to have me sent back to the states.

After I regained my strength I was sent to NCO school and then back to Vietnam.

It was great to see the guys again, and I was ready.

I had no problems the rest of the tour. I even started liking it. Except for the last 30 days. That's when you get short. I started to get anxious and began to think about American women. It was time to go home.

NOTES: The four patrol members killed that day were as follows:
Armitage, Robert L. Pfc. 2314872; 19; Everett, Washington
Shafer, Robert L. Cpl. 22085833; 22; Windsor, Illinois
Smith, Edward F. Pfc. 2290347; 19; Easton, Massachusetts
Starbuck, Robert F. Sgt. 1939063; 25; Montgomery, New York

The other patrol members were:
Chaplin, Raymond L. Pfc. 230082; Albany, New York
Davis, Charles H. Pvt. 2128172; Alabama
O'Leary, James R. Pfc. 2249415; Fall River, Massachusetts
Rowe, James H. III LCpl. 2174252; Philadelphia, Pennsylvania
Smith, Roger S. Pfc. 2200251; Jacksonville, Florida
Urbaniak, Klaus H. Pfc. 2260319;
Verheyn, David A. LCpl. 2117334; 21; Lenoxdale, Massachusetts

David Verheyn was awarded the Navy Cross for his heroism this day.

The Silver Star was posthumously awarded to Sgt. Robert Starbuck.

Vice President Hubert Humphrey presents
The Navy Cross to Sgt. David Verheyn

* * * *

Captain Joseph R. Tenney from Cape Cod, Massachusetts was the commanding officer of K-3-5 on the day that Operation Swift began. The following excerpt is taken from Tenney's unpublished manuscript and is used with his permission.

"Spit shined boots and starched utilities
don't belong in a combat zone."

Capt. Kenneth D. Jordan
3rd Recon Battalion
Silver Star

9
THE VALLEY OF THE SHADOW

Operation Swift began on the fourth of September 1967. Delta Company of 1st Battalion 5th Marines was badly mauled by a large NVA force while operating in the central part of the Que Son Valley.

Initially, Bravo Company was sent to assist. However, they too were pinned down. Captain Morgan of Delta Company had been killed. At this point, Kilo and Mike Company were placed under the 1st Battalion 5th Marines and attacked west after being inserted to the east of the Bravo and Delta's position.

The action on the fourth was heavy but the action on the sixth was a major fight of Operation Swift.

Five September was spent resupplying and licking our wounds from the fighting on the fourth. India Company was fresh. M Company was chewed up. The Battalion Chaplain had been killed along with about 23 Marines. J.D. Murray had done a superb job as the new CO but he had taken the brunt of the casualties. I had taken one killed, the Corpsman from the 2nd Platoon, and several wounded including my brand new XO of one day, 1stLt. Ed Easton.

The Company had fought well but the men were tired. We had been on the move since early August with less than a day off the line or out of the field.

The morning of the 6th the Battalion Command Group from 3-5 arrived. After about an hour, we moved out with India Company on the left and Kilo Company on the right now moving to the south with M Company in reserve.

Initially, we moved south behind 1st Battalion 5th Marines which was now a composite unit of Bravo, Delta and Charlie. Delta was down to less than platoon strength. It was made up of rear area people brought out from the 1-5 Base Camp.

After about an hour, we wheeled on an axis formed by India Company and headed east basically four Companies abreast. However, the two Battalions were about a thousand yards apart. Units were not tied in and began to fan out so that eventually India and Kilo were about a thousand yards apart. India made contact and began to maneuver against it.

I called Frank Burke on the radio and told him I could move up to support since I was not in contact. The India CO requested us to stand clear and stay out of his way because they had the situation under control.

About five minutes later, I was told by Battalion to halt my advance until India could reduce their contact. We set up in a village at about 1300 and waited. The firing persisted to our flank and well ahead of us.

Ironically, we had taken one casualty to a loose water buffalo that had charged one of the troops trampling him. The trooper was injured but not critically and would have to be carried.

I was monitoring the reports and noted that India's situation was following an all too familiar pattern. It was a small contact initially. But, each maneuver was met with fire pinning down each maneuver element. Finally a Company or patrol would find itself pinned down by fire and strung out on a line.

Suddenly, at about 1700 I received a call from India Company requesting immediate assistance. The call was on the Battalion Tactical Radio net asking the Battalion operations officer to monitor. Silence would be assumed as approval. No countermand order was given, so Kilo was on its way to a date with destiny.

Time was on the side of the enemy.

I knew Frank's Company was to the north and east—a good 1000 to 2000 yards away. The ground was rolling, wooded and broken into paddies, and the light was failing. If I couldn't reach him before dark, we might both be in serious trouble. It was a grim situation.

Lt. Dave Blizzard had the point. I was behind him with Lt. Wayne Brandon's First Platoon. The rear was Lt. Jim McCool's 3rd Platoon carrying the injured man. This was slowing our progress.

Somewhere ahead of us was India Company and an enemy beginning to encircle for the kill. This meant we would have to advance rapidly. Too rapidly! We did not fire because of fear of hitting our own troops. At the same time we were running the risk of walking into an ambush or being fired on by our own troops in India Company.

India was firing flares to guide us to their location. The light was failing. I was getting more concerned as were all of us. We were moving ahead too fast now. We would have to slow down soon.

Then—FINALLY! CONTACT!

With it came fire from our right flank to the southeast wounding several members of the 2nd Platoon including Lt. Blizzard.

Blizzard had moved up with his point unit and had made the difference on us moving more rapidly.

Contact had been made. We were now able to start to move forward.

Unfortunately, the worst was yet to come. I was to learn later that Captain Burke's situation was worse than either he or we realized. It turned out that India had 28 killed along with a number wounded some still forward of our position.

I moved my command group up. Since Captain Burke was the senior officer present, I placed my men at his disposal.

Burke elected to withdraw up the hill to form the rear and one flank. We held the front and the other flank.

The problem now was the NVA attacking my rear element and splitting it. We were cut off from Jim McCool and two squads from the 3rd Platoon. His third squad was still with me. The second Platoon had a wounded Platoon Commander. I elected to move the 1st Platoon through to take the northern flank, leave the second Platoon where it was but spread it north to meet the 1st Platoon and my Headquarters group who had moved into what we thought was India's CP, only to find we were on the front lines in the center.

In any case, after some milling and confusion we decided on a plan.

By now it was virtually dark. India Company would withdraw on the flanks while remnants pulled through us and up the hill. It was a poor man's "circle the wagons." But it was better than nothing.

As previously stated, Captain Burke had Command of the Operation, but I was on the front lines and in the thick of the fight when it came.

We had hastily dug in behind a narrow bamboo thicket. We were at the base of the hill with the bamboo working as a shield against the enemy's advance. The first assault was repulsed but casualties were taken. We still had a patrol out in front of us.

I was becoming more alarmed. I had lost radio contact with the Second Platoon Commander after I had ordered two of his men to bring him into the position.

As it turned out, Dave was okay. He had stayed with his men and was tying in, but his radio was on the blink. Jim McCool was on the radio but cut off from us still to the south. He wanted to move in, but I told him to sit tight.

I couldn't see anybody else moving. I was missing the first Platoon leader who had moved out on a recovery mission after setting in his men and leaving the Platoon Sergeant in charge.

At this point, the first attack hit! It was what I like to call a probe in force. I really don't think it was well organized. I think the enemy was deceived as to where our line really was. We were able to handle it.

The second one was much stronger! In fact, the sky lit up green from all the green tracers. The hillside above was an eerie green color from all the tracers flashing around. U.S. tracers are red and NVA were generally either green or white.

I remember talking to people in Battalion later. They were convinced we had been wiped out since there appeared to be nothing but the enemy firing by the glow in the sky. Actually, we were firing. Initially, no tracers were used because I felt they gave away our position. Only the machineguns had tracers and then less than usual. The NVA would advance with tracers marking their lanes until they went into the assault.

I kept shouting to the men moving along our line, "Hold your fire until you have a target! Then, shoot at the tracer's source!"

It worked.

On our left flank was a machinegun—the key to our defense. I had already replaced one. Now, Bob Hawks was working it as the XO. I was in the center. The Gunny was on the right flank.

In the midst of the firing, Bob Hawks came staggering down the line. He had been hit twice. Men were trying to get him down. He didn't fall until he reached me.

With the left flank gun gone, the enemy was closing in.

I moved in that direction through the dark along the line.

Just before reaching the location there was an increase in the firing. Shells were cracking all around me!

I dove forward—there was a blast in front of me!

The NVA were swarming through the gap in the bamboo and over the gun. I don't remember how long it took, but it was fast.

I ran at the position. About five yards away I stopped. I fired until my pistol emptied! I caught the NVA who were in the position by surprise since they had just gotten there.

I know that I hit two of them and possibly a third. I threw my pistol at him. I either hit him with the pistol or he had already been shot because he crouched down.

I then ran forward groping for my K-bar knife. As I reached the position, I felt it in my right hand. With my left hand, I straight-armed the soldier. We fell backward into the position.

As I struggled with the soldier, more of Kilo Company met the breakthrough.

The fighting was hand-to-hand and furious!

More of the company moved in with men mostly from adjacent positions.

In seconds, we were back in the position with the gun operating. The gun crew was now beginning to take its toll.

Later, we would learn that the NVA had found themselves in a crossfire with Lt. Wayne Brandon's men attacking their rear mortars and machineguns.

The fighting began to subside. Although we did not know it, the NVA had apparently made their last effort.

We received more probes but Mike Company was now on its way to reinforce us. It was later determined that these probes were a covering action while the enemy disengaged.

The next few hours were spent licking our wounds and getting organized.

I learned a good lesson from the Company Acting Gunnery Sergeant, SSgt. Orlett. After the second assault he had moved over on the left flank as we refused our flanks and moved to tie into a solid perimeter with India Company.

Battalion wanted our status. Regiment wanted us to disengage and move south to help 1-5 that was also under heavy pressure.

I called the Gunny asking what his status was and generally showing my alarm at not being able to contact all my people.

The Gunny responded that the people I was missing were with him and were in good shape and ready in case of another attack.

Later, when I reached him we talked. I asked how the men were doing. He responded that he didn't know where they were.

I looked at him in disbelief, and then he explained. When Lt. Brandon had returned he had reported that one of his radios had been lost and presumably captured by the enemy. If they were monitoring, we wanted the enemy to think we were as strong as possible. I've often wondered whether that one transmission might have had any effect on the enemy's decision to withdraw.

Sometime later, I found Lt. Hawks. I had figured him to be a goner—propped up and taped up—though in pain, very much alive!

Dave Blizzard, although shot in both legs and unable to move, was still running his platoon. The two men who had earlier carried him were still with him.

Even Jim McCool was confident with his one small separated force.

The tide had turned.

The morning dawned clear and was, somehow, almost cool. Daylight always makes things look better and 7 September was no exception. Although we had nearly 50 wounded, we had only lost five men killed. India had 29 killed from the earlier fighting and a like number of wounded.

The seventh was a day of reorganization. Frank took over the medivac mission while I went about expanding our positions. Sometime that morning III MAF CG and the Regimental CO flew in by helicopter. Captain Burke briefed General Cushman and Colonel Davis and then they flew to the Battalion CP located about a click to our rear.

Operation Swift would continue for several more days. Like many of the operations in Vietnam, it started with a contact and grew into a major operation. Before it was over, three medals of Honor, seven Navy Crosses, eighteen Silver Stars, numerous Bronze Stars and over 150 Purple Hearts would be awarded to participants that included both Navy and Marine personnel.

As for Kilo Company, we would fight in three major actions on the 4th, the 6th and the 12th losing only six men killed while accounting for 143 NVA confirmed killed. I suspect even more that we couldn't confirm.

NOTES:
Operation Swift took place between September 4, 1967 and September 15, 1967.

K Company 3rd Battalion Fifth Marines was given the nickname Killer Kilo because of its consistent high kill ratio. In six months between May and November 1967 Kilo had over 300 confirmed NVA killed while losing 23 Marines in seven major operations and numerous small unit actions.

Captain Morgan, the commanding officer of D-1-5, killed on Sept. 4 was:
Morgan, Robert F. Capt. 079825; 28; Glen Ellyn, Illinois

The six members of K-3-5 killed on 9/6/67 were as follows:
Arnold, Reid C. Cpl. 2154074; 19; Largo, Florida
Carota, John T. Sgt. 2039618; 24; Milton, Massachusetts
Rust, James H. Pfc. 2190891; 22; Malone, New York
Stewart, David S. HN B501494; 18; Peoria, Illinois
Swafford, Robert W. Pfc. 2131001; 23; Fallon, Missouri
Willow, Robert G. Pfc. 2209544; 18; Johnsburg, Pennsylvania

The Medal of Honor was awarded to three men on Operation Swift: Navy Lieutenant Vincent R. Capodanno the Battalion Chaplain for 3-5, Sgt. Lawrence D. Peters of M-3-5, and Sgt. Rodney M. Davis of B-1-5. All three of the awards were posthumous.

Six Marines and a Navy Corpsman earned the Navy Cross:
LCpl. Thomas B. Driscoll of D-1-5; LCpl. Thomas W. Fisher of M-3-5; HN Armando G. Leal, Jr. of M-3-5; Capt. John D. Murray of M-3-5; Sgt. Thomas C. Panian of I-3-5; 2dLt. Dennie D. Peterson, FO for 2-11; and, Maj. David L. Ross of VMO-2. The awards to Leal and Peterson were posthumous.

The Silver Star was awarded to Maj. Charles H. Black the Operating Officer for 1-5, 2dLt. Wayne H. Brandon of K-3-5, Sgt. Richard J. Brown of K-3-5, Maj. Francis M. Burke of I-3-5, LCpl. John G. Call of B-1-5, Col. Stanley Davis CO of the Fifth Marines, 2dLt. Carlton W. Fulford of D-1-5, LtCol. Peter L. Hilgartner CO of 1-5, Cpl. Stephen L. Irwin of H-2-5, Sgt. Charles E. Jenkins of D-1-5, Sgt. Robert F. Johnson, II of K-3-5, Sgt. Howard T. Manfra Jr. of M-3-5, Pfc. Curtis Mitchell of B-1-5, Maj. Edmond J. Murphy of HMM-363, Sgt. Paul J. Orlett of K-3-5, Sgt. Joel Rousseau of I-3-5, Capt. Joseph R. Tenney of K-3-5, 1stLt. Robert O. Tilley of K-3-5 and Sgt. Harold E. Wadley of H-2-5. The awards to Richard Brown, Call, Irwin and Mitchell were posthumous.

Lieutenant General Robert E. Cushman, 05062, was the commanding officer of the III Marine Amphibious Corps in Vietnam. He had earned the Navy Cross during WWII for heroism on Guam from July 21 to August 20, 1944. Cushman would later become the first post-Vietnam Commandant.

Sgt. Charles E. Jenkins, 21, from Pittsburgh, Pennsylvania was a squad leader in D-1-5 during Operation Swift. He earned a Silver Star for heroism on September 4. Here Jenkins shares his recollections of that operation:

On the morning of September 3, we moved out at daybreak on a company-sized patrol of about 90 men. One platoon was left at the base camp for security. There were no major firefights with Charley during the day except for the usual sniping.

Just before dark, we set up our night defensive positions. There was a little ville just to the west of our position and we could hear the inhabitants banging pots and pans. Little did we know at the time that these gooks were signaling the other gooks of our presence in the area.

About 0400 the listening post in front of my platoon started taking small arms fire and the company was taking incoming mortar fire. Charley had infiltrated our company position and was all over the perimeter. I sent Smitty to check our platoon positions to the left and I went to the right. That was the last time I saw Smitty alive. The gooks were inside the perimeter and our CO Capt. Morgan was killed.

As it started to get light the gooks were still inside our perimeter. I went down the trench line throwing grenades, and I killed at least a couple of the gooks. I can remember some Marines firing at some objects in the rocks on the perimeter, and they turned out to be Marines. I know at least one was killed by friendly fire.

We finally killed all of the gooks that were inside our position. I stood over one gook that was badly wounded and finished him off.

The emotion of the fight was overwhelming. I found my own little space and cried.

We lined up our 13 KIA's in ponchos and body bags for their final trip back to the world. One of the choppers coming in to pick up our wounded and dead was shot down inside our little corner of the world. The reinforcements that were sent to help were also ambushed and suffered heavy casualties.

Later that day after the terrible heat of the afternoon, we started removing the dead gooks from inside our perimeter. I will never forget the stench of death in the heat. As we were picking them up parts of their arms came off. It was probably because they had been lying in the sun for so long.

After spending that night and the next day recuperating and being resupplied we moved out. We were to join up with the rest of the battalion that was conducting a search and destroy operation.

On the afternoon of 6 September, Charlie hit us again. My platoon had the rear security of the company, and Charlie was lobbing in Mortar rounds and machine gun fire.

I looked to my right and less than 25 yards away was a squad of NVA on line sweeping across the open area. They didn't know where we were and kept on firing and moving.

As we were moving to keep up with the rest of the company, we came across one of our machine gunners. He was lying across his M-60. Half of the side of his head was missing. I had one of my squad take the gun so that Charlie wouldn't get it. I was afraid that they would use it on us.

A short time later, a mortar round exploded a short distance from me sending shrapnel into my arms and legs. Fortunately, it wasn't very serious. I could keep moving with the help of some of my men.

As we were moving to link up with the battalion I came across a spider hole and threw in a grenade. I thought that there might have been a gook in the hole.

That night the pain of my wound became almost unbearable. We set up a defensive position with the rest of the battalion. The wounded and the dead had to wait until morning to be evacuated. We had gooks all over the area and incoming mortars throughout the night. I lay in a partially dug foxhole and hoped that the mortar rounds would not fall on my head. The good Lord was with me that night.

The next morning I was medivaced out and spent the next 3 weeks at Cam Ranh Bay recuperating from my wounds. The wounds weren't serious enough for a trip back to the world. I ended up back out in the bush.

The helicopter shot down within the Company D perimeter was from VMO-2 and was piloted by Maj. David L. Ross. Here he shares his recollection of that night:

I was assigned to an armed UH-1E that was providing escort for a UH-34 helicopter flying a medical evacuation mission.

As the UH-34 made its approach we began our firing runs hoping to suppress the enemy fire. Both helicopters sustained several hits and were forced to set down within the perimeter.

On the ground I made my way to the command post and talked briefly to Capt. Morgan before he died. I changed my radio call sign from "Deadlock" to "Deadlock on the Deck." I continued to help direct air strikes on the NVA.

I can remember one Marine, LCpl. Thomas Driscoll, who picked up a strobe light and used it to guide the medevac helicopters into the landing zone. He repeatedly exposed himself to enemy fire. I kept expecting the NVA to knock him down. They never did.

Dave Blizzard was a 26-year-old Second Lieutenant when he received orders to Vietnam. He would earn a Silver Star as an advisor on 11/9/71 during a second tour in Vietnam. In the following paragraphs he describes what he recalls about Operation Swift and his time in Vietnam:

When I arrived I was put up in the transient officers quarters at the headquarters of the 1st Marine Division near Danang.

My first night in country I was witness to the largest attack of the war on the Danang Air Base. Needless to say, I was really wondering what I had gotten myself into.

At any rate, the next day I reported to the G-1 for my assignment. When I walked in, there was a wormy little 2nd Lt. named Lisenby sitting behind a desk. Since we were of equal rank, theoretically, (in reality, if another Lt. had one more day in country than you, he was convinced he out-ranked you) I just told him straight out that I was here to be assigned to Force Recon.

Lisenby just laughed as he looked up and said something like, "Got some hot news for you. You're not going to Recon. The Fifth Marines just took heavy casualties during an operation, and I'm sending you there to be an infantry platoon commander."

Thus began my first thirteen-month tour in Nam.

I flew by means of the old CH-34 to Hill 63 where the Fifth Marine Regiment had a provisional headquarters. It was a low hill surrounded by wire and fighting positions. The regiment was headquartered in GP tents; two other newly arrived 2dLts. were escorted to the Personnel Officer for in processing.

After that we were taken to the office tent of the C.O. for the Fifth Marines. We waited for a very long time to be ushered into Colonel Davis office. When finally ordered in, we snapped to attention in front of him as he sat at his small field desk poring over some report. We stood at rigid attention for some minutes before the Colonel finally looked up. When he did we saw a craggy face with a bone-deep sunburn and a look of exhaustion in his eyes.

I guess we all expected the standard "welcome aboard" motivational speech. What we got instead was something of a blow to our eager anticipation.

The only words out the Colonel's mouth were, "If you three don't know how to read a map, I guarantee that in the next thirteen months you will be killed, wounded or relieved. Dismissed!"

Nevertheless, we were all very well schooled in map reading and land navigation.

Of the three of us who reported in that day, one Lieutenant was later killed. One was subsequently relieved of command. I was wounded several months later.

Of the three possibilities that the Colonel presented to us as dedicated Marine Officers the most dreadful prospect was being relieved of command—a fate worse than death!

After our fateful meeting with the C.O., we were each hustled off to a different battalion. I was assigned to the 3rd battalion of the Fifth Marines.

When I arrived at their out-posted headquarters, I was introduced to LtCol. Webster, the 3rd Battalion C.O. I immediately liked him. He was much more forthcoming and communicative than the regimental commander. Webster informed me that he was assigning me to Kilo Company as an infantry platoon commander.

After that meeting I was taken down to the company and introduced to the C.O., Captain Joe Tenney. I noticed as Tenney turned to greet me in the tent that he had an ugly scar around the back of his head extending from the rear of one ear to the other. This was the result of having been shot by a sniper. As the bullet penetrated his helmet, it deflected and sliced around the back of his skull. The impact had knocked him cold leaving what John Wayne referred to as "Nothin' but a flesh wound."

Joe Tenney was a fine guy and a good commander. He wasted no time in giving me the run down on the situation with the company and assigned me as commander of the Third Platoon.

I was replacing 1stLt. Bob Hawks who was moving up to be the company executive officer. He was very helpful to me, and we were to become friends as the result of developments beyond our control.

Bob was later seriously wounded on the same day I was hit. We ended up in the same hospital room in Yokosuka, Japan.

After talks with Joe Tenney and Bob Hawks, I was taken some miles away to the location of my platoon. They were in a temporary defensive position guarding a bridge.

I met my Marines with a sense of confidence and anticipation. My Platoon Sergeant was named Brown. My squad leaders were Cpl. Leo Tablizio, Sgt. John Carota and Cpl. Greg Rossof. I had three other young Marines who stand out in my mind, an American Indian of the Pima tribe named F.W. Weahkee (the troops called him "Fearless Warrior" for his initials), a Polynesian named Joseph Momoa and a black named McMillan. The other platoon commanders were Wayne Brandon, Jim McCool and John Corr.

McCool had been a football player at the University of Delaware.

Cpl. Tablizio, I believe, was a Mexican American from the West Coast.

Sgt. Carota was a quiet but very effective and courageous leader.

Momoa and Fearless Warrior Weahkee were best of friends. If one was assigned point, the other wanted to be next in file. Both were wounded on a number of occasions and both had refused Purple Hearts since they didn't want to be sent home.

Cpl. Greg Rossof was the most senior Marine left standing after I got hit.

Sgt. Carota was killed. He and I communicated throughout the night of 6-7 Sept. He did a great job after I got hit. I believe he was awarded a Silver Star for the action. If he didn't, he should have!

I'm not sure if the black Corporal's name was McMillan, it could have been McDonald, etc. But, we all called him Mac. Mac's memory is burned into my brain — a terrific lad!

John Corr, 23, from Wilton, Connecticut, The India Company Platoon Commander, was hit about the same time as I. He was lying near me. John was a source of inspiration to me that night as he displayed great spirit. He recovered from this wound and returned to Vietnam. John was killed on 12/28/67 in Quang Nam Province.

Chaplain Vincent Capodanno was killed on Operation Swift. I still carry the St. Christopher medal he gave to me when I travel. He was a Catholic. Although I am a Lutheran I used to go to his field services— any port in a storm, so to speak. The Chaplain was a very inspiring guy.

In a Marine infantry platoon the table of organization calls for squad leaders to be sergeants and the platoon sergeant is a staff sergeant. However, I was soon to learn that for the Marines in Viet Nam upward mobility was a fact of life. The longevity of a sergeant, staff sergeant, and lieutenant was rather limited. When you lost a sergeant as a squad leader you replaced him with the best corporal in the squad and so forth. The meat grinder was a well-oiled machine that operated at peak efficiency, twenty-four hours per day.

We spent a few days on this position. We had it pretty easy, running patrols out from our position, listening to Armed Forces Radio.

Every day at 0600 the announcer really did screech, "Good morning Viet Nam!"

Then we were pulled back to the company area and were briefed on an upcoming operation.

During this time, one incident stands out in my mind in vivid detail. We were moving across an open paddy bordered by dikes and heavy vegetation. Shots aimed at my platoon rang out in rapid succession from the tree line. We all went to ground.

I shouted, "Anyone hit!"

I scanned my men and saw one black hand raised. Since I was nearest to him, I ran to his position and plopped down next to him. It was Mac. I asked him where he was hit. He told me he took one in the leg.

I ran my hands down both sides of the leg, feeling for any bone displacement. As I did so, the most amazing thing happened. The bullet fell out of the wound into my hand.

As I grasped it, I said to Mac, "I've got an incredible war souvenir for you."

Just as I got the words out of my mouth, the sniper opened up again. As the rounds kicked up dust just inches from us, I lurched and the bullet flew out of my hand.

At that point, I figured, "Only one thing to do now-get the hell out of here".

I picked up Mac and ran with a speed I had never been blessed with in my former life.

This later took an interesting turn when I ended up in the hospital in Yokuska. The first two familiar faces I saw were that of Bob Hawks and Mac. Bob was my roommate. Mac came from another ward to see me. During the time I was confined to a wheelchair, Mac came every day to wheel me to the movie.

When I finally reached Yoksuka, I was feeling a bit sorry for myself with wounds through both legs. That was until they rolled me into my room. I saw Bob Hawks laying there with tubes coming out of his chest and a breathing apparatus hooked to him. He had been shot through the chest. Bob was shot again down the top of the shoulder as he fell forward. The second bullet shattered his scapula and lodged near his heart. Bob was evacuated to St. Alban's in New York as far as I recall.

Bob was a great guy. He was a graduate of Syracuse where I believe he wrestled. Bob also dressed as an Indian and rode the mascot horse for Syracuse football games.

From that point on it was one operation after another. The conditions under which we lived and operated were abysmal. We were moving constantly on foot and rarely being transported on helicopters. Our feet were always wet and diarrhea was a constant. None of us wore socks. It just didn't make sense since it was impossible to change them often enough to keep our feet dry.

One time, as we were preparing to move out on an operation I got this stabbing pain in the heel of my right foot. I took my boot off and discovered that a thick callus had split wide open down to the red meat. When I walked I experienced excruciating pain as my heel struck the ground. I was scrambling to find some method of taking the pressure off my heel in order to keep up on the operation.

I found that with a piece of broomstick wired to the instep of my boot, I could hobble along at a respectable pace. I cut the broomstick to about five inches and carefully affixed it to the steel instep of my boot with comm wire and tape.

I walked for the next twenty-one days that way never taking my boot off. I was afraid that I wouldn't be able to get the contraption back on properly. When I finally did take the boot off, I found the gash completely healed.

Life in the field for an infantry Marine was just about as elemental as it can get. Survival was the number one priority.

One day, platoon commander Wayne Brandon and I were sitting on top of a hill that was devoid of vegetation because of a napalm drop. The battalion had stopped to regroup.

We broke out some C-rats. Wayne had a can of fruit cocktail, which was the most coveted thing in any of the C-rats.

Brandon looked at me as the sweat poured off him and said, "Dave life it so basic right now that if I found out you stole my fruit cocktail, I'd blow your friggin' head off!"

On the 6th of September 1967 my life changed forever. It was late in the afternoon, perhaps 1700. We were fighting our way to the relief of "Charlie" Company that, according to radio reports, had suffered some 38 Marines killed in action that afternoon. "Charlie" Company was positioned on top of a hill and was surrounded by North Vietnamese regular units.

My platoon was in the lead of our company as we prepared to punch through the NVA positions. I was with the lead squad in my platoon approaching an open area that encircled the entire hill.

Moving forward, we noted considerable enemy movement in the open area. I set up a base of fire with the squad on my right, and we began to advance by fire and movement.

About halfway across the open area my radio operator shouted, "There's a machine gun to the right!"

The radio operator had barely gotten these words out when the NVA gunner fired a burst at me. I was hit twice in the legs and went down.

My Marines reacted well. The grenadier fired a round that impacted on a rock next to the gunner, killing the NVA soldier instantly. My corpsman and radio operator dragged me forward under a heavy volume of fire and into the lines of "Charlie" Company.

We took heavy casualties as we broke through. All my platoon members, minus those who had been killed, made it through to "Charlie".

The remainder of the Company, however, was unable to follow and was cut off as the NVA closed their lines behind our platoon.

Later in the night another platoon made it through with the command group of Joe Tenney and Bob Hawks. The NVA lobbed mortars on us throughout the night and made several assaults as they attempted to over-run our position. During one of the assaults, they wiped out a two-man listening post located some distance in front of our main position.

One of the Marines was still alive and Bob Hawks ran out to try to drag him back. Bob later told me that an NVA was hidden in foliage lying in wait near the wounded Marine. When Bob reached the Marine, he was reaching down to pick him up when the NVA soldier opened up with a burst that hit Bob twice in the chest. Somehow Bob survived to tell me this story later in the hospital.

That night platoon sergeant Carota and corpsmen David Stewart were among those who were killed in action. Another corpsman as well as numerous others were seriously wounded.

It was a very long night. Finally, reinforcements got through to us and the NVA pulled back. They slowly moved all the casualties to an LZ and lined us up in four groups on the ground.

It was a triage operation. Those who didn't make it were placed off to the side. The first helicopter came in later in the morning. They began evacuating the most seriously wounded immediately. There was no attempt to treat wounds on the LZ, only efforts to stop heavy bleeding, clear airways and give morphine. I was towards the end of the evacuation priorities since my wounds were not life threatening.

That night as I lay there, I said to myself, "Nothing could be worse than this!"

A little while later, I leaned over to say something to another seriously wounded Marine. He didn't respond. I realized that he had just died. At that point a momentous lesson in life was driven home to me: things can always be a lot worse than they seem at the moment.

Late in the morning, 15 or 16 hours after I had been hit, a CH-34 finally lifted me out. In the mud with only field bandages covering my wounds, infection got a good foothold.

I was evacuated to Charlie Med, the Navy equivalent to the Mobile

Army Surgical Hospital (MASH) with some refinements. I waited for quite awhile in the open-air passageway outside the surgical suite.

When they finally rolled me in, they gave me a spinal and began the process of cutting away infected tissue and muscle. It went down fast because these guys had plenty of practice and obviously would be working well into the night.

My last recollection was that one of the surgeons leaned over and asked me, "Are you an officer or an enlisted man?"

Not imagining any reason for such a question, I merely said, "I'm a Second Lieutenant."

The surgeon then turned to his accomplice and said, "Sam, put those stitches closer together. He's an officer".

I was kind of foggy at the time. It didn't dawn on me until later that it was with such humor these guys dealt with the grisly carnage of their daily duties for one year of their lives.

I realized after surgery that I would probably never again run as fast or jump as high. The fact is that I never did run so fast or jump real high, so this wasn't going to be any great handicap.

From surgery they rolled me to a holding area, where I remained until late at night. I asked several times where I might be going, but nobody knew the answer. I was thinking that there were several possibilities. They could keep me in country to recover—unlikely. They could fly me to the Navy hospital ship Repose stationed off the coast. Or, they could fly me directly home! Of course, I was banking on a one-way ticket home. Wrong!

They flew me to Clarke Air Force Base in the Philippines. After one very short night there, I was flown to Yokosuka Naval Hospital in Japan.

To say that life for a Marine in an infantry outfit in the Nam was a dismal existence is a pure and unadulterated understatement. For an officer or NCO it was slightly better than it was for the rest of their fellow Marines. This was certainly not due to the perks (nonexistent) that came with the job. Rather, it was because those in leadership positions had to concentrate on the welfare of their men. That tended to deflect attention from one's own welfare and misery.

The all too common image of the skies filled with choppers moving large numbers of men in relative comfort into conflictive areas was certainly not the norm for the Fifth Marines. Nor was it for most other Marine infantry units in Viet Nam. We mainly humped in never—ending overland movements. Two C-Rations meals a day and water rationing, coupled with the oppressive heat and constant diarrhea tended to take the edge off one slightly.

With no end to the war in sight, one tended to concentrate on getting through one day at a time. When it really drove you down, you were reduced to just putting one foot in front of the other without stepping on a mine.

Were we as Marines good in battle? You bet we were because that's when all the fury, frustration and personal misery was released. Was the average Marine good? No, he was magnificent in his resilience, perseverance and courage under fire!

With regard to perseverance, I remember one day vividly. We were moving out on what was anticipated to be a long operation. My platoon was in the lead of my company. I was at the head of my platoon.

The last Marine in the column ahead of me appeared to be struggling as he walked. After awhile I noticed a brown stain spreading on the seat of his cammies. He couldn't control his bowels and obviously had a case of the very common dysentery. Nevertheless, he would not fall out of his unit. We moved throughout the day in those relative positions and that lad hung in there until we stopped near a stream where he could clean himself.

Were they good? No, they were magnificent!

Harold Wadley, 33, from Stanley, Idaho was a Platoon Sergeant with H-2-5 on Operation Swift. His account is as follows:

It might strike you strange to find a 33 year old sergeant in Vietnam. Well, here's a long story shortened of just such a one.

I had fought, been wounded and decorated with the Fifth Marines in Korea. I was later honorably discharged. Then went to and graduated from forestry college. I got a good job and had a wife and two small sons.

When Vietnam started, I couldn't bear to watch the news and see those young Marines in the mud and dying again.

The old salts from the Pacific Islands sure made a difference with us young jarheads in Korea and helped keep us alive. I didn't see any veterans in the daily news in Vietnam.

I wrote to the Commandant and asked to go to Vietnam giving him my reasons. I got a call from a colonel in the Commandants office.

The only thing he asked me was, "Are you still in shape?"

I assured him I was. After all, I ran the ridges of Idaho after cougar.

In three weeks I received direct orders to Vietnam and was back with the Fifth Marines!

I stopped in Camp Pendleton for a refresher on new weapons and hooked up with a replacement unit. We then stepped off the plane at DaNang and went to Hotel Company, Second Battalion, Fifth Marines.

Once again I was with my beloved Fifth Marines!

The United States Marine Corps is indeed a small outfit! Some of us keep popping up!

It turned out that the company gunny was Roberto Gutierrez who had also fought in Korea with the Seventh Marines. He had been on a bad outpost battle called Outpost Vegas!

On my last operation in Vietnam, Operation Swift, a tall lanky officer came trotting across the paddy to brief us. I knew the walk! It was Wayne King. He was now a Captain and the C.O. of Bravo Company, First Battalion, Fifth Marines. He and I were both wounded on the same raid on a Chinese hill called UnGok in Korea! We were sergeants then. We just called the war to a halt and lay at the tree line catching up on 14 years!

I haven't seen him since. I hope he made it out.

I was shot up and medevaced to Danang then to Japan and finally Oak Knoll Hospital in California before being medically discharged.

What a Wonderful bunch of Marines! From Captain Gene Bowers— one of the best—right down to the last private!

On that last day our reinforced platoon jumped off on what turned out to be a company sized NVA unit. It was one of those times when you immediately know it is certain death but you have to go ahead.

Our three man point of Wolf, Braswell and Stutes was dropped quickly. All hell broke loose!

I grabbed "Doc" Dennis Noah and took his corpsman bag telling him to keep his skinny ass right behind me. I knew they would kill the corpsman with the bag and that would leave Doc the chance to save Wolf, Braswell and Stutes.

I shot our way out to them.

Stutes was dying, Wolf was dead.

I grabbed Braswell by the neck where he had been shot at close range. As I did an NVA raised up about 10 feet away and shot Braswell through the head.

I shot and killed the NVA soldier and turned to the others dug in just a few feet away.

Steve Rader about 30 yards behind me rose up with a LAW to take the .50 cal that was really hammering us. The damn thing wouldn't close the circuit to fire!

Rader spit on his fingers, reached back and held the wire connection together and fired taking out the gun bunker.

Another of our Marines in 60mm mortars tried to bring suppression fire around me. I looked back to see him sitting up with no base plate—just the tube—with his right leg wrapped around it and holding it with his hand, aiming and dropping rounds in!

The Marine was so close to me—about 35 yards behind. He used no increments or maybe just one. The round barely made it to the top of the bamboo before falling fins first and slowly turning nose down just before it hit the deck!

In training we talk about "Danger Close" in firing mortars, which is considerably farther than what he did that day! He was killed.

Things finally got so bad after the bolt plug pins in our three M60 machineguns broke and the gunners hit.

John Jessmore, a machine gunner that had replaced the wounded radioman Harold Jenkins was now on the radio. I had him call for arty on our position as I heard the clacking signals of the NVA getting ready for a counterattack. I knew most of us were hit and wouldn't be able to stop them. The same with the napalm strike and boy it nearly took our breath away.

Mike Company came that night along with Captain Bowers and our third platoon to get us out.

We had a great bunch. I see their faces everyday.

Sergeant Stutes, who died that day, left me a special gift that I received twenty-five years later when my phone rang.

A voice asked, "Do you remember my Dad, William Stutes who died in Vietnam?"

"Remember?" I exclaimed! "How could I forget!"

The caller turned out to be Stutes daughter Catherine who was a baby at the time of his death.

Catherine came to visit me. At the time my son was on leave from the Marine Corps and also got to meet her.

Catherine is now my daughter-in-law.

William's gift to me is two fold. She has given me a grandson. The little boy is named William after his other grandfather.

Someday I will sit William down and tell him all about how wonderful his other grandpa was!

Looking at Catherine is like looking at a ghost, but a very sweet one indeed.

The following H-2-5 Marines were killed on 9/10/67:
Aukland, Leo C. LCpl. 2310862; 20; Bison, South Dakota
Braswell, James P. Jr. LCpl. 2320151; 20; New York, New York
Horvath, Charles W. LCpl. 2279840; 23; Bethlehem, Pennsylvania
Irvin, Stephen L. Cpl. 2305659; 20; Columbia, Missouri
Johnson, Kenneth C. LCpl. 2250094; 20; Bradley, Illinois
Stutes, William B. Sgt. 1930167; 25; Oceanside, California
Wolf, Michael F. LCpl. 2260001; 21; Beulah, North Dakota

Others mentioned by Harold Wadley are:
Bowers, Gene W. Capt.
Jessmore, John J. LCpl. 2309057
Noah, Dennis
Rader, Steve Pfc. 2223062

Wayne Carr was a squad leader with H-2-5 on 9/10/67. He shares his recollection of that day:

I had the first squad and Braswell and Wolfe were with me when we got hit. I remember that day like it was yesterday. We lost a lot of good men and a lot were wounded. We were pinned down for what seemed like days and the next morning pulling out the bodies of all my friends was tough. I knew Stutes well. He was platoon sergeant. I also remember Harold Wadley. After I was wounded Doc Noah bandaged me up and put me on the chopper. It was my third Purple Heart and I was going out of country.

Captain Joe Tenney makes this final comment about his service in Vietnam:

As I look back now on it, my memory is dim in some areas and crystal clear in others. The War has left its mark both physically and mentally. The scar on the back of my head will always remind me that I am alive today by the grace of God and that I have much to be thankful for. Mentally, as war does for most men, it makes one humble. I proved things to myself and when all is said and done, that is the person you can never fool. I was proud of what I had accomplished and the medals I had received. I was a bit disappointed in the general attitude of the country I returned to. The War would become increasingly less popular at home. My medals classified me as a war hero in another war but not this one. This was a war without heroes. The men who fought in the Valley of the Shadow had shared an experience in life that would make them better men. For my money, they were all heroes.

Brandon, Hawks, Blizzard, Tenney, Waggoner, McCool

*   *   *   *

Richard Allen Russell from Milford, Michigan was eighteen years old when sent to Vietnam in 1967. He was assigned to Fox Company, Second Battalion, Ninth Marines, which was assigned to the Phu Bai area.

By the spring of 1967 the new M-16 rifle was issued to the Marines who had originally been armed with the reliable M-14 rifle. Where as the M-14 fired a heavy 7.62mm cartridge, the new M-16 used a much lighter 5.56-mm cartridge. Under orders, the Marines reluctantly parted with the trusty M-14's.

Of the new M-16 rifle MacAvoy Lane wrote:

> When the M-16 rifle had a stoppage,
> One could feel enemy eyes
> Climbing
> His
> Bones
> Like
> Ivy.

It is May in Northern Quang Tri Province as we join Russell and the Marines of F-2-9.

Grateful acknowledgement is made to Richard Allen Russell for permission to reprint previously published material. The following excerpt is taken from *Hell In A Helmet: Memoirs of a Marine Infantryman Vietnam 1967* © 1989 by Richard Allen Russell by permission of Richard Allen Russell.

10
THE IMPERIAL HUNTING GROUNDS

In early May, before I asked for the transfer, we took off for a sweep in Northern Quang Tri Province. We slowly wound through the foot hills and soon saw our objective looming in the distance. The trip this time was to climb the mountain ridge that separated Laos from Vietnam and put a blocking action on the well- camouflaged highway up there, a highway that was better known as the Ho Chi Minh Trail.

The area we were in was once The Imperial Hunting Ground of the royal families of Vietnam. Although it had been an infiltration route for years and blasted to shit in places by Japs, Frenchies and us, the place was still fantastic. The jungle canopy was nearly one hundred feet off the ground in places and so thick that it precluded sunlight. It gave the illusion of perpetual twilight. Monstrous trees, plants, insects and animals abounded. Leeches dripped from the trees along with condensing water drops.

We patrolled the general area for a while and finally climbed up to Ho's road. The trail was a marvel of primitive engineering techniques coupled with third world construction technology. At the crest of the massive ridgeline we found the trail an easy hump, eight feet wide with easy grades and a level tread.

Along the ridge run, the enemy used an ingenious method of lashing three bicycles together with bamboo poles enabling them to have three men push six hundred pounds over the mountains. The deep fresh tracks gave evidence of recent bike convoys.

We climbed up above the trail and set in for the night in an area that had been bombed clear of big trees during an earlier war. Bob, Walt, and I dug in and bivouacked. It felt like old times, like when I first arrived and was in Bob's fire team - all three of us Michigan Homies together again. Usually Bob set up with the radioman and corpsman, while I set up with my own team and Walt set up with the newly formed elite interbattalion "pathfinders" group. That evening before dark we talked of familiar experiences and places and remembered the good in the world and in each other. It was to be our last night together.

At dawn, my platoon drew the point for our unit, and we took off down the mountain trail. We were two-thirds of the way down when the enemy sprung an ambush on our rear element. The cry rang out; and for reasons known only to God and the Marine Corps, my platoon, which was farthest down the slope, was called all the way back up. I was given the dubious honor of being the first one to go back out into the open and assault the two, thirty cal machine guns and AK's.

My first objective was a pretty good size tree stump on the far side of the bombed out clearing about thirty meters away. Except for my FAM

Fire (familiarization firing) with my brand new M16, this would be the first time I had to use it for real. I took a couple big breaths of air and psyched myself up.

My basic plan was to run like hell and fire short bursts from my hip to make the gook gunners duck. I dug my toes in well back from the opening, crouched like when running track and lit off like a rocket. By the time I hit the opening I was at full stride. I pulled the trigger for the first burst. The rifle fired one round and jammed. There I was forty feet from safety with two machine guns and eight or ten automatic rifles beaded in on me. I shifted into max-overdrive and dove about the last fifteen feet through the air. The enemy slugs followed me like a shadow, tearing the ground and showering me with sawdust from the stump I had managed to get behind.

I could see the lieutenant and several of my guys from where I was and hollered between machine gun bursts, "Jammed!!!" and pointed to my rifle. During class on the new M16's many of us had wondered at the armorers' (weapon specialists) insistence that all of us carry a cleaning rod and a full pint of oil to clean and lube the barrel. The M14's we had been trained with never jammed, and one cleaning rod and a pint of oil might be used by six men.

I took a round out of my mag, punched the pin out, broke down the barrel and assembled my cleaning rod. Meanwhile the lieutenant sent another guy out and up the other side of the opening. He got about twenty feet and dove behind a log with a jammed M16. I punched out the jammed shell casing, snapped the barrel down, replaced the pin and let go again. "Bang." jam. The lieutenant sent another guy out. "Bang." jam, and dive for cover, again and again till about eight of us were eating sawdust and clearing our 16's.

I poured a healthy squirt of oil into the breach. This time the rifle didn't jam but let go both a hearty hail of fire and a smoke display that would have made a steam locomotive proud. A great white plume of smoke rose straight over my head exactly pinpointing my position. More sawdust. As each guy's smoke column plumed up, the enemy zeroed in. They were having a field day.

Things were starting to look a little grim when an American Indian machine gunner we called "Injun Joe" charged out into the opening with his sixty blazing. He half walked and half ran straight up the slope into the enemy guns. He was hit twice and grazed twice but made it all the way up, dispatching three NVA's and scattering the rest. Later, he was awarded the Vietnamese Cross of Gallantry for this action.

We found the face of the slope covered with dead marines; one of them was my friend, Walt. Almost every one of them had been shot between the eyes and had an assembled cleaning rod and an open can of oil near them. Jammed 16's and pinpoint smoke plumes add up to dead marines, anyway you cut it. None of us that were there that day ever had faith in the black stick again.

While searching the area, we found a large enemy arms cache containing rice, Chicom (Chinese communist) grenades and a whole mess of brand-new Chinese SKS rifles. They had bayonets that flipped out of the side of the barrel like giant switchblade knives. I picked a real nice one (a mistake because my captain took it home with him), tagged it and never saw it again.

We called for choppers to bring in water and carry out several heat exhaustion cases. Due to the extreme angle of the slope, the choppers could not land but had to hover instead. They threw all the five-gallon water cans out the door, which promptly smashed to bits when they hit the ground. There was not enough water left for ten men to wet their whistle.

After bombarding us with exploding water cans, the choppers lowered lines for the heat exhaustion cases. It was with no small degree of satisfaction that I noticed a formerly skeptical Battalion Aide Surgeon being raised forlornly into the waiting chopper with exactly the same symptoms he had accused heat exhaustion victims of faking to avoid combat. There was no question that he now believed how real such an experience could be.

In order to get the dead and new cases of heat stress off the mountain, we had to build an elevated L.Z. out of trees and bush. Grunts cut and stacked a pile of wood about twelve feet high. The banana-shaped chinooks (helicopters) pulled into the slope one by one, touched with the back wheels and hovered the front end, just above our woodpile. Because of the angle of the hill, the back door was blocked shut; and everything and everybody had to be passed up a human chain -to the chopper's side door near the front. Five or six guys would lift a corpse and begin the long and treacherous climb down the slope to the L.Z.

After carrying my third body down, I was taking a break with my team when a different group of Grunts came by us with another body.

The corpse had the whole top of his head blown off; and when the grunts lifted him over a log in the trail, his brains spilled out, all pink and yellow-like, splatting heavily on the ground. A staff sergeant standing nearby summed it up for all of us when he said, "This fucking war sucks."

Resuming the climb my legs began to cramp up. Soon I was laying alongside the trail writhing in pain with my body locked in severe heat cramps. All the major muscles cramped, along with muscles I never even knew I had. My nostrils, my tongue, my eyes, and even my ears were locked hard in seizure. Such pain is impossible to describe to one who has never experienced it, similar perhaps to leg cramps only in every muscle throughout the body doing the same thing at one time only harder, much, much harder.

No water, one hundred twenty degrees and humping bodies down the mountain caused many marines to drop that day. I soon found myself being pried out of the ball shape I always cramped into and laid out straight near the L.Z. To attempt to move would throw me right into a cramp ball again, so I could only glance a little and ever so slightly try to speak when I had to. I noticed a pair of boots near my head and quietly asked, "Who are you? Are you all right?" No reply.

Soon I was passed up the chain to the arms of the chopper crew chief and placed on a slightly raised stretcher directly under the rear rotor of the helicopter. My head rested on a pack board, and I was totally paralyzed by the heat cramps into a straightened- out shape. My eyes looked straight down the chopper body, as they loaded the guy, whose boots I had been talking to, on board. The reason he did not respond was because the whole left top of his head was blown clean off.

The rest of the bodies were thrown on board, and we began ascending. I looked to the left and there was Burger, the very same guy who had shot Phil back in the Cobie Tahn Tahn Valley beneath Hill #51. He had caught a case of back blast and had one eye patched. On the other side was a network newsman who had come in to see what was happening and was wisely getting the fuck out on the next available chopper. Both guys were peering anxiously out the windows along with everyone else that could look down both sides of the chopper.

As the angle of ascent increased, the dead black corporal laying in front of me began to slide down the deck. I realized the corpse was going to slide right into my feet and tried to move, but no luck. Instead, the attempt caused the cramps to grip me even tighter. The dead man's head slid right up to my feet, as I stared with eyes that dared not shift. I was totally unable to move and enveloped in an electrifying bolt of pain. I was reminded of every nightmare I had ever dreamt in my life, but this was real.

I could not move, and the heel of my left foot was in a dead man's head. My arch was right on the top of the bridge of his nose, and all his blood was draining town the back of my legs and settling in the low spots on the stretcher. What few pitiful sounds I could utter were drowned out by the rotor as the ascent and my horror increased.

Of all the times of my life, this was the very worst. This is the scene I still see in my re-occurring nightmares-my foot in a dead man's head, and all his blood draining out on me.

Finally, after a million years, Burger casually looked down, immediately, registering shock and horror on his face. He grabbed the corpse and yanked it off my foot. Then he bent his head to mine. "My legs, my legs," was all I could say. They hurt so bad from the cramps that I was afraid the muscles would break the bones. Burger grabbed the network newsman, and both guys went to work trying to massage the concrete out of my legs.

By the time we landed in Phu Bai the cramps had eased some, but they began again when the corpsmen lifted up the stretcher. My heels locked over the end, and the dead corporal's blood began draining onto the ground, leaving a thick trail all the way to the Triage. There, several Asians and Troopies, standing near the Triage, stepped back in horror when they saw the blood cascading onto the rear stretcher-bearer's feet.

They threw me on a table, cut off all my clothes (including my medevac tag) and flopped me around looking for big holes. Each flip hurt like hell; and I wanted to tell them I was a heat exhaustion victim, but my tongue was cramped along with everything else. Finally they searched my discarded clothes, found the tag and started massaging me and sticking saline solution in my veins.

A day later I was dragging my aching body out front to watch the sunset when a medevac corpsman came up to me and said, "Jesus Christ, I thought you'd be dead by now." I told him about the dead guy's blood, but he left still looking at me like he had seen a ghost.

NOTES:

The poem at the beginning of this chapter is entitled "*Guns*". It was

134

written by former Marine MacAvoy Layne and can be found in his novel-in-verse, *How Audie Murphy Died in Vietnam*. Anchor Books published the book in 1973.

Walt, Russell's friend from Michigan, was actually Pfc. Ronald Walter Sanders, 18, from Wayne, Michigan.

Gary D. Murtha was a Marine with F-2-7 in the spring of 1967 when the change in weapons occurred. His comments on this change follow:

Grateful acknowledgement is made to Gary D. Murtha for permission to reprint previously published material. The following excerpt is taken from *Timefighter* © 1985 by Gary D. Murtha by permission of Gary D. Murtha.

APRIL 1967

First we had to get new weapons.

We assembled in our compound for a pep rally on the benefits of our new weapon. We were told that turning in our M-14 rifles would be voluntary. The M-16 looked like a toy and soon our leaders had a minor revolt on their hands. Nobody wanted to make the trade. Threats of office hours soon had us standing in line to make the reluctant trade. Everyone was leary of this new gun. Little did we know that our fears would be justified. Loaded with our new toys, Foxtrot was now at full strength and ready for a new assignment. Our new home would be in the Danang area.

JULY 1967

The last few months of combat had proven the M-16 to be a very poor and dangerous weapon. You were guaranteed a jam after each shot. It was so bad that everybody carried their cleaning rods, fully assembled, in their belt. It reminded you of the Revolutionary War when the shooting started. One shot, then ram the rod down the barrel to free the jam. After that shot, and it was up to three if you were lucky, you had to find a place to hide while you cleared your weapon. Luckily Charlie didn't know the problems we were having, as he didn't take advantage of several bad situations.

We received word one day that a team of rifle experts were coming to the bridge to have us test fire our rifles and hopefully find ways of curing the rifles ills. We shot our weapons off the bridge into the water. For an hour or so the experts walked up and down the lines with eyes peeled. Then they left without any explanation.

Within a few weeks their report helped to turn the M-16 into an excellent weapon. They had discovered that the rifle had two basic problems. The rifle was too fast for itself. The incoming round hit the spent outgoing round before it had a chance to leave the weapon. They corrected this by putting a heavier buffer in. This slowed the rifle down. The other problem concerned the ammunition. The casing of the bullet was too soft and as the extractor tried to grab hold they would rip. No matter how many times the rifle tried to eject the spent cartridge, it failed. The rounds currently being used had a red dot on the back. They came out with blue dot ammo with a harder case. That solved the problem. A problem with a weak magazine spring didn't prove to be a real problem. By putting a few less rounds in, it kept the temper in the spring so it didn't wear out so fast. The M-16 was now a superb weapon with no equal.

Gary Murtha

George Navadel was a hard charging Marine who commanded five different rifle companies during his tour in Vietnam. He had the reputation of being a Marines Marine. Navadel was fiercely devoted to the individual Marine and was held in high regard. He was considered a take no prisoner's type when it came to matters of integrity and combat readiness of the troops. Navadel also had a realistic idea of what could be expected of rifle companies in terms of distance and movement. He understood tactics and was a professional in every sense of the word.

The Third Battalion, Ninth Marines had suffered from poor leadership for many months but were about to make a change for the better. M-3-9 was about to come under new management. George Navadel who could always be counted on to choose the difficult right over the easy wrong was about to take over the company.

The following account was written by George Navadel and is his description of the action that occurred in the area of Hill 94 in Quan Gio Linh Province on June 1, 1967. He earned a Silver Star for his actions this day.

"Can't you keep a Sorry Ass Job in this Sorry Ass Marine Corps?"

GySgt. John C. "Horrible" Hatfield
K-3-9
Silver Star

11
TROUBLESHOOTER

M-3-9 had just taken a bloody beating on Operation Hickory. They took casualties, and their CO pulled back. He simply did not have the stomach to close with the enemy. They did not recover their dead until the following day. This was the second time this had happened.

The first was at Hill 881 South in March. I was the S-4 at the time following rehab of the Battalion on Okinawa. The CO was relieved and I was brought in by helicopter. About the same time, K-3-9 was improperly committed by Battalion and was reduced to 50% effective strength. Read Gerry Giles' account in *Operation Buffalo*. It will also give you a pretty accurate picture of the type of Battalion leadership we had been experiencing for the previous nine months. It was bad, really bad!

Mercifully, Division stepped in and relieved the Battalion CO, XO and S-3. Maj Jim Woodring who had earned the Silver Star on Operation Buffalo was brought in.. All of these changes took place on May 30-31.

Woody was brought to Kilo's position by helicopter. The only contact he had with Troy Shirley, the commanding officer of L-3-9, and I was over the radio—we were off on the approach march—contact eminent on 1 June. We had yet to meet him physically.

I had all of 36 hours to get to know my unit leaders. About half of the staff and officers knew me by reputation in the Battalion, but I was a mystery to the squad and fire team leaders. Fortunately, the H&S attachments had been in the field with me and knew what to expect.

On the evening of the 31st replacements were brought in by helicopter while we were on the move. Mike Company got a new corpsman. I climbed into a hole with him and the squad leader he was assigned to.

Along with my "Welcome to Vietnam" dos and don'ts speech, I got right in his face and told him, "You are not to do a damn thing unless your squad leader tells you to. The last thing I want to have to do is alter the attack to pick up your dead ass trying to take care of a wounded Marine. You wait until we uncover his position. You are not to go forward of your squad leader."

Before Lima was hit, India had seen many signs of NVA in the area. Trails crossed deep inside the wood line and included Machine Gun cart tire tracks and a badly mutilated snake. The NVA hated snakes.

We heard the NVA open up on Lima Company. Troy Shirley reported his situation over the Battalion Tactical Net and asked for assistance to break contact so that they could evacuate the dead and wounded. Company commanders in 3-9 had become accustomed to working things out with each other because the previous Battalion staff was of no appreciable help.

I came on the net and told Troy that I would be in position to sweep the flank and rear of the NVA position as soon as possible. I expressed concern about Lima's fire as we closed the enemy and told Troy I would keep Mike's fire low and rely on grenades and point blank fire to prevent our rounds from carrying into Lima's position.

At this time Woodring came on the net and informed us that he was in charge and would coordinate our actions.

Both Troy and I expressed amazement and relief. We both responded with a hardy, "Yes Sir!"

Leadership had been lacking at the Battalion level for the past nine months.

At this time Mike was directed to secure a safe helicopter zone that Lima could move to once mobility was regained so that casualties could be evacuated. I sent the trail platoon that was securing our left exposed flank to the east of Lima to accomplish this task. I was now without my reserve. The company command group and our attached supporting personnel would have to do the job when and if required.

Mike pressed forward silently, covered by the noise and distraction the NVA was having with the Lima firefight. Tree branches were falling on us as Lima's long rounds were shooting them off.

I gave the order that no M-16s would be set on automatic fire. Only low, well-aimed shots were to be fired.

Simultaneously, the second platoon that was sweeping forward inside the wood line surprised a wheel mounted Machine gun dug in position. On the left flank, third platoon encountered NVA in fighting holes and communication positions in the enemy's rear area.

The Second had no problem and quickly eliminated the first MG. The five NVA were armed with the machinegun, some hand grenades and rifle propelled grenades. They could not bring the machine gun to bear.

The NVA were taken completely by surprise. They simply did not prepare for a Marine unit to attack out of the woods. For good reason of past experience, the NVA prepared for Marines to attack into the woods from areas where maneuver and control is easier. The open areas.

The NVA desperately tried to establish a defensive line in front of Mike's attack, which was now heading steeply down hill into the gully that was the center of the NVA position. They did not set up on the hilltops because the Marines would routinely pound them with artillery and would concentrate their attacks there.

As they pulled back, the pressure was relieved on Lima. As they pulled out of their prepared positions facing Lima, they were exposed to the enfilade fire of Mike. Mike could now use machinegun and 3.5 Rocket fire, as it would no longer carry into Lima's position.

As the fight got hot from one end of Mike's line to the other I passed the word to all the troops, "You are in a real fire fight now. Relax and enjoy it."

I then gave them the same instructions that they had learned during their boot camp rifle range days, "Sight alignment and trigger squeeze - hold them and squeeze them. Only hits count!"

The third Platoon surprised the enemy in his rear area. The NVA were initially firing with rifles out of individual positions. At this time, a tough, red headed H&S Company wireman moved past me to the point of the heaviest firing. He always seemed to attach himself to any company that I commanded whether we needed wire laid or not.

As the wireman passed he commented, "I'm going to kill me an NVA."

Less than a minute later, he passed me on the way to the rear with a big grin on his face. He had a corpsman's casualty tag and blood was streaming down from his neck.

"I got me my NVA Skipper," was his comment.

What the guy had done was to climb right into the holes with the enemy. His action was an inspiration to all the troops and opened the way to the rear of the enemy's position.

The second platoon that was under an experienced First Lieutenant was doing well rolling up the NVA positions along the edge of the wood line.

The third platoon well inside the woods was encountering heavier resistance as the enemy pulled troops away from firing at Lima in an attempt to prevent being cut off from the rear. A fine Sergeant who had moved up from platoon guide when the Lieutenant went on R&R and the platoon sergeant rotated led it. This Sergeant and E-3's and E-4's were carrying out the heaviest fighting.

I moved to the Sergeant's side as we slithered down the side of the gully into the now disorganized NVA. We were being hit by branches and chunks of bark caused by high enemy fire.

Then we started to get hit with a storm of debris that was being churned up by machinegun fire. This fire was coming from the NVA's wheel mounted machineguns. They were located in the bottom of the gully and could not elevate their muzzles high enough to hit us directly until we were on top of them. It was a very strange feeling when we were hugging the ground knowing the heels of our boots were at a higher elevation than our heads.

At about this time, my Sergeant platoon commander exclaimed, "I'm hit!"

I looked at him as he lay next to me. He had a perfectly round bullet hole right in the middle of his chest a little below his neck. As he looked at me in bewilderment the blood sort of oozed out.

I exclaimed, "Why aren't you dead?"

He shot back, "I don't know sir but this is my third wound."

I asked him if he could make it back to the first platoon which was securing the Landing Zone on it's own. He nodded and I told him to get going.

This left the young Marine Lance Corporal machine gunner in charge. He was directing traffic to my immediate left front. The action was now intense.

The machine gunner may not have been the senior man at the time, but he definitely took charge of the ensuing platoon fighting. I did not know who was senior for I had only been in charge of the company for a few days. He would designate which NVA position to concentrate the assault on while also spreading fire to keep other enemy positions from putting effective fire on the advancing Marines. We all had learned that fire discipline was critical in a sustained engagement or you would run out of ammunition and lose.

The Lance Corporal used a simple but very effective tactic to eliminate each successive position that was offering resistance. He would identify it with a burst of machinegun fire. We are talking about point blank range.

He would begin each assault with the shout, "Let me heat it up!"

He did this with a long burst of fire as the Marines closed to short grenade range. The limit of advance was the explosion of our extremely good M-26 grenade. As soon as the explosion went off a Marine would rush right to the center of it while the smoke and dust was still in the air, rifle firing to finish off any dazed but often still kicking NVA.

In the middle of this process, I had a close to near death experience. (I had come this close to being killed only three other times while with 3-9.) The NVA opened up with a wheel-mounted machinegun that they had pulled out of their front line, which was facing Lima. It was so close that I saw not only the muzzle flash but also the muzzle. Somehow, the

NVA elevated the muzzle high enough to fire into our advance. Luckily they had the elevation set a little too high and the bullets that could have been meant for me went just a scoosh over my head and heels.

I tossed my last grenade from as prone a position as possible for a non-burrowing creature. The gun fell silent.

Just for good measure I thought I would toss the white phosphorus grenade I carried for marking targets. As my arm went up, a branch caught my sleeve. I never had much of an arm anyway, but the impedance of that damn branch caused the WP to dribble about 7 yards to my front. It went off after what seemed like an eternity as I reviewed what to do for white phosphorus burns. The smoking stuff was on all sides of me. Close but no cigar!

At that moment, my machine gunner yelled, "There they go!"

A group of NVA had had enough of Mike and started running south, down the ravine. This was one of the few times that I know of where the Marines had the opportunity to shoot at fleeing NVA. All I had to do in this situation was to control the individual trooper. They had a tendency to become overly enthusiastic and would expose themselves to get a better shot.

The cry up and down the line was, "Aimed shots. Hits count!"

I have never been more proud of my Marines in a firefight as I was at that moment.

At this time, a Huie was buzzing the tops of the trees.

Woodring came on the net and said, "I'm overhead and have the machineguns loaded. Where do you want the fire?"

By this time, the smoke from the WP grenade was drifting south down the ravine with the NVA. I notified him of this fact and Woodring acknowledged that he could see the WP, and the helicopter began to pour fire into the ravine.

About this time two events occurred that were detrimental to the progress of Co M.

The Platoon Sergeant of the first platoon was SSgt. Thomas J. Hamm. He was sent with the Company Gunnery Sergeant, Nolan, to secure the Landing Zone for Lima Company to use to withdraw. Hamm was a large man and was extremely aggressive. I got a call on the Co Tac Net that the LZ was secure and that Hamm, and one squad was hot to join the fight.

I was delighted with this development because I needed a unit to cover the exposed left flank as we got deeper into the NVA position. I knew that the fleeing unit could regroup and counter attack. At the very least, they would deliver enfilade fire from the flank. I gave explicit instructions for the reinforcing squad to enter our line from well to the rear where we had cleared the wood line.

In his haste to get to the fight, Hamm tried to cut the angle to our position in the woods. In making this approach, his squad ran into a string of trip wired ChiCom grenades and claymores. The NVA used these to secure their flanks when they were in an ambush position.

In sweeping the edge of the wood line, the second platoon had reported seeing these impediments. When Hamm was wounded and could no longer lead the uninjured members of the squad to the fight they gathered the wounded and returned to the LZ to await medivac.

It was during this time when machine gunner Brown was "heating things up" for the NVA that I received the word that we had sustained a KIA. The heartsick feeling that had hit me on three other occasions was smothering. It was the new corpsman.

A Marine was wounded and before the squad leader could stop him, "Doc" dashed to the wounded man. When he reached the fallen Marine he stopped and knelt down. As he attempted to access his medical kit he took a high NVA round to the head and was killed instantly.

The wounded Marine was recovered and would survive.

The fire was intense and it took a considerable amount of time to uncover the area in which the body of the corpsman lay. We did not attempt to recover the corpsman's body until we were certain that no one else would be exposed to enemy fire. If the enthusiasm of the young petty officer could have been tempered with a little more time in country and with a few lessons taught by his fellow corpsmen, his life would not have been lost. The extra effort and time used to recover his body could have been better spent keeping pressure on the enemy.

At this time in the fight we were almost to the bottom of the gully. We were about to start our assault up the other side. This had been the original march objective for the Battalion. I was very concerned about our left flank. We had no way of knowing what the NVA had in the way of forces to commit against us. We were just entering evening nautical twilight, which would leave me about twenty minutes of light to orientate our attack. Our supply of grenades was also exhausted and the ammo count was not encouraging. I was starting to anchor the left flank and LCpl. Brown and pivoting the second platoon up the face of the slope.

The third platoon could provide fire in front of the advance. I was not looking forward to this at night. Control would be by the flash of the rifles.

Thankfully, things became calm. It was as if nothing had gone on for the last few hours. Woodring came on the net after assessing the situation and directed Mike Company to consolidate with Lima at the LZ and establish night defensive positions.

I must admit I was relieved and a sudden weariness came over all the fighting men in the woods. It took a lot of leadership by the squad and fire team leaders to keep all hands alert as we moved to the LZ. We walked over ground where a lot of blood had been shed just a few moments-minutes-hours before.

As Mike Company tied into a 360 defense with Lima Company, I had time to reassess the NVA's actions. A Marine company raising havoc in the woods to their rear had compromised the enemy position. This was an undefended area. I was convinced they had pulled out and were moving south at night toward Route 9. Then they would turn west and north to escape the Marine units deployed along the DMZ on Operation Hickory. With the Third Division deployed, as they were this NVA unit was in a very bad situation and was threatened with annihilation.

I knew that the NVA had been in this position for some time. This was determined by the amount of wire radio equipment that we picked up during the assault. We also found more of the same the following week when counting enemy bodies for political purposes. It was at least a battalion command unit defended by a reinforced company. I would like to think it was the unit that fought India Company back in March in the same general location.

Mike Getlin, the India CO, was killed fighting valiantly. He earned the Navy Cross and Lt. John Bobo received a posthumous Medal of Honor.

India had been my first command in August and September near An Hoa. During Hickory, India was detached to the Balong Valley to stop infiltration south of Dong Hoa.

Woodring was still with Kilo. They had been mauled a few days before (See GILES - OP BUFFALO). I radioed my assessment to Woodring. He was moving with Kilo to join up with Troy and myself to jump off in the attack just as soon as we could get an ammo resupply in the morning.

Keep in mind that Monday in Manila is Sunday in San Francisco. The action on 1 June was 31 May in the U.S., and it was close to the end of the week. A big deal was made in the Press any time the KIA count reached three figures. The President and the Pentagon did not want the KIA count to exceed 99 in any one-week and they watched the monthly totals as well. As we were to learn later, it did not make a bit of difference that we had paid the price to make decisive contact with the enemy. It did not matter that he was about to become ours. 3-9 was told to hold off on the pursuit. This meant that we were to let the NVA get away without a fight. We could not risk the loss of another American fighting man.

I was furious and afraid the troops could sense my frustration. We were being told to let the enemy off the hook. Opportunities like this seldom occurred in Vietnam.

I can only recall one other occasion when this did happen. That was Operation Star Light. We were told to hold our position until supporting arms would soften up the NVA position. The NVA left in the position were all dead and I do not think the guys we shot the hell out of as they fled south down the ravine would be reoccupying.

That night was spent redistributing ammo and C-rations. There is nothing like a prolonged, hot firefight at close quarters to burn up the calories and create an intense hunger. We had all sorts of night, defensive, artillery fire land close. Too damn close!

Lima had a hot shot, mouthy arty FO who claimed he could bring it in real close. He sure did. He brought in his 8" battery so close that it blew the Lt and his radio talker completely out of their hole on the perimeter.

Although badly shaken up, they were not wounded. The "Hot Shot" Lieutenant suffered damage to his pride and a temporary loss of hearing. He was never known to call in close fire again.. The exhaustion of the day took over and the troopers got some sleep when not on alert.

I should add here that the arty FO with Mike was an extremely competent officer. He was 1stLt. J.C. Bennett from F-2-12. As night was falling during the day's assault, he was working on illumination fires so Mike could keep the attack going.

About 0400 I got the message to pull off my position. It was across from the wood line from the previous day's assault. At 0730 we were to move to Woodring and Kilo's position so that air strikes with 2,000-pound bombs could be brought in to destroy the enemy bunkers. We had already over run these same bunkers. I guess the authorities wanted to be sure the NVA were really dead.

Any way, as ordered, precisely at 0730 my rear guard was clearing the forward military crest of the hill. To my shock, precisely at 0730 a flight of four A-4 Sky Hawks pealed in on their bombing run. Their target was about fifty meters from my rear guard unit. The air attack was NOT - I REPEAT -NOT being controlled by a ground FAC. Some big thinker in an air-conditioned bunker in Danang had this all under control. I was about to crap my pants.

The basic rule of thumb is you want the separation between friendlies and the bomb burst to be one yard (meters in the New Corps) for every pound of bomb. It doesn't take a whole lot of math to see that 50 yards is a long way from 2,000. I was always concerned about the one-pound bomb. Do you think one yard would be enough separation?

I then shouted one of my shortest commands, "RUN!!!"

Thankfully, The A-4's were loaded with napalm to mark the edge of the wood line. But, from the angle of their attack that came right over Mike's route of withdrawal, a normal No-No. It looked like the tumbling napalm tanks would land right into my trail squad. I think I must have set the record for a lap around the rosary beads. It sure did not hurt. The tanks just did clear the topographical crest and smashed right into the edge of the woods. It would have been terrific if any of the NVA were home.

We were not home free yet. The next flight consisted of F-4 Phantoms. We knew that they were loaded with 2,000-pound Daisy Cutters. It was amazing how fast heavily loaded, combat weary troops could move when being hurried along by debris being thrown up by 2,000-pound bombs. Trunks of trees were still beating us back toward our rendezvous with Major Woodring. I was really looking forward to seeing him for the first time.

NOTES:

The corpsman killed on June 1,1967 was:
Whinery, Roger L. HN B605148; 22; Fredonia, Kansas

HM3 James W. Ashby a corpsman with I-3-9 was also killed this day. He would later be awarded the Navy Cross posthumously.

Other Marines mentioned in this chapter were:
Bennett, J.C. 1stLt. 093860; F-2-12

Brown, Roy LCpl. 2215674; M-3-9
Bobo, John P. 2dLt. 092986; I-3-9; 24; Niagra Falls, New York
Getlin, Michael P. Capt. 086661; I-3-9; 27; Lagrange, Illinois
Giles, Jerrald E. Capt. K-3-9
Hamm, Thomas J. SSgt. 1622488; M-3-9
Navadel, George D. Capt. 075389; M-3-9; 30; Buffalo, New York
Shirley, Troy T. Capt. 081360; L-3-9
Woodring, Willard J. Jr. Maj. 059686; CO-3-9; 40; Springfield, Missouri

LCpl. Lawrence R.
"Two-Step" Brown
FO I-3-9, Silver Star 9/5/66

Sgt. Garrette W. Peck, III
H-2-9, Silver Star 8/2/66

* * * *

On July 28, 1967 about 800 Marines of the Second Battalion, Ninth Regiment invaded the southern half of the demilitarized zone between North and South Vietnam. Their targets were the North Vietnamese mortar and artillery positions that had been shelling Marine positions just south of the zone. This was Operation Kingfisher.

Again, we join F-2-9 and Richard Russell.

> "Instead of running, they just kind of floated.
> We'd get 'em and they just kept coming.
> They had to be doped up."
> Said Lt. Chadwick Floyd, 22, Washington, D.C.

Grateful acknowledgement is made to Richard Allen Russell for permission to reprint previously published material. The following excerpt is taken from *Hell In A Helmet. Memoirs of a Marine Infantryman Vietnam 1967* © 1989 by Richard Allen Russell by permission of Richard Allen Russell.

12

A SHOW OF FORCE

We set out from north of Cam Lo in battalion strength on July 28, 1967. I remember this hump well, as it was the only time I saw a guy I knew from home, While we cleared the way to make room for a convoy, I noticed, in a group of doggies (Army - distinguished by their arm patches), a face from my tenth grade science class. I was too dumbfounded to make a move, and the group sped off to Con Thien before I had a chance to call out. Ten years later I ran into the same guy, and he said he had been at Con Thien at the time, a small and sad, on its way to sadder, world.

We marshaled west of Con Thien and were ordered to leave our packs and put one day's C's in our jungle pants' pockets. As this was an unusual order, scuttlebutt flew with unparalleled fervor. When Bob returned from the squad leaders' meeting, our worst fears were confirmed. We were not only going into the Z, but we were going all the way to Song Bien Ha River, literally a stone's throw away from North Vietnam.

"What the fuck for?" we asked.

"'Cuz the big boys want to show the enemy we can do it. They call it a show of force."

A great swarm of Huey's, thirty-four's, and Chinooks (helicopters) plucked us up and hopped us the three miles to Hill #37. Fully expecting to be shot the second I hit the ground, I had no great pleasure in noting, as we wopped our way in, that I was in line to be the first one off the chopper. Fifteen feet from the ground the extremely anxious crew chief motioned, "All right, Number One, let's go!"

I looked down. "This asshole's nuts. That's fifteen fucking feet!" I looked at him. He ain't kidding, and he outranks me. I bailed out the door. I hit the ground like a beanbag, amazed that I had not been shot and had lived through the fall apparently intact.

While Fox Company formed a Three-Sixty on top of Hill #37, the rest of the battalion joined up with the tanks and ontoses (small armored vehicles) in an old French village a couple of miles down river. Nothing happened, as in ZIP, ZERO, ZILCH, no incoming fire of any kind, nothing - just the trucks droning in North Vietnam, lots of trucks, all night long.

Just before dawn, our east perimeter got pounded pretty good by a couple dozen mortar rounds (I have always felt that some of the guys down there, being pouges and cooks, made too much noise setting up and cooking their food, instead of eating it cold like we did, and gave their position away.). Simultaneously, the enemy began pounding the rest of the battalion down river much heavier. For the rest of the morning we fought a slow, rear-guard action with a large enemy contingent that was not giving us all they had. They could hit from a lot of quarters, but they only gave us a little bit, slowly moving us toward the road.

The constant barrage of sniper fire mixed with the occasional mortar round contributed no more to our morale than watching a navy jet fighter dive, guns blazing, into an incredible hail of fire. As the large caliber slugs thumped into the fuselage, the plane made a one-way trip to eternity, exploding with tremendous ferocity and spraying us grunts with white hot, blown-up, jet fragments.

When the battalion pulled abreast our position, we witnessed a pathetic sight. The tanks were covered with so many dead and wounded men, that other than the cannon and tracks, one could barely see metal. I noticed amongst the wounded my former mustang lieutenant, half his face covered with a bloody battle dressing. He looked hurt and as scared as the rest of us.

In as much as Fox Company had not been under the heavy fire everyone else had and were relatively fresh, we were delegated to take the point. Actually, I was delegated to take the point. Through an incredible twist of fate, first my company, then my platoon, then my squad, then finally my fire team were up front. Because the two lance corporals in my team were very short, I ended up with the honors, not wanting to have them killed with so little time left in country. I set off on the longest and hardest hump of my life, followed (not real closely) by several hundred, tired, scared and wounded men.

I moved out slowly at first, very much aware of hundreds of enemy eyes on me. As I went down the road, I peered into the impenetrable brush that offered a wall so thick, that if one could shove his fist into it, he would not be able to open his hand. The road was partially covered by a jungle canopy, and nearby the enemy had previously hacked out and camouflaged their positions so well that even the best eyes in our battalion could not see them until it was too late. Although the rest of the battalion was under continual harassing fire, not one cap was popped at me. The enemy was eager for me to keep moving, too eager.

After what seemed like a thousand miles, but was probably a thousand meters, I cleared the top of the hill, immediately dropping to the ground. I quickly pulled my weapon to fire, spotting three figures in the valley below. Just as quickly, I realized they were too big to be NVA and must be marines. Stunned, I released my hold. There were not supposed to be any Marines until Con Thien.

"Who are you, and what the fuck are you doing here?" I yelled down the hill. Going toward them I saw that one was a corpse, one was a corpsman and the last was an Echo Company platoon commander.

The platoon commander replied, "We left before dawn on a recon patrol and got stomped."

"The battalion's coming just behind the hill. Let's get the hell out of here!"

The platoon commander answered back, "This is it. This is as far as we're going.

I looked at him to see if he was shell-shocked. "What the fuck are you talking about?"

He turned back and motioned to the left of the road in front of where we were standing and noted, "They've got a fifty (machine gun) in a fortified bunker over there and another one on the other side. They've got rockets and mortars. I estimate a battalion of NVA regulars have dug in on our right flank!"

My mouth was hanging open down to my knees. "You mean, when the rest of our battalion gets here..." The words trailed off.

"Exactly," he concurred.

Just then the barrel of the first tank cleared the hill, a metal signal if there ever was one. My squad was close at hand, so I hollered and made the signs of ambush. "Hit the dirt! Hit the deck!" In as much as no one was shooting at us yet, they moved slowly but took cover. As the other platoons came up, they began yelling at us, "Come on; let's go" and other such shit. Everyone started milling around, waiting to be told what to do. I passed the word to Bob, yelling over the confusion. He, in turn, radioed and got most of our platoon's men down.

At this point I left the trail and fought through the brush until I found a very shallow irrigation ditch, which ran parallel to the road. Most of my squad was in the surrounding area when the first tank pulled up even with us and was hit dead nuts by a RPG rocket, signaling the enemy attack. Immediately the air was full of metal. The fifties ripped in a withering crossfire, as mortars and rockets exploded off the tanks, sending shrapnel into the huddling masses.

For what seemed like a lifetime, and it was for many, the cascading crescendo of ultimate chaos descended upon us. Trees cut neatly by the crossfire were falling every second or so, as screams and deafening explosions rattled us to our souls. On and on it went; all concepts of time and normalcy stopped. Unable to budge an inch, we just pulled in close to ol' Mother Earth. I thought of my dad's copy of Upfront by Bill Maulden. Joe looks at Willy under a withering barrage of fire and says, "I can't get no lower, Willy. Me buttons is in the way."

The battle raged on. I caught a glimpse of Bob crawling near the burning tank, which was blocking the road. The dense vegetation was quickly becoming mulch, and visibility was improving. I hollered at him, and we crawled toward each other. He told me he had located our missing machine gun and motioned across the road. There was Bill, slumped over his gun exactly where he'd been when the fifties opened up, about ten meters in front of the tank on the east side of the road.

Bob hollered, "I'm going to get him."

I yelled back, "He ain't moved since they sprung the ambush. He can't be alive. Don't go out there; it's a cross-fire!"

He looked down the line, looked at Bill, looked back at me and said, "I got to try!"

He got about five good steps before he was hit in the heel from a slug of one of the fifties. The force of the blow knocked him down, and the twin fifties centered in on him. As each slug hit him, it rolled him over. In this manner they moved him about six feet. We threw everything we had at the muzzle flashes of the fifties, while our corpsman raced out to Bob and dragged him back to cover.

Bob had been hit at least five times with the slugs; and though a smaller man would have been cut to pieces, he was still alive. I called for the thump gun, but all the M seventy-nines, as well as most of the machine guns, had been drawn back to protect the command group. Finally, Angel managed to get one, crawled out under the tank barrel and began letting rounds go toward the bunker on the left. Crawling back for more ammo, he was hit. This was technically his homeward ticket, as it was the third time he had been wounded. Angel crawled back to the tank with more ammo he had scrounged and let go again and was also shot again. After his third trip into the crossfire and his fifth purple heart, the corpsman had to hold him down and run him up with morphine to keep him from bleeding to death.

When the smoke cleared, the left bunker was silent. Angel had knocked it out with sheer determination and guts. He later received the Navy Cross for this action. With the fire reduced by half in the front, the decision was made to load the wounded on the tanks and ontosses and have them make a run for Con Thien. When the next tank in line pushed the burning hulk of the rocketed tank off the road, they all made a blast toward safety. Before they were around the next corner, the NVA were raking the wounded off with automatic weapon fire. I later heard only one tank made it back to Con Thien.

Suddenly, a great clamor rose to our right flank - whistles, bugles and yelling. The NVA were getting out of their pre-dug fighting positions and charging enmasse across an area they had cleared just beyond our sight. As I searched for a position on the firing line, I was startled to see a Phantom jet at treetop level. Because it was at the bottom of a six hundred mile per hour power dive, the images I saw were there longer than the jet was. The first image was that of the jet itself -huge and imposing, fifty feet over my head. Next, the sun glanced off the pilot's face shield, then off the four tubes of napalm he had just released. The jet was gone, but the napalm tubes just sort of hung there for a millisecond and rolled slowly, end over end, into the enemy.

The exposed NVA also saw their oncoming emulation and raised a cry of horror that went far beyond my wildest concept of fear, a cry I can hear right now and will hear till I join them. The napalm kawumped into the enemy; all the nearby oxygen was pulled into the fire. A tremendous rush of air yanked me right off balance, and I was quickly thrown back to the opposite direction and hard into the ground as the enemy's ammunition exploded. My tooth was broken, and my glasses were shattered, but I was still breathing. Several seconds passed when someone yelled the one thing that makes even the toughest grunt cringe, "GAS!"

A great black and foul cloud began crossing our perimeter, causing men to cough and retch. Because I had left my gas mask - so had everyone else - back in the rear, I took off my sweat towel and poured most of my remaining water on it. I then got in the fetal position, covering my eyes, nose and mouth and kissed my ass goodbye. As foul as the cloud was, it did not kill anyone because it was not gas, but incinerated NVA soldiers. A rotting corpse ripped from the ground smells like magnolias compared to burnt human flesh and hair. And, as their cries still ring in my ears, their sizzling skeletons still singe my nose. The perfect timing and placement of the napalm took the snap out of the enemy's punch, for a short while, and we took advantage of the drop in incoming fire to draw in our positions and dig in.

We formed a tight three-sixty and placed our wounded down both sides of the road within the circle. We next brought up our battalion eighty-one mm mortar teams and called in the artillery support. Because of the close proximity of the enemy, we directed our friendly fire so close we were constantly showered with dirt and shrapnel from our own guns.

Twilight fell. Our corpsman came to tell me that Bob wanted to talk to me. I made my way back to where he was lying. He was covered from the waist down by a poncho and was amazingly lucid considering his wounds and the morphine. He first asked about the squad, and I gave him some relief by telling him we were doing all right. He then said, "Well, Russ, it doesn't look like we'll be partying at my cabin back in

Michigan next year."

I tried to play down his impending death by saying, "Sure, we'll be there. Just wait. Everything will be fine." But he wouldn't buy it.

He said, "No, Russ, this is it. I was supposed to rotate today, and I'm, going home all right, but I won't be partying anymore."

I wanted to talk. I wanted to cry. And, I wanted to scream. My best friend, my teacher, my mentor, bleeding to death on the very day he was to have left the field after twelve months and twenty days in combat. I wanted to tell him, "Thank you for my life," but no words would come out. Finally, I put my hand on his shoulder and looked into his blue eyes for the last time. He sort of nodded, smiled and put his hand on top of mine, kind of like, "Don't worry, it will be all right." A half hour later, the corpsman crawled out to my position to tell me Bob had finally gone home.

At the time, I registered numb, like we all did, to the horrors that surrounded us. But today, and everyday I feel a loss of one of the greatest men of my lifetime, through the greatest irony I've ever known.

Total fatigue had us all by the throat - no food, no water and hour after hour of incessant pounding. About three o'clock in the morning total pandemonium set in. Three or four naked NVA sappers killed the guards on the road and ran down the middle spraying their AK's and throwing satchel charges (explosives) at the many wounded lying on the side. They did a lot of damage very quickly and ran right out the other end of the perimeter, unscathed.

Dawn found the battle still going, but greatly reduced. Finally, three/four, which was on the float, came in, surrounded us and helped us out of the mess. We started marching down the road toward Con Thien; my mind, body, and soul were so whacked out that everything seemed like a jerky-action, over lit cartoon. There were Bob's thirteen's sticking out from underneath the bloody, smelly poncho, which was lined up with dozens of other bloody, smelly ponchos covering bodies. There were hundreds of wounded lying on the hillside near the LZ waiting to be flown out on choppers, vulnerable to hotshot gook gunners who were blasting away at them.

My legs began the now-familiar seizing and cramping that always precedes my attacks of heat exhaustion/ stroke. I knew I would soon be in searing pain. I felt something snap inside me, but I kept marching forward. At this point I noticed two cameramen standing on top of a knoll ahead. Rage filled my body, the likes of which I have never experienced before or since.

"You goddamn trite assholes! Not only did you miss the whole fucking twenty four hour battle, but now you'll be showing us with our tails dragging on network television tonight, so people will have something to watch while they eat dinner!" My heart was pounding, and I flipped the safety off my weapon and began raising it and aiming it toward the two cameramen. Suddenly my body went limp, and reason returned. I realized I could not kill them without getting into some pretty deep shit. In as much as the battle was over, I dropped the weapon to my side and flipped them the best middle finger "Fuck You" I could muster. They looked at me like I was crazy (maybe I was). When they edited their film that night, I bet they never realized they had come within a hair's breadth of being former cameramen.

Two hundred meters further I collapsed into a white-hot ball of debilitating pain. I limped, then was dragged and finally carried to the nearest waterhole, but it was too late. The attack was already too far advanced. The corpsman got me out of the waterhole and onto a tank for the hot and bumpy ride to the LZ. This part of the event is foggiest in my mind. I remember bits and pieces, but no more than that. I remember a large corpsman sitting on me, pouring water on me and slapping me, while he yelled at the top of his lungs, "Come on, wake up! Don't die, you asshole!" I remember being put on a chopper and then nothing.

The next day I was at Delta Med, hobbling like a ninety-year-old man from the effects of the cramps. I limped across the compound, and a medevac: corpsman ran up to me and, like the medevac at Charley Med on May eighth, cried, "Jesus Christ, I thought you'd be dead by now!" He said they put me on board first before a guy with his leg blown off. He was stable; I was not. He had had to run me up with adrenalin to keep my ticker going. Apparently I had died a little more than was usual on this OP, but then I already knew that.

NOTES:

The following were members of the Ninth Marines and were killed on 7/29/67:

Bennefield, Steven H. Pfc. 2240325; G-2-9; 19; Girard, Kansas
Bernard, Henry W. LCpl. 2322441; H&S-2-9; 19; Willimantic, Conn.
Dudley, John M. Pfc. 2237746; F-2-9; 20; Glen Rock, Pennsylvania

Ellison, Robert L. Cpl. 2245473; F-2-9; 20; Charlotte, Michigan
Gaffney, Michael F. LCpl. 2323201; 20; Chicago, Illinois
Gaspar, Alfred J. Cpl. 2114661; H-2-9; 20; Fall River, Massachusetts
Gibson, Walter C. LCpl. 2225545; F-2-9; 21; Denver, Colorado
Jacob, Phillip LCpl. 2229007; G-2-9; 20; Toledo, Ohio
Johnson, Richard H. LCpl. 2309178; G-2-9; 18; Wolcott, New York
Kinard, Larry V. LCpl. 2174885; G-2-9; 21; Philadelphia, Pennsylvania
Leach, Anthony M. LCpl. 2251182; G-2-9; 18; Lynwood, Washington
McGovern, James G. LCpl. 2270963; H-2-9; 19; Riverdale, Maryland
Prentice, David S. GySgt. 1447461; H-2-9; 43; Anchorage, Alaska
Roberts, Eddie L. Pfc. 2232999; F-2-9; 18; Hope, Arkansas
Seveney, William F. Pfc. 2238703; F-2-9; 20; Ware, Massachusetts
Taylor, Richard H. Pfc. 2280646; F-2-9; 20; Pittsburgh, Pennsylvania

The Navy Cross was awarded to "Angel" which was the nickname given to Cpl. Miguel A. Rivera Sotomayor by his Marine Corps buddies.

The Silver Star was awarded to Pfc. Billy J. Bennett, LCpl. Henry W. Bernard, Jr., LCpl. Michael F. Gaffney and LCpl. James P. Proctor.

Richard Russell's best friend Bob who was killed in action was Cpl. Robert L. Ellison.

LCpl. Daniel L. Lanham
D-1-5 Silver Star 8/29/68

William D. Ehrhart from Perkasie, Pennsylvania spent thirteen months in Vietnam with H&S-1-1. He went to Vietnam in February of 1967 as an eighteen-year-old Private First Class. Ehrhart left at the end of February of 1968 as a Corporal, having served in the intelligence section of 1-1. While in Vietnam, he was wounded during the battle for Hue by a B-40 rocket but was not evacuated. He was also on more than a dozen other operations including the siege of Con Thien.

After serving his time in the Marine Corps, Ehrhart became active with Vietnam Veterans Against the War. He has written several books which include *Vietnam-Perkasie* and *In the Shadow of Vietnam*.

"Swearing is an insult. War is an insult. It all goes together. We are violent men who practice violence like a game. Swearing is an essential part of our brotherhood. It sets us apart from the world, which has set itself apart from us.
Fuck 'em you know?"

1stLt. Ernest Spencer
D-1-26
From *Welcome to Vietnam, Macho Man*

Grateful acknowledgement is made to McFarland & Company for permission to reprint previously published material.
The following excerpt is taken:
From *In the Shadow of Vietnam: Essays, 1977-1991* © 1977, 1978, 1980, 1981, 1983, 1984, 1986, 1987, 1989, 1990, 1991 by W.D. Ehrhart by permission of McFarland & Company, Inc., Publishers, Jefferson, North Carolina 28640.

13
PLACES AND WAYS TO LIVE

Undoubtedly, the most useless piece of equipment issued by the United

States Marine Corps in Vietnam was the shelter half. A holdover from the War of 1812, this was a heavy piece of canvas shaped to form one half of a small field tent commonly known as a pup tent. Along with the shelter half, you were issued half the total number of pegs needed for the whole tent, one of the two necessary poles (which came apart into three sections when not in use), and one of the two necessary support ropes. Some of the shelter halves had buttons along the seam that connected to the other half; others had buttonholes. Every Marine learned in boot camp the proper step-by-step procedure for constructing the tent.

However, unless you were willing to settle for half a tent (which is silly), in order to construct the tent successfully, you needed to find someone who fit all of the following requirements: he had to have a shelter half that was the opposite of yours (that is, if yours had buttons, his had to have buttonholes, and vice versa); he had to possess his full complement of pegs, pole sections and rope; he had to be able to remember the proper step-by-step procedure he'd learned in boot camp; and he had to be someone with whom you did not mind sleeping at close proximity.

If you actually managed to find someone who filled all of these requirements, and the two of you succeeded in getting your tent constructed before the sun rose and you had to pack up and leave again, you still had problems. The heavy canvas material rapidly caused the air inside the tent to become uncomfortably hot and stagnant. If the weather was good enough to enable you to open the end flap and let in fresh air, then you didn't need the tent in the first place. And if it was raining, you couldn't open the flap because you would get wet. In addition, to say that the tent held two people is very much like those pudding mixes that say, "Makes four generous servings." (People in 1812 weren't as big as people are now. I went to Mount Vernon once and saw George Washington's bed; it was very small.) Moreover, if your body happened to touch the canvas while it was raining, which was impossible to prevent in the small confines of the tent, no matter how close you slept to your buddy, the waterproof seal on the canvas would be broken and the tent would leak for the rest of the night. Furthermore, the tent often fell down in the middle of the night because of faulty construction or the inability of the sandy soil in Vietnam to hold the short tent pegs under the strain caused by the weight of the heavy canvas. Finally, when not in use, the shelter half and its accessories were a cumbersome extra weight to be lugged around -a consideration worthy of the highest respect by all sensible infantrymen.

I threw my shelter half away at the earliest opportunity. So did nearly everyone else. One always tried to stay as far away as possible from anyone with a shelter half, for it was widely believed that anyone who lacked the sense to get rid of his shelter half would sooner or later manage to get you killed, though I don't believe the connection was ever actually proven since no one kept statistics on this, fond as the Pentagon was of numbers.

All sensible grunts carried ponchos instead of shelter halves. These were also useless for the purpose for which they were designed-that is, to be worn while walking in the rain-since the poncho covered everything you were carrying with many folds of loose material, and made access to things like ammunition and grenades extremely difficult in emergencies. Rain suits were much better because they kept you dry and alive at the same time. These were just rubberized pants and pullover shirts with hoods that were worn over your utility uniform but under your equipment. They were in short supply in the Marine Corps (as were all useful things), but you could always barter them off the Navy Seabees (Construction Battalion) or the Air Force for a disarmed Chinese grenade or an authentic Viet Cong battle flag made by one of the local tailors.

The poncho, however, was useful as a ground cloth when there was no need for a tent, which was the case during most of the dry season from April to September. And during the monsoons, the poncho became worth its weight in letters from home, for it made an easily constructed, remarkably efficient one-man tent.

To make a one-man poncho tent, you needed only your poncho, four little sticks, one stick about two feet long, and a bit of string (which usually came attached to the poncho). First, you pulled the drawstring tight on the face hole. Then you laid the poncho out in a loose rectangle on a flat bit of ground, and staked down the four corners with the little sticks. Then you reached inside with the long stick, poked it up into the poncho hood, and stood the stick upright, which would lift the poncho up from the center and stretch it into a taut, four-sided pyramid. Finally, you took the string and ran it from the center grommet on one side of the poncho to a nearby tree, bush or tank at about knee height in order to form a little entrance to the tent. If you wanted to get fancy, you could throw in a little brush or some banana leaves for a mattress. You were then ready to crawl in, curl up around the center pole, and go to sleep.

The one-man poncho tent took about three minutes to construct, almost never fell down because of its light weight and low profile, was fully waterproof because it was made of rubber rather than canvas, allowed ventilation in the rain, could be constructed even in the dark without assistance, and permitted you to sleep in privacy.

Furthermore, since it took so little time to construct, and demanded no time at all to locate a buddy who fulfilled all of the requirements for constructing a proper pup tent, the one-man poncho tent allowed you more time to spend digging your fighting hole. Every night you spent in the field, you had to dig a fighting hole with your entrenching tool. If you were on an operation and slept fifteen different places on fifteen different nights, you dug fifteen different fighting holes. Some nights you'd think, "Shit, I been walking all day; I'm too tired to dig." Then Tinney would remind you what Sullivan looked like after the mortar round landed next to him the night he'd been too tired. And when you thought about it, you were never really too tired to dig a fighting hole.

It didn't have to be anything grandiose -just enough to get you below ground level so that shrapnel from incoming mortar rounds and grenades would go over you instead of through you, and to give you a little cover to shoot from should the need arise. In fact, you could always tell the new guys because they'd spend half the night digging vast craters big enough to park a jeep in. Sensible grunts dug little slit trenches just long enough to get your body into and deep enough to get your head down. Anything else was wasted energy, and sensible grunts seldom wasted energy unless they were ordered to do so.

On rare occasions, you had to spend whole nights in your fighting hole because the Viet Cong made it perfectly clear they were not going to let you sleep. Usually, however, they were not so considerate; they'd let you get to sleep first, then wake you up. You always dug your fighting hole right by the entrance to your poncho tent so that, when you were abruptly awakened in the middle of the night, you didn't have to waste time trying to wake up enough to remember where your fighting hole was. I got so good, I could grab my rifle, throw on my flak jacket and helmet, and be lying in my fighting hole without ever opening my eyes or rising more than eight inches off the ground. It took about two-tenths of a second.

Of course, you didn't always sleep in the bushes (we called them the "boonies" or boondocks). During the first eight months I was in Vietnam, from February to September 1967, my battalion was located in the same place continuously, and the battalion headquarters and the four rifle companies each had more or less permanent command posts. You might go on patrol for a few days or even weeks, but somebody always stayed behind, and you always returned to the same place. Since I was in battalion intelligence, when I wasn't in the field, I always worked out of the battalion command post.

Thus, I got to live in relative luxury, for the living shelters at battalion CP were strongback tents. (We called them hooches. Any living quarters more permanent than a simple tent were called hooches, including the houses of the Vietnamese.) Strongback tents were not really tents at all, but rather plywood one-room houses with canvas roofs built by the Sea Bees. They had plywood frames and plywood floors, a walk-in screen door at either end, and screen-covered windows with hinged plywood covers that could be raised out to form plywood awnings. The whole structure was draped with a large general purpose tent that formed the roof.

Strongbacks were very roomy, sleeping eight to twelve men on fold-up cots, and when the camp generator was working, you got electric light from naked bulbs suspended from the roof beams though, of course, there was no running water or plumbing. If you were lucky, you had an air mattress as well (which we called "rubber ladies"- not nearly so good as the real thing, but quite comfortable under the circumstances), and you could use empty wooden artillery shell boxes as storage compartments and foot lockers. Some guys even had mosquito nets. I had a mosquito net on my cot for awhile, but I got rid of it after the night the battalion CP got hit by a VC rocket attack.

This was not your ordinary everyday artillery or mortar assault. These were real rockets: Russian-made self-propelled 130 milli-meter rockets which were aimed by pointing them in the general direction of the target and launched from bamboo chutes. They had been used previously against the big airbase at Danang, but I believe we were the first field unit in the Vietnam war to be introduced to the Russian rockets. History in the making.

There was always noise at night in Vietnam: aircraft, helicopters, artillery, small-arms fire, you name it. If you were to jump at everything, you would never get any sleep ever. So without really trying, you learned quickly to identify sounds in your sleep. The big guns in the CP-we had three different artillery batteries and an 81 millimeter mortar platoon-could fire all night, and though they shook your hooch and nearly blew out your eardrums, you never woke up. But the slightest sound out of the ordinary and your brain would shout, "Wake up; I think there's trouble," and you'd be up and running for the nearest of the deep sandbagged open bunkers that surrounded the hooches before you even knew what was happening.

So while none of us had ever heard rockets before, and though everybody in my hooch was sound asleep at the time, the instant that strange whooshing sound broke the regular nonsilence of the Vietnam night, there was a mad scramble of bodies piling out the door and diving headlong into the nearest bunker, ending up in a cursing, laughing, confused tangle of arms, legs, elbows, wrenched knees, bent backs, jammed fingers and bloody noses many seconds before the first rockets impacted. (Time plays funny tricks in stress situations, as anyone who's ever been in an automobile accident knows. Things which take only a few seconds seem to unravel in slow motion, leaving vivid recollections of each small detail etched into the memory.)

You could see the rockets coming in two waves, the first wave already at the apex of their trajectory, the second still rising out of the horizon to the south. They were relatively slow-moving, and made a very loud noise like water rushing from a high-pressure fire hose; and each rocket left a thin orange trail of sparks and fire like an aerial torpedo. It was curious and novel, and we all watched for awhile (maybe a second or two), until we realized the rockets were right on target and had to paste ourselves to the bottom of the open bunker as the earth around us erupted in columns of smoke, noise, sand, shattered wood, shredded canvas, steel slivers and fire.

Our hooch was not hit, and nobody in my bunker got wounded. But in the rush to get out of the hooch, I had gotten wrapped up in my mosquito net, tripped over another cot, and hit the door frame with my shoulder on the way out the door. It didn't slow me down at all, but it hurt like hell and I ended up with a bruised shin and a very sore shoulder. The morning after the rocket attack, I traded my mosquito net to a guy from Baltimore for a fine pair of padded cartridge belt suspenders he'd swiped off a soldier at the U.S. Army compound in Hoi An the week before. He was happy with the deal, and so was I. I didn't tell him about my shin or my shoulder. And I never used a mosquito net again. Damn things didn't work all that well anyway; every time you got under the net, a whole bunch of the little bastards would climb in with you, and you'd have to spend the rest of the night trying to squash them all.

I thought the good life was over forever when the battalion had to leave its old digs south of Danang and head up north toward the Demilitarized Zone. From then on, we spent a whole lot of time living in one-man poncho tents while we humped through the boondocks in search of the wily VC and their "big brothers," the North Vietnamese regular army. No more strongback hooches, or electricity or weekly cold showers. No more greasy field kitchens with their three tubs of scalding water -one with soap and a toilet brush to swab out your mess kit, two to rinse and sterilize it. No more comfortable walk-up four-hole sit-down outhouses. From here on, it was going to be candles and Coleman gas lanterns, wash when and where you can, eat out of cans, and dig a little cat hole to shit in.

But we did sit still occasionally for a few weeks at a time, and then we'd dig right in like busy beavers and fix up a home. The first place we sat in, after two weeks in the field on Operation Medina in early October 1967, was a new airfield the Sea Bees were building near Ai Tu, between Quang Tri and Dong Ha. We provided security for the Sea Bees, and the intelligence scouts had a little section of the perimeter overlooking a river. The river was right there, not twenty feet away; the current was swift and the water was clean, and you could swim and bathe at the same time, a few guys in the water while others posted guard on the bank. It was really very pleasant.

Anyway, the first night there, I just threw up a one-man poncho tent, dug a fighting hole in the sandy soil, and went to sleep. I was tired. Unfortunately, the wily VC were not. Middle of the night, here comes the welcoming committee: you could hear them dropping in before the first mortar rounds exploded - 20 or 30 of them before the VC let up. We took a whole lot of casualties that night, and though none of the scouts were hit, me and Kenny Takenaga and Rolly Maas decided the next morning that what we needed were real fortifications. No more of this getting up in the middle of the night crap.

We spent the whole day building a magnificent three-man hooch. First we dug a rectangular pit large enough to sleep three and about eighteen inches deep. Then we filled a mess of sandbags (I filled a lot of sandbags in thirteen months; I never go to the beach anymore without having to deliberately force myself not to try to calculate how many sandbags it would take to make the beach completely disappear), lined the pit with them, and added three more layers above ground, making a total inside vertical wall of about three feet. To the head and foot walls we added two more rows of sandbags, each shorter than the one below, to form a sloped roof support so that rain water would be carried off. Then we bummed a two-by-four board from the Sea Bees to use as a roof beam, and hooked two of our ponchos together over the center beam to form the actual roof. The third poncho we used as a ground cloth. We got a Coleman lantern and hung it from the roof beam, removed a few sandbags from one wall to form an entrance, and by damned if we didn't have the finest house on the block-sleeping quarters, reading room and fighting hole all in one. A regular fortified bedroom. Real estate values soared.

As the fortunes of war would have it, of course, the battalion headed back into the field before we ever got the chance to see how well our castle would hold up under siege but I sure slept soundly for those few weeks there by the river. Which is more than I can say for one particularly memorable night on Operation Kentucky just a week or so later. We had formed a perimeter for the night on a hilltop somewhere between Dong Ha and Con Thien. I had thrown up my trusty poncho tent, and dug my fighting hole -but I had neglected to bother digging the little trench around the base of the tent that helps divert rain water rather than allowing it to flow in under the tent. Some people have to learn everything the hard way -though I must say in my defense that I was used to the sandier soil farther south that absorbed rainwater quickly. Anyway, I woke up in the middle of the night to discover that it was pouring down rain and, because I was on a hillside, I was lying in the middle of a small but furious river. I was totally, irredeemably soaked, and very cold, and there wasn't a damned thing I could do about it by then. So I just lay there shivering in the water until dawn. It was the longest night of my life, and I never made that mistake again. About the only good thing I can say for the night is that the VC didn't bother to hassle us-no doubt they were all trying to stay dry.

The next place the battalion went, just before Thanksgiving 1967, was Con Thien, one of the northernmost Marine outposts along the DMZ. No need for one-man poncho tents there; we all lived in damp, muddy underground sandbagged bunkers just like the Doughboys in France. I liked the house by the river much better. But after thirty-three days of "Over There" and "Mademoiselle from Armentiers," we were sent back down to a place just south of Quang Tri where we spent the next month.

Me and Randy Hill scrounged up a good-sized tent from an anti-tank battalion big enough to stand up in, threw in two cots swiped from the battalion first aid station (no one can scrounge like a Marine; if you can't scrounge in the Marine Corps, you don't get nothin'), and we were in business.

Of course, since this was the monsoon season, you were wet all the time. The temperature seldom went below 55 or 60 degrees, but because you were always wet and because your body was accustomed to temperatures into the hundreds, it was cold. (I even had a pair of long underwear dyed green and sent over as a Christmas present by my mother. Everything you wore was green. Even the small white V of a teeshirt sticking up below the neck stood out like a bullseye on a clear night.) At night, you slept with your clothes on, which were wet, under a wet blanket. But if you put your poncho over your blanket, the sealed rubber kept the heat in, and after awhile you would warm up from your own body heat. You were still wet when you woke up, because moisture condensed on the inside of the poncho, but you stayed warm and toasty. It wasn't so bad.

In fact, New Year's Eve, when Randy and I sat on ammo boxes in front of the tent watching the fireworks display, we were feeling like princes. We had a pint of Johnny Walker Red Label scotch that John Pifer, a high school buddy, had mailed to me stuffed inside a hollowed out loaf of French bread. (A few years later, I helped Pifer get a Conscientious Objector's deferment from the draft -I owed him one for the scotch, and I couldn't see anybody else having to learn about Vietnam the hard way if he could avoid it.) At midnight, flares of every imaginable color and kind went up against orders - from every Marine outpost all the way to the DMZ. Happy New Year! It was beautiful. It made us homesick. Everything made us homesick. The next day, Randy and I celebrated the New Year with a picnic thrown together from the ingredients of care packages from home: salami, cheese, saltines, raisins, chocolate and cookies all laid out on top of a box of 81 millimeter mortar rounds. The sun even made a cameo appearance, and it was a grand way to begin another year.

Finally, toward the end of January, the battalion was sent down to the big base at Phu Bai for a rest after four months constantly on the move. We got to live in strongback tents again, and with only a month to go in Vietnam, I thought I was going out in style and comfort. Ah, but the fortunes of war -just a few days later, I found myself in Hue City in the middle of the biggest battle of the war: the Tet Offensive of 1968. I spent the next month mostly not sleeping at all, and when I did sleep, it was wherever I could put my head -in abandoned houses, in abandoned convents, in abandoned churches, in abandoned businesses (everything was abandoned). But at least you didn't have to build anything. Or dig anything. And sometimes you found an old mattress to sleep on. It was better than a shelter half, and no questions asked.

NOTES:

In W.D. Ehrhart latest book, *Ordinary Lives: Platoon 1005 and the Vietnam War,* he writes that, "Though I came to hate the American War in Vietnam, I have never hated the Marine Corps, and I will always be grateful to Staff Sergeant J.J. Oliver, Sergeant T.W. Evans, and Sergeant D.S. Bosch, and to the training program for which they served as point men, for preparing me as well as anyone could have prepared me to bear up under the awful obscenity of war."

Other Marines mentioned in the story were Cpl. Randall W. Hill 2318427, Cpl. Roland E. Maas 2313865 and Cpl. Kazunor Takenaga 2320456.

President Lyndon Johnson presents the Navy Cross
to GySgt. Leroy N. Poulson, VMO-6

*   *   *   *

The son of a Marine, Jeff "T.J." Kelly joined the Marine Corps in 1965. As a reservist, he volunteered for duty in Vietnam in 1967. Upon arrival in Vietnam he was assigned to the communications platoon, Tactical Air Control Party section, Third Battalion, Third Regiment. We join him in early February 1968 in northern Quang Tri Province along McNamara's infamous Trace. He has been assigned to M-3-3.

> "I think our platoon was somewhere around thirty-five
> to forty men. Most of the fellows went down either
> killed or wounded in the initial few minutes."
>
> Cpl. Gary Conner, K-3-3
> From *No Shining Armor*
> by Otto J. Lehrack

Grateful acknowledgement is made to McFarland & Company, Inc. for permission to reprint previously published material. The following excerpt is taken:
From *DMZ Diary: A Combat Marine's Vietnam Memoir* © 1991 Jeff Kelly by permission of McFarland & Company, Inc., Publishers, Jefferson, North Carolina 28640.

14
KILO HAS CONTACT!

My empty stomach growled. It was 1000 hours-two more to go before Frenchy was due. Since my FUO (fever of unknown origin), I was back at Alpha 3 doing little besides pulling a four-hour radio watch in the COC each day and reading the Stars and Stripes coverage of the Tet fighting. The doctor's order of light duty kept me from returning to Hill 28.

I dreaded watch in the COC. There was nothing to do. My letter writing was caught up; I wrote Sue the letters I owed her, and we weren't allowed to read magazines. I just sat and stared at the hissing remote unit that connected to the TAC Party radio. Only Kilo Company was outside the wire, and they didn't have a 1-4 man. It was a lonely network I monitored.

Beside me Matt was busy working eight of them. He had Reg TAC I and 2, Battalion TAC I and 2, and four others used for admin and to monitor the companies. All his radios were on squelch, so he didn't have any annoying static hissing at him. Past Matt and lining the walls of the oversize dye-marker were the other sections: 2-4 artillery, S-3 operations, and S-2 intelligence. They were all busy or at least occupied.

Suddenly Matt was on his feet. "Roger, Kilo. Roger, Kilo," he said to Hammer through the handset, then shouted, "Kilo has contact!" to everyone in the COC. Matt listened, his face intense. "They were ambushed near Highway One and the MSR [main supply route]. Third is pinned down and second is moving up."

I looked at my idle remote unit. Jesus, they should have a One-Four man, I thought.

Major Findley, the operations officer, rushed around the table and took the handset from Matt. "Kilo six, Mad three." He listened as Kilo six briefed him. "Okay, hang on. We're on our way," he said. He fired orders at his assistant. "Get Lima saddled up and headed out to Kilo. Tell India to take over Lima's lines. Call Mike and put them on alert. Get all available people from H and S to fill in on line watch. And get hold of Corporal Moore in Comm. Tell him to make up my pack and stand by to go out."

The lieutenant cranked furiously on the field telephone. The major turned to me. "One-Four, do you have comm with Kilo yet?"

"Negative, sir. They don't have an operator."

"Why the hell not?" he barked, anger visible in his eyes. "Get them an AO anyway," he said calmly, his outburst over.

In a few minutes a voice came on the 1-4 net identifying as Kilo. The background noise sounded like corn popping.

"Okay, Kilo, this is Fighting Mad One-Four," I said. "I'm going to help you with your air support. The first thing we do is take your radio off squelch. You can't hear the aircraft if it's on squelch. You copy that?"

"This is Kilo, A ... Roger, Fighting Mad ... A One-Four."

He was untrained with the radio. I talked him through the procedure to set the squelch to off, and he rogered that. No sooner was that done when the AO checked in with us. Right away Kilo started using the battalion's brevity code. Instead of using words like *company* or *platoon*, he used our code words, which were *knight* for company and *rook* for platoon. This made no sense to the AO. There was no way the AOs and pilots could memorize each battalion's brevity code.

"Kilo, this is One-Four," I broke in. "Forget the brevity code. Send everything in the clear. Just tell the AO where you are and what's happening. "

The AO worked well with Kilo. "Fighting Mad Kilo, this is Southern Delta. Okay, real good. Now I'm flying down the road. When you see me get over your position, you let me know. Okay, babe?"

After Southern Delta was over the ambush site he talked to Major Findley. "I've never seen such a concentration of NVA," he said. "They have an extensive bunker complex down there. It looks fresh. There are connecting trenches crisscrossing the whole thing. I estimate their strength in the hundreds, maybe two to four hundred men. Maybe more. My front seat concurs with that estimate, sir. Go."

The remote-unit speaker played the conversation to the COC. The knot of officers leaning over my shoulder groaned and cursed softly when they heard the numbers. We listened as Kilo tried to consolidate. They could not advance to the trapped platoon because of an intense crossfire in the clearing where they went down. It was all they could do to hold their ground against repeated NVA rushes, and in fact their hasty perimeter was soon broached. The AO was running gunships on the NVA, but it was in the center of the bunker complex, not close to Kilo where it was most needed. He couldn't get it closer because Kilo and the NVA were mixed together.

Frenchy was at the COC at noon to relieve me, but it took almost an hour before I could get away. Actually, I never briefed Frenchy. He sat beside me until he knew what was going on and told me I could leave. I went back to the Peon Bunker-mentally drained. In the quiet bunker I heated a can of chow and appreciated the cozy solitude, looking forward to relieving both my tension and my hunger with a quiet meal before going on line watch. My beans were almost heated when the telephone clicked. "TJ", they want you to take a radio up to the COC," said Brownie. Resigned to one more task before my break, I shoveled down a couple of spoonfuls of beans and rushed out to the comm o's bunker for a radio.

Cherry Red on switchboard watch hollered the instant I ducked into the door. "Goddamn, TJ! They've been screaming like crazy for you. You better get your butt up to the COC on the double, " he said. I guessed they had comm trouble and wanted to switch out a radio unit. I grabbed a field radio and ran with it. I figured I'd take off the carrying harness when I got there.

Frenchy was outside the COC waiting. "Catch Mike Company. They're going out the east gate. Haul ass, man!" he yelled.

"Who do I give the radio to?" I asked.

"You keep it. You're One-Four Mike. Find Moore and the three and stay with them. Hurry! They're almost through the safe lane."

"Jesus fucking Christ!" I shouted as it sunk in. I was on my way to a big-ass firefight completely unprepared. I had no first aid kit, no water, no entrenching tool. I didn't even have food in my stomach, let alone my pack. Mud sucked at my boots as I crossed Alpha 3, and I remembered I wasn't even wearing socks. My mind whirled at how fast the cozy bunker disappeared. "Fucking Brownie," I muttered. He should have told me.

Mike's rear guard was starting through the safe lane when I reached the east gate. I kept running down the safe lane, passing men and looking for Moore and the CP group. Above me the whistling sound of an incoming round triggered a conditioned response, and I dived to the dirt road. A flash and a cloud of black smoke hit the road fifty feet away-where I had just been. I saw an object flying up out of the smoke. It was a body arching ten feet over the barbed wire on a trajectory that took it into the minefield. A 152 round scored a direct hit on a Mike Company man. The body-I could see he was black-landed on his head and shoulders, then flipped over on his back. His legs were missing from the knees down. He lay motionless.

"Good God, it hit Rossaw!" said the man between me and where the round hit. On the road were a pair of boots surrounded with smoking trouser material and bits of flesh. No one moved for what seemed like a long time as we looked from the dead Marine in the minefield to his feet still on the road, then back. We were too stunned by what we saw. Then I realized that (1) I still had to find Moore, and (2) the gook artillery crew must be preparing to fire another round. I sprang to my feet and started running. The rest of the rear guard followed my lead. They were screaming for the stalled column to move out, but no one waited for an answer. It was a mad scramble to get out of the safe lane and find some cover.

"Break up this cluster fuck. You're making a target for the gook FO," shouted a staff sergeant. In our haste to clear the minefield we had bunched up at the end of the road. As if on cue, more incoming exploded on the just vacated safe lane. Now I knew why the gooks shelled the dump so often. The safe lane ran right past it. They had been registering the safe lane for just such an opportunity. As we dispersed the cluster, I continued down the column looking for Moore and Major Findley. I found them huddled with Captain Zensen from Lima and Captain McAdam from Mike. The reason we were held up on the safe lane was that Lima was crossing in front of us. I exchanged a hurried greeting with Harris as Lima moved south into the woods. Mike proceeded toward Kilo, skirting the trees on the south side of the Trace.

Kilo's firefight was easy to locate. Apart from the crackle of small-arms fire, there were the choppers and AOs buzzing over it. Behind us we heard Lima open up with M-16 fire, and Harris called to report two NVA KIAs, probably an LP (listening post). As we drew closer to Kilo, I steered a course from one crater to the next, never more than a step or two from the safety of a hole. I expected incoming. The gook FO had to see Mike walking down the open Trace. The impression that body made hitting and doing its slow flip was hard to shake. I appreciated the many craters and old fighting holes the Trace offered after lying exposed on the hard-packed dirt of the safe lane.

We turned south off the Trace heading for a linkup, and I spotted movement in the treeline. I drew my pistol and saw that Major Findley had one in his hand, too. A pop and a wink of light in the shadows sent all of us diving for the deck and firing positions as a loud hissing came from the treeline. I aimed at the movement with my .45, wishing for an M-16, cursing myself for letting Red put me off when I asked for one. Then a pop overhead was followed by a green star cluster floating in the sky between us and the treeline. A Marine stepped from the treeline and waved, his relief evident from a broad smile. We had found Kilo.

The sky darkened with rain clouds, and the wind picked up just then, giving the afternoon the look of dusk. The sporadic rain began to fall again, large drops striking us with a splatter, and the lowering ceiling sent the choppers and AO scurrying back to Quang Tri for fuel. They promised to return after the storm passed.

Major Findley met with Captain Frank, Kilo's six, to plan their next move. Kilo's platoons-first, second, weapons, and what was left of third-were strung out in a tactical withdrawal. They carried a number of wounded with them. I want to go back in," said Kilo six. "We have people in there. There might be some alive."

The decisions belonged to the major. There had been no word from the missing platoon for hours. The NVA was dug in and waiting for us in vastly superior numbers. Current weather denied us air support and decreased visibility to near night conditions. I watched the major's face twisting in concentration as he bit the inside of his cheek and stared at the NVAs position. The captain continued to plead his case for an immediate assault. I was grateful I wasn't in Findley's boots.

"We're going to pull back to the Trace and dig in," he said. "Come first light we're going to get some more firepower in here and go after them." The decision was made.

We set up a two-company perimeter in a graveyard outside Gio Linh ville and geared for a night assault. Lima was most vulnerable in the woods, so they slipped back to Alpha 3. Moore had a good start on a hole, and I took turns relieving him on the entrenching tool; it was a way to keep warm. Major Findley was included, so we were working on a three-man hole, enough work to keep warm for a while. The frantic pace we had maintained since morning was beginning to slacken as everyone settled in for the night. In a short time the hole we were digging turned into a mud pit. We scooped out the sticky mud and water, hitting dry earth again, but that soon dissolved into paste as well.

Occasional gunfire sounded from the NVA position, and I asked the major what they were shooting at. "I don't know. Maybe they have itchy trigger fingers," he said. Looking pained, he added, "Maybe they're killing wounded."

After dark the 1-4 Actual called me. He sounded tense as he explained they were getting a flare ship for us and gave me a quick lesson on how to use it. "Now, the winds aloft will be pushing the flares in different directions at different altitudes, but you just worry about them from when you get a solid tallyho to the time they hit the deck. Make sure you illuminate the area between you and the woods. Can you do that for me, buddy?"

"Roger, sir, no sweat."

"Okay. His call sign is 'Basketball,' and we're only going to use him if it looks like the gooks are going to penetrate your defenses. Understand what I mean?"

"That's a rog. I copy."

"The Mad three will help you with this, but he might be busy. Remember, your job is directing flares, nothing else."

After he signed off I cracked, "Scare the shit out of me, why don't you?" Both Moore and the major laughed.

Basketball called saying he was orbiting over the ocean and would be dropping flares three minutes after my call. He called again at 0100 saying he was low on fuel and returning to Da Nang. I asked the three if we should get a replacement.

"No. They would have hit us by now if they were coming," he said. He slid down into the hole to get some sleep. "The enemy is no different than us. He gets cold and wet and sleepy. He's sleeping now, getting rested for tomorrow. You might as well do the same."

"Do officers get cold like us enlisted men, sir?" Moore joked. We were soaked with rain and mud, and the stiff wind had us shivering.

"Of course not, Corporal Moore. You know that. We just look cold so the men won't feel bad. Inside we're warm as toast."

There was a bond between these two. It was kind of stiff, but I could see they cared about each other. It was typical of the major. He exuded formality. He didn't share in the banter that most officers had with the radio operators in the COC. He studied his maps and papers and wrote out plans in a lined copybook. Sometimes he snapped at the journal clerks for letting his Coleman lantern get dim, but normally he was civil. When it dawned on me that what he worked on with such seriousness affected my personal safety, I saw him in a new light. I no longer resented his cold personality. Nice guys were plentiful, but tactical genius was a rare commodity.

It was a miserable night. Wet mud numbed the cheeks of my ass, and chilling rain swirled into the hole. Moore and I used our flak jackets as a crude blanket, but it didn't do much good. After a while we were hugging like young lovers. None of us slept, really, just grabbed snatches of sleep here and there. When Moore and I thought the major was dozing we sneaked a cigarette, cupping it so the gooks-and the major-couldn't see its glowing tip. When the long night ended we warmed our bones with C-ration coffee and more cigarettes.

Artillery prep fires blasted the NVA bunker complex while we waited for a section of tanks to arrive from Gio Linh. A gray ceiling of clouds above the woods left a thin layer of visibility, enough for an AO to slip in and report movement in the NVAs position. Near our hole a wounded rifleman sat calmly, his attention fixed on the NVA stronghold. Mud and blood marbled on his flak jacket and spread to his green sling and tan bandages. His eyes never left the woods as he spoke: "We got to get those sneaky cocksuckers, man. We got to kill every fucking one of them."

Kilo six asked permission to lead the assault, and the major granted it with a nod. Mike left for their assigned position on the flank and the major, Moore, and I stayed with Kilo. We formed up two companies and three tanks on line. "Move out!" was called, and we began the advance. There was little talking, just some commands from squad leaders adjusting the formation. Then the tanks engaged gears, and the morning stillness was broken by clanking steel and rumbling engines. Patches of fog hung in the morning air, and dew moistened our legs.

One hundred meters from the first hedgerow a flight of huey gunships asked permission to join the assault. I gave it, setting them up in a racetrack formation that put their strafing runs parallel to our on-line formation. Ash had explained this to me, but this was my first time doing it. "Make your run-in from west to east with a pull-out left, sir. You're cleared to fire only as long as you got a visual on us." With only two hundred feet of flying room between the treetops and the clouds, I was afraid they would lose track of us and then mistake us for gooks. Their strafing run was answered by green tracers coming up from the woods.

"Recon by fire!" yelled Captain Frank when we were twenty meters from the hedgerow. A fusillade erupted along the length of our line that caused bushes to quiver and sawed off tree branches. The tanks joined in with their heavy machine guns. Kilo's men were cursing at the NVA, calling them out to die. Brown exhaust from the tanks rose through the white mist.

The NVA waited until we were approaching the road before they began firing. A man ten meters to my left went down with a bullet in his hip. Only a corpsman stopped to help him; the rest of the line pressed on, firing and changing magazines as we advanced slowly on the bunkers. Any muzzle flash, any sign of movement drew our concentrated fire, tearing that spot unmercifully.

As we entered the woods I sent the gunships high and dry. Our formation was splitting, and control was impossible. The Arty FO had his fires shut off, too. It was all grunts now.

Abruptly a group of NVA bolted from a trench, racing deeper into the bunker complex. They were killed in seconds, getting no farther than a few steps before being knocked off their feet, spun around, and sent reeling as pieces of their bodies flew into the air. Other NVA panicked and ran, with similar results. Now Kilo was the grim reaper, killing anything that moved as they assaulted through the NVA trenches and bunkers in a tactic so simple and direct I was amazed by its effectiveness. Their firepower was a wave of destruction surging before them, overwhelming the enemy. It was over quickly.

Across the road was the thickest part of the woods, almost dense enough to be called a jungle. Running perpendicular to the road was a small footpath. Three sides of the intersection were wooded; the other was an open field. It was in the field that we found the missing platoon.

The first thing I saw when I crossed the road was a bloody jungle boot. Ours, I thought, somehow reassured by its familiarity. As I stepped over it I looked down and saw it still held a foot. A cream-colored shaft of bone protruded from a bloody mess that had once been someone's ankle. Bone chips littered the ground around the boot, and flies buzzed and landed. My stomach dropped, and an involuntary sound came from my throat like I'd been jabbed in the solar plexus. "Don't stop. Don't look at that stuff," ordered Moore.

Most of Kilo's third platoon were lying on their backs with wounds in the chest and upper body. Hit by the initial burst, they were killed before they could react in any way. Most never returned fire. I stared at a dead radioman, his face peaceful and relaxed, eyes closed. His arms were outstretched, almost Christ-like, held there by small bushes beneath him, the leaves stained dark by large amounts of his blood. His face was turned skyward as if he were sunbathing-catching rays. His hand still gripped the handset. I could hear transmissions coming from it.

I looked up and saw Hammer walking across the field of sprawled bodies. His flak jacket was newly stained with blood and was getting worse as he cradled a PRC-25, wiping it with a rag. A tight smile hung on his face but would not hide the hurt in his eyes. "Hey, TJ, I didn't know you were out here," he said.

"How you doing, dude? I didn't see you last night," I said.

"It was a motherfucker here yesterday, man. We had gooks all around us. I was right over there by those bushes helping a friend with a chest wound." He pointed steadily at the blood-covered grass. "Right fucking there." He paused and blinked. "Four NVA carrying a machine gun ran right past me. I could've touched them." Hammer's eyes widened and he talked in spurts about the ambush. Sometimes a smile passed across his face that bore no correlation to his words. "Fucking gooks are some English speaking sons a bitches, too, man. They got one of our squids by yelling "Corpsman, I'm hit!" He fell silent, continuing to wipe blood off the radio's antenna base. I didn't know what to say.

"This is Willie's radio. That's him there." The words caught in his throat. All he could get out was, "Fuck, TJ, it was awful." He turned and walked away.

I listened to two grunts from Mike Company discussing the ambush in analytical terms. "Look, see the way the ground is chewed up in front of the KIAs? They started firing at the ground in front of the platoon and let their AKs rise right into them. Smart. Real smart. Get a line of rifleman doing that, and you can chew up a platoon fast. I'll bet a lot of rounds bounced off the ground and up into Kilo."

I wandered around the gruesome scene. The combined effect of gunship strikes, artillery, and Kilos walking assault was piles of North Vietnamese bodies. A commotion at a nearby bunker, men jostling to look inside, drew me there. I took my turn and saw a dead NVA with a severed arm and massive head damage. "Look. The fucker killed hisself," said a grunt, putting forth the theory that he pulled the string on a chi comm grenade and held it to his head.

Through the woods came the sound of another firefight, Lima ambushing retreating NVA. Ten minutes after it started the firing stopped. Harris called, saying, "Tell the Kilo dudes we just got nineteen confirmed for them. That's kick-in-the-head, piss-in-the-face confirms."

A rifleman from Mike came sprinting down the road and told Captain Frank in breathless gasps that his squad had found four wounded and a corpsman hiding under a bush. The corpsman, unhit during the ambush, had kept the wounded alive, propped rifles in the shoulders of those who could squeeze a trigger, and somehow managed to evade NVA looting parties. We ran to the spot, and I led a parade of wounded, limping and being carried, out of the woods and called in my first medevac. Including the wounded from the day before and the few we sustained in the assault, thirty men were wearing medevac tags. Five were emergencies. One, a black Marine from under the bush, was chalky gray from loss of blood. Only his hair and nostrils distinguished him as black. He shivered as corpsmen replaced lost blood with IV solution. The exit wound in his back was a three-inch pink crater of flesh that no longer bled, the torn tissue only slightly moistened with clear fluid.

Med Evac Chase, a huey gunship, was the first to arrive. I showed him Kilo and Mike's positions, and Harris showed him Lima's. He wanted clearance to fire, but I restricted him to the areas south of the woods-the only one I knew held no Marines-and then only if fired on. Med Evac Chase led the pickup birds into the zone, simplifying my job. The misty rain and fog cut the ceiling to a hundred feet and visibility to half a mile. Hill 31 across the Trace was completely whited out by the weather. The medevac birds, older CH-34s, carried six wounded each. That took the pressure off, with all the emergencies and most of the priorities getting out. While the 34s were going to the hospital ship, the gunship patrolled aggressively south of the woods. He called saying he had a small column of ten men moving south and requested permission to fire.

"Stand by, Chase, let me double-check to see if we have anybody in that area," I said as I ran to check with the major. "Med Evac Chase, they're not ours. Blow them away," I said after verifying with Major Findley.

" Roger, Fighting Mad. Ah ... be advised there is no question who these people are. They are carrying AK-47s and two radios. Probably the CP group from that bunch you tangled with. We're rolling in hot." His machine guns chattered, and his rockets ignited and left the pods. "Okay, we got six confirmed and four probables. I think we got them all but only see six bodies."

When the 34s returned, visibility was almost nil. The ceiling was so low they were flying around trees rather than over them. They requested this be their last trip. We loaded aboard everyone who couldn't walk, and after a few rolling bounces on the Trace the 34s gained altitude.

Three piles left on the LZ were the NVA gear, the American gear, and the American dead. The tanks pulled alongside, and we loaded the NVA gear on one tank and the American dead on the other two. It was absolutely quiet except for the groans of the loaders and the sounds made by the bodies of the dead being dragged to the tanks. They were stacked four high-one on his back, the next on his stomach-the heads and arms placed between the legs of the body underneath to lock in the stack and prevent it from toppling. Rigor mortis had the bodies rigid as statues, arms and legs thrusting out aimlessly.

The tank crews watched in horror. Thick blood and body fluids oozed from under the stack and dripped off the steel fenders. Twenty-nine dead Americans rode the tanks back to Gio Linh. I watched them until they disappeared in the mist.

All the gear of the dead and wounded had to be carried back to Alpha 3. There was a huge row. I carried an extra radio for Hammer and half a dozen M-16s. When we got back to the supply bunker, I turned in the radio and five rifles. I kept one for myself.

NOTES:

The following Marines were killed in the ambush:
Archer, Sanford K. LCpl. 2222550; K-3-3; 20; Melrose, Montana
Adger, Willie H. LCpl. 2338245; M-3-3; 20; Greensboro, N. C.
Chaplin, Lawrence Pvt. 2236894; K-3-3; 21; Frogmore, South Carolina
Couch, Michael A. Pfc. 2352668; K-3-3; 18; Pacific City, Oregon
Deeter, Michael A. 2dLt. 0103433; K-3-3; 23; Coolville, Ohio
Durham, James W. LCpl. 2350288; K-3-3; 20; Washington, D.C.
Ford, Manzelle A. Pfc. 2284545; K-3-3; 20; Mount Pleasant, Iowa
Holbrook, Gary W. Cpl. 2175826; K-3-3; 21; Trenton, Michigan
Jackson, Calvin O. Pfc. 2345500; K-3-3; 20; Columbus, Georgia
Jensen, Robert A. Pfc. 2326495; K-3-3; 19; Stroudsburg, Pennsylvania
Johnston, Evaristo P. LCpl. 2151295; K-3-3; 22; Columbus, Ohio
Justice, Everett E. Pfc. 2365625; K-3-3; 18; Mount Airy, Maryland
Kane, Larry W. Pfc. 2317354; K-3-3; 19; Ashland, Ohio
Kaplan, Daniel J. LCpl. 2284467; K-3-3; 19; Cedar Rapids, Iowa
Marshall, Samuel T. LCpl. 1851538; K-3-3; 26; Covington, Kentucky
McPherson, David L. Pfc. 2337903; K-3-3; 18; Martins Ferry, Ohio
Medley, Tommy R. Pfc. 2252956; K-3-3; 18; Newton, Texas
Nelson, Donald L. Pfc. 2349680; K-3-3; 18; Santa Susana, California
Ortiz, Arturo M. LCpl. 2235332; K-3-3; 19; Los Angeles, California
Osborne, Joseph Jr. Pfc. 2359846; K-3-3; 21; Chicago, Illinois
Owens, Larrington LCpl. 2351648; K-3-3; 19; Palmyra, Virginia
Powell, Larry K. Pfc. 2246453; K-3-3; 19; Fort Worth, Texas
Prather, Ronald R. Jr. Sgt. 2177783; K-3-3; 23; Cave Junction, Oregon
Quick, Robert L. Pfc. 2395468; K-3-3; 18; Wallaceton, Pennsylvania
Rice, James J. Pfc. 2290281; K-3-3; 21; Newtonville, Massachusetts
Ripley, Larry D. Cpl. 2227092; K-3-3; 21; London, Ohio
Robbins, Wayne D. Sgt. 2041121; K-3-3; 23; Southington, Connecticut
Robinson, James E. LCpl. 2260835; K-3-3; 18; Winchester, Tennessee
Russaw, Preston I. Pfc. 2384265; M-3-3; 19; Diboll, Texas
Strate, Bruce E. Cpl. 2268029; K-3-3; 21; Vincennes, Indiana

Swanson, Lawrence H. LCpl. 2259942; K-3-3; 19; Hastings, Minnesota

LCpl. Tony A. Cisneros and Cpl. Victor Jinkerson of K-3-3 were awarded the Silver Star for heroism on this day.

Allan Sams was the Corpsman who survived the ambush. The four wounded Marines whose lives he helped save were Jim Ferguson, Mike Granberry, Bob Manter and John Shelton. Sams would later receive the Bronze Star for his actions.

Bob Richards, 21, from Bowling Green, Kentucky was a squad leader with the first platoon of K-3-3 on the day of the ambush. Here he recalls the events of the day:

We were on the left flank and we were running a mine sweep on the road. We thought we were out for a stroll. Then we heard firing. The second platoon had taken fire as they walked through a bunker complex. They should have stopped. Their platoon commander made a big mistake. I think his name was Deeter. Our Lieutenant got us on line and we moved to the sound of the firing. As we got closer the firing increased in volume. It was the most intense fire that I experienced in my 13-month tour. The noise from small arms fire was unbelievable.

As we crossed the road and the fire increased the Lieutenant stopped us and told us to pull back. As I turned and started back, I noticed that the two Marines, Bob Jensen and Sam Marshall, who had been on either side of me, were no longer there. I turned to see why they had not come. Both were lying on their backs with a look of surprise on their faces. Both had a single bullet wound directly between the eyes. Why I was not hit, I will never know. The machine gunner must have traversed past me between rounds.

Marshall was older than the rest of us and had been in the Corps a while. He was somewhat backwards. He would do whatever he was told and would continue to do so until ordered to stop. In my opinion, he should not have been in the infantry.

Jensen had been a baseball player before joining the Corps. His goal was to play baseball in the Major Leagues for the Philadelphia Phillies. Jensen could throw a grenade further than anyone I ever saw. He would hit what he was aiming at with uncanny accuracy. For awhile after he was killed, his mother would write to Marines in the platoon asking that we lay down our arms and come home.

These two were the only Marines from our platoon killed that day. Almost all of the casualties were from the second platoon. They were almost wiped out. The Marines from M Company, who were called to our rescue, had a field day. They literally slaughtered the NVA. Many told me afterwards that the killing of the enemy soldiers was so exciting that it was almost fun.

Sgt. Carl E. "Tank" Elliot shares his recollection of that day:

I was with the third platoon of M-3-3. We ran a patrol to the village that morning but we never left the tree line. Our point man, Billy Watson, didn't feel right for there was no movement or sound coming from the village. We radioed back and moved north to the graveyard and held up. We were then directed to return to A-3 as Kilo was on its way out. We returned by a different route and never hooked up with Kilo. Before we could take our gear off we were on our way out again. The shit had hit the fan! SSgt. Lee Veteto was the Platoon commander and I was the Platoon Sergeant. Thank god for Billy Watson being point. If not for him they would have killed us all because we were only a platoon.

The Marines mentioned in this chapter were:
Frenchy was the nickname for LCpl. Donald L. Dufoe 2221350.
Hammer was the nickname for Pfc. Thomas Hamer, 2147438
Moore was a pseudonym for LCpl. Raymond K. Blair 2322889.
Harris was a pseudonym for Pfc. Robert H. Garrett, 2320105

The others were:
Ferguson, James L. LCpl. 2233617
Findley, Raymond Maj. 078214; Oceanside, California
Frank, Donald R. Capt. 087775
Granberry, Michael Cpl. 2323324
Kelly, Thomas J. LCpl. 2074464;
Manter, Robert W. Pfc. 2261184
McAdam, William H. Capt. 028370; San Diego, California
Richards, Robert Cpl. 2100481; 21; Bowling Green, Kentucky
Sams, Allan HM3 630167
Shelton, John Cpl. 2223241
Veteto, Lee E. SSgt. 153263

* * * *

On January 30-31, 1968, the Vietnamese Communist mounted a surprise offensive throughout South Vietnam. It was the Vietnamese lunar New Year. It commenced what has become known as the Tet Offensive. Most of these attacks were carried out by local units of the Viet Cong with the exception of the month long battle for Hue City. In Hue, front line, North Vietnamese Army troops were employed.

Hue was the former imperial capital of Vietnam and was considered by many the cultural center of the country. It was actually two cities divided by the Perfume River. North of the river was the Citadel, the ancient walled city of the emperors. The modern city lay south of the river.

By daylight of January 31, the NVA had complete control of the Citadel and most of southern Hue.

Marines from recently formed Task Force X-Ray were ordered to the city. The first to arrive was A-1-1, commanded by Capt. Gordon Batcheller. Soon after crossing the An Cuu Bridge into the city they came under heavy fire and sustained many casualties. Among the more severely wounded was Batcheller.

Marines from H&S-1-1 and G-2-5 rushed to the aid of the embattled company. Within a short period, Company G lost nearly a third of its men either killed or wounded.

Reinforcements in the form of F-2-5 entered the city on February 1. The next day, after some progress was made, H-2-5 joined the fray. On the morning of the fourth, B-1-1 joined LtCol. Marcus J. Gravel's battalion.

By February 10 Hue was indeed a divided city with the Marines in control of the southern part and the NVA in control of the Citadel. The Marines had accounted for over 1,000 enemy dead. Their casualties were 38 dead and over 320 wounded.

With an impending assault on the Citadel forthcoming the First Battalion, Fifth Marines, under Maj. Robert H. Thompson was injected into the battle. This unit included 1stLt. Scott A. Nelson's, Company C. The first platoon of this company was led by 2ndLt. Nicholas Warr and consisted of 51 members.

Warr, who had been raised on a small farm in Oregon, arrived in

Vietnam on November 15, 1967. He was "wet behind the ears and scared nearly speechless."

Warr was later to write the finest combat memoir to come out of the Vietnam War. It rivals Eugene B. Sledge's *With the Old Breed: at Peleliu and Okinawa* as the finest book written about Marines in combat in any war.

Phase Line Green is a classic. It is a realistic, no holds barred approach to the description of the brutal fighting in the streets of Hue.

This anthology would have been remiss had it not included an excerpt from Warr's book.

"This is it. This is Vietnam."
Anonymous Sergeant
Hue City

Grateful acknowledgement is made to the Naval Institute Press; Annapolis, Maryland for permission to reprint previously published material.

15
PHASE LINE GREEN

Early on the morning of 13 February 1968, the Marines of 1-5 left the relative safety of the First ARVN Division compound and headed southeast toward our designated line of departure, phase line green. Alpha Company followed closely behind with Charlie One, as usual, on company point. One platoon from Delta Company provided rear security for the battalion CP group.

Dawn had reluctantly and halfheartedly defeated the dismal darkness of the previous night, but the winter sun could not penetrate a thick, low-hanging, gloomy cloud cover with anything other than a minimum of illumination. The only thing complimentary about the weather conditions was that the rain also appeared reluctant to show itself, and we were dry, at least for the time being.

Walking slowly, keeping at least a ten-meter interval between each man, the Marines of C-1-5 maintained a staggered column on either side of the street called Dinh Bo Linh after a fifth-century Vietnamese king. Dinh Bo Linh was a two-lane city street parallel to the eastern wall of the Citadel. Dinh Bo Linh would eventually deliver us from the First ARVN Division compound to phase line green. Alpha Company, as 1/5's point element and responsible for coverage of the eastern Citadel wall and the narrow city block adjacent to the wall, would turn left one block before they reached phase line green. Phase line green was, of course, a street, and its actual name was Mai Thuc Loan. Mai Thuc Loan was named in honor of a Vietnamese general who fought against both the Chinese and the French as they both encroached on Vietnamese soil during the sixteenth century.

Alpha Company would make the appropriate turn to the east and then deploy parallel to phase line green and move through the houses until they reached the point of departure. Charlie Company would move up behind them, deploy in a similar fashion along the three blocks of our responsibility, cover each other's flanks, and move forward until we reached phase line green. Once we were in position on phase line green, we would be given the word to commence a coordinated frontal assault on the NVA who were waiting for us, according to all the available intelligence reports, somewhere south of phase line green.

Because of the ten-meter interval and the deliberately slow and careful pace established by Alpha Company through the quiet, ancient suburbia of Hue inside the Citadel walls, it was very easy to become distracted by the sights. Spacious old estates were the dominant theme along both sides of Dinh Bo Linh, our present route of approach. Dinh Bo Linh was lined by several mansions, surrounded and separated by a mature and somewhat overgrown landscape of trees, shrubs, and spacious grounds, interspersed with reflecting ponds. The mansions were all surrounded by substantial stone walls, four to six feet high, and occupied large chunks of each city block. As we progressed southward, the larger estates gave way to a more normal suburban setting, consisting of many smaller houses in orderly rows facing the east-west running streets. The only thing consistent about the larger estates and the smaller houses was the distinctly discomforting lack of noise coming from them. It was as though this section of Hue was utterly void of humanity. Inside the Citadel, Hue was a ghost town.

My attention was abruptly wrenched away from the immediate scenery and back in the direction of Alpha Company by the all-too familiar "whump" of a mortar or rocket explosion, followed by several more of the same, punctuated by a ragged trickle and then a rushing torrent of small-arms fire. Alpha Company, whose point element was several hundred meters ahead of us and who had made their designated left turn several minutes before, had stepped in the shit, no question about it. A healthy firefight was under way, obviously involving Alpha Company.

Without the necessity of commands, the Marines of Charlie Company took cover as best they could along the walls lining Dinh Bo Linh and waited. Finally, after what seemed like hours but was probably only several minutes, the rear element of Alpha Company started to move again, and they turned the comer. Charlie One's point fire team started to move out after them, following about fifty meters behind Alpha's rear element. In my normal position, following just behind the Point fire team, I was one of the first Charlie Company Marines to find out what had happened to Alpha Company.

As I began to make the appropriate left turn, Benny and I Stopped cold as we were confronted by a fearful sight. Walking slowly and painfully toward us, 1st Lt. F.R. Wilbourne, Alpha Company's executive officer, was carefully making his way on his own, back toward the battalion rear area. Wilbourne had actually been the company commander of Alpha Company for a short time before 1/5 headed toward Hue, but he had been bumped down the ladder of command just a couple of days before by a Capt. J.J. Bowe, and Wilbourne was now the executive officer.

If we hadn't heard the firefight, if we hadn't seen the blood that covered his entire body from head to toe, we would have been tempted to ask him if he had shit his pants, since he was walking, with stiff legs and arms, like someone who had rectally embarrassed himself. But as he approached us it quickly became obvious that Lieutenant Wilbourne had been hit by a shower of shrapnel, and though none of his wounds appeared to be life-threatening, the cumulative effect was that Alpha's XO had become a bloody sieve.

Recognizing me as a Charlie Company platoon commander, Lieutenant Wilbourne stopped his arduous trek momentarily. Although it obviously pained him to do so, he pointed out that several of my men were in an exposed position, still nonchalantly turning the corner of the intersection, and he quietly chewed my butt.

Wilbourne said, "The Alpha CP group just got wasted because we were standing right out in the middle of an intersection, a block behind phase line green, clusterfucked around an M-48 tank The gooks ran out into the street about a block and a half in front of us and fired three RPG rockets, hitting the M-48 directly in the turret with their first shot. Shit, the skipper and the gunny were both blown away, and Alpha has been effectively eliminated on the battalion's left flank. Delta is moving up to take our places, and we'll be falling back to provide rear security. Fuck, the tank commander had his head blown off. Now, you tell your people that if they keep ditty-bopping across the damned streets, they're gonna get themselves blown away, too!"

Having said his piece, he started his painful trek toward the rear of the battalion column once again. As he walked away, he continued to mutter at me that we should get our collective heads out of our asses, get out of the middle of the fucking street, and make goddamned sure to stay alert and keep our heads down.

As I turned away from Wilbourne's unwelcome visage, I noticed that I didn't have to say a damned thing. Most of Charlie One had seen and heard him, and they were taking a distinctly lower stance along the sides of the road and were moving very quickly across the open areas when they had to cross the intersection. Shit. Alpha Company was history before the battle had even begun.

The battalion's assault was delayed for what again seemed like hours as a platoon from Delta Company moved up and relieved Alpha Company, and we got positioned along Tang Bat Ho, another street named for ancient Vietnamese royalty. The street ran parallel to phase line green, one block north of our point of departure. A shallow, muddy ditch ran alongside Tang Bat Ho, and Charlie One hunkered down in the ditch as the rest of Charlie Company got into position and as Delta switched positions with Alpha. As we waited, I resisted letting my attention wander toward the scene of destruction surrounding the now-disabled M-48 tank about fifty meters away and tried to concentrate on other things besides the frantic efforts to save the critically injured and to evacuate the dead members of the Alpha Company CP, but we couldn't avoid knowing exactly what was happening. During the first brief skirmish inside the Citadel, the NVA had struck unexpectedly and viciously, and as a result several KIAs (killed in action) and many WIAs (wounded in action) had rendered the Alpha CP group totally ineffective as a command unit. Alpha would have to fall back into battalion reserve status and regroup.

As Benny's Prick-25 squawked to life, the orders from Charlie Six tersely broke into my thoughts. "Move out. Maintain contact on both Ranks. Move up to the line of departure, and prepare to attack across phase line green."

Charlie One's three squads had lined up three abreast, broken into their fire team units. Slowly and cautiously, we moved into and around each house, taking our time, making sure that we weren't going to accidentally walk past any hidden enemy positions, constantly conscious and fearful of a counterattack from the rear. The houses in this block were much smaller than the estates we had passed on our way; they were very close together and often very difficult to walk around. This was not really a problem, because we had to clear each house anyway, but we still checked the narrow, brushy spaces between the houses to make sure we weren't missing anything.

The shouts of Marines communicating with each other as they practiced for the first time the tactics of house-to-house fighting penetrated the sullen air, muffled by the walls and the damp morning air. These barking commands, obviously made by Americans, reached my ears and gave me some comfort that at least the men of Charlie One were taking this very seriously. They had seen the instant destruction of the Alpha CP group, and they didn't want to be hit unexpectedly.

As was normal when Charlie One was in a frontal assault formation, Benny and I tagged along behind the center squad, Ed Estes's squad, in the middle of the block and kept in touch with the other two squads via their PRC-6 radios, much smaller and much less effective communication devices than the Prick-25.

The Prick-6, resembling an overgrown walkie-talkie, quickly proved to be ineffective in penetrating the walls of the houses that the Charlie One Marines were clearing, and it quickly became clear that we would have to rely on runners for a lot of our intraplatoon communications. Each platoon of a Marine company had one Prick-25, for communications with the company CP group and the battalion and support nets for calling in artillery and air support and we had three or four Prick-6s, which were designed for close-in communications between squads. The Prick-25s worked great; the Prick-6s were completely useless.

Charlie One was organized into three squads, each of roughly thirteen Marines, broken down farther into three fire teams and a squad leader. Each squad was further reinforced by a team who lugged and handled the awesome and devastating firepower of the M-60 machine guns. Sometimes they had the added luxury of an M-79 man, who carried the forty-millimeter grenade launcher and somewhere between forty and sixty rounds of accurate and deadly high-explosive firepower. On the morning of 13 February 1968, Charlie One's table of organization was comprised of a total of fifty-one Marines, including the attached M-60 teams, me, Benny Benwaring, and the two Navy corpsmen assigned to travel with us. The Marine fire team is the basic and fundamental tactical unit of the U.S. Marine Corps, and many hours of every Marine's training after boot camp were focused on the maneuvers of the fire team. The Marines of every fire team were drilled not only on individual movements and covering their buddy's back but also on the importance of maintaining the integrity of their fire team. Thus it was natural in our current situation that one fire team would be responsible for clearing one house at a time. This tactic worked out very conveniently in the first block, which contained fifteen or sixteen houses, half of them facing north along Tang Bat Ho and half of them facing south along Mai Thuc Loan (phase line green). In this particular block, unlike most other blocks in southeast Hue inside the Citadel, the houses and their respective yards were separated by a narrow alley. The nine fire teams of Charlie One, with Benny and me trailing the center fire team of the center squad, cleared the first seven or eight houses facing Tang Bat Ho. Then, making sure that their flanks were covered on both sides, the men moved slowly and cautiously across the narrow alley, through old, flimsy gates defining the back yards of the houses facing phase line green, and entered the back doors of the eight or so houses along phase line green almost simultaneously.

As Benny and I waited for the fire team ahead of us to clear their assigned house, I checked out the intersecting alley and noticed that although it was very overgrown, it defined a pathway that went all the way to both sides of the block. I could clearly see both of the streets that intersected phase line green and defined Charlie One's left and right flanks. As it was very overgrown, I was not at all disturbed that I couldn't see any Marines across the street on our left flank. An M-48 tank rumbled slowly past the alley on the street to our right and inched toward phase line green. I wondered momentarily how the tank crews were feeling, with their hands tied by not being able to fire their ninety-millimeter cannons and knowing that one of their group had been eliminated from the battle already.

Estes came back out the back door and signaled that this center house was cleared, and Benny and I moved in through the back door. Although these homes were small by American standards, they were very substantial by Vietnamese standards, at least from our limited experience in the paddies and jungles in other parts of I Corps. We stepped up three low steps onto a raised wooden floor and immediately entered a hallway leading from the rear to the front of the house; a stairway led to a second floor. Walking past the stairway into an empty front room, which was lined at the front by multipaned windows framing the front door, we walked through the eerily empty front room. The dim daylight illuminated the front room, and the street, Mai Thuc Loan, phase line green, was dimly visible through the front windows.

As Estes and Benny, just ahead of me, walked through the front room, through the front door, and out into the street, something nagged at me. Something wasn't right here. My feet kept walking. My mind knew that something was terribly wrong, but it couldn't grasp the problem, and my feet kept walking.

As I passed through the front door of that dreary small house out on Mai Thuc Loan and turned my head to the left and then back to the right I saw my men all standing there along the narrow sidewalk that lined the north side of phase line green. Some of them crouched behind the inadequate trunks of the shade trees lining this side of the street. I couldn't formulate any of the words in my mind. But I knew then, and I will know for the rest of my life, just exactly what was wrong. They had followed my orders to the letter. None of them had crossed the street, none of them had crossed phase line green, but every damned one of them, every swinging dick of Charlie One, was completely exposed out in the street. Charlie One was a collective sitting duck, standing out in the open along the narrow sidewalk in front of the houses. Some of them were crouching behind the trees, but most of them were just standing there, looking at each other, looking at me as I walked out of the front door of the center house.

My mind had no coherent thoughts in that one moment, that one heartbeat that will live forever as a cancer in my soul. I have had uncounted moments since then, during which I've eternally debated what my first words, at that crucial moment, should have been. The raging debate in my soul swings from the extremes of. "Charge!!" to "Shit! to "What the fuck are you idiots doing out in the street? Didn't common sense tell you to stay inside the houses until I give you the order to attack?" These debates are all totally useless; they are nothing more than a futile raging, and they will never be anything more than wishful thinking.

Here's what came out of my mouth: "GET THE FUCK OUTTA THE STREET!!"

I wish that the next few seconds had ticked away at normal speed, but with contemptuous certainty, time instantly changed into the slow motion of frustrating nightmares, of trying to run away from unseen but hideous monsters, only to be hindered by glue-covered feet or concrete shoes. I was only in that street that morning for a few seconds, but trying to escape the inevitable explosion of the well-prepared ambush of the entrenched NVA thirty feet in front of us, those seconds seemed like hours. Part of me will be there, in that street, for those terrible moments, for the rest of my days.

I have no idea why I didn't just turn around and run back inside the house I had just walked out of. That would have been the most obvious and fastest route to safety. I have no idea why I didn't turn left, or charge straight ahead I have no idea why I turned to the right, screaming those immortal words at the top of my lungs and running as fast as my legs have ever run before or since, yet taking forever to get to wherever it was that I thought that I was going. I turned to the right and I was following other Marines, my men, as the shit royally hit the fan.

The NVA were dug in and waiting for us on the other side of the street. They occupied the first- and second-floor windows, and many of the NVA were on the roofs. Several automatic weapons raked the street from our left flank, from the tower that protected the eastern entrance to the Citadel. And I ran, and ran, and ran, and I got nowhere fast.

There was no place to hide; I was shit outta luck.

Just before reaching the intersection of Mai Time Loan and Dinh Bo Linh, my first nightmare of that fateful day came to a spectacular and horrible conclusion. I was following a man from Charlie One Charlie, the third squad of Charlie One. He was one of its fire team leaders, a lance corporal named Gibson. Running one step in front of me, he was shot through the back by the NVA. The combined force of his running body and the AK-47 round that had slammed into him proved just enough to flatten a corner courtyard gate, winch became my escape valve. As Lance Corporal Gibson's bleeding body knocked down the gate, my feet propelled me into the safety of the corner courtyard as I leaped over his crumbling body. I was closely followed by Benny Benwaring, who had gone where his leader had led him, regardless of the insanity of the direction. The peaceful sanctity of this small corner courtyard had been shattered by our abrupt arrival. The scene was a nightmare, something out of Dante's Inferno, with the severely bleeding lance corporal sprawled on top of the wrecked remnants of the gate and several other shocked Marines huddled in the corner, protected by a substantial six-foot-high masonry wall but unable to return fire effectively. Doc English, one of Charlie One's Navy corpsmen, was one of the men in the courtyard, and he immediately began working on the severe wounds that were threatening to take the life of Lance Corporal Gibson. The ferocity of the enemy small-arms fire had not abated; it sounded like an NVA battalion was just on the other side of the street, shooting at us with everything they had. We had really stepped in the shit this time.

I asked Benny Benwaring to get the other squads on the Prick-6, but after a few frustrating attempts that resulted in a very unsatisfactory and unhelpful squelch of static noise, it was clear that if I wanted to find out what was going on, I would have to communicate by runner. Benny was monitoring the company radio net on the Prick-25, and it was very quickly evident that everyone else in the battalion was fully engaged with an entrenched enemy on the other side of phase line green. Charlie Six's instructions were to take care of our casualties, make damned sure of the integrity of our present positions, return fire, and await further instructions.

The leader of this squad, Charlie One Charlie, had begun to assert his leadership; he had made sure that the other Marines in the courtyard had good cover and were returning fire to the best of their ability. Doc English was doing everything he could for the wounded man, and it was killing me not to know what was going on with the rest of my platoon. I decided to go find out for myself.

Instructing Benny to stay with Doc English in case he needed help evacuating the injured man and to monitor the company net, I took off out the back gate of the corner courtyard into the alley. Turning right into the alley that would allow me to get to the other squads, I started running down the narrow, vine-draped alley. As I ran past a well, I tripped on something and nearly fell on my face, but whatever I had tripped on was a small hindrance, and I kept my feet and continued running. Two more heartbeats went by before the booby-trapped grenade exploded, knocking me forward onto my hands and knees, but my feet kept pumping, and I kind of skipped off my hands and knees, bounced back on my feet, and just kept running. The force of the grenade's explosion had hit my legs and lower back, but nothing hurt at the moment. My mind didn't even register that I might be wounded and numb. I just kept running. (I didn't think much about the incident until three weeks later, back in a GP tent in Phu Bai, when I was finally able to take off my utility trousers for the first time, and four small pieces of shrapnel clinked to the floor. I had been running so fast, and the NVA had been so inept at setting up booby traps, that I was out of the effective range of the shrapnel by the time it had exploded. When I saw those pieces of shrapnel fall from my trousers in Phu Bai, I thanked my lucky stars that it had been an NVA who had set up the booby trap, and not a Viet Cong. The latter would have known to remove the time-delay fuse from the detonator of the booby-trapped grenade, creating an instant explosion rather than one that happened a few seconds after the pin had been pulled out by the trip wire.

Crazily at that moment, running down the alley, I was taken back to my childhood for a few seconds. Once again I was sitting by my four brothers in the living room of the farmhouse on the Coos River in southwestern Oregon, watching the family's eight-millimeter home movies. We were all laughing like crazy as we made my older brother, Steve, go back and forth, forward and reverse, from the back door of my grandmother's house to her outhouse. My father, who had been a fanatic with the old hand-crank eight-millimeter movie projector and who was also a frustrated actor/director, had on many occasions enlisted us boys to be actors in his crackpot, slapstick productions. On this particular occasion, Dad had thought it would be hilarious if Steve would burst out the back door of Grandma's old house, run down the four back steps, along the fifty-foot boardwalk that connected the back of the house with the outhouse, running as fast as possible, with the obvious theme that Steve was running to save his clean britches. In one of those rare and impromptu moments, Steve had slipped on the rain-soaked, ancient wooden slats of the boardwalk while Dad was filming and had fallen on his butt when his feet flew out from under him. But he had amazingly kept his feet pumping, and without losing any ground speed, Steve had bounced off his butt, regained his feet, and completed his urgent journey. All of this had been captured on film, and with the help of the reverse switch on the ancient eight-millimeter projector, my family spent many hilarious evenings forcing Steve to run back and forth, back and forth, while assaulting him verbally with appropriate comments like, "Hey, Steve, why'd you keep running9 You probably did it in your pants when you hit the boardwalk, so the emergency was over." You get the drift.

At that moment, running down that shrouded alleyway, I giggled, just briefly, at the similarity of the events, but I quickly smothered that thought because there was nothing funny about any of this. I needed to know what was going on with the other squads, and fast.

Running to the opposite end of the alley, I ran inside the last building on the east corner of the block and found the squad leader of Charlie One Bravo, the squad who had covered the left side of our frontal assault formation. I quickly discerned that our situation was not good. Staff Sergeant Mullan, who had been traveling with Charlie One Bravo on our left flank, was gone. He had been standing out in the street like the rest of Charlie One and had been shot in the head during the initial burst of fire. The squad leader shakily told me that although Sergeant Mullan had been alive when they took him on a quickly improvised stretcher back toward the battalion rear for medevac, it didn't look like he could possibly survive. The side of his head had been severely wounded, probably by an AK-47, and he was unconscious and just barely breathing when he was carried away. Doc Lowdermilk, who had administered first aid, didn't give him much hope of survival.

The blow of losing Sergeant Mullan, who had truly been the leader of this platoon and my mentor while I was going through on-the-job training, was devastating, but there was no time to mourn or even to consider this loss, because we had a much worse situation on our hands. According to the squad leader, there were at least three dead Marines still out in the street, and he thought that Estes's squad had a wounded man down in the street as well. The wounded man was still alive, but stuck out in the street and exposed to enemy gunfire.

Making sure that Charlie One Bravo kept returning fire at the suspected enemy positions and that they kept their heads down as much as possible, I ran back into the alley and retraced my earlier steps following

Estes's squad through the back yard and into the back door of the house that had been my initial entry into phase line green.

Bedlam greeted me. Exposed as they were in the front room, several Marines were returning fire toward the enemy across the street. Estes was hunched down in the hallway and was using the stairway for cover When I came up behind him, he turned toward me with a look of anger and frustration that immediately spelled out the disastrous situation. There truly were three men down in the street right in front of this house, right where I had stood when I had first walked into phase line green and screamed those immortal words. I realized momentarily that if I had turned around and tried to go back inside this house through the front door, there was a very high likelihood that either Benny or I would have been one of the Marines down in the street.

Estes looked at me with a terrible burning fire in his eyes, and he quickly summed up the most serious problem. "Morgan is still alive, Lieutenant. He's hit bad, but we could hear him yelling at us to come get him just a couple of minutes ago. He's totally exposed, but he's hit bad and he can't move. We gotta get him outta there."

Enemy gunfire continued to rake the front room of the house, having long since shattered the windows, and effectively pinned down the Marines in the front room, making the effectiveness of their return fire questionable. From our position in the hallway, I couldn't see Morgan, but I could see two other green-clad bodies a little further out in the street. "How about those other two guys, Estes?"

"They're definitely wasted, Lieutenant. They were knocked down in the initial burst, and they've taken a lot more hits since. Neither of them have moved, and we haven't heard any sounds from them at all. But Morgan is still alive. What the fuck are we going to do?"

I said, "Let's try to give him some cover with smoke grenades, and then ask for a volunteer to go out and get him." Morgan's fire team leader, hunkering down under the window sill in the front room, immediately volunteered to make the effort. After sending two other Marines via the alley to the adjacent squads to tell them to lay down a heavy volume of fire when they saw the smoke pop in the street, we executed the plan.

Two smoke grenades went out the shattered front window, one on either side of Morgan's position, and the fire team leader, a lance corporal named Hallmark, rushed out into the hellfire. The volume of the small-arms fire, both incoming and outgoing, increased immediately, and after three long seconds, Lance Corporal Hallmark staggered back into the front room, blood gushing like a water faucet from his lower left leg. He collapsed in the hallway, screaming and holding his leg, as Doc Lowdermilk pounced on him and started the first aid necessary to stop the flow of blood and save the young man's life. Although the bone was most likely broken and he was in a great deal of pain, the young man had a hard time keeping a grin off his face, because he knew that this wound would put him on the sidelines and get him the hell out of Hue. But the grin vanished immediately when we asked him about Morgan.

Hallmark looked up at me through his pain and said, "Fuck me, Lieutenant, I couldn't tell if he was dead or alive. The shit is really hitting the fan out there, and I lost my grip on him when I got hit. I couldn't drag him over the curb, he's just too goddamned heavy. He might still be alive, but he's unconscious for sure. I think he got hit a couple more times when I tried to get him."

Estes and I helped Doc Lowdermilk carry the young hero out to the back yard and assigned another Marine to help him limp back to the battalion rear for medevac. As I watched them leave out the back gate, my mind was racing a million miles per hour, but none of my thoughts were at all helpful. Morgan was still down in the street, and we didn't know for sure if he was dead or alive. The Marine Corps has long had a proud tradition of making every effort possible to evacuate the dead and wounded from the battlefield, but the cards were stacked against us. Every time we sent more men into the street to try to recover the wounded or dead, even with the cover of smoke, it looked like we were just going to take more casualties, making a terrible situation even worse.

As I turned back toward the house, my vision fixed on LCpl. Ed Estes, who was obviously having the same terrible thoughts, but who was now insanely maddened by one other fact: Morgan was not just another Marine, he was his friend. They had been together for over six months, had survived the daisy-chain command-detonated mine outside Hoi An together, and had shared many night ambush patrols and uncountable daytime hours filled with terror and uncertainty. And now Morgan was down in the street and probably still alive. Estes was his squad leader, and he felt completely responsible.

As these thoughts surged through his mind, they were obvious to me as the emotions played across his angry face. Estes was turning slowly in place, walking in a tight circle, frustrated by Morgan's situation, scared to death like the rest of us about the prospects of making another attempt to go get him. As I watched this horrible internal struggle with himself, Estes made a complete 360-degree pivot, as though his right foot was staked to the ground. Our eyes connected for only a moment, and I instantly knew what Estes was going to do. I froze, unable to move, unable to make a sound. Estes completed his pivot, and when he saw the back door to the house, he screamed in fury, "Morgan!!" Unable to believe that Estes was going to run out into that damnable hell, I could only scream his name, "Estes!!!"

LCpl. Edward S. Estes knew what he was running to face, but Ed Estes was unable to stop himself. His friend, PFC Charles R. Morgan, was down in the street, and it was up to Estes to help him. Estes ran into the house, down the hallway, through the front room, and out the front door into a terrible hail of enemy gunfire, which was now concentrated on the front door. The smoke in the street was dissipating, and by the time I got inside the back door, finally able to move, Estes was lost to my view for a moment in the smoke. But just for a moment.

Ed Estes didn't even make it to Morgan. He had hardly stepped outside the doorway when an AK-47 round tore through his neck, entering his Adam's apple. Knowing then that Morgan was dead and that he was also probably dead, Ed Estes turned around and, still trying to run, stumbled back into the house, back through the front room, and collapsed at my feet in the hallway. He had been grasping his neck, but I had clearly seen the entry bullet hole in his Adam's apple. A thick, steady stream of blood was gushing from the hole, leaking heavily through his fingers.

Doc Lowdermilk was also Ed Estes's friend, and now Ed was dying. Doc Lowdermilk jumped on him and rolled him over on his back and onto my lap. Doc pulled Ed's hand away from his neck so that he could assess the damage and do what he could to save his friend's life.

Doc looked over at me with despair in his eyes and said, "We gotta do an emergency tracheotomy; his windpipe's crushed. I need a tube, something to stick into the opening when I cut into his windpipe."

I was stunned, stupid, unable to think or to move. None of the other Marines was any more help. Estes was dying on my lap, making feeble convulsive motions, and I couldn't move.

"Break down your .45, Lieutenant, goddammit. I can use the barrel as a temporary airway."

Still stunned, I was just barely able to pull my never-used pistol out of my Marine Corps-issue holster and break it down without looking at it as I had done so many times at Quantico and Basic School. I handed Doc Lowdermilk the barrel after he cut Estes's throat, and then he inserted the barrel into the bloody opening. Estes had stopped breathing, and Doc Lowdermilk started to push down on his chest to try to jump-start his breathing, when we noticed the terrible pool of blood forming under Estes and leaking from under his body.

Doc Lowdermilk gently turned Estes over, and we all knew at that moment that Estes was beyond any help that we could give him. The NVA bullet had entered his windpipe, and if it had gone straight back out his neck he might have had a chance for survival. But this particular NVA must have been shooting through a second-story window or from the roof of the house across the street, because the trajectory had been downward. The bullet had traveled through Estes's heart and out his lower back, probably shattering his spine for good measure.

Ed Estes, Squad Leader for Charlie One Alpha, was dead.

Stunned as we all were in that dim hallway, we were all forced to start living again when another Marine from Estes's squad was shot through the chest. He had been in the front room sitting up against a side wall, and an NVA gunner had moved into a position where he could shoot down into the front room. We dragged him out of the front room, and I yelled at the rest of the Marines in the front room to get out of there and to take up positions upstairs or on the roof. This particular front room had become way too deadly.

We carried Estes's body out of the house into the back yard and laid him out on an old outdoor table. The firing in the street had diminished to a less frantic and more sporadic level, and I stood there for a while, looking at Estes. I was in shock, and I think I would have remained standing there for a long time, but flies started to buzz around Estes' head, and his face started to take on the ugly greenish cast of the newly deceased. I couldn't bear to look at him any more. I pulled this wasted young man's poncho over his face, picked up his discarded M-16 rifle that had been propped up against the table by one of the other men, and turned my back on Ed Estes forever.

I don't remember too much about the next hour or so. I think time stopped for me. I vaguely remember returning to the house and walking into a back room that the owners had stuffed with the furniture from the front room and sitting down in a rocking chair. I closed my eyes an started rocking.

I remember rocking in that chair and thinking about the small dairy farm where I had grown up in Coos River, Oregon, and my pet cow, Honey, and the peaceful summer afternoons when I would lie on Honey's side and soak up the welcome and infrequent sunshine. Those were the most peaceful and least disturbing moments of my life, and my mind was subconsciously trying to submerge itself in memories of a peaceful moment. I could just not deal with the cruelty and savagery of our situation on phase line green and the death of many good men, in particular the death of Ed Estes. He was a young man who had accepted the responsibility of fighting for his country, of taking care of his men, and who had paid the ultimate penalty for facing up to those responsibilities.

So I sat in that rocking chair, holding Estes's M-16 in my hands between my knees, and rocked away God knows how many minutes. The other Marines from what remained of Estes's squad were reluctant to disturb me, and I probably spent nearly a half hour as a seven-year old again, finding some peace with a cow named Honey.

Finally, Benny Benwaring brought me back into the present. He had left the comer courtyard and followed my footsteps into that house. Seeing me sitting there, blank-eyed, rocking gently and quietly, he probably figured I had gone off my rocker, so to speak, but he had summoned the courage to shake my arm and force me back into the present.

Benny spoke quietly but insistently: "Lieutenant, the skipper is trying to reach you. We've got orders from battalion to attack across the street."

Part of me came back to life and I somehow reassumed the role and responsibilities of Marine platoon commander, Charlie One Actual. Another part of me stayed in that rocking chair and is still there today, rocking away, thinking about the torn lives and destruction focused on that bloody street. Many of the events I witnessed and participated in on that street that day and the terrible days that followed are so etched in my memory banks that I can hear the sounds, smell the smells, and scream the screams in my mind as though they happened yesterday.

Charlie One was ordered to attack across phase line green three times that day, so the Marines of Charlie One attacked across the deadly avenue three times that day. After the first attack, it quickly became obvious that the main concentration of the NVA's forces were established right across the street from Charlie One and our battalion commander had now decided that if we could successfully attack and penetrate the enemy's defenses at this point, we could break the back of their resistance and overwhelm them.

Repeated attempts were made to reverse the orders that restricted our heavy support. I pleaded with Scott Nelson to plead with Major Thompson to get us some artillery or air support. At least the major could allow the M-48 tanks to fire their ninety-millimeter cannons into the enemy positions, to soften the positions somewhat, to do something to force our enemy to get his head down, so that we had even a shred of a chance at success in a frontal assault.

My frantic requests for heavy firepower were all turned down flat. At one point, Charlie Six Actual got on the radio with me directly, reminded me of our orders, and told me to pull my men together and to assault the enemy. Running from position to position, Benny Benwaring and I set up the initial attack as best we could, which required one fire team in each squad to attack across the street, while the other fire teams provided covering fire. It didn't work; no one even got halfway across the street. The awful result was several more wounded Marines and another KIA. Now there was yet another dead Marine down in the street.

During the first abortive assault, I noticed that we were taking a high volume of enemy fire from our left flank, from the tower that guarded the east entrance to the Citadel. The NVA apparently occupied the tower in force and had many automatic weapons. From about a block and a half away, a distance of little more than a hundred meters, this firepower was devastating to the Marines who were trying to cross the street in full view of the NVA gunners in their tower positions.

After reporting back to Scott Nelson that we had been unsuccessful in getting a foothold on the other side of the street, he maintained that our orders hadn't changed and that we should get ready to try again. I was getting an awful feeling about the security of our left flank, so Benny and I took off down the alley to its intersection with the street that defined our connection with Delta Company on our left. When I got to the corner of the alley and the street, my heart sank. The M-48 tank that had been the center of the attack on the Alpha Company CP group, having been assigned a new tank commander and put back into action (albeit still under strict orders not to fire its cannon) was now positioned behind the intersection of the alley and the street. Furthermore, I couldn't see any Marines from Delta Company in their assigned positions along phase line green.

Benny and I ran across the street and dived behind the tank, as enemy gunners spotted us and started shooting in our direction. I asked for the whereabouts of the Delta Company platoon commander who was responsible for covering our left flank, and I finally found him in a house behind the alley. When I confronted him and tried to explain that they were not in position at phase line green, he looked at me like I was crazy and said that his men were in position where they were supposed to be and that they were taking terrible enemy fire from the tower. The Delta Company platoon had stopped their forward movement at the alley, and the platoon commander refused to look closely at his map or even consider that they were a half block back of their assigned positions.

Leaving him in disgust, I returned to the back of the tank, got on the direct telephone that was designed for the trailing infantry to communicate with the tank commander, and ordered him to move up past the alley to the street corner and at least open up with his machine guns: The tank commander, repeating what the Delta platoon commander said, refused to budge. Charlie One's left flank was totally exposed, and it looked like it was going to stay that way.

Running back across the street into the alley, I called Scott Nelson and reported this news. He said he would check it out with battalion and get back to me, and in the meantime, we were to get ready to attack.

After only a couple of minutes, Nelson called me back, forcefully letting me know that I must be mistaken, because the Delta Company platoon commander had assured battalion that he was in the correct position, right on the north side of phase line green. Another frantic request to provide artillery or air support was immediately rejected by Nelson. We were on our own, and we were to attack again within the next ten minutes.

Our second attack involved selecting one squad-the right-most squad (the furthest from our left flank)—to be the assault force, with the remaining two squads setting up covering fire. As ordered, the Marines from Charlie One Charlie, the right-flank squad, attacked across the street, but they were again forced back by a ferocious concentration of enemy fire. The results were predictable: more wounded and yet another dead Marine down in the street.

Benny and I found ourselves back in the corner courtyard after the second assault, trying to assess the damage. Doc English was still there in the courtyard, working frantically on two more wounded Marines who had been hit in the second assault. Doc told me about the Marine down in the street; he could see him through the knocked-down gate from his position, which provided some security from the enemy fire because of the angles, and he knew that this Marine was dead. There were now, by my best count, five dead Charlie One Marines in the street; two more dead, including Estes, who had been evacuated; and many, many wounded. Our fighting strength had been cut in half, and we hadn't been able to budge the enemy an inch.

At this point, as I pleaded yet again with Scott Nelson that our left flank was exposed and that we needed artillery and air support or at least let the goddamned tanks start firing their cannons, SSgt. Robert H. Odum came running into the small corner courtyard from across the street that separated our platoons. He was the platoon sergeant for Charlie Three, the Charlie Company platoon that was assigned the next block on our right flank and that was taking heavy enemy fire from its immediate front. His platoon, however, had yet to be ordered to attack and had not had any Marines knocked down in an exposed position in the street. He was obviously pissed, and although he handled the situation with respect for my rank and the chain of command drilled into all Marines throughout their careers, he was obviously upset with me, that a Marine platoon commander could allow one of his men to stay out in the street without some attempts being made to recover his body.

"Lieutenant, one of your men is down in the street, right out in front of that tank. Maybe you weren't aware, sir?" Sergeant Odum's voice barely covered the sarcasm that was obviously intended to urge me to action.

I replied, "I am well aware of that, Sergeant Odum, and while I appreciate your efforts at running over here to inform me of this fact, I'd appreciate it if you would go back to your men."

Sergeant Odum said, "Sir, with all due respect, we must try to get that man back out of the street" Sergeant Odum was a very good staff NCO, well liked by his platoon commander and his men alike, and he was going to persist.

Rather testily now, I said, "Sergeant Odum, that man is dead. Doc English saw him get hit. He took at least one hit in the head, and he's been shot several times since. He's dead. I've lost several other Marines attempting to get their buddies out of the street, and while I appreciate your concern for that Marine and for the Marine Corps' traditions, I will not lose another Marine trying to get dead bodies out of the street. If I had any hope that he was still alive, which he is not, I'd be making the effort to get him right now without your help. Now, go back to your platoon."

Sergeant Odum looked me right in the eye, started taking his pack off, and said, "Well, Lieutenant, if you won't make an effort, I will. If it's not too much trouble, sir, have your men give me some covering fire."

No more words were spoken. He was determined, and there was no way that I was going to stop him. The few remaining Marines from Charlie One Charlie didn't have to be told to start shooting at the enemy positions across the street. Sergeant Odum tightened up his helmet's chin strap, made sure his flak jacket was buttoned all the way to the top, set his M-16 aside temporarily, took out his .45-caliber pistol, pulled back the slide, and seated a round in the chamber. His plan was to go back to the alley and crawl back forward behind the M-48 tank sitting just on the other side of the courtyard wall. Then he would crawl between the tank and the wall, until he got to the street. When he finally got into this position, he would leave his position of cover, rush to the downed Marine, and drag him out of the street in between the wall and the tank.

The Marines in the courtyard increased their covering fire, and Sergeant Odum crawled forward.

I couldn't directly see what happened to Sergeant Odum out in the street, but Doc English could, and since I had a clear view of Doc English's face, I could watch the events in the street by watching the changing expressions on Doc English's face. Doc English saw, from his barely protected position as he worked frantically on a wounded Marine, everything that happened in graphic detail. He could not avoid watching what happened to Sergeant Odum, and I could see it all very clearly, reflected on Doc English's face. When Sergeant Odum made his move, the enemy gunners, no more than fifty feet away from him, saw him immediately and opened up. Doc English's face was already filled with anguish at everything going on all around him-the wounded man in his lap, the dead man in the street, and the heroic and very dangerous effort Sergeant Odum had decided to make to recover the dead Marine. Then the expression on Doc English's face got worse; for a moment his face looked like death itself. I am absolutely positive that this one second in Doc English's life will remain with him forever; the look on his face will remain seared into my brain forever. Sergeant Odum was shot in the face, his lower jaw blown off by an AK-47 round.

I thought from the look on Doc English's face that Sergeant Odum was dead, but he was not. Sergeant Odum did realize then that he would not be able to save the poor dead Marine in the street, though, and he had the presence of mind or enough life-preserving instincts to abandon the dead Marine and crawl back behind the tank and back into the courtyard.

Sergeant Odum couldn't say anything. He tried, looking me right in the eye, but I had no way of knowing if he was saying that I had been right or if he was calling me a cowardly asshole. The AK-47 round had entered his face just below his left eye and had exited his face below his chin. Everything below his upper lip had been blown into mushy strips of flesh and blood. There was no mouth; there were no teeth. There were just shreds of bloody skin.

Sergeant Odum stood up, carefully holstered his pistol, and pulled out a canteen from his utility belt pouch. He calmly poured the contents of his canteen over his shattered lower face, as if he believed that he could simply wash out this nightmare as he would wash out a badly done watercolor portrait and then attempt to paint his lower jaw back in. Doc English quickly finished his bandaging efforts on the other wounded Marine that he had been working on, broke out several more bandages from his medical kit, and crawled across the gate's opening to assist Sergeant Odum. There wasn't much he could do for him except apply the bandages and hope the bleeding would slow down long enough to get him safely medevacced. Without my needing to speak a word, Doc English knew that I wanted him to help Sergeant Odum get to the rear. Sergeant Odum resisted all attempts to have him lie down on a poncho stretcher, however, and the last time I saw him he was walking under his own power, with Doc English and a small entourage of Charlie One Charlie Marines carrying the other wounded men back to the battalion rear for medevac. That was the last time, with one notable exception, that Charlie Company made any attempts to recover dead Marines from an exposed position in a street during the battle for Hue. There were many heroic efforts made to help wounded men while they were still alive, but after Sergeant Odum walked away from phase line green, all recovery efforts for the dead were made after darkness provided at least the illusion of cover. The only other time that an obviously dead Marine was recovered from the street in daylight hours took place several days later, and it was under highly unusual circumstances. But that story will wait.

As harsh as it sounded, and although it was very contrary to Marine Corps tradition, I gave direct orders to the rest of Charlie One that no further attempts would be made to get any dead Marines out of the street. We would do whatever we could to help save wounded men in exposed positions, but we would take no further risks by trying to retrieve dead bodies during daylight hours. After my brief and unhappy debate with Sergeant Odum on the subject, there were no further arguments.

One more attempt was made to assault across phase line green in the waning hours of that miserable afternoon. Scott Nelson and Major Thompson still did not believe that our left flank was exposed, and they resisted all pleas to provide heavy firepower. The powers that be had established the rules of engagement, and we would go forward across phase line green using the limited firepower of our small-arms weapons, or we would die. And, so, Charlie One died.

Our third attempt to assault across phase line green resulted in getting two Marines completely across the street, but it also resulted in several more wounded and two more KIAs. The two Marines who made it across the street were immediately pinned down behind two separate, low walls. They had made it across the street, but both of them were totally pinned down, unable to move right or left without dying. One of these men, an E-5 sergeant named Bossert, who had taken over as Charlie One's platoon sergeant after we lost Sergeant Mullan, had a PRC-6 radio with him. Since he was out in the street and we had good line of sight from the roof of the house that Estes had died in, we could talk with him. He didn't want to talk above a whisper, because he could hear the NVA talking very close by, and he was afraid that if they knew he was across the street and still alive, they'd find him and blow him away. He could communicate, by hand signals, with the other Marine who had made it across further down the street. Sergeant Bossert was able to tell him to hold on until after dark and then run back across the street to our side when he thought it was safe.

Benny and I had climbed up on the roof of the two-story house along with a couple more Marines from Charlie One Alpha before the third assault, but we couldn't stay on the roof very long before several NVA gunners spotted us and started pouring small-arms fire in our direction. After we had lobbed some M-79 grenades from the blooper, they had quickly figured out where we were and we had to get back down off the roof post haste.

Returning to our right flank once again for the umpteenth time that day, I crawled out behind the M-48 tank that had sat on the corner all afternoon long without once firing its cannon and got the tank commander on the phone. In as demented and angry a voice as I could muster, I told him that if he didn't start shooting his cannon at the enemy across the street, I would blow his tank up with a satchel charge. Either I wasn't very convincing, or he just didn't give a shit. He repeated that his orders were not to fire the cannon, but his machine guns did start shooting faster than they had up to that point.

I finally convinced Scott Nelson that there was no way that we could effectively assault an entrenched enemy across that street without heavy support, and that our left flank was exposed to boot. A few minutes later, he showed up in the corner courtyard.

Without speaking, I led him down the alley to our exposed left flank, and pointed out Delta Company's positions, half a block behind phase line green. He finally agreed that our left flank was exposed. As we moved back down the alley, we made contact with each squad, and by the time we got back to the corner courtyard, our head count was down to twenty-three Marines still able to fight. Eight Charlie One Marines had died that day, 13 February 1968, and twenty more had been seriously wounded and had to be medevacced.

As we huddled in that shattered courtyard, I think Scott Nelson was just starting to believe me, and he started to get just a little pissed off at Major Thompson. He got on his Prick-25, gave a terse report, and after a long wait, he was told to move back away from phase line green after we had recovered the two live Marines who had made it across the street and our dead bodies in the street and to take up defensive positions in the houses on the north side of the alley. The decision had been made to replace Charlie One with Alpha Company (complete with a newly assigned company commander) the next morning, so that they could execute the attack orders that we had not been able to carry out.

Late that night, after we had recovered our lost Marines under the cover of darkness and after I had made sure that both our flanks were secure and our defensive positions were well prepared to repel any counterattack or any attempt to sneak through our lines, I told Benny to wake me for the early morning radio watch. I found a dry bed in a corner of a small house, crawled under the mosquito netting, and dropped immediately into the sleep of the damned.

NOTES:

The following Marines were killed in Hue that day:
Couto, Jimmy M. LCpl. 2249377; 23; North Reading, Massachusetts
Craspe, Wayne F. Pfc. 2236831; 18; Brunson, South Carolina
Estes, Edward S. LCpl. 2329731; C-1-5; 23; Dallas, Texas
Harris, Eddie C. Pfc. 2384306; 18; Lufkin, Texas
Langrock, Dennis R. Pfc. 2327902; C-1-5; 19; Sacramento, California
Lopez, Perfecto N. LCpl. 2360891; B-1-5; 20; Peoria, Arizona
Morgan, Charles R. Pfc. 2252099; C-1-5; 19; Rayville, Louisiana
Mounts, Jerry D. Pfc. 2377637; C-1-5; 19; Wichita, Kansas
Nelson, Robert J. LCpl. 2290632; 21; Lynn, Massachusetts
Schuett, Jerome A. Pvt. 2351498; 19; Reedsburg, Wisconsin
Shields, Ronald W. LCpl. 2257649; 18; A-1-5; Enid, Oklahoma

The Silver Star was awarded to Cpl. Lawrence E. Desmond, LCpl. Edward S. Estes and Pfc. Joseph P. Lopez for their actions on this day.

Many years later John Mullan was awarded the Bronze Star.

Other Marines mentioned in the chapter were as follows:
Bossert, Robert R. Sgt.
Gibson, Emmett E. LCpl. 2390862;
Mullan, John A. SSgt. 1659026; 27; Detroit, Michigan
Nelson, Scott A. 1stLt. 095393;
Odum, Robert H. SSgt. 1906638
Wilbourne, Frank R. 1stLt. 095155;

In the following paragraph, Nicholas Warr shares his feelings about John Mullan:

I can't begin to tell you how I felt when I saw the pictures of John Mullan. As you may know, we all thought that he had been killed when he got hit in Hue. We heard several weeks later that he had survived, when we received a short letter from him in a very shaky hand. Understandable, under the circumstances. It does my heart good to see that he is alive and well, and living in Mesa, Arizona. Thank you so much for sending your copy of the book to John. I hope he likes it, and I hope he can read between the lines to discover how very much he meant to all of us. As a green-behind-the-ears 2nd Lieutenant, new in country, and scared to death that I would do something stupid which would result in death or injury to a member of my platoon, I can remember with great clarity the relief I felt when John agreed to quietly "train" me in the realities of combat, Vietnam-style, for those first few weeks. I know that it made a great difference, both to me and to the men. I can still see his flashing smile, his bellowed "Good Morning, Vietnam," which happened like clockwork at first light of every morning in late '67 and early '68. I can still remember how devastated I was at his loss. It will be the most important thing that happens as a direct result of the book, when I see him again, shake his hand, and thank him for his help and his contribution to the Marines of Charlie One. I will be writing to him next.

Sgt. Ronald T. Curley   Capt. George R. Christmas
F-2-26 Navy Cross 5/16/67   H-2-5 Navy Cross 2/5/68

*　*　*　*

On February 12, 1968 General William Westmoreland, the Commander of U.S. forces in Vietnam, sent in an emergency request for 10,500 additional troops to be sent to Vietnam. This request was quickly approved.

The 27th Marine Regiment was one of the military units selected to help make up this augmentation.

The 3rd Battalion, 27th Marine Regiment that was located at Camp Pendleton, California was woefully undermanned. In order to bring the Battalion up to strength every available Marine at Camp Pendleton was taken. A majority of its men were not even infantrymen. A variety of MOS's made up the ranks. There were cooks, bakers and candlestick makers with, here and there, an occasional rifleman.

The old Marine Corps axiom "Every Marine A Rifleman," came into play. The Marines of 3/27 were jokingly referred to as the Bastard Battalion.

Without any practical combat training, 3/27 was sent to Vietnam.

Upon arrival on February 18, the Battalion immediately began combat patrols.

One of these Marines was Cpl. Bob Simonsen 2297603, 20, from Santa Monica, California. He had been a construction surveyor with the 13th Engineers at Pendleton and volunteered to join 3/27. Years later, he would write a fine oral history of this Battalion and its activities in Vietnam. Not yet published, it is entitled *Every Marine: An Oral History of A Marine Battalion in 1968 Vietnam.*

Pfc. Dale Camp 2344304, 19, from Enid, Oklahoma had been assigned as an automobile mechanic to H&S Co., 5th Tanks before being ordered to join 3/27. Upon his arrival, he was then assigned as a rifleman to Company I.

Operation Allen Brook began on May 4 and was originally under control of 2/7.

As heavy fighting continued, 3/27 was notified that it would participate in this Operation and join the assault on the NVA staging area on Go Noi Island.

On May 13, 3/27 joined the fight.

The following excerpt is taken from *Every Marine.* It is reprinted with written permission from Robert Simonsen and commentator Dale Camp. We now join Camp on May 16 as he describes the action.

"Gunny, get this green Marine Corps shit off of me."
Cpl. Melvin (Mud Flap) Cox
I-3-27

16
THE WORST DAY OF MY LIFE

We marched onto the Island under cover of darkness. Later in the morning, the column began taking fire. Our columns were spread out and we couldn't tell if the bullets flying by were from Marines or the enemy.

First platoon with Lt Thompson, his radioman Cpl Jan Mitscher and SSgt Shelby Monk moved forward with 1st squad in the lead. We moved into a tree line and found several new fighting holes. One still had a small e-tool in it. These holes had square corners and sides that were straight up and down with perfectly smooth sides. Very different from ours. Because of the e-tool and a camo hat lying there, we got the impression that the NVA had just gotten up and ran.

We all got into a trench line facing an open area with a small house in the middle. An NVA in full uniform with a rifle walked out of the house and was going to our left across the field.

We all jumped up to shoot, but SSgt. Monk said, "I'll do it."

Monk shot and critically wounded the NVA.

Immediately after this, we were ordered to assault the opposite tree line.

First Platoon, Co I, under 1stLt. Stephen B. Thompson then probably made the smartest move of the day. Although no enemy could be seen, they began sweeping on line and firing into the approaching tree lines. The hidden NVA, not knowing that they hadn't been observed, started returning fire.

We were all firing as we crossed the open area. As we moved into the tree line we were firing forward of us but couldn't tell if we were taking incoming.

At one point Pfc. Vincent S. Coles and I were taking cover next to the remnant of a brick wall. We were being hit in the face with little sand grains or something. I remember looking at Coles and asking what was happening. He didn't know either.

All at once, we noticed that bullets were hitting the bricks, inches from me and we were being splattered with pieces of brick. This was when we first knew we were taking incoming.

We got the hell out of there and moved forward to an NVA bunker. We took cover behind the bunker, a mound of earth 3 feet tall and 6 feet wide, and began firing. The NVA were only 50 feet or so in front of us, in bunkers, trenches and bomb craters.

As Coles rose up to fire over the top of the bunker, he was shot once in the center of his chest and died immediately.

Coles was a good friend who kept me laughing and tormented me with his descriptions of food dishes he learned to prepare in school.

As I resumed firing, I noticed dirt popping up from an NVA muzzle blast. I could not see the soldier firing. There was what looked like a small sign, shaped like a 'T' in front of his position. I just kept firing at that area until I hit him. I hit him in the neck and his head just fell forward. Until then I had not seen him. I remember thinking when I saw him fall that it looked just like the movies.

My next thought was that I was getting very weird.

Very soon after this I heard shouting to my left. Guys were yelling for a new Private to get down. He was standing up behind a banana tree, firing away. They didn't tell him at ITR (Infantry Training Regiment) that a banana tree wouldn't stop a bullet. We finally got his attention and he hit the deck. We were actually laughing at him. What a strange place to find yourself laughing.

I think right after that was when Cpl. Bob Simonsen was shot. I looked to my left just as the bullet hit his head. It threw him backward through the air and he landed in a heap. This was my second good friend to die in the last few minutes and I just couldn't believe they were gone.

We kept on fighting. Lt. Thompson urged us forward. Marines were running from bunker to bunker, throwing grenades along the way.

An enemy grenade went off within 10 feet of me, but I wasn't hit.

I was behind a bunker reloading the magazines for my M-14. I had fired more than 100 rounds on single fire and only had one full magazine left.

The FO with me was on his third M-16 because of malfunctions. Lt. Thompson was yelling for us to move up, but the only place to move up to was the NVA bunkers. We weren't going anywhere.

Pfc. Juan "Speedy" Gonzalez jumped up and ran forward to a bunker. The FO started firing, but his M-16 had a malfunction. He grabbed my M-14 and continued firing. He said that an NVA on top of the bunker had shot Speedy.

I wrestled my weapon away from the FO just in time to draw a bead on an NVA as he ran from behind the bunker.

Just as I was about to fire, the FO yelled. "Don't fire, that's Speedy."

I hesitated because the NVA did kind of look like Speedy. He had black hair, a green uniform, cartridge belt and rifle. When he came out of his Ho Chi Minh sandals, I started firing. I don't know if I hit him or not.

While others covered us Mitch, another guy and I ran up to get Speedy. He was shot up pretty bad. Mitch and the other grunt dropped their gear and picked up Speedy.

They ran back with him to one of our bunkers. I grabbed all the gear and ran back to the same bunker. We were getting shot at the whole time.

We had killed or run off all the NVA in the bunker complex and had advanced 100 yards or so.

While searching a bamboo grove on our right flank, I discovered a pack with uniforms, sandals, medicine, etc. One of the guys gave me the AK-47 of the man I had killed. It was covered with his blood.

I think it was Pvt. Hinden who passed out NVA cigarette lighters that he had taken off their dead. During this time some of us were holed up in a pagoda that was to the front of the bunker complex.

When we moved back, I found Sgt. Deleon and showed him the pack and rifle. He thought we had done great. He was just going on and on about how well we fought. I asked Deleon of our dead, and he told me that Simonsen was alive. You could have knocked me over with a feather.

I found Bob lying down with bandages on his head. As soon as I got over to him, Bob told me to go get his helmet. I found it and was amazed to see an entry hole, dead center in front, and a big exit hole in the rear.

When Bob and I were looking at it we saw that for some reason the bullet went around the inside, between the liner and the steel pot. Bob was the luckiest guy I ever knew.

17 MAY

We moved out early with India on point. Just before dawn we were moving down a trail with trees and jungle on each side.

Up ahead we began to hear and smell the sounds of morning. Pots and pans were rattling, people were talking, cooking fires were smoking. I smelled Vietnamese tobacco. A young woman laughed.

All hell broke loose as fire erupted ahead of us. We hit the deck and looked for targets, but saw nothing.

Up ahead there was a pretty good firefight going on. Bullets zipping by kept us down. To our left we heard the mortars fire. We waited and listened.

Soon the mortars whistled down on top of us. We were somewhat protected by the depression of the trail, but their mortars walked down the trail.

I heard the Marines ahead of me cry out as they were hit.

For one of the few times in Nam, I prayed for God to protect me.

The mortar attack ended abruptly.

First squad had 2 or 3 walking wounded and so did other squads. First squad was assigned to take them back to an LZ for evacuation. My squad was down to 4 with Cpl Massey (Tex) as squad leader.

The rest of the company moved on.

We delivered the wounded and turned back to catch up.

By now in the operation I think I was starting to loose my nerve a little. I asked Cpl Massey how we could get back to the company because we had to go back through the scene of the firefight. He yelled at me to shut up and get going.

Just as we caught up with tail end Charlie, the point was ambushed. There was a tremendous amount of shooting and explosions up there. It was terrifying.

Massey said we must catch up with our platoon. We ran all the way across the huge open field that sloped down to the ambush site at the river. We passed Golf-2-7 and some of India and made it to the riverbank.

The incoming was tearing the place up. Bullets were hitting all around us and cutting down the tall grass. We were laying in some tank tracks. There was no cover at all. The bodies of the dead and wounded were lying all over.

Hospital Corpsman, Mike Lutz, was with us. He saw a wounded Marine down in the dry riverbed and told Massey that we had to get him out of there.

Massey said, "Come on Camp".

Lutz, Massey, Ciezki, and I ran down the tank tracks to the river. Dead Marines were lying along the tracks as we ran and they reminded me of photos of Marine dead lying on the beaches of WWII. How could my mind think of that with so much going on around me?

Lutz was yelling for us to get the guy up and make him run. We didn't stop running ourselves as we swooped him up and ran for the safety of the opposite river bank.

With only 20 feet or so to go we all fell.

That was it for me. I only had one thought and that was to get out of that river. I will always live with the guilt of leaving my squad and crawling for my life. Bullets hit all around me as I crawled like a madman.

When I reached the shelter of the bank I heard Lutz yelling for me. He was still a little ways out in the river and was wounded. I ran to him and grabbed his arm, where blood was shooting 6 feet in the air. I wanted to put pressure on this arterial bleeder as we had been taught.

Lutz was so cool. He told me to get his unit one and apply pressure bandages to the wounds. The bullet hit him behind the left thumb, on his wrist and traveled through his forearm and blew out his elbow. He was bleeding from 3 arteries. I used one bandage after another and they all became soaked with blood.

I asked Lutz if we should use a tourniquet because I was afraid he would bleed to death. He told me no because he knew if we did, he would lose his arm. I questioned his reasoning but he told me he knew what he was doing.

About this time grunts down to our left started yelling for a Corpsman. Since I had the Unit One I ran down to see if I could help. It was my friend Robert Burke. He had 4 or 5 bullet holes in his chest and was already dead. We all know the story of his bravery. I believe that many of us would not have made it across the river without his help. He died so we could live.

When I got back to Lutz, he was really hurting. He told me to reach in his pocket and get the morphine he kept there. I gave it to him in his left shoulder, and in a while he felt a little better.

Of the four of us who ran into the river after the wounded guy two were hit, Lutz and Massey. The wounded guy was hit again but survived.

Ironically, Massey was also hit in the wrist but not as bad as Lutz. When I gave him morphine for his pain he laid a guilt trip on me that has lasted all these years. I guess he was mad about me not helping him out of the river, cause he told me to quit looking out for myself and to start looking out for others. I still feel like I let him down even though he and I didn't like each other. He was making the hard decisions that I was afraid to.

The battle raged on around us. The NVA behind us were pouring fire across the river into India and Golf. The sniper on our right flank was hitting one grunt after another. Men were screaming, crying, begging for help, and asking for their mothers.

And, we who were safe behind the riverbank felt helpless. Our leadership gone, we just didn't know what to do. We talked about what to do but no one seemed to know the answer. All I really knew was, I wanted to survive this.

Artillery screamed into the NVA bunkers behind us but didn't seem to slow them down. Marine jets showed up and we laid out colored panels on the bank above us. We lay against the bank as they started their dives. They looked like they were coming down at us. The NVA fired up at them as they came down and quit just before the jets dropped their loads. When those bombs went off 100 feet behind us the earth rolled under us like waves on the ocean. They made run after run to no avail. The snipers continued to kill Marines.

All our water was given to the wounded and now the incredible heat was trying to kill us.

A Marine across the river just stood up and started walking away. We all yelled at him to get down but he was crazed by dehydration and heat and just walked away.

Our friend 'Senator Mudflap' from Joplin, Missouri had been laying in the riverbed all day and everyone thought he was dead. He started yelling at us, telling us that he was going to run to us and to cover him. We were very afraid that he would be killed and we told him to stay put. He moved a little and the sniper shot him in the ass. 'Senator Mudflap' quit moving.

I had sat next to Lutz all day, talking to him and checking his bandages. I had 13 pressure bandages on his arm and the bleeding had stopped. My clothes and his were soaked in blood and the smell of blood that day stays in my memory. We had all run out of water and I started to get delirious. I realized that I was crying. I remember thinking that I shouldn't be crying cause I was a Marine, but I couldn't stop. Some one threw water in my face and I snapped out of it. They gave me a drink and I came back to my senses.

Some of the guys were getting water from a dirty, little pond on our right flank. Grunts would fire into the trees and where we thought the sniper was and others would run out and get water in their helmets. It saved our lives. Many trips were made to the pond as we fired cover fire.

Phillip Miller our 1st squad radioman tried to get water without cover fire and was shot by the sniper. We got him back to the bank but he was shot through the right lung and died a short while later.

Many of the men on my side of the river were wounded but one stands out because of his special wound. He had been shot in the balls and the bag looked like a surgeon had opened it. The testicles were untouched. We rigged a shade over him and every time someone went by he asked them to look and see if his balls were going to be all right. In typical grunt black humor we thought this was somewhat funny.

Only one person came across the river to us during the day. He was a young officer who was the FO. He ran across and asked for water. He never said another thing all day and we all knew that he had gone over the edge from the horror of that side of the river.

The hot, tragic day drug on.

The other companies from 3-27 were dropped behind the NVA bunker complex and started moving toward us. We could hear the battle raging.

This action flushed out some NVA doctors and nurses who tried to escape by crossing up river from us. They ran into the dry riverbed still wearing their white gowns and we all jumped up and tried to kill them. They ran back the way they came.

Firing in our area had slowed down and the sniper had been killed by fire from the grassy field.

Darkness was coming.

With darkness we prepared to cross back over the river. Although we were in the safest place on the battlefield, we felt cut off from our company, and felt a strong need to get back to them. We picked up our wounded and started to the other side. Lutz, who was pretty high on morphine, wanted to walk by himself. He passed out when he stood up and another grunt and I carried him across.

Bodies' lay everywhere. Some were already lined up under ponchos.

I found Lt. Stephen Thompson who was the only India Company officer left alive. He grabbed me and told me that he had been told early in the day that I was dead. It was great to see him.

We added our dead to the line. The wounded were medevaced. I looked for the only other member of my squad and found out that he had broken his leg carrying wounded back from across the river.

I was the only one left from 1st squad. I dug a shallow hole, crawled in and went to sleep.

The worst day of my life had ended.

NOTES:

Among the Marines mentioned in this chapter were:
Ciezki, Allen W. LCpl. 2366194, Milwaukee, Wisconsin
Cox, Melvin R. Pfc. 2114892; Joplin, Missouri
DeLeon, Domingo Sgt. 2110363, Texas
Gonzales, Juan Pfc. 2256442, Texas
Hinden, Carleton Pvt. 2327447
Lutz, Michael HM, 19, Hatboro, Pennsylvania
Massey, Gary L. Cpl. 2211046, Texas
Mitscher, Jan E. Cpl. 2142113
Monk, Shelby E. SSgt. 1432857, 31, Escondido, California
Thompson, Stephen B. 1stLt. 0101540, Gary, Indiana

Eighteen-year-old Robert C. Burke of Monticello, Illinois was posthumously awarded the Medal of Honor for his actions on May 17. When others were hesitant to move he set an example by calmly moving from position to position and maintaining a steady volume of fire until he was killed. He was the youngest person to receive this medal in the Vietnam War.

On Operation Allen Brook the Navy Cross was awarded to LCpl. Richard W. Buchanan and Pfc. Charles R. Yordy of 3-27.

The Silver Star Medal was earned by 1stLt. Joseph H. Belser, Jr., Pfc. Burton K. Bower, Sgt. John T. Burton, Pfc. Vincent N. Chiofiolo, Cpl. John E. Hazelwood, Cpl. Marlin W. Jackson, Pfc. Herbert A. Jester, LCpl.

Gary W. Much, Cpl. Hiahwhanah R. Neal, Pfc. Thomas E. Sharpe, Cpl. Michael D. Stoppa, LCpl. Thomas R. Thuesen, Sgt. Charles J. Whyte and LtCol. Tullis J. Woodham. The awards to Burton, Hazelwood, Sharpe and Whyte were posthumous.

The following Marines from 3-27 were killed on Go Noi Island on May 16, 1968:
Coles, Vincent S. Pfc. 2355251; I-3-27; 18; Newark, New Jersey
Henderson, Jack Jr. Pfc. 2381508; I-3-27; 18; Chicago, Illinois

The following Marines from 3-27 were killed in the heavy fighting that occurred on May 17,1968:
Bauer, Robert L. Pfc. 2420225; I-3-27; 25; Port Huron, Michigan
Bills, Lyle P. Pfc. 2334520; I-3-27; 19; Council Bluffs, Iowa
Blalock, Gherald E. Pfc. 2384261; K-3-27; 19; Houston, Texas
Burke, Robert C. Pfc. 2359360; I-3-27; 18; Monticello, Illinois
Crook, Thomas H. Pvt. 2067712; I-3-27; 22; Kansas City, Missouri
Gibson, John A. LCpl. 2129828; I-3-27; 20; Chicago, Illinois
Gorton, Jack B. Sgt. 2118132; L-3-27; 21; Culver City, California
Green, Allen R. LCpl. 2273738; I-3-27; 18; Hanley Hills, Missouri
Hawkins, Albert W. Pfc. 2342534; I-3-27; 27; Columbus, Ohio
Himes, Bernard M. LCpl. 2337456; I-3-27; 18; Anita, Pennsylvania
Jones, Bennie R. Pvt. 2306552; I-3-27; 19; Jackson, Tennessee
Lee, Nate F. Sgt. 1613109; I-3-27; 29; Hazelton, Pennsylvania
Metzker, Franklin H. Pvt. 2387884; K-3-27; 20; Hillside, Maryland
Miller, Philip D. Pfc. 2287410; I-3-27; 18; Grand Junction, Colorado
Schettl, David L. LCpl. 2285861; I-3-27; 21; Manitowoc, Wisconsin
Schweig, Victor J. Pvt. 2415675; I-3-27; 18; Chicago, Illinois
Thomas, George Jr. Pfc. 2406478; K-3-27; 20; Cincinnati, Ohio
Turner, Richard Cpl. 2155965; I-3-27; 23; Washington, D.C.
Tyler, Sylvester G. Pfc. 2417114; I-3-27; 19; Washington, D.C.
Walker, Gary L. Pvt. 2376553; K-3-27; 21; Cudahy, California
West, Larry J. LCpl. 2269654; I-3-27; 19; Morenci, Arizona
White, Jack L. Cpl. 2220022; I-3-27; 23; Tacoma, Washington

Restlessness, a disinterest in college and a desire for independence led Ronald Winter to join to join the Marine Corps in January of 1966. Everything he did after high school graduation turned him in the direction of the Corps and eventually to Vietnam. The war was just heating up back then, yet Winter felt that he was destined to be there.

In August of 1968 Winter was a member of Marine Medium Helicopter 161 (HMM-161) commanded by Lieutenant Colonel Paul W. Niesen. He joined this squadron in 1966 and remained with it through most of his thirteen month tour in Vietnam. Aside for a couple of weeks with HMM-364 the remainder of his tour was with HMM-164.

Trained as a helicopter electrician Winter flew three hundred missions as an aerial gunner and earned many distinguished service decorations. They include fifteen Air Medals, Combat Air Crew Wings and the Vietnamese Cross of Gallantry.

In the following excerpt taken from *Masters of the Art*, Winter's fine memoir of his time in the Corps, he gives a vivid description of a helicopter door gunner. It is thorough, complete and enthralling.

"When things are so bad that they're too tough for everyone else,
I smile, because then they're just right for me."

Sgt. Robert F. Starbuck
Drill Instructor
Platoon 214
Parris Island, South Carolina
Winter 1966

Grateful acknowledgement is made to Ronald Winter for permission to reprint material previously published by Carlton Press, Inc. of New York. The following excerpt is taken from *Masters of the Art: A Marine's Memoir of Parris Island and Vietnam* © 1989 by Ronald Winter by permission of Ronald Winter.

17
DOOR GUNNER

"Fire in the zone! We're taking hits!"

I heard the message crackle over the headset in my helmet, and tried to see where the shots were coming from. I was the starboard gunner on the third aircraft in a flight of four. We were making the initial assault, and we were the first wave. Three more flights of four helicopters each were behind us and each of the helicopters carried a squad of infantrymen from the fourth Marine regiment.

It was August 1968 and we were over rolling, heavily grassed and jungled terrain, south of Khe Sanh and just east of the Laotian border. The LZ was a grassy knoll, with heavy tree lines and ravines to the north. We were coming in from the east and that meant the fire was on my side!

I had been locked and loaded since we had cleared the concertina wire back at Quang Tri that morning, and now it was just a matter of finding out where the Vietnamese were, and firing back before we started getting hit.

"We've got muzzle flashes. In a gully fifty meters north of the zone."

At least now we knew where to look for them.

Another message from the lead bird said more muzzle flashes had been seen coming from a hill about two hundred yards away.

I leaned out the window, got a glimpse of the area ahead, and swung my .50-caliber as far ahead as it would go. The machine guns were mounted on swivels, which were bolted into the side of the helicopter. They had mechanical stops to limit movement forward and back, up and down. We had excellent mobility as it was, but the stops were there for a purpose, If the gun was swung too far forward the bullets would be going right through the pilot's head, too far back or downward, and the external fuel cells would be ruptured. If the gun was pointed too high it could chop off sections of the rotor blades.

We were coming in low and extremely fast, somewhere above sixty knots, to avoid as much fire as possible, so all of this was happening quickly. I glimpsed the area the lead bird had warned of, and as soon as it came into my line of fire I opened up. Three rounds, four rounds, three rounds, again four. I kept up the bursts, slamming the heavy bullets into any likely spots I could see.

I kept waiting for the by-now familiar bwaaang, the sharp metallic sound you hear when their bullets start finding their target. As our tour had progressed, many crews had encountered small-arms fire, machine-gun fire and occasional shots from .37mm anti-aircraft guns. When the North Vietnamese found their mark, the bullets slammed through the metal skin of our aircraft with extreme force, bwaaang! bwaaang! They filled the inside with shrapnel and played havoc with people and flight systems.

As we closed on the Vietnamese positions, I upped my rate of fire to five rounds, six, seven, eight rounds to a burst. It was getting more frantic with each second.

So far no one had been injured. The enemy bullets were going too high and passing harmlessly by. But it was a donnybrook and a half! Out of the corner of my eye I saw J.D. Cross, the crew chief, shooting out of the starboard hatchway with his M-14 rifle on full automatic. Cross was shorter, and weighed even less than I, and the recoil from his rifle kept knocking him backward several steps. But each time he'd recover and come right back firing again. He had full magazines taped together in twos, each upside down from the other, so when one ran out he could eject it, turn it upside down and insert the other. It kept reloading time to a minimum.

Speaking of which, I had run out of the 50 rounds in the ammo box strapped to the side of my machine gun and had to reload, immediately! I flipped up the cover over the .50's chamber, threw the empty ammo box to the side and grabbed for another. A grunt sitting next to my gun, looking helpless and scared half to death, jumped up to help me reload. He yanked the top off the box, passed it to me in one swift motion, I reloaded and resumed firing.

As brave as they were, a lot of grunts hated being in those helicopters when we started taking hits because they generally couldn't fire back and there was no place to go for cover. I always felt safer inside than outside, but being more familiar with ground activities they felt just the opposite. I imagine the guy helping me was just happy to have something to do until he could get the hell out of there.

Eight rounds. Nine rounds. I was putting out longer bursts. Aircraft further back reported taking hits, and they were opening up too.

Still, no one in our bird was hit, but my adrenalin was flowing, and I felt as if all my senses were on overdrive, keyed to pinpoint responsiveness. I placed the thumb of my right hand over the butterfly trigger, wrapped my fingers around the handle near the trigger, on the rear of the .50, said "Fuck this" and leaned right out the window.

Partly I was doing it for a better view, but I also did it because I didn't want to succumb to fear. So in reaction, I went nuts. I screamed at the Vietnamese out there, wherever they were.

"You want a piece of this shit, motherfucker? Come on! Here it is cocksuckers, take a shot!"

All the time I kept firing, watching the tracers, yelling, swearing, even spitting at someone whom I couldn't see, but who was trying to kill me!

And suddenly I felt the flare of the rotor blades as we settled into the LZ. I saw other grunts on the ground forming defensive positions. Our ramp went down, the squad headed out and the grunt who'd helped me reload made a beeline for the ground, his idea of safety. At the end of the ramp he stood for a split second, shot me back a 'thumbs up' and headed out to do battle. The whole engagement had lasted only about a minute. But it was a minute of total insanity, which is what war is anyway.

I never planned to act the way I did, but when the shooting started, something came over me and I acted on instinct. If you had asked me back then if I was ever scared in battle, I honestly could have answered 'No!' Because whether I knew it was coming or it just happened, my reaction was always the same. I felt the only way to survive was to use the adrenalin flowing in my blood to go far, far beyond fear.

"Staying on the offensive is 90 percent of winning a fight," Starbuck had told us. If it was crazy, fine! At least it kept you alive.

Combat isn't a quiet chess game or a gentlemanly sports match. The punishment for losing is death. I had no intention of dying, and none of the others in the squadron acted as though they were opting for suicide either. Sometimes you just had to push yourself to a point of insanity. You could go outwardly crazy, or appear calm as hell. But inside you were boiling, and if you could channel that energy to direct and accurate action, you had much better chances for survival.

We'd only been in Vietnam for three months in August, but I already was closing in on 100 missions. Many of the crew chiefs, including Doug Braman and Al Munoz, had already surpassed that milestone. We had arrived off the coast of Vietnam on May 16, and off loaded on May 17. We had one day of indoctrination and then started flying combat missions. For the first couple of days we flew with HMM-262 aircraft as escorts until our pilots and crews were familiar with the terrain. Then we were on our own and HMM-161 went to work.

I had to cool my heels for a week and a half because my primary job was aircraft electrician, not door gunner, and only a limited number of people from each job assignment could fly each month. Those days until the end of May passed very slowly, it seemed, until I was authorized to fly gunner. I really wanted to be part of the battle.

I wanted to fly. I wanted to fly all the time, and I wanted to be where the action was.

Luckily for me, not everyone in the squadron felt that way. There were a few guys with wives and children back home, for instance, who didn't want to stick their necks out any more than necessary, unless they absolutely had to, and flew just enough to earn their gunners wings and a couple of air medals. Gunners wings were silver, with a gold center, and three stars across the top. The stars were for each of your first three battles, but in addition to getting into battles three times, you had to fly a total of twenty missions before you qualified for the wings.

A mission was counted when an aircraft went into a hot zone, whether it was on a resupply, med-evac, extracting or landing troops. After twenty missions crews were awarded their wings, if they had actually engaged the enemy three times, and were awarded their first air medal. For some guys, that was enough to show their bravery. Then they opted for ground assignments. Which was fine by me, because it opened up more opportunities for me to fly. And I found out what war was really about, almost immediately!

Khe Sanh was still an active little place in early June, even though the siege had been over for two months, and it still took shellings from the North Vietnamese. The hills surrounding the base, which were manned by our infantry and artillery, were regularly probed, usually at night. We worked incredibly long days, resupplying the hills, med-evacing wounded Marines, carrying troops on assaults and dropping reconnaissance Marines into remote locations where they could monitor enemy movements.

On June 3, my third day of flying, we launched an assault into the same area near the Laotian border where, two months later, I would get into the firefight described above. I was flying as starboard gunner, Chuck Palmer was crew chief, and Bob Thompson, another electrician was port gunner. That area hadn't been probed much in recent months, mainly because of the Tet offensive and the siege at Khe Sanh.

Again, I was in the first flight of four, but we didn't draw fire. We landed safely, and the grunts jumped out to form a perimeter. I was leaning out the window, watching closely to be sure where our troops were. One thing I never wanted to do in Vietnam, and never did do, was to shoot our own people because of uncertainty over their location versus the North Vietnamese.

We lifted off, flew low over the forming perimeter, and suddenly I saw what appeared to be a garden. For a second I couldn't believe what I was seeing! What the hell was a garden doing out here in the middle of the jungle? Obviously, I thought later, the VC and NVA regulars were growing food out there. But those thoughts were rudely interrupted by a sound which would soon become familiar.

Bwaaang! We had taken a hit!

It was the first time I had been shot at, and every nerve in my body seemed to explode. I couldn't tell whether I had been hit or not, and remembered being told by people who had been wounded that the first thing they felt was numb. And as those thoughts were going through my mind, I saw just past the garden, a black pajama clad figure, wearing a straw conical-shaped hat, running like hell for an opening in the jungle.

Without thinking, I opened up with my .50. It all seemed like slow motion, that figure running, tracers from my barrel following him, and then both disappearing into the dark greenness.

I felt a tap on my shoulder and looked up. It was Palmer, and he was pointing down at my feet.

I looked, and there, an inch from the heel of my right boot, a bullet had plowed a furrow into the deck. When we landed for fuel, Chuck and I looked the exterior over and found the bullet had entered in the bottom, by a rotating beacon light that is used as a warning device for aircraft flying at a lower altitude. We had disconnected all those lights on our aircraft, but the VC still used them as an aiming point. The bullet had torn through the skin, slammed into a cargo roller, started it spinning and ricocheted into the deck at my feet. Later I regretted that I didn't dig that bullet out of the floor and keep it as a souvenir.

I never knew for sure whether the VC who shot at us died or not. Thompson said he later heard that the grunts found a body in that location, but I didn't press the issue.

Action of that nature had quickly become routine for our squadron.

HMM-161 had come to Vietnam as a well-trained, highly motivated group of people with the best of equipment and we wasted no time in establishing ourselves. In June we set an all time flight record for a squadron of CH-46 helicopters logging 2,400 flight hours. By the end of July the squadron had flown 5,524 hours, 3,968 missions, 22,814 sorties, 2,954 medical evacuations and carried 4,257 tons of cargo. For all of that, though, we often had to go to extremes to find the NVA and VC.

Back home, the media had made the Tet offensive appear as a major defeat for the U.S. It apparently didn't occur to the armchair experts back at the briefing centers in Da Nang and Saigon that soldiers who had been fighting for over thirty years in some cases could mount a coordinated offensive, especially when it was on a familiar battleground. But in doing so the North Vietnamese had taken a terrible beating. Our airstrip at Quang Tri was the northernmost helicopter base in South Vietnam, and was only 15 miles from the DMZ. Yet, throughout the summer of 1968, rocket attacks and attempts to penetrate our perimeter were sharply reduced.

So the Marine infantry was hounding those remnants of the army that had attacked in February, rooting it out wherever northern soldiers or southern guerillas could be found. Often that meant major forays into the DMZ or operations along the infiltration routes from Laos.

Wherever the grunts were, we went. We'd start on an initial assault, tearing into a landing zone in some remote section of jungle, dropping hundreds of Marines in within an hour or so. If the action was intense, we'd sometimes divert to do gun runs, strafing enemy positions as the infantry prepared to assault from the ground.

We often were accompanied by Huey gunships from VMO-6, also stationed at Quang Tri, which had compiled a formidable record of 1,300 confirmed enemy kills from September 1965 to April 1968. If we encountered mortars or anti-aircraft positions the Hueys or jet aircraft would unleash their rockets. When a firebase was established and the infantry started making patrols, or conducting search and destroy missions, we'd resupply them with everything from food, water and ammunition to mail, and occasionally beer. When engagements with the North Vietnamese produced casualties, we were there to med-evac them to aid stations or to hospital ships off the coast if the injuries were severe. We regularly worked with the 1st, 3rd, 4th, 5th, 7th, 9th, and 26th Marine Regiments. It often was dangerous, since most LZ's were hostile. It also could be grueling.

As a rule, the pilots, numbering roughly three for each aircraft, were split into two shifts. One shift would take off between dawn and 7 a.m., depending on the morning's missions, returning to Quang Tri in the afternoon when another set of pilots would take over and fly all afternoon and into the evening. The crews, meanwhile, remained on board. If the aircraft you were assigned to had an early flight, say resupplying a firebase that had been under attack all night, you could leave at 5 a.m. and fly nearly continuously until eight p.m. or so. We also had two or three helicopters on standby for emergency resupply and emergency med-evacs all night.

If you didn't get assigned to night flights, you still had to remove the machine guns from the helicopter, take them to a shack that housed cleaning equipment, dismantle them, give them a good scrubbing, and reassemble them. The machine guns were stored in the squadron armory, which was actually a makeshift room on one side of a tin hangar. When that was done you could collapse in your hooch, a twelve-by-twenty foot building made of two-by four frames, plywood floors and walls, with screens comprising the upper half of the walls for ventilation, and corrugated tin roofs.

Then at about 4:30 a.m. it started all over. The pace was exhausting, but it was necessary, and it was taken seriously. We had waited more than two years for the chance to join the war and we weren't going to do things half-heartedly.

Early in the war years there was much more activity from local Viet Cong than from North Vietnamese regulars. Often death was dealt from concealed booby traps, or by snipers, while engagements with full-force units were still a rarity. But by 1968 our fighting was against well trained, well equipped, regular troops. They had rockets, artillery, machine guns, mortars, RPG's-rocket-propelled grenades-which were extremely dangerous against helicopters, along with Russian-made AK-47 assault rifles, and Swedish SKS rifles, both of which were accurate and sturdy.

Our most dangerous encounters usually came either on initial assaults, where you might drop right into a concentration of enemy troops, or during insertions and retractions of reconnaissance Marines.

Recons, as they were known, represented the cream of the Marine Corps ground operations. They were trained in surveillance, camouflage, guerilla warfare, counter-insurgency, scuba diving, parachute jumping, infiltration, and virtually every form of unconventional warfare that existed. They considered themselves a cut above every other form of Marine, refused to acknowledge the existence of the U.S. Army, Green Berets or Navy SEALS, and were absolutely convinced that one Recon was the equivalent of at least ten enemy soldiers. Judging from what I saw during my tour in Vietnam, I have to agree with them.

An insertion was the term for picking up a team of Recons either at Quang Tri, where some of them were stationed, at Dong Ha, a supply base five miles further north, or at LZ Stud, a staging area ten miles west of Dong Ha, and then taking them out to enemy territory where they were dropped off. An extraction meant picking up that team, at a predesignated point or time, usually a week or so later, or yanking them out in a hurry if they ran into a real problem.

Going out with the Recons was always an experience. They always went to some off-the-wall location in the middle of what was called Indian Country, where encounters with infiltrating North Vietnamese troops were a likelihood rather than a possibility. Sometimes five to eight Recons would go out for ten days to two weeks, just to keep an eye on things and call artillery strikes on top of infiltrating troops. Sometimes as many as fifteen would go together for the expressed purpose of killing Vietnamese. Sometimes they'd barely get out of the helicopter before they would be "compromised" meaning seen by the enemy, and would have to call for an emergency extraction.

That happened on one of my first flights as gunner during a day of Recon work.

We went to the headquarters at Quang Tri, where a briefing was held. I felt kind of privileged to be there as Recon officers discussed enemy infiltration movements and the missions of the teams we would insert that day. We started taking teams out, mostly in the Laotian border area, and it went well for the first two insertions. Then, on the third mission that day, we dropped a team off in a grassy area fifteen miles or so southeast of Khe Sanh where the flat plain turned to rolling hills.

We weren't out of the zone two minutes before the team leader radioed us.

"Sir, we are compromised!"

We turned back toward the insertion point immediately, and the pilot asked the team leader where they had moved since we dropped them off. The leader said the enemy troops were so close that he didn't want to give specific directions, since they may have been monitoring our radio transmissions.

There was no questioning his sincerity. As we listened to his conversation with the pilot we realized that every word spoken from the ground as whispered!

To overcome the problem of the Vietnamese listening in, the pilot and team leader discussed the winning team in the previous year's North-South football game, and which direction the Recons had taken, related to the designation of the winner or loser. Ultimately it was decided that the team was about 100 yards north of the zone where we had dropped them off.

To pinpoint the location, the co-pilot radioed, "Pop a yellow smoke!" That meant, pull the pin on a yellow smoke grenade, which would billow out a cloud of yellow on the ground, showing where the team was.

Major mistake!

The Vietnamese were listening, and as I looked down, I suddenly saw no less than four clouds of yellow smoke emerge from the high grass!

"Shit," I thought. "Those guys are fucking surrounded!"

Still, we didn't know which yellow smoke cloud marked the Recon team's location. If we went to the wrong one, we'd be shot to shit.

The pilot radioed the situation to the ground, and then recommended, "Pop a smoke, and then tell us which color it is."

Suddenly a green smoke cloud appeared, along with radio transmission that the team had indeed popped a green smoke. We headed for it while the team leader, still whispering, told us they could hear the Vietnamese moving towards their position. From the air it looked as though less than 100 yards separated the good guys from the bad guys. We dropped down for the extraction, into an area of tall elephant grass. It appeared to be fifteen feet high or so, and was a great cover for everyone, the Recons and the Vietnamese. The pilot didn't like that one bit, and gave me the most all encompassing order I ever received as a Marine.

"If you see something move, kill it!"

"Yes, Sir!"

"If you think you see something move, kill it!"

"Yes, Sir!"

"If you think you see something thinking about moving, kill it!"

"Yes, Sir!"

"If someone lights a cigarette, kill him. If you think you see someone light a cigarette, kill him! Kill every rock, tree, and blade of grass out there. I don't want anything left alive when we leave!"

We landed, the Recons ran on board and typically pulled one of the stunts that Recons were noted for. They kicked out the two remaining Plexiglas windows on the helicopter and prepared to start shooting.

As soon as the ramp lifted, insuring that the whole team was inside, I opened up, as did the port gunner. We tore the shit out of that place! If the NVA were coming they ran into a solid wall of bullets. The Recons were firing with everything they had, and as far as I know, nothing was left alive in that LZ when we left. I'd bet that if I went back to that little part of Vietnam today, there still is a pile of dead rocks and barren ground there.

For all of our efforts, and our successes, however, there was bound to be a time when we also took our losses. That time came on June 19, one month to the day after we started combat operations in Vietnam. It was at Khe Sanh, not surprisingly, but didn't involve a direct engagement with enemy troops.

Our helicopters were picking up troops at the north end of the runway as part of an assault at another location. An old village, once quiet and unmolested, had stood slightly north of Khe Sanh. The thatched-roof hooches were there, along with several trees that had survived both the incredible bombardment that had gone on from January to April, and the occasional flurries of activity that continued even after the siege ended. When the siege was in full swing the base had been resupplied by C-130 Hercules Aircraft, and other cargo aircraft capable of dropping supplies out of rear cargo hatches. The cargo had been attached to parachutes, which brought it to earth intact. But many of those parachutes were cut loose, only to end up caught in the trees at the north end of the base.

On June 19, 1968 helicopters from HMM-161 landed at the north end of Khe Sanh, in a place called LZ Turkey, where Marine infantrymen were gathered waiting to move out.

An aircraft piloted by Capt. Lufkin S. Sharp, with 1st Lt. Michael D. Helmstetler as co-pilot, landed and lowered its ramp.

As a squad of infantrymen ran on board, the rotor wash began whipping a parachute out of a nearby tree. Suddenly it was freed, blowing wildly in the wind, and then was drawn straight into the. rotor blades. The huge sheet caught in the blades, throwing them out of synchronization. The aft rotor head tilted, then went completely out of control. Miraculously, the infantrymen and crew were not injured. But the blades smashed through the cockpit, killing Sharp and Helmstetler.

Later the squadron sent technicians and mechanics to recover salvageable parts of the destroyed aircraft. The bodies had already been recovered and sent home for burial. They were good people, good pilots and good Marines. They were liked and respected, and they were missed. The squadron cruise book, a yearbook detailing a unit's achievements, was dedicated to them, and a memorial service was held in their honor in a hangar at Quang Tri.

It was the first memorial service for a member of HMM-161 who died in combat during its 1968-1969 tour. It would prove to be far, far from the last.

NOTES:

The two pilots from HMM-161 killed on June 19, 1968 were:
Helmstetler, Michael D. 1stLt. 0102685; 23; High Point, N.C.
Sharp, Lufkin S. Capt. 088503; 26; Gainesville, Georgia

Other Marines mentioned in this chapter were as follows:
Braman, Douglas M. LCpl. 2163535; Lebanon, Connecticut
Cross, Jeffery D. LCpl. 2204020; Gresham, Oregon
Munoz, Anselmo Jr. LCpl. 2185565; Wharton, Texas
Niesen, Paul W. LtCol. 051752; Pensacola, Florida
Palmer, Charles W. Cpl. 2177239
Thompson, Robert L. Pfc.; New Hampshire
Winter, Ronald E. LCpl. 2208381; 20; Wynantskill, New York
Starbuck, Robert F. Sgt. 1939063; 25; Montgomery, New York

MEDAL OF HONOR

Name	Service #	Unit	Date	Age	Hometown
Anderson, James Jr Pfc	2241921	F-2-3	2/28/67*	20	Compton, California
Anderson, Richard A LCpl	450842089	E-3-Recon	8/24/69*	21	Houston, Texas
Austin, Oscar P Pfc	2472757	E-2-7	2/23/69*	21	Phoenix, Arizona
Barker, Jedh C Cpl	2207369	F-2-4	9/21/67*	22	Franklin, New Hampshire
Barnum, Harvey C Jr 1stLt	084262	H-2-9	12/18/65	25	Waterbury, Connecticut
Bobo, John P 2dLt	092986	3-9	3/30/67*	24	Niagara Falls, New York
Bruce, Daniel D Pfc	2485891	H&S-3-5	3/1/69*	18	Beverly Shores, Indiana
Burke, Robert C Pfc	2359360	I-3-27	5/17/68*	18	Monticello, Illinois
Carter, Bruce W Pfc	261961399	H-2-3	8/7/69*	19	Miami Springs, Florida
Clausen, Raymond F Jr Pfc	2258929	HMM-263	1/31/70	22	New Orleans, Louisiana
Coker, Ronald L Pfc	2452732	M-3-3	3/24/69*	21	Alliance, Colorado
Connor, Peter S SSgt	1280832	F-2-3	3/8/66*	33	East Orange, New Jersey
Cook, Donald G Col	105263773	POW	12/64-12/67	45	New York, New York
Creek, Thomas E LCpl	2403648	I-3-9	2/13/69*	18	Amarillo, Texas
Davis, Rodney M Sgt	1978754	B-1-5	9/6/67*	25	Macon, Georgia
De La Garza, Emilio A LCpl	313526485	E-2-1	4/11/70*	20	East Chicago, Indiana
Dias, Ralph E Pfc	195381053	D-1-7	11/12/69*	19	Shelocta, Pennsylvania
Dickey, Douglas E Pfc	2199321	C-1-4	3/26/67*	20	Rossburg, Ohio
Foster, Paul H Sgt	1903536	2-4	10/14/67*	28	San Francisco, California
Fox, Wesley L 1stLt	096702	A-1-9	2/22/69	40	Round Hill, Virginia
Gonzalez, Alfredo Sgt	2142473	A-1-1	1/31/68*	21	Edinburg, Texas
Graham, James A Capt	088847	F-2-5	6/3/67*	26	Frostburg, Maryland
Graves, Terrence C 2dLt	0101090	3-F-Recon	2/17/68*	22	Groton, New York
Howard, Jimmie E GySgt	1130610	C-1-Recon	6/16/66	37	Burlington, Iowa
Howe, James D LCpl	248846637	I-3-7	5/6/70*	21	Liberty,South Carolina
Jenkins, Robert H Jr Pfc	2428700	3-Recon	3/5/69*	20	Interlachen, Florida
Jimenez, Jose F LCpl	527602916	K-3-7	8/28/69*	23	Red Rock, Arizona
Johnson, Ralph H Pfc	2356797	A-1-Recon	3/5/68*	19	Charleston, South Carolina
Keith, Miguel LCpl	456844128	CAP-1-2-3	5/8/70*	18	Omaha, Nebraska
Kellog, Allan J Jr GySgt		G-2-5	3/11/70	26	Bridgeport, Connecticut
Lee, Howard V Capt	069961	E-2-4	8/8-9/66	33	Dumfries, Virginia
Livingston, James E Capt		E-2-4	4/30/68	28	McRae, Georgia
Martini, Gary W Pfc	2217825	F-2-1	4/21/67*	18	Portland, Oregon
Maxam, Larry L Cpl	2141892	D-1-4	2/2/68*	20	Glendale, California
Mc Ginty, John J III SSgt	1602718	K-3-4	7/18/66	26	Boston, Massachusetts
Modrzejewski, R J Capt	073356	K-3-4	7/15-18/66	32	Milwaukee, Wisconsin
Morgan, William D Cpl	2337025	H-2-9	2/25/69*	21	Mount Lebanon, Penn
Newlin, Melvin E Pfc	2229466	2-5	7/4/67*	18	Wellsville, Ohio
Noonan, Thomas P Jr LCpl	2292900	G-2-9	2/5/69*	25	Maspeth, New York
O'Malley, Robert E Cpl	1972161	I-3-3	8/18/65	22	Woodside, New York
Paul, Joe C LCpl	2033358	H-2-4	8/19/65*	19	Dayton, Ohio
Perkins, William T Jr Cpl	2296240	C-1-1	10/12/67*	20	Sepulveda, California
Peters, Lawrence D Sgt	2004158	M-3-5	9/4/67*	20	Binghamton, New York
Phipps, Jimmy W Pfc	2412145	B-1-Eng	5/27/69*	18	Culver City, California
Pittman, Richard A Sgt		I-3-5	7/24/66	21	San Joaquin,California
Pless, Stephen W Maj	079156	VMO-6	8/19/67	27	Decatur, Georgia
Prom, William R LCpl	2421504	I-3-3	2/9/69*	20	Pittsburgh, Pennsylvania
Reasoner, Frank S 1stLt	085378	A-3-Recon	7/12/65*	27	Kellog,g,. Idaho
Singleton, Walter K Sgt	2056158	A-1-9	3/24/67*	22	Memphis, Tennessee
Smedley, Larry E Cpl	2274116	D-1-7	12/21/67*	18	Orlando, Florida
Taylor, Karl G SSgt	1862790	I-3-26	12/8/68*	29	Avella, Pennsylvania
Vargas, Jay R Capt		G-2-4	4/30-5/2/68	29	Winslow, Arizona

229

Weber, Lester W LCpl	2323793	M-3-7	2/23/69	20	Hinsdale, Illinois
Wheat, Roy M LCpl	2242728	K-3-7	8/11/67*	20	Moselle, Mississippi
Williams, Dewayne T Pfc	2420506	H-2-1	9/18/68*	19	St. Clair, Michigan
Wilson, Alfred M Pfc	2421744	M-3-9	3/3/69*	21	Odessa, Texas
Worley, Kenneth L LCpl	2230824	3-7	8/12/68*	20	Modesto, California

NAVY CORPSMAN

Ballard, Donald E HC2c		M-3-4	5/16/68	22	Kansas City, Missouri
Caron, Wayne M HM3	B116083	H&S-3-7	7/28/68	21	Middleboro, Massachusetts
Ingram, Robert R HM3		C-1-7	3/28/66		
Ray, David R HM2	B308634	2-11	3/19/69	24	McMinnville, Tennessee

CHAPLAIN

Capodanno, Vincent R Lt	656197	3/5	9/4/67	38	Honolulu, Hawaii

*Posthumous

Maj. Stephen W. Pless
VMO-6 Medal of Honor 8/19/67

NAVY CROSS

Name	Service #	Unit	Date	Age	Hometown
Abrams, Lewis H Col	150222864	VMA-242	10/25/67*	48	Montclair, New Jersey
Abshire, Bobby W Cpl	1979928	VMO-2	5/21/66		
Abshire, Richard F Sgt	2125809	G-2-4	5/2/68*	23	Abbeville, Louisiana
Adams, John T LCpl	2033889	C-1-Recon	6/16/66*	22	Covington, Oklahoma
Adams, Laurence R III Capt	092937	HMM-165	1/12/69		
Alfonso, Vincent Pfc		A-1-3	7/20/66		
Allen, Yale G Cpl		C-1-4	3/5/69		
Almeida, Russell V LCpl	2083359	C-3-Eng	12/20/65*	19	South Dartmouth, Massachusetts
Ambrose, Gerald D LCpl		M-3-1	1/8/70		
Amendola, Willet R Cpl	2303053	M-3-7	11/2/67*	19	Deposit, New York
Anderson, John J Sgt		I-3-9	10/27/65		
Armstrong, Russell P SSgt	1970190	I-3-26	9/7-8/67	24	Ft. Calhoun, Nebraska
Arquero, Elpidio A SSgt	1694536	B-1-3	5/10/67*	27	Honolulu, Hawaii
Aston, James M Pfc	2450092	H-2-26	3/19/69*	18	Wichita Falls, Texas
Ayers, Darrell Sgt	538341301	1-Recon	3/19/70*	32	Alderwood Manor, Washington
Badnek, Samuel J Pvt	2012032	H-2-4	8/18/65		
Baggett, Curtis F SSgt	1384825	K-3-5	2/6/68*	31	Raleigh, North Carolina
Bailey, Walter F Sgt		E-2-5	3/21/70		
Barnes, Robert C SSgt		B-3-Recon	12/17/66		
Barnett, Robert L Cp		A-1-5	5/9/69		
Barrett, James J Cpl		I-3-26	9/19/67		
Barrett, John J Capt	085356	HMM-263	2/26/69	30	Minneapolis, Minnesota
Baskin, Richard W Sgt		H&S-1-26	6/6/67		
Batcheller, Gordon D Capt	080672	A-1-1	1/31/68	28	Hingham, Massachusetts
Bateman, Kent C Maj		VMA-533	10/25/67		
Beaulieu, Leo V Pfc	2162804	E-2-5	5/16/66*	21	Lengby, Minnesota
Bell, Van D Jr LtCol	044563	CO-1-1	6/6/66	48	Miami, Florida
Bendorf, David G LCpl	2247275	L-3-9	5/20/67*	20	Livingston, Wisconsin
Benoit, Ronald R 2dLt		D-1-Recon	2/25/67		
Berger, Donald J 2dLt		HMM-163	3/11-12/66		
Binns, Ricardo C LCpl	2031505	C-1-Recon	6/16/66		
Bird, William C Pfc		E-2-5	5/15/69		
Blann, Stephen L Cpl	2391078	E-2-9	2/16/69*	23	Pompano Beach, Florida
Blevins, Thomas L Jr Cpl	2255036	C-1-26	5/31/69*	21	Middletown, New Jersey
Bogan, Richard E LCpl		C-1-5	4/12/68		
Brady, Eugene R LtCol	64228075	HMM-364	5/15/69	41	York, Pennsylvania
Brandtner, Martin L Capt	080625	D-1-5	9/3/68	31	Minneapolis, Minnesota
Brandtner, Martin L Capt	080625	D-1-5	9/11/68	31	Minneapolis, Minnesota
Brantley, Leroy Cpl	2392215	G-2-5	3/28/69*	20	Charleston, South Carolina
Brindley, Thomas D 2dLt	0101761	I-3-26	1/20/68*	24	St.. Paul, Minnesota
Brown, Charles E Cpl		CAP-H-8	1/31/68		
Brown, David H Sgt	2056298	L-3-26	9/10/67*	21	Saltillo, Tennessee
Browning, Randall A Cpl		A-3-ATanks	9/10/67		
Bryan, Charles W Cpl	2307311	B-3-Recon	1/20/67*	20	McKinney, Texas
Bryant, Jarold O LCpl		K-3-1	3/21/66		
Buchanan, Richard W LCpl	2113260	M-3-27	5/24/68	23	Moraga, California
Burke, John R Cpl	2200142	H&S-1-26	6/6/67*	23	Clearwater, Florida
Burnham, Thomas R Cpl		F-2-5	10/1/67	31	Pennsylvania
Burns, Leon R SSgt		B-1-9	7/2/67		
Caine, Lawrence B III Cpl		I-3-5	5/13/67		
Calhoun, John C LCpl	2328321	CAP-H-6	1/7/68*	20	South Boston, Massachusetts
Campbell, Joseph T 1stLt	0101784	I-3-5	6/15/68*	23	Stoneham, Massachusetts

Name	Service No.	Unit	Date	Age	Hometown
Canley, "J" "L" GySgt	1455946	A-1-1	1/31-2/6/68		
Carroll, James J Capt	079583	K-3-4	9/27-10/5/66*	29	Miami Beach, Florida
Carter, Marshall N Capt		C-1-1	1/14/67		
Casebolt, Henry C Cpl	1933907	F-2-1	2/28/66*	24	St. Joseph, Missouri
Casey, Michael J 2dLt	095659	C-1-1	3/18/68*	23	Dalton, Massachusetts
Casey, Thomas J Jr LCpl	2422191	D-1-7	2/16/69*	22	Milton, Massachusetts
Castillo, William Pfc		E-2-4	2/25/69		
Cavanaugh, Thomas J Cpl	2136906	F-2-7	9/19/68*	22	Waterbury, Connecticutt
Cheatham, Ernest C Jr LtCol		CO-2-5	2/3-3/3/68		
Cheatwood, Paul R LCpl	2345578	B-1-5	2/16/68	19	Tallapoosa, Georgia
Christensen, Paul K Cpl		3-CAG	11/19/67		
Christy, Kenneth L 2dLt		I-3-4	1/18/68		
Christman, William J III 2dLt	0106531	A-1-9	2/22/69*	23	Gaithersburg, Maryland
Christmas, George R Capt	085447	H-2-5	2/5/68	28	Yeadon, Pennsylvania
Cisneros, Roy Cpl	2341534	B-1-3	9/11/68*	19	San Antonio, Texas
Claybin,Edward A Pfc		D-2-11	6/20/66		
Cobb, Paul F 2dLt	0103410	A-1-7	5/16/68*	24	Roanoke, Virginia
Cochran, Robert F Jr 2dLt	089648	A-1-Amphib	8/18/65*	23	Poplarville. Mississippi
Coffman, Clovis C Jr GySgt		C-1-Recon	10/10/66		
Collins, Bryant C Cpl		A-3-Recon	7/12/65		
Cone, Fred "J" Maj		VMA-242	10/24/67		
Conklin, Richard F Cpl		D-2-13	5/10/68		
Coolican, James J Capt		HMAC	1/31/68		Carbondale, Pennsylvania
Corsetti, Harry J Cpl		3-Recon	8/15/68		
Cousins, Merritt T LCpl	2295242	B-1-12	7/8/67*	19	Clinton, Iowa
Covella, Joseph F GySgt	1001220	Advisor	1/3/66*	37	New York, New York
Cover, Robert L MSg		VMO-2	3/17/67		
Crockett, Joseph R Jr Sgt		1-1-Recon	4/23/69		
Cummings, Roger W Pfc	2470680	K-3-7	4/20/69*	21	Bloomington, Indiana
Curley, Ronald T Sgt		F-2-26	5/16/67		
Curtis, Russell W GySgt		FFSR	8/21/67		
Dalton, Robert G Cpl		K-3-3	5/25/69		
Danner, David J Sgt		A-3-Tanks	5/8/67		
Darnell, Dana C LCpl	2208738	B-1-9	4/24/67*	19	Greenville, South Carolina
Davis, Dennis D Pfc	578667690	K-3-7	8/28/69*	20	Capitol Heights, Maryland
Dawson, John R 2dLt	0100987	G-3-12	10/27/67*	23	Adrian, Michigan
Day, Edward L Cpl	2283719	L-3-3	8/26/68*	19	Philadelphia, Pennsylvania
De Bona, Andrew D Capt	185268563	M-3-26	9/10/67	30	Ebensburg, Pennsylvania
De Planche, Mark B Cpl		G-2-9	1/13-14/66		
Devries, Marvin H 1stLt		E-2-3	8/10/69		
Dickson, Grover L Cpl	1508294	K-3-3	11/11/66*	28	New Orleans, Louisiana
Dillard, Henry C Cpl		M-3-4	5/29/67		
Dittman, Carl R Cpl		IS-3	11/14/68		
Donaldson, Billy M SSgt	1461338	1-3-Recon	8/8/66	30	Valliant, Oklahoma
Donovan, Joseph P 1stLt	0101005	HMM-364	2/22/69	27	Waxahachie, Texas
Donovan, Joseph P 1stLt	0101005	HMM-364	4/21/69	27	Waxahachie, Texas
Dorris, Claude H SSgt	1547450	CAP-H-6	1/7/68*	29	Louisville, Kentucky
Dowd, John A LtCol	157224808	CO-1-7	8/12-13/69*	37	Elizabeth, New Jersey
Downing, Talmadge R GySgt		M-3-1	3/5/66		
Driscoll, Thomas B Cpl		D-1-5	9/4,6/67		
Duff, Barry W Cpl	2098848	C-1-9	5/21/66*	21	Baltimore, Maryland
Duncan, Richard W Cpl	2327745	M-3-5	11/8/67*	19	Livermore, California
Eades, Lawrence M LCpl		CAC-P-3	2/2/68		
Ebbert, Terry J 1stLt	091101	E-2-5	12/24/66	24	Chicago, Illinois
Edwards, Craig A 1stLt		H-2-7	8/20/70		
Estrada, Manuel A LCpl	2361066	A-3-Recon	8/15-16/68	20	Phoenix, Arizona
Evans, Richard A Jr Pfc	2427562	D-1-5	8/29/68*	18	Independence, Missouri

232

Name	Service #	Unit	Date	Age	Hometown
Fairfield, Rupert E Jr Capt		VMO-6	8/19/67		
Fante, Robert G Cpl	2175781	F-2-5	8/6/68*	20	Roseville, Michigan
Federowski, Robert A Cpl	2204671	D-1-5	5/24/68*	19	Lansing, Illinois
Feerrar, Donald L Cpl		G-2-1	3/20/67		
Felton, Samuel L Jr Pfc		C-1-5	6/11/69		
Finley, Michael P LCpl	2204950	A-1-4	5/8/67*	20	Big Rock, Illinois
Fisher, Thomas W LCpl	2244800	M-3-5	9/4/67*	20	Allentown, Pennsylvania
Floren, Jimmy E Cpl	2325565	H-2-5	11/6/67*	21	Klamath Falls, Oregon
Fowler, Earl W Cpl		C-1-7	3/28/66		
Frederick, John W Jr CWO	333240838	POW	6/67-8/68*	48	Manito, Illinois
Fryman, Roy A SSgt	1356690	1-Recon	4/29/68	34	Paris, Kentucky
Fuller, John L Jr 2dLt	094257	E-2-5	3/23/67*	22	Atlanta, Georgia
Galbreath, Bobby F Capt	070303	VMO-6	2/16/68*	37	Amarillo, Texas
Gale, Alvin R Pfc	2393859	G-2-26	1/28/69*	21	Hyde Park, Massachusetts
Gallagher, Patrick LCpl		H-2-4	7/18/66		
Gauthier, Brian J Cpl	2007664	A-1-3	7/11/65*	20	Mansura, Louisiana
Getlin, Michael P Capt	086661	I-3-9	3/30/67*	27	Lagrange, Illinois
Gibson, George R Cpl		B-2-4	8/8/66		
Gilleland, Richard M Sgt	2260688	M-3-7	2/23/69	22	Nashville, Tennessee
Gillingham Richard K Cpl	2118093	H-2-9	5/19/67*	20	Valatie, New York
Gomez, Ernesto LCpl	2151708	HMM-262	1/25/68	20	Pasadena, California
Gonzales, Daniel G Cpl		B-1-7	6/7/69		
Goodsell, William J Maj	055282	VMO-6	6/16/66*	37	Seattle, Washington
Gray, George E LCpl		E-2-9	2/2/68		
Green, John S GySgt		F-2-5	6/2/67		
Green, Maurice O V 1stLt	0103516	IO-1-5	10/27/68		Birmingham, Alabama
Gregory, Robert B Jr LCpl		CAP2-1-2	2/23,25/69		
Gresham, Michael E Sgt		D-1-5	9/11/68		
Gresko, Richard W LCpl		H&S-3-5	3/11/70		
Grimes, Paul E Jr LCpl		F-2-7	3/4/67		
Grosz, Nicholas H Jr 1stLt	086541	H&S-2-7	12/18/65	25	River Edge, New Jersey
Guarino, Timothy S Pfc		G-2-9	6/1/69		
Guay, Robert P Maj		HMM-261	3/19/66		
Guerra, Victor J SSgt		L-3-1	10/27/69		
Halstead, Lee M 1stLt	094751	HMM-167	8/29/68*	23	Lansing, Michigan
Harrington, Myron C Capt	081869	D-1-5	2/23/68	27	Georgia
Hartsoe, David E Pfc	2279897	L-3-9	5/20/67*	20	Coatesville, Pennsylvania
Hayes, Daniel J LCpl		L-3-5	11/28/68		
Hazelbaker, Vincil W Maj	063157	VMO-2	8/8/66	39	Grangeville, Idaho
Helle, Ronald B Sgt	2146818	G-2-5	1/28/71	23	Toledo, Ohio
Henderson, Billy K LCpl		H-2-1	7/17/69		
Hendricks, Robert L Cpl		H-2-7	2/19/68		
Herrea, Felipe LCpl	2341619	A-1-Recon	9/20/68*	20	San Antonio, Texas
Herron, Lee R 1stLt	0102874	A-1-9	2/22/69*	23	Lubbock, Texas
Hilgers, John J W Capt		OO-2-4	8/23-24/66		
Hill, Lamont D Pfc	2229088	I-3-4	3/6/67*	20	Massillon, Ohio
Hoapili, John GySgt		K-3-26	5/9/68		
Hodgkins, Guy M SSgt	1490687	I-3-9	9/3/66*	30	Los Alamos, New Mexico
Hoff, John R Jr 2dLt		E-1-Recon	4/7/70		
Holmes, Walter C Sgt		B-1-9	11/27/65		
Honeycutt, James E Pfc	2356099	3-Recon	2/16/68*	20	Haynes, Arkansas
Hopkins, Michael E Pfc	2037164	K-3-9	7/4/66*	21	Norfolk, Virginia
Houghton, Kenneth J Col		CO-5	5/26-6/5/67		
House, Charles A LtCol		HMM-163	3/9-10/66		
Howard, Billy GySgt	554586	E-2-4	3/21/66*	39	Hialeah, Florida
Howell, Gatlin J 1stLt	093190	IO-1-9	7/2-7/67*	31	Colma, California
Hubbard, Robert W Capt	088752	Advisor	1/31-2/4/68*	27	Auburn, Alabama

233

Name	Service No.	Unit	Date	Age	Hometown
Huffcut, William H II Maj		VMO-6	9/28/69		
Huggins, Michael A Pfc		G-2-4	6/27/69		
Hughes, Stanley S Col	012654	CO-1	2/3/68		
Hunnicutt, Hubert H III Cpl		C-1-9	4/16-18/68		
Jaehne, Richard L 2dLt	0106958	K-3-7	8/28/69		
Jmaeff, Alan C Cpl	2436055	C-1-4	3/1/69*	23	Canada, XC
Johnson, James L Jr Cpl		E-2-9	2/17/69		
Johnston, Clement B Jr LCpl	2116397	D-1-Recon	4/28/66*	18	Pittsburgh, Pennsylvania
Jones, Phillip B 2dLt	0106589	G-2-26	1/28/69*	21	Slater, Iowa
Joys, John W SSgt	1624442	A-1-4	8/26/66*	27	San Francisco, California
Judge, Mark W Pfc	2235869	E-2-4	9/21/67*	20	Torrance, California
Kaler, Richard D Cpl	2031739	H-2-4	7/21/66*	22	Patchogue, New York
Kaufman, David M 1stSgt	1016850	E-2-3	6/15/69*	42	Plaquemine, Louisiana
Keck, Russell F Cpl	2201914	A-1-3	5/18/67*	20	Okmulgee, Oklahoma
Kelley, Edwin C Jr 1stLt	0104244	M-3-4	3/13/69	25	Shillington, Pennsylvania
Kelly, James R III Cpl	2040353	I-3-3	3/24/67*	22	Sacramento, California
Kelly, Robert A 1stLt		I-3-9	9/3,5/66		
Kemp, Marwick L SSgt		E-2-4	3/21/66		
Kenison, Benjamin A LCpl	2098437	D-1-4	9/16/66*	20	Jefferson, New Hampshire
Kennedy, Johnnie M GySgt		Advisor	4/19/65		
Keys, William M Capt		D-1-9	3/2/67		
Koelper, Donald E Maj	060953		2/18/64*	32	Northbrook, Illinois
Koontz, Lenoard Cpl		M-3-4	5/27/68		
Korkow, Kenneth A Cpl	2258125	B-1-26	3/30/68	21	Blunt, South Dakota
Kowalyk, William LCpl		G-3-12	8/26/66		
Kuzma, Marc J Pfc	2391847	A-1-4	4/26/68*	19	South Hadley Falls, Mass
Lain, Bobby D Capt		B-1-1	2/19/67		
Lankford, Albert J III 1stLt	0106303	G-2-9	4/21/69	24	Montgomery, Alabama
La Pointe, Alvin S Pfc	2083443	C-1-7	3/28/66	19	Sudbury, Massachusetts
La Porte, Alfred P Jr Sgt	2076173	H-2-4	2/25/69		
Laraway, William D LCpl	2210088	CAC-H-4	4/11/67*	23	Seymour, Indiana
Lauer, Charles R Cpl		A-3-Amphib	6/18/67*		
Lazaro, Lawrence J Cpl		E-2-7	9/19/66		
Lebas, Claude G LCpl		B-1-3	4/2/66		
Ledbetter, Walter R Jr LtCol	063973	HMM-263	1/31/70	40	Shreveport, Louisiana
Lefler, Alan C LCpl		VMO-2	3/17/69		
Leftwich, William G Jr Maj	413465361	Advisor	3/9/65	39	Germantown, Tennessee
Lineberry, Jerry E SSgt	239624713	B-1-7	2/12/70*	28	Wadesboro, North Carolina
Livingston, Lawrence H Capt		Advisor	7/11/72		
Long, Melvin M Sgt		F-2-5	6/2/67		
Lopez, Jose G Sgt		B-3-Recon	9/2/67		
Lopez, Steven D Pfc		A-3-Recon	5/9-10/67	18	Silver Springs, Maryland
Loweranitis, John L Cpl	2052170	I-3-9	3/30/67*	22	Dubois, Pennsylvania
Lowery, Steven M Cpl		C-3-Recon	3/5/69		
Lownds, David E Col	015530	CO-KSCB	11/67-3/68	47	Westerly, Rhode Island
Luca, Joseph Sgt		F-2-7	3/5/67		
Lumbard, Donald W LCpl		B-1-Amphib	7/4/66		
Lunsford, Glen T Sgt	2101197	D-1-7	2/3/68*	20	Danville, Virginia
Mac Vane, Matthew C Cpl		CAC-F-H	8/14/67		
Malone, George M 2dLt		A-1-9	2/22/69		
Mann, Bennie H Jr Maj	060180	HMM-163	3/31/65		
Marlantes, Karl A 1stLt		C-1-4	3/1-6/69		
Martin, Raymond C Sgt	1511600	F-2-9	3/18/66*	28	Pomona, California
Mc Afee, Carlos K Capt	067830	Advisor	6/12/66	32	Oklahoma City, Oklahoma
Mc Cauley, Bertram W Maj	058997	HMM-263	9/5/66	37	New Albany, Indiana
Mc Cormick, Michael P 2dLt	0107462	D-1-4	3/20/69*	24	Wellston, Ohio
Mc Donald, Thomas C Capt		HMM-167	3/28/71		

Mc Henry, William D Cpl		H&S-1-5	2/1/68		
Mc Rae, Arthur G Cpl		F-2-7	3/16/67		
Mc Whorter, James E LCpl	452760963	L-3-3	8/22/69*	20	Beaverton, Oregon
Meier, Terrance L SSgt	1999759	M-3-3	7/21/67*	22	Portland, Oregon
Mendez, Angel Sgt	2030367	F-2-7	3/16/67*	20	New York, New York
Meuse, John R Pfc	2249495	E-2-3	5/3/67*	18	Malden, Massachusetts
Miller, Cleatus A Jr Pfc		K-3-7	10/25/69		
Mitchell, Robert G Maj	070988	HMM-165	11/29/68		
Moe, Robert F SSgt		L-3-3	12/9/65		
Moffit, Richard E Sgt		G-2-26	5/16-17/67		
Monahan, Frederick G LCpl		E-2-3	5/3/67		
Monahan, Robert E LCpl	2121721	D-1-9	5/28/67*	20	Swedesboro, New Jersey
Montgomery, Robin L 2dLt		M-1-5	6/8/69		
Moore, Freddie L LCpl		B-1-7	8/12/69		
Moore, Ronald A LCpl	2241747	I-3-7	7/19/67*	20	Manhattan Beach, California
Mosher, Christopher K LCpl		K-3-5	5/13/67		
Muir, Joseph E LtCol	049816	CO-3-3	8/18-24/65*	37	Meadow Bridge, West Virginia
Mulloy, James E Jr Sgt		H&S-3-3	8/18/65		
Murphy, James E Capt		AO-2-4	10/26/67		
Murray, John D Capt		M-3-5	9/4/67		
Myers, William H Pfc	2315999	D-1-5	5/12/67*	20	Salem, Indiana
Neil, Michael I 2dLt		D-1-7	12/20/67		
Noel, Thomas E 2dLt	0106151	C-1-4	3/1/69	22	Tulsa, Oklahoma
Noon, Patrick J Jr Sgt		F-2-4	8/24/66		
Norris, James A LCpl	478640914	I-3-5	8/13/69*	19	Des Moines, Iowa
Norton, John J Capt		E-2-5	4/21/68	31	Foster City, California
Norwood, George O LCpl		G-2-7	3/4/66		
Oakley, John L LCpl		G-2-3	8/22/66		
O'Conner, Martin E Maj	072430	Advisor	11/5/69	36	Rahway, New Jersey
Panian, Thomas C Sgt		I-3-5	9/6/67		
Parrott, Lee R GySgt	1533280	MP-2-3	8/10/69	31	Noblesville, Indiana
Paskevich, Anthony Jr 1stLt	094196	VMO-2	3/17/69	25	Chagrin Falls, Ohio
Peczeli, Joseph S GySgt		1-AAmphib	3/24/67		
Peters, William L Jr 1stLt	0102208	HMM-165	4/12/69*	26	Fort Dodge, Iowa
Peterson, Dennie D 2dLt	0100590	FO-2-11	9/6/67*	24	Los Angeles, California
Phelps, John J LCpl		VMO-6	8/19/67		
Piatt, Louis R 2dLt	0106014	M-3-7	2/23/69	23	New Orleans, Louisiana
Pichon, Louis A Jr GySgt	605087	I-3-3	3/24/67*	39	Slidell, Louisiana
Pierpan, Herbert E Maj	082433	OO-1-4	3/20-22/69	30	North Adams, Massachusetts
Pitts, Roy E Pfc	2425604	G-2-9	2/17/69*	18	North Highlands, California
Popp, James A Pfc	2246112	F-2-4	4/8/67*	21	Hemlock, Michigan
Poulson, Leroy N GySgt	1209285	VMO-6	8/19/67	35	Newell, Iowa
Powell, Charles T Sgt	2085259	L-3-7	5/31/68*	23	Columbus, Georgia
Quick, Robert L Pfc	2395468	K-3-3	2/7/68*	18	Wallaceton, Pennsylvania
Ralya, Warren H Jr Cpl	2287779	A-1-Amphib	1/20/68*	21	Shalimar, Florida
Rash, Donald R Pfc	2230103	B-1-26	3/30/68*	19	Pocahontas, Virginia
Ray, Darrell T Pfc	2108299	C-2-1	2/28/66*	18	Olympia, Washington
Reid, John M Cpl	2145615	C-1-3	5/10/67*	20	Magnolia, New Jersey
Reilly, Donald J Maj	061230	VMO-2	12/9/65*	36	St. Louis, Missouri
Reilly, James R Pfc	2042266	G-2-3	3/17/66*	20	Esopus, New York
Reis, Tiago Cpl	2209245	F-2-4	9/21/67*	20	New Bedford, Massachusetts
Richards, Thomas A Cpl		H-2-9	6/5-6/69		
Riensche, Harold A SSgt		B-3-Tanks	3/24/69		
Ripley, John W Capt		Advisor	4/2/72	32	Radford, Virginia
Rivera, Jose L LCpl		L-3-5	3/26/69		
Rivera Sotomayor, Miguel A Cpl	2174861	F-2-9	7/29/67		
Rivers, Jettie Jr 2dLt	1300239	D-1-9	5/14-15/67*	34	Nashville, Tennessee

Name	Service No.	Unit	Date	Age	Hometown
Roberson, James J 2dLt		1-AAmphib	3/24/67		
Rodrigues, Joe G Jr Sgt	2058221	L-3-4	2/22-3/3/69*	22	Dallas, Texas
Rogers, Raymond G Jr 1stSgt		I-3-9	3/30/67		
Roller, Robert T Sgt		F-2-5	10/13/66		
Rollings, Wayne E 1stLt		1-Recon	9/18/69		
Romine, Richard E LtCol		HMM-165	6/3-4/67		
Rosenberger, Roger D Pfc	2484828	M-3-3	6/17/69*	18	Swartz Creek, Michigan
Ross, David L Maj	074837	VMO-2	9/4/67	35	Cabool, Missouri
Rusher, Robert C Cpl	2278308	CAP-H-6	1/7/68*	25	Tracy, California
Russell, Timothy W Cpl		D-1-4	2/2/68		
Russell, William E Capt		E-2-3	5/28/68		
Rusth, John E Cpl		C-1-5	5/10/67		
Sadler, Charles D Cpl	2130908	A-1-9	5/21/66		
Sampson, Gerald H Capt	245607597	B-1-3	8/28/69*	32	Williamsport, Pennsylvania
Sanders, Thomas Cpl	2169627	C-1-3	5/10/67*	22	East Elmhurst, New York
Sargent, George T Jr LtCol	051686	CO-1-4	3/20/69*	39	Auburn, Alabama
Schley, Robert J Cpl	2162020	M-3-3	4/30/67*	23	Oregon, Wisconsin
Schreiber, Klaus D 1stLt	010653	C-1-Recon	10/14/67		
Schunck, Henry M Cpl		D-2-13	5/10/68		
Scott, Donald W Sgt		D-1-26	9/18/66		
See, Roger D Cpl	2382260	A-3-Recon	6/8/69	20	Indianapolis, Indiana
Sexton, Charles T Cpl		3-Recon	2/5/70		Columbia, South Carolina
Sexton, Harry E LtCol		HMM-367	9/11/70		
Sexton, Merlyn A Capt		I-3-4	6/19-7/8/68		
Sherman, Andrew M 2dLt	097870	E-2-4	8/8/66*	32	Doylestown, Ohio
Sipple, Conrad A Cpl	2043729	C-2-4	3/5/66*	22	Salem, Indiana
Sirousa, Michael A Pfc	332383951	C-1-7	2/12/70*	25	Chicago, Illinois
Skibbe, David W 2dLt	332388613	C-1-Recon	3/2/70*	23	Des Plaines, Illinois
Skweres, Jeff C Cpl		HMM-364	6/1/70		
Slater, Albert C Jr Capt	084435	A-1-9	7/6-7/67	26	Venice, California
Slater, Robert M S 1sLt		Advisor	1/5-11/68		
Sleigh, Duncan B 2dLt	0105657	M-3-7	11/6/68*	23	Marblehead, Massachusetts
Sliby, Dennis M LCpl		A-1-5	3/30/68		
Smith, Ray L Capt	0102290	Advisor	3/30-4/1/72	26	Shidler, Oklahoma
Snyder, Stephen F 2dLt	093446	F-2-4	8/24/66*	23	Sunbury, Pennsylvania
Soliz, Thomas Cpl	2180067	A-1-Amphib	9/6/67*	19	Bakersfield, California
Spark, Michael M Col	049041	CO-3-3	1/15/69*	41	New York, New York
Spicer, Jonathan N Pfc	2390916	C-3-MB	3/8/68*	19	Miami, Florida
Srsen, Steve A Pfc	2196925	A-1-3	1/27/67*	20	San Lorenzo, California
Stahl, Mykle E Sgt		K-3-26	1/21/68		
Starrett, Edward F LCpl		G-2-5	12/9/70		
St. Clair, Clarence H Jr Cpl		K-3-7	8/28/69		
Stewart, Michael E LCpl	2135524	A-1-9	5/13/67*	18	Culpepper, Virginia
Stockman, Robert D Sgt		3-MPB	1/14/70		
Stuckey, James L LCpl	2114059	C-1-9	7/6/67	21	Seminole, Florida
Sullivan, Daniel F Jr Cpl		L-3-4	4/11/66		
Sullivan, George R 2dLt		L-3-4	3/17/67		
Thatcher, Charles D LCpl		A-3-Tanks	5/8/67		
Thomas, Michael H 2dLt	0102330	I-3-26	1/20/68*	25	Pawnee, Oklahoma
Thompson, Brock I Cpl		E-2-7	10/19/67		
Thompson, Clinton W Cpl		M-3-4	3/13-14/69		
Thompson, Jerrald R Cpl	1892012	C-1-Recon	6/16/66*	24	Columbus, Ohio
Thompson, John C Sgt		HMM-364	4/30/64		
Thompson, Robert H LtCol		CO-1-5	3/3/68		
Thoryk, Barry L Cpl		A-1-9	4/4/68		
Thouvenel, Armand R Pfc	2272239	M-3-4	5/29/67*	24	Wheatridge, Colorado
Timmons, James M Pfc	2389485	M-3-7	11/6/68*	20	Groveport, Ohio

Tonkyn, Michael S LCpl	2255465	C-1-5	6/11/69	19	Mendham, New Jersey
Trent, William D LCpl	2381048	M-3-5	5/9/68*	19	East Peoria, Illinois
Tycz, James N Sgt	2082767	A-3-Recon	5/9/67*	22	Milwaukee, Wisconsin
Tyrone, Willie D SSgt	1221421	Advisor	5/30-31/65*	32	Carbon, Texas
Underwood, David F Capt	088999	HMM-163	2/16/68	27	Waynesville, North Carol
Vancor, Norman W LCpl	2418325	C-3-Recon	5/7/69	22	Ashfield, Massachusetts
Vasquez, Jesus R Sgt	2126694	FFSR	1/30/68*	20	El Paso, Texas
Verheyn, David A LCpl	2117334	A-1-Recon	2/3/67	21	Lenoxdale, Mass
Wallace, Ernie W Cpl	2034491	H-2-4	8/18/65	22	Wayne, West Virginia
Ward, James C Cpl	2439597	D-1-5	5/9/69*	21	Alexandria, Virginia
Warren, Roger O LCpl		F-2-5	2/3/68		
Webb, Bruce D Capt	068857	I-3-3	8/18/65*	31	Wheaton, Illinois
Webb, James H Jr 1stLt		D-1-5	7/10/69	23	St. Joseph, Missouri
Weise, William LtCol	057704	CO-2-4	4/30-5/2/68	39	Philadelphia, Penn
Widger, Robert I Cpl		K-3-1	6/7/69		
Williams, Robert S 1stLt		I-3-5	7/24-25/66		
Wilson, Willis C 1stLt		B-1-3	4/2/66		
Wirick, William C Cpl	2386310	I-3-26	12/8/68*	20	Toledo, Ohio
Woods, Lloyd Cpl		F-2-5	6/2/67		
Wynn, Edward H Pfc	2424476	E-2-4	5/25/68	20	Napa, California
Yarber, Vernon L LCpl	2366678	L-3-3	8/26/68*	18	Jacksonville, Florida
Yates, John C SSgt	0108133	B-1-Amphib	10/17/68*	26	Fergus Falls, Minn
Yordy, Charles R Pfc	2420003	K-3-27	5/24/68	20	Fruitport, Michigan
Young, William H Cpl		A-1-3	3/7/68		

NAVY CORPSMAN

Ashby, James W HM3	9140268	L-3-9	6/1/67*	23	Park Rapids, Minnesota
Barber, William B HM3		I-3-4	11/25/68		
Benoit, Francis A. HN	9140346	E-2-9	3/16/67*	22	Red Lake Falls, Minnesota
Burns, Dewey R Jr HM3	461900253	CAP-1-3-9	9/13/69*	20	Sulphur Springs, Texas
Casey, Robert M HM3	B111377	G-2-7	5/16/68*	19	Guttenberg, New Jersey
Clay, Raymond D HN		G-2-7	9/24/66		
Crawford, Charles H HM3	6874759	M-3-4	5/29/67*	26	Batavia, Ohio
Cruse, James D HN	1392506	M-3-4	6/15/68*	22	Paducah, Kentucky
Gerrish, Alan R HN	B116456	3-MPB	9/7/68*	19	Woburn, Massachusetts
Gillespie, Martin L Jr HM2	9027756	D-1-4	3/21/66*	26	East Boston, Massachusetts
Grant, Gollie L HN	6833808	B-1-26	9/19/66*	22	Old Fort, North Carolina
Hancock, Eugene S HM2	B317923	I-3-7	2/24/69*	22	Gainesville, Florida
Holmes, Billie D. HM3		C-1-Recon			
Hickey, William L HM2		K-3-9	7/4/66		
James, Alan C HM2		B-1-3	9/9/68		
Leal, Armando G Jr HN	B704027	M-3-5	9/4/67*	20	San Antonio, Texas
Mack, Francis W HM3	5950010	F-2-4	8/17/66*	24	Jersey City, New Jersey
Mayton, James A. HM1	2973461	VMO-2	5/21/66	33	Manchester, Tennessee
Mercer, William I. HM2	B980863	M-3-4	6/15/68*	21	Los Angeles, California
Orlando, Samuel G HN	5910304	H-2-7	3/4/66*	21	Birmingham, Alabama
Phillips, John C HN		C-1-7	12/19/68		
Powell, Richard L HN	B418314	L-3-7	8/29/68*	20	Youngstown, Ohio
Rudd, Donald L HM2	B502831		3/3/69*	23	Tecumseh, Michigan
Valdez, Phil I HN	9997731	B-1-1	1/29/67*	20	Dixon, New Mexico
Wilhelm, Mack H BM3	B713921	D-1-9	2/19/69	23	Rockport, Texas
Willeford, Franklin P HN	3537852	F-2-4	12/14/68*	25	Lawton, Oklahoma
Work, Warren A Jr HM3			4/8/67		

*Posthumous

SILVER STAR

Name	Service #	Unit	Date	Age	Hometown
Aaron, Robert J Jr 1stLt		A-1-9	3/24/67		
Abely, John LCpl					
Achterhoff, James P LCpl	2385864	E-2-4	3/18/68*	18	Muskegon, Michigan
Adams, George W III Cpl		C-1-26	6/7/69		
Adams, Laurence R III Capt	092937	HMM-165	12/15/68		
Aguilar, Vincente Jr Pfc		G-2-4	5/1/68		
Akers, Jerry R 2dLt					
Albers, Vincent A Jr LtCol	057287	CO-2-7	9/11/70	40	Houston, Texas
Albrecht, John A 1stLt	086107	D-1-4	3/21-24/66		
Albright, Edward J Sgt		A-3-Tank	4/29/69		
Alderette, Arnold L Cpl		A-1-9	2/8/68		
Alexander, Robert B Capt		B-1-4	3/20-26/66		
Alexander, Robert B Maj		OO-1-7	8/12/69		
Allen, Carl Jr Capt		L-3-26	2/28/69		
Allen, David C Pfc			2/28/66		
Allen, Don W Cpl	2337744	D-1-3	7/15/66		
Allen, Donald W LCpl	2337744	K-3-7	4/10/68		
Allen, Fred A LCpl		I-3-1	1/31/70		
Allen, Joe E 2dLt	0103089	D-1-5	5/24/68*	22	Bay St. Louis, Mississippi
Allen, Melvin L LCpl	2232029	B-1-3	5/4/67*	21	Chicago, Illinois
Allen, Paul D C Pfc	2090875	H-2-1	2/28/66		
Allen, Ronald L Capt	080654	F-2-4	6/26-27/66	24	Sabula, Iowa
Almanza, Ricky J Cpl	2379991	M-3-5	9/03/68*	20	Moline, Illinois
Alo, Ta'Aloga S SSgt		3-3	9/28/67		
Altazan, Kenneth A Sgt	2303933	HMM-364	5/9/69	23	Baton Rouge, Louisiana
Althoff, David L Maj	064955	HMM-262	2/2/68	35	Chandler, Arizona
Althoff, David L Maj	064955	HMM-262	5/13/68	35	Chandler, Arizona
Althoff, David L Maj	064955	HMM-262	5/18/68	35	Chandler, Arizona
Alvarado, Jose J SSgt					
Alvarez, Enrique Cpl					
Alvarez, Robert Pfc	2193505	C-1-4	3/24/67*	20	Clint, Texas
Amendola, Willet R Cpl	2303053		11/2/67*	19	Deposit, New York
Anasiewicz, Richard J Pfc	2169441	M-3-5	7/18/66*	20	New Brunswick, New Jersey
Anderson, Clinton H Jr 2dLt	0100013		7/4/67*	22	El Segundo, California
Anderson, Donald F Pfc		B-3-Tanks	9/19/66		
Anderson, John J Sgt	1646153	I-3-9	10/27/65		
Anderson, Joseph S Pfc		E-2-4	3/13/68		
Anderson, Lee H 2dLt		L-3-5	7/24/66		
Anderson, Ralph C 1stLt		HMM-262	7/31/69		
Anderson, Ralph T LCpl	2366871	H-2-4	5/2/68*	18	St. Petersburg, Florida
Anderson, Ronald D Pfc	2320067	H&S-2-26	4/6/67*	18	New York, New York
Anderson, Terry C Pfc					
Anderst, James L Capt	082185	VMA-242	10/25/67	29	Plankton, South Dakota
Andrews, James F III 1stLt	0902684	HMM-265	3/13/69		
Angle, Peter F Capt	081994				
Angle, Peter F Capt	081994	HMM-161	7/8/68		
Anzaldua, Alberto T Sgt	451740476	A-1-3	8/10/69*	23	Santa Rosa, Texas
Apodaca, Ramon LCpl		G-2-1	3/4/68		
Araujo, Espiridion Jr LCpl	2423491	C-1-27			
Arbogast, Allen G Cpl			4/13/68		
Ariss, David W Capt	082292	HMM-265	2/8/68	28	Pomona, California
Arizmendez, Daniel M Cpl	2202057	B-1-26	5/29/68	22	Holland, Michigan

Name	ID	Unit	Date	Age	Hometown
Armer, Billy R GySgt	1196747	G-2-4	4/27/68		
Armes, Willard P 2dLt		M-3-9	2/10/69		
Armstrong, Elton Pfc	2424349	H-2-5	5/11/69		
Armstrong, John C Cpl		G-2-9	4/21/69		
Arthur, Lawrence K Pfc	2380637		5/28/68*	18	Lowville, New York
Ashby, James C Pvt		M-3-1	4/14/67		
Ashley, Maurice C Jr LtCol					
Atkins, William LCpl		D-1-26	6/9/68		
Austin, Randall W LtCol	075337	CO-2-9	5/15/75	38	Glenside, Pennsylvania
Avalos, Manuel Jr Cpl	2080450	B-1-3	4/2/66		
Avery, John M GySgt	1518220	B-3-1	10/25/68*	31	Cottondale, Alabama
Axley, Lawrence A LCpl		L-3-3	8/22/69		
Babb, Wayne A Capt	085006		3/19/69	29	Brevard, North Carolina
Babitz, Donald M Maj	073760	HMM-165	11/14/66	32	Cicero, Illinois
Bach, Albert W Sgt	1994442	B-3-Recon	1/18/67	22	Hialeah, Florida
Bachta, Thomas E Sgt		1-Recon	8/8/66		
Backeberg, Bruce B Pfc	2100837	D-1-26	9/19/66*	19	Helena, Montana
Baez, Jose M LCpl		D-1-4	10/26/67		
Bailey, Gene E Maj		HMM-367	3/28/71		
Bailey, Thomas B Cpl		D-3-Recon	9/2/68		
Baird, John R Jr LCpl	2423144	A-1-9	2/22/69*	19	Oak Lawn, Illinois
Baker, Billy R LCpl	453966023	H-2-7	4/24/70*	19	Leesville, Texas
Baker, Clyde L 2dlt		D-1-4	2/25/67		
Baker, David R Cpl	2032366	L-3-7	3/22/66		
Baker, Fred J LCpl	2147111	A-3-Recon	4/25/67	21	Piedmont, Alabama
Baker, Harvey L Pfc					
Baker, Herbert G SSgt		D-1-1	7/2/68		
Baker, Kenneth A SSgt	1471002	D-1-1	11/22/68*	32	New Bedford, Massachusetts
Baker, Sam R II Sgt		A-1-5	8/10/66		
Baker, Sydney A 1stLt	0105860	HMM-367	9/11/70	24	San Antonio, Texas
Baker, William H Sgt	2036045	G-2-7	3/4/66		
Balanco, John J Sgt		CAP-0-1	1/21/68		
Balfanz, Duane A Capt		Advisor	11/6/69		
Balignasay, Pedro L GySgt					
Ballew, Donald L GySgt	649328	Advisor	2/7/66		
Ballew, Henry Jr LCpl	256784132	A-1-3	7/27/69*	18	Atlanta, Georgia
Ballin, Joe M Jr LCpl	2127236	D-1-4	9/16/66*	19	Fresno, California
Banks, Adam J Jr SSgt		M-3-5	11/8/67		
Banks, Andrew B Jr Maj					
Banks, Edward J Capt		H-2-1	1/31/67		
Banks, Johnny L Pfc					
Banning, John J 2dLt		A-1-Tanks	5/25/68		
Barber, Russell M Sgt	1866636	K-3-4	7/18/66		
Barclay, Boyd L Capt	087876	VMO-3	6/8/67	27	Oklahoma City, Oklahoma
Barden, Roosevelt Jr LCpl					
Barents, Brent J Capt					
Barham, Robert L II Sgt		D-3-Recon	1/4/67		
Barnard, Roger H Lt Col		CO-3-7	5/15/68		
Barnes, Alan R Pfc					
Barnes, Eric M 1stLt		C-1-26	9/24/66		
Barnes, Louis Cpl					
Barnes, Robert C LCpl		B-3-Recon	10/3/66		
Barnes, Robert L 1stLt		HMM-367	12/8/69		
Barnett, Meredith L Sgt	281508098	I-3-1	11/6/70*	20	Belpre, Ohio
Barr, James B Capt					
Barrett, Clarance A Pfc		L-3-5	3/1/68		
Barrett, James A Cpl		C-1-Recon	10/10/66		

Name	Service #	Unit	Date	Age	Hometown
Barrett, James J Cpl					
Barrett, John J Capt	085356	HMM-263	2/10/69	30	Minneapolis, Minnesota
Barrett, John J Capt	085356	HMM-263	4/3/69	30	Minneapolis, Minnesota
Barrett, John J Capt	085356	HMM-263	5/26/69	30	Minneapolis, Minnesota
Barron, Jeffrey M Cpl	2296415	G-3-12	2/25/69*	20	La Puente, California
Barrow, Thomas M Jr Pfc	2308150	K-3-3	4/26/67*	18	Atlanta, Georgia
Bartlett, Dan M LCpl		E-2-5	5/16/66		
Bartlett, Gary R Sgt		F-2-3	7/20/66		
Bartolotti, Joseph Cpl					
Bartolotti, Richard J LCpl		L-3-7	2/7/68		
Bartusevics, John Sgt		C-1-Tanks	1/15/67		
Basel, John M 1stLt					
Baskin, Richard W Sgt			6/5-6/67		
Bateman, James A Sgt	2102290	CAP-2-8-1	5/15/69*	23	Mundelein, Illinois
Bates, Robert A 1stLt	091299	G-2-3	10/22/66*	24	Lake Forest, Illinois
Bathurst, Sheldon J Sgt	1820763	E-2-1	7/18/66	25	Baltimore, Maryland
Battista, Anthony J 2dLt	091530		4/16/66*	23	Dunmore, Pennsylvania
Bauer, William A LCpl		K-5	7/24/66		
Beans, James D Maj	072931	Advisor	5/2/71	37	Annapolis, Maryland
Beard, Lary G LCpl		E-2-1	5/17/68		
Beaver, Donald E GySgt	1201018	HMM-164	9/2/66	32	Selinsgrove, Pennsylvania
Becham, Gary V LCpl		G-2-9	2/17/69		
Beckman, Bruce E 1stLt		VMA-262	2/23/68		
Beckman, Bruce M 1stLt					
Beebe, William A II 1stLt		HMM-364	4/8/69		
Beeler, Robert A Capt	089734	I-3-5	8/13/69	27	Louisville, Kentucky
Belko, Laurence E Sgt		I-3-3	5/26/68		
Bell, Earl W SSgt		H&S-3-Rec	3/24/67		
Bell, James E Sgt	1083156	G-2-4	3/22/66		
Bell, Marcus R Cpl					
Bell, Thomas J Sgt		F-2-4	6/25/66		
Bell, Van D Jr LtCol	044563	CO-1-1	2/18-22/67	47	Miami, Florida
Below, Jack W SSgt		A-1-Recon	3/20/67		
Belser, Joseph H Jr 1stLt		K-3-27	5/24/68		
Bem, Walter P Pfc	2490068	B-1-7	4/30/69*	18	Indiana, Pennsylvania
Bench, Arnold E LtCol		CO-2-4	7/18-24/66		
Bench, Edmund Jr LCpl		G-2-9	6/1/69		
Bendell, Lee R LtCol	050744	CO-3-4	1/24/68	40	Melrose Park, Illinois
Bender, Lawrence J II Capt	095847	Advisor	5/14-15/70	33	Cleveland, Ohio
Benet, Peter E Maj		HMM-263	6/14/70		
Benfatti, Raymond C 1stLt		L-3-9	2/17/69		
Benjamin, John Cpl		H-2-7	3/4/66		
Bennett, Billy J Pfc	2327147	F-2-9	7/29/67*	19	Chattanooga, Tennessee
Bennett, Jesse D Jr Maj					
Bennett, Kenneth D Cpl					
Bergeron, Robert H SSgt	1375888	K-3-4	9/27/66		
Bergerson, John F 2dLt	092624	B-1-1	1/29/67*	23	Mercer Island, Washington
Bergman, Carl E Capt	092979	HMM-163	2/16/68	24	Kenmare, North Dakota
Berman, Stuart C 2dLt		C-1-Tanks	3/21/67		
Bernard, Henry W Jr LCpl	2322441	H&S-2-9	7/29/67*	19	Willimantic, Connecticutt
Berry, Johnny K GySgt		I-3-1	12/22/67		
Berry, Larry J Cpl		F-3-1			
Betts, Albert L SSgt	1982176	D-1-1	2/6/68	24	West Palm Beach, Florida
Beyerlein, David Sgt		A-1-9	2/22/69		
Bianchino, Richard L Capt	088193	HMM-364	4/14/69	28	Albany, New York
Bibeau, Arthur K Cpl		C-11-Eng	3/24/69		
Biber, Joseph F Sgt	2198273	E-3-Recon	9/19/68*	22	Lompoc, California

Bickert, Edward T Jr LCpl		2-CAG	2/7/68		
Bickford, Thomas E 2dLt	096171	FO-3-11	9/18-25/66	36	Flandreau, South Dakota
Bickley, Leroy A Maj		OO-1-5	2/26/70		
Biddulph, Stephen G 1stLt		1-Anglico	7/11-13/72		
Biehl, Michael C Cpl					
Biggers, Archie J 1stLt					
Biggs, Jimmy D Pfc	2451993	A-1-7	12/7/68*	19	Kansas City, Missouri
Billings, Roger L LCpl	2361338	D-1-5	2/22/68		
Billups, Josh LCpl		K-3-9	2/12/69		
Bingenheimer, James Sgt	156346736	A-1-Recon	3/15/71*	23	Atlantic City, New Jersey
Bird, Charles U Jr Sgt					
Bird, Loren W SSgt		H-3-7	1/11/68		
Biskey, Robert A Pfc	1871095	I-3-1	3/5/66		
Black, Charles H Maj		OO-1-5	9/6/67		
Black, Robert A Jr Capt	087392	B-1-1	7/6/68		
Blackburn, Glenn J Pvt		D-1-3	5/4/67		
Blackman, Thomas J Pfc	2398632		5/10/68*	19	Racine, Wisconsin
Blackwell, Kenneth G LCpl	2400695	I-3-26	2/23/69*	20	Tucson, Arizona
Blades, Arthur C 1stLt	090430	1-1	8/10/66	24	Westhampton Beach, New York
Blair, Frank S III 1stLt		F-2-4	10/14/67		
Blair, Frank S III 1stLt		F-2-4	9/21/67		
Blair, John D Cpl		I-3-4	1/27/68		
Blair, Lawrence K III Sgt		B-1-26	9/16/66		
Bland, Richard P L Capt		HMM-364	6/4/68		
Blankenship, Dennis R SSgt		I-F-Recon	5/20/66		
Blankenship, Sidney H SSgt					
Blanton, Charles G Sgt		I-3-Recon	12/16/65		
Bleacher, Ronald T Cpl	2283664	H-2-5	10/29/68*	19	Marshallton, Delaware
Blizzard, David W Capt	0100870	Advisor	11/9/71	30	Ocean City, New Jersey
Blocker, Eugene SSgt		A-1-9	2/21/67		
Bloomberg, Richard N Capt		VMA-121	5/10/68		
Boatman, Michael L Pfc	2373653	G-2-7	5/7/68	19	Lakewood, Colorado
Bobak, Raymond W Pfc					
Bobian, Ralph D LCpl	2304829	D-1-7	12/20/67*	18	Denver, Colorado
Boeck, Gary R LCpl	472643165	L-3-5	1/6/71*	20	Braham, Minnesota
Bogart, John G 2dLt	0106510	3-3	6/16/69	24	Chappaqua, New York
Bohn, Robert D Col	037498	CO-5	12/27/67		
Boillot, David A 2dLt		A-1-27	6/19/68		
Boldes, James M LCpl			10/3-5/66		
Bolding, Benjamin F Cpl	2257470	M-3-26	2/15/69*	20	Moore, Oklahoma
Bolduc, George J 2dLt		L-3-7	2/7/68		
Bolduc, George J 2dLt		L-3-7	5/18/68		
Boles, James M LCpl		I-3-9			
Bollman, Henry C Capt		HMM-165	7/11/72		
Bolton, Gilbert H SSgt		M-3-7	11/2/67	26	Portsmouth, Ohio
Bolton, Michael L Cpl		D-1-3	9/18/68		
Bonnelycke, Clyde L Sgt	1806021	C-1-3	1/19/68	28	Honolulu, Hawaii
Bonsper, Donald E Capt		Advisor	1/9/68		
Book, Floyd G Jr LCpl			6/5/67		
Boomer, Walter E Capt	079957	H-2-4	2/5/67	29	Rich Square, North Carolina
Boomer, Walter E Maj	079957	Advisor	3/30-4/3/72	34	Rich Square, North Carolina
Boone, Samuel Jr Cpl	2294933	B-1-26	3/30/68		
Booty, Larry O J Cpl	2062303	F-2-9	1/8/66*	21	Greenwell Springs, Louisiana
Bosley, Charles W Pfc	2122523	C-1-Recon	6/16/66		
Boss, Otis E Jr LCpl	2363521	F-2-4	5/2/68		
Bosser, Johnny S LCpl	521685259	K-3-7	9/28/69*	19	Fort Lupton, Colorado
Bost, Barry N Cpl		A-1-7	5/17/68		

Botello, Alfred L		E-2-5	12/19/66		
Bott, Daniel J SSgt		D-1-1	9/25/68		
Bourne, Frank L Jr LtCol		CO-3-4	6/16/68		
Bower, Burton K Pfc	2238843	L-3-27	5/18/68		
Boyer, Robert L Cpl	2234967	E-2-3	12/28/67*	21	Long Beach, California
Braddock, Harold T Jr Cpl		E-2-5	5/16/66		
Braddon, John R Maj	057518	HMM-364	4/27/64	34	Wellsville, New York
Brady, Phillip O 1stLt	082115	Advisor	12/31/64		
Bradley, Gerald G Cpl	2394208	E-2-1	1/15/69*	21	Braintree, Massachusetts
Bradley, John M LCpl		M-3-1	12/27/68		
Brady, Eugene R LtCol	164228075	HMM-364	2/26/69	40	York, Pennsylvania
Brandon, Jack A Maj					
Brandon, Wayne H 2dLt	0100069	K-3-5	9/6/67	23	Martin, Tennessee
Brank, Walter S III LCpl	2212179	HMM-165	5/5/68		
Branscombe, Robert A Sgt	2157195	CAP-B-1	2/6/68	20	Glendale, California
Breeding, Earle G Maj		E-2-26	2/5/68		
Brennan, John L 1stLt	0100072	HMM-364	2/12/69		
Brenno, Wesley C Pfc		C-1-1	3/20/67		
Brent, Lawrence J Cpl		A-1-3	7/20/66		
Brewer, Herman R Jr Sgt		A-1-Amphib	3/6/67		
Brick, George E Cpl		M-3-5	8/17/68		
Brickey, Billy J SSgt		I-3-5	7/22/66		
Bright, Robert III Cpl		3-Recon	10/21/66		
Brisco, Joseph O Cpl		H-2-4	8/20/69		
Britt, Ted D Pfc	2378809	B-1-26	3/30/68*	19	Decatur, Georgia
Britton, Albert K SSgt	1820832				
Broadtman, Henry R Jr Pfc	2384975	L-3-3	1/26/69*	18	Waggaman, Louisiana
Brodrick, Steven P 1stLt	0103916	F-2-4	12/11/68*	25	Selma, California
Bronars, Edward J Maj		Advisor	7/22/65		
Brooks, Robert P Capt		K-3-9	7/4/66		
Brophy, Daniel R 1stLt					
Broquist, Steven A 2dLt	094500	D-1-9	5/14/67*	22	Champaign, Illinois
Broughton, Frankie D GySgt					
Brown, Calvin F SSgt		C-1-1	1/14/67		
Brown, Charles L Sgt		L-3-9	2/24/69		
Brown, David B Capt	082465	F-2-5	9/30/68	29	Shillington, Pennsylvania
Brown, Gary E 1stLt		E-2-4	3/21/66		
Brown, James G LCpl	2080108	H-2-5	4/21/66*	21	Gatesville, Texas
Brown, James H 1stLt					
Brown, James S Jr 1stLt					
Brown, Jerome W Maj	295289076		2/13/69	35	Cincinnati, Ohio
Brown, Joseph C Cpl	2047608	B-3-Tanks	7/30/66*	20	Pasadena, Maryland
Brown, Lawrence R LCpl	2089250	I-3-9	9/5/66	19	Cincinnati, Ohio
Brown, Leslie E Col	019930	CO-MAG-12	10/28/65		
Brown, Marc A Pfc	2297413	M-3-1	4/21/67*	19	Long Beach, California
Brown, Michael A LCpl		G-2-4	3/11/69		
Brown, Michael R Sgt		3-5	8/9/68		
Brown, Richard J Sgt	2031415	K-3-5	9/6/67*	23	Pine Beach, New Jersey
Brown, Robert H LCpl					
Brown, Terry R Pfc		A-1-Recon	10/28/68		
Brown, Willie LCpl	2476128		4/24/69*	20	Tallahassee, Florida
Browning, Michael L LCpl	2251278	B-1-7	10/24/67*	19	Fullerton, California
Broyer, Clifton L Cpl	2249149	C-1-4	2/28/69*	23	Cataumet, Massachusetts
Bruggeman, David C 1stLt	172386431	1-Anglico	4/1/72*	25	Pittsburgh, Pennsylvania
Bruinekool, Dewayne G Cpl		M-3-3	7/21/67		
Bruno, Edward LCpl	072381541	F-2-3	8/6/69*	21	Long Beach, New York
Bryan, Byron E Jr 1stLt		K-3-9	4/30/68		

Bryant, David P LCpl	2205916	FO-3-9	10/1/67		
Bryant, Donald L Sgt		G-2-26	10/4/68		
Buchholz, Edward A LCpl	2088095	H-2-4	7/23/66		
Buchs, Christopher J LCpl	2107157	I-3-3	8/18/65		Fraser, Michigan
Buckles, William T LCpl	2333245	M-3-5	2/6/68*	19	Hollywood, Florida
Buckley, Alton LCpl		E-2-9	2/2/68		
Buckner, Gordon H II Maj	065539	HMM-362	11/18/65		
Budd, Talman C III Maj		Advisor	7/30-31/67		
Bulger, Thomas E LtCol	050747	CO-3-1	4/4/69	42	Staten Island, New York
Bull, Edward D Cpl		C-1-4	3/1/69		
Bunda, George J 1stLt	093008	HMM-265			
Burch, James M 1stLt		H-2-3	8/20-26/?		
Burchett, Donald D Cpl					
Burchette, Johnny R Pfc		H-2-1	1/29/67		
Burgess, Glenn F 1stLt					
Burgett, George S Capt		F-2-5	10/13/66		
Burghardt, James E LCpl	2215780	I-3-9	3/30/67	20	Belmont, California
Burke, Francis M Maj		I-3-5	9/6/67		
Burke, John R Cpl	2200142		6/6/67*	23	Clearwater, Florida
Burke, Nicholas E Capt					
Burkhardt, Douglas K Pfc		1-Recon	3/5/68		
Burleson, Eugene B Jr Capt		C-1-3	10/11/67		
Burns, John R Jr 2dLt	0101776	M-3-4	1/18/68*	24	St. Louis, Missouri
Burns, Raymond M Capt		VMA-242	10/27/67		
Burns, Roy T Pvt		B-3-Recon	9/2/67		Garyville, Florida
Burns, Terry P Capt					
Burr, Stewart S Pfc	2255287	E-2-9	4/23/69*	20	Passaic, New Jersey
Burton, John T Sgt	2109309	E-2-7	5/18/68*	21	Mount Juliet, Tennessee
Burton, Ronald E LCpl			5/12/68		
Burtsell, Ronald L 1stSgt		A-1-27	8/23/68		
Butler, Christopher P SSgt		H&S-212	10/20/66		
Butler, James T Capt		HMM-164	2/12/68		
Butler, John C SSgt		CAC-1-1	5/9/68		
Butler, Robert H Jr Sgt	1968622	M-3-5	7/18/66		Indianapolis, Indiana
Butt, Thomas E LCpl		I -3-9	3/30/67	20	Rockville, Maryland
Buttry, Robert L Jr LCpl					
Buttry, Robert L Jr LCpl		D-1-1	9/1/67		
Butts, John D Sgt		CAC-1	1/10/68		
Byers, James N IV 2dLt		D-1-5	9/11/68		
Byler, Earl D 2dLt					
Byrne, Gerald J Jr Pfc	2208181	H/2/5	9/10/67		
Byrne, Joseph L Jr Pfc	2116537		7/20/66*	19	Roscoe, Pennsylvania
Byron, Michael J 1stLt	088284	A-1-3	7/1/65		
Cabrera, Alfredo Sgt					
Caceres, Edgardo LCpl	2108262	B-1-9	5/12/66*	21	Tacoma, Washington
Cahoon, Curtis R LCpl		I-3-7	6/19/69		
Cain, Jerome F Pfc		B-5-Tanks	6/15/68		
Calabria, Joseph R Sgt		H&S-11-Eng	5/8/67		
Calderone, Thomas Cpl	2207193	B-1-1	5/31/68		
Caldon, David L Capt	089878	TAC-2-26	4/6/68	25	Cheshire, Connecticutt
Caldwell, Robert P Pfc		C-1-1	3/18/68		
Call, John G LCpl	2308135	B-1-5	9/4/67*	19	Columbus, Georgia
Callaham, Robert LCpl		E-2-3	12/28/67		
Callahan, Melvin R LCpl	2105660	A-1-1	10/30/65		
Callaway, Johnny P Pfc		B-1-Recon	11/29/68		
Camp, Aubie Pfc	2083796	A-1-1	10/30/65	19	Apison, Tennessee
Campbell, Donald A Cpl	2128722	B-1-3	9/9/68*	21	Glouster, Ohio

Campbell, Harold J Jr Capt	085928	HMM-265	1/27/67	28	Somerville, Massachusetts
Campbell, Kenneth C Sgt		1-Anglico	2/1/67		
Campbell, Thomas E Capt	1543461	Advisor	6/29/66	28	Dallas, Texas
Campbell, Wallace L 1stLt		MAG-11	5-6/67?		
Candelario, Rafael A Sgt		A-1-5	5/9/69		
Canney, George T LCpl		B-1-3	9/17/67		
Cannon, James R 2dLt	093569	E-2-3	5/3/67	31	Fredericksburg , Virginia
Cannon, James T Jr SSgt					
Cantieny, John B LtCol		CO-1-13	2/23/69	37	Minneapolis, Minnesota
Cantu, Andres Jr Cpl		I-3-3	9/11/68		
Caple, Edward F Pfc		K-3-3	9/15/69		
Capozzoli, Orlando S Cpl	2022090	M-3-7	4/21/66	22	Chicago, Illinois
Capraro, Claud W Cpl	2373669	K-3-7	12/3/68*	19	Penrose, Colorado
Car, John P Jr Cpl					
Carey, Michael D 1stLt	091723	I-3-5	7/22/66	25	Torrance, California
Carey, Michael D 1stLt	091723	I-3-5	7/24/66	25	Torrance, California
Carey, Thomas W LCpl	2262396	F-2-9			
Carl, Daniel R Sgt		H-2-7	7/13/70		
Carlin, John P Capt					
Carlisi, Ignatius Pfc	2170881	C-1-Recon	6/16/66*	20	New York, New York
Carlisle, Jimmy D Sgt	2164281	I-3-5	8/29/70	25	Zillah, Washington
Carlisle, Richard P Maj		Advisor	3/25/71		
Carlson, Clarence R LCpl		A-3-Recon	5/9/67		
Carlson, Gary E Capt		Advisor	6/29/66		
Carlton, David J Cpl	2259576	C-1-1	8/1/67*	20	St. Paul, Minnesota
Carlton, John D Maj		ReconSquad-1	4/16/72		
Carmean, Paul R Jr Cpl		MABS-36	3/17/68		
Carmody, John J 1stLt					
Caro, Alexander J LCpl		M-3-4	1/27/68		
Carolan, Fredrick A Capt	072088	MAG-11	5/6/67		
Carpenter, Peter B 2dLt		C-1-Recon	1/16/69		
Carr, John D Capt	083158	L-3-4	1/18/68	34	Belfast, Maine
Carr, Richard W Maj	068300	HMM-161	4/18/69	36	Anderson, S C
Carr, William D 1stLt	083966	VMA-513	2/21/68	35	New York, New York
Carrel, Jeffery L LCpl					
Carroll, Peter R LCpl	2375967	H-2-1	1/15/69*	20	Winters, California
Carter, Johnnie III Pfc					
Carter, Thomas C 1stLt	088603	B-1-7	9/10/65		
Carter, Timothy G LCpl	530380598	F-2-1	7/1/69*	20	Ely, Nevada
Carter, Wallace M SSgt		G-2-5	12/19/66		
Caruolo, Richard A LCpl	2011788	K-3-7	3/22/66*	21	Providence, Rhode Island
Cashman, Cornelius J LCpl	291426576	D-1-7	8/12/69*	19	North Royalton, Ohio
Cassidy, John J 1stLt	090418	B-3-Recon	3/15/66	23	Central Islip, New York
Castagnetti, Gene E Capt	031285536	B-1-5	6/9/69	30	Needham, Massachusetts
Castaneda, Robert L Sgt 7/23/70					
Castania, Donald W LCpl		C-3-Recon	2/17/69		
Castillo, Alfredo R L Cpl		A-1-1	4/9/67		
Castillo, Charles R LCpl			6/5-6/67		Detroit, Michigan
Castor, James W Cpl	513505308	I-3-5	8/13/69*	20	Natoma, Kansas
Caswell, Russell J Capt					
Catalogne, Paul R Capt		C-3-Eng	7/30/67		
Cauble, John D Jr SSgt		HMM-262	1/25/68		
Caudle, Jerry W 1stLt		HMM-361	10/30/66		Winston-Salem, N C
Cecil, Richard D Sgt	1127963	C-3-Tanks	5/20/66	32	San Diego, California
Centers, Jack Cpl					
Centers, Normand B 1stLt		A-1-26	6/7/67		
Centers, Ronald L Pfc	2128537	H-2-4	8/18/65		

Name	Service No.	Unit	Date	Age	Hometown
Cerda, Rene Cpl		B-3-Tanks	5/19/68		
Cerna, Narciso R Jr LCpl	2110587	K-3-4	7/15/66*	18	San Antonio, Texas
Chacon, David A LCpl	2409589	A-1-9	2/22/69*	20	Gilcrest, Colorado
Chacon, Richard S Jr Sgt	1371893	K-3-3	7/7/68		
Chadwick, Leon G III Capt	087306	PMO-6	10/31/66*	26	Raleigh, North Carolina
Chaisson, John R Col		G-3	4/9/66		
Chamberlain, Gene Pfc		I-3-9	3/30/67		
Chambers, John C Cpl		A-3-Tanks	05/19/67		
Chambers, Lester E Pfc	2336047	A-1-Atanks	2/24/68*	21	Dallas, Texas
Chambliss,Carl S LCpl					
Champe, Charles R 1stLt					
Chapa, Richard E 1stLt					
Chapman, Darrell H LCpl		A-1-9	2/22/69	20	Claremont, New Hampshire
Chapman, Harlan P LtCol		POW	7/66-10/67		
Chapman, William W SSgt		B-1-9	8/22/68		
Charlie, Peter LCpl	585305795		8/8/70*	21	Farmington, New Mexico
Charlton, Albert K LtCol	066768		9/21/69	37	Spokane, Washington
Chase, Jerry D 2dLt	095902	I-3-3	3/24/67	31	Vestal, New York
Chavarria, Manuel T SSgt		B-1-4	3/22/67		
Chaves, Allen F Pfc	2269791	D-3-Recon	5/4/67*	19	Winslow, Arizona
Cheatham, Charles W 1stLt	089036	I-3-12	7/28-29/66	24	Burlington, North Carolina
Cheff, Stanley W 1stLt	088234	C-1-Recon	10/16/65	24	Grand Rapids, Michigan
Chesnut, Robert E LCpl					
Chidgey, Donald J LCpl	2181762	C-1-1Recon	10/10/66		
Childress, Arthur C LCpl					
Chiofolo, Vincent N Pfc	2417922	K-3-27	5/17/68		
Chism, Samuel M Sgt		B-1-13	6/17/68		
Christensen, Harry C Cpl		B-3-Tanks	1/24/68		
Christensen, Paul K Cpl					
Christmas, George R Capt	085447			27	Yeadon, Pennsylvania
Christy, Howard A Capt	069814	A-1-9	5/21/66		Provo, Utah
Cincotta, Thomas A Pfc	2483094	L-3-9	6/28/69*	18	San Rafael, California
Cisneros, Tony A LCpl	2327825	K-3-3	2/7/68		
Clancy, John J III 1stLt	085172	A-1-4	3/20/66		
Clark, Delbert E Cpl	2036461	C-1-3	6/5/65		
Clark, Frank A LtCol		CO-1-7	11/12/69		
Clark, John L Jr Maj	4720662	VMO-2	5/5/68	31	Omaha, Nebraska
Clark, Read M Capt		I-3-7	1/30/67	31	Winston-Salem, N C
Clark, Robert N Jr 2dLt	093883	D-1-9	3/4/67*	24	Indianapolis, Indiana
Clark, Stephen W Capt	091131	VMA-235	5/3/68*	26	Plymouth, California
Clay, Henry H Pfc					
Cleary, Robert E GySgt	1223540	G-2-1	6/25/66		
Clements, Charles G Sgt					
Clements, Marvin W Cpl		L-3-7	8/29/68		
Cleven, Wayne R 1stLt		H&S-12	5/5/68		
Clute, Michael A Pfc	2454839	J-2-9	2/17/69*	19	Hinsdale, New York
Coachman, Albert Cpl		M-3-1	2/2/68		
Coats, Charles T LCpl	2352780	G-2-9	4/19/68*	18	Klamath Falls, Oregon
Cobb, Daniel J III Capt		M-O-6	12/22/67		
Cody, Richard L Capt	085109	A-1-5	10/7/68	30	Richmond, California
Coe, Michael G 2dLt		A-1-7	2/6/68		
Colasanti, Robert J Sgt		G-2-4	5/2/68		
Colby, Brian L LCpl	2261912	F-2-7	2/28/67*	19	Lansing, Michigan
Coleman, David M Cpl		G-2-3	4/30/67		
Coleman, George W 2dLt	0103411	D-1-7	3/17/68*	25	Wildwood Crest, New Jersey
Coleman, Matthew Pfc		L-3-1	1/1/67		
Collins, David L Cpl	2127450	F-2-5	2/1/68*	20	Carson City, California

Collins, Edward Jr Pfc		B-1-26	3/30/68		
Collins, James A Pfc	2086051	3-26	1/20/68*	22	Broadwell, Illinois
Collins, Patrick G Capt	076230	D-3-Recon	5/14/65		
Compton, James L Maj		B-3-Recon	3/13-15/66		
Conatser, Bernis B Capt		Advisor	1/22/70		
Conger, William A Capt					
Connell, George M 1stLt	089342	C-1-9	5/21/66		
Connelly, Edward W Jr Capt	093033	HMM-165	5/5/68*	24	Agawam, Massachusetts
Connelly, William 1stLt		C-1-9	4/16/68		
Conner, Samuel D LCpl	2122469	G-2-9	1/13/66		
Conti, Robert F 1stLt	326403952	E-2-5	11/24/69*	23	Emmaus, Pennsylvania
Contreras, Anselmo Cpl		K-3-3	3/24/67		
Convery, Joseph F Jr Pfc	2347401	F-2-3	2/6/68*	19	Chester, Pennsylvania
Cooke, Harold T Pfc	1686983	F-2-9	1/30/66*	27	San Diego, California
Coomer, Richard R Cpl	2397845	A-1-1	10/27/68*	21	Placentia, California
Cooper, James L Maj		E-2-5	6/21/66		
Cooper, Thomas M Capt	085558		1/7/69	30	Elizabethtown, Kentucky
Copeland, Randolph G Capt		G-2-1	3/4/68		
Copeland, Shalor II LCpl		B-1-3	8/17/65		
Corbett, Wayne Jr Pfc		3-Recon	12/17/66		
Corliss, Gregory A Maj					
Cornett, Charles B Cpl		VMO-2	1/6/69		
Corsino, Eddie N LCpl	278449236	I-3-4	9/17/69*	20	Lorain, Ohio
Costello, William F LCpl	2097787	F-2-7	3/4/66		
Cothran, Terry E Cpl	2010356	D-3-Recon	5/14/65	21	Houston, Texas
Cotter, Richard L 2dLt	0105059	H&S-1-Amphib	2/10/69*	23	Peabody, Massachusetts
Courtney, Paul H Capt	088591	HMM-363	4/13/67	25	Leavenworth, Kansas
Cowart, David L LCpl	2281133	A-1-1	9/25/67*	20	Aliquippa, Pennsylvania
Cox, Eugene P Capt		T-F-77	4/16/72		
Cox, George W Jr Maj	066082	HMM-364	5/7/69	38	Overland Park, Kansas
Cox, Lester E Jr Cpl		HMM-165	7/11/72		
Cox, Robert K Pfc 3/4/69		E-2-4	3/4/69		
Craft, David F Sgt					
Cramer, Robert M Maj	076778	HMM-362	1/8/68*	32	Stoutland, Missouri
Crawford, Curtis E Cpl	2127011	G-2-3	2/28/67*	19	Dunkirk, New York
Crawl, Daniel Jr LCpl		FLSGA	9/3/67		
Creech, Jimmie A Maj	077879	VMO-2	7/26/69	33	Jenkins, Kentucky
Creed, Jerry L Capt		Recon	11/5/70		
Creel, John B Jr 2dLt	089621	A-1-9	9/9/65		
Creel, John B Jr Capt					
Creelman, Malcolm W Pfc		H-2-1	9/16/68		
Crespocruz, Antonoi Cpl					
Crews, Curtis T. Capt					
Croft, Harold A Pfc		K-3-3	3/25/67		
Crooks, Ronald L Cpl	2214965	B-1-26	6/7/67*	21	Hickory, North Carolina
Cross, Robert J Jr 1stLt		I-3-4	8/16/68		
Crouch, George M SSgt	1938468	A-1-Recon	4/15/69		
Crouch, Jack E Jr LCpl	2115687	C-1-26	9/22/66*	18	Mount Vernon, Illinois
Crowder, David L Cpl					
Cruz, Luis A LCpl	087421797	B-1-5	11/4/70*	20	New York, New York
Cuddy, Francis J Jr Capt	094240	HMM-265	6/8/69	29	Samford, Connecticut
Cudnik, Edmund V Pfc	2421050	M-3-7	12/26/68*	19	Detroit, Michigan
Cullen, Terence M 2dLt		L-3-9	6/1/67		
Culver, Richard O Jr Capt		H-2-3	7/21/67		
Cumbie, William T Cpl	2308561	I-3-3	2/9/69*	19	Jacksonville, Florida
Cummings, Charles H Pfc	2359128	C-3-Recon	9/14/68	18	Washington, Illinois
Cummings, John D Capt					

Cunningham, Frederick R 1stLt		M-3-1	2/2/68		
Curd, James H R Capt	070637	C-1-9	3/4/67		
Curd, James H R Capt	070637	C-1-9	3/24/67		
Curry, Jimmy D Cpl	2196774	F-2-4	9/21/67*	21	San Jose, California
Curry, Richard T Pfc		A-1-1	8/12/67		
Cushman, Earl D Jr Cpl		C-3-Eng.	4/10/68		
Cutbirth, Richard E LCpl	2377740		5/28/68*	19	Marionville, Missouri
Cutshall, David W LCpl	2217976		3/8/68*	21	Rapid City, South Dakota
Dabney, William H Capt		I-3-26	1/20/68		
Dagger, Carl R Cpl	2304358	I-3-4	5/17/68*	20	Urbana, Ohio
Daigle, Isreal J Sgt	1637938	G-2-1	12/16/65		
Dalbey, Rolland M 1stLt		HMM-165	5/26/67		
Daley, Edmund W Pfc		H&S-3-3	3/24/67		
Dalhouse, John D 1stLt	089075	D-1-3	2/14/66	26	Montgomery, Alabama
Dally, David J Sgt		L-3-4	6/15/68		
Danielson, Darrell C Maj					
Danis, John A Sgt		G-2-9	6/14/66		
Darden, Ronald C Cpl		L-3-3	9/7/67		
Darlington, Earl G 2dLt	096498	D-1-Recon	11/22/66	36	New Braunfels, Texas
Darrh, Floyd J GySgt	1297336	F-2-3	3/14/68	34	Constantia, New York
Dartt, Robert J Cpl	2049979	C-1-9	12/25/65	20	Maunie, Illinois
Dartt, Robert J. Cpl	2049979	C-1-9			Maunie, Illinois
David, George J Cpl		D-1-Recon	9/13/67		
Davis, Allan D Maj	065655	HMM-165	12/31/68		
Davis, Alan F Capt	092159	HMM-262	9/20/68	25	Albany, New York
Davis, Bruce Cpl	2035575	F-2-7	3/4/66	20	Gilbert, Louisiana
Davis, Bruce W Cpl		A-1-Tanks	2/23/69		
Davis, Earl R SSgt		B-1-9	5/12/66		
Davis, Edward D Pfc	2309471	C-1-9	7/6/67		
Davis, Garry D Cpl					
Davis, Gene F SSgt		C-1-1	7/24/66		
Davis, George B 1stLt		D-1-7	11/12/69		
Davis, James R Capt		Advisor	5/20/67		
Davis, Jerry M LCpl		A-1-7	2/24/69		
Davis, Michael H Pfc		5th	2/7/68		
Davis, Stanley Col		CO-5	9/4-15/67	45	Niagara Falls, New York
Davis, Thomas R Cpl	2416988	C-1-3	1/31/69*	20	Frostburg, Maryland
Davis, William J LtCol	049480				
Dawson, John R 2dLt	0100987		10/27/67*	23	Adrian, Michigan
Day, James L Maj	056003		3/2-4/67	41	Illinois
Day, Wesley D Pfc	2365134	L-3-7	11/26/67*	19	Grand Rapids, Michigan
Deal, Earl M LCpl	2351262	H&S-1-5	1/18/68		
Deatley, Hillmer F LtCol		CO-3-1	2/12-18/67		
Deatley, Hillmer F LtCol		CO-3-1	4/21/67		
DeBlanc, Daniel J 1stLt		VMO-2	3/17/69		
Deegan, Gene A Capt	075623	F-2-1	4/21/67	30	St. James, Minnesota
DeForest, Roy E Maj	082183	OO-3-3	6/17/69		
Deichman, Jack E Capt		G-2-4	4/30/68		
Delong, Earl R LtCol	292910	CO-2-3	5/9/67		
Demartino, Pasquale W Capt	068915	CO-3-3	12/9/65	34	Cumberland, Maryland
Demille. Roy W Pfc			5/3/67		
Dempsey, F Jr Sgt					
Dennis, Dan M Cpl	2053890	M-3-5	5/13/67*	21	Houston, Texas
Dennis, Phillip V Pfc	2433936	D-3-Recon	12/17/68	22	Toms River, New Jersey
Denton, Charles L Cpl	2073195	C-3-Tanks	8/18/65		
Dermody, Denis J Cpl		MATS-152	3/17/68		
Derryberry, A R III LCpl	2259201		3/7/68*	18	Shreveport, Louisiana

Deschuytner, Victor R LtCol		AOO-9	11/17/65		
Desmond, Lawrence E Cpl	2240370	C-1-5	2/13/68		
Desselle, Thomas W Pfc	2434898	G-2-7	11/20/68*	20	San Antonio, Texas
Detora, Ernest F Jr Cpl	2222067	L-3-3	8/21/67		
DeTrempe, Barry V Cpl	2231831	H&S-1-Amp	2/10/69*	19	Peoria, Illinois
Dewey, Henry C Maj		VMA-242	10/27/67		
DeWilde, Peter F Pfc	2484172	C-3-Recon	3/5/69*	18	Lansing, Michigan
Dewlen, Michael L 2dLt	0102756	C-1-12	6/11/68*	24	Amarillo, Texas
Dextraze, Richard P	2416530	E-2-9	4/23/69*	21	Canada, XC
Dias, Raymond R III Pvt		A-1-9	4/16/68		
Diaz, Frank E Sgt					
Dickey, Dwight R Maj		1-Tanks	2/6/68		
Dickey, Thomas R Pfc	2465956	L-3-9	2/10/69*	19	Concord, Massachusetts
Dillberg, David W Cpl		G-2-1	1/22/68		
Dinota, Dennis T SSgt	1858560	M-3-5	2/1/67	25	Clearwater, Florida
Dirr, Michael A LCpl		D-3-Recon	9/3/69		
Dito, Raymond E 2dLt	0103445	F-2-3	5/28/68	24	San Francisco, California
Doan, Thomas L 2dLt	0105493	L-3-4	12/8/68	28	Danville, Illinois
Dobbins, Kent E 1stLt					
Dobbs, John W Jr LCpl	1910349	D-E-Recon	5/14/65	22	Tuscumbia, Alabama
Dockendorff, Gary D 2dLt		M-3-9	8/20/66		
Dodge, Harvey J Pfc	2129286	G-2-9	1/13/66		
Dodson, James A Cpl		CAP-2-3-2	3/17/69		
Dodson, Robert G 1stLt	0101865	C-1-1	7/7/68*	25	Bloomfield, New Jersey
Doherty, Jerome J Jr Capt		H-2-5	1/26/67		
Doherty, John B 2dLt		L-3-4	7/18/66		
Dolan, David L Pfc					
Dombrova, Louis A 1stLt	0101867	E-2-4	8/2/68		
Doneghy, James M SSgt					
Donnelly, Alan C LCpl	2391481	B-1-Eng	11/12/68*	20	Gloversville, New York
Donnelly, William R Jr 2dLt	0101619	A-1-1	2/4/68		
Donofrio, Ernest Jr LCpl	2237518	HMM-165	3/3/67	20	Enola, Pennsylvania
Donovan, Joseph P 1stLt	0101005	HMM-364	5/9/69	27	Waxahachie, Texas
Dooley, Dennis D 2dLt		C-1-4	3/26/67		
Dopko, Theodore G Capt	079129	FLSG	1/30/66		
Doss, James G Jr Maj	051888	CO-3-Tanks	8/17/66	40	Phoenix, Arizona
Doss, Larry D LCpl	2370576	G-2-7	9/20/68*	19	Nashville, Tennessee
Doublet, Alvin J Capt	060073	H&S-2-7	12/18/65	37	Pittsburgh, Pennsylvania
Dougherty, James E Sgt	2096769	B-1-5	2/7/68		
Dougherty, Steven J Cpl					
Douglas, William L Jr Cpl	2103224	K-3-4	7/15/66*	19	Canal Fulton, Ohio
Douthit, Roger W. SSgt					
Dowd, John A LtCol	157224808	CO-1-7	4/21/69	37	Elizabeth, New Jersey
Dowd, Lawrence K LCpl	016408052	E-2-3	8/10/69	19	Bridgewater, Massachusetts
Downing, William K Cpl	2201839	E-2-3	5/3/67*	20	Fort Gibson, Oklahoma
Downs, Edward J Cpl	2350684	K-3-7	7/28/68*	19	Washington, DC
Downs, Michael P Capt	081727	F-2-5	2/3-7/68	27	Oak Bluffs, Massachusetts
Downs, Vernon L Jr Cpl	2306783	H&S-3-9	2/14/68*	19	Huntsville, Alabama
Drake, Benjamin A Cpl	2385832	H-2-1	3/3-4/69	18	Grand Rapids, Michigan
Drake, Warren G Sgt		HMM-165	1/28/67		
Draude, Thomas V Capt	089211	M-3-7	4/21/66		
Draude, Thomas V Capt	089211	M-3-7	7/15/66		
Drollinger, Harry B 2dLt	0101014	B-1-5	2/1/68	24	Dallas, Texas
Drone, Frank K Cpl		M-3-3	3/24/69		
Drury, Paul S LCpl	2376703	D-1-5	8/4/68		
Dulude, Daniel D LCpl	2186420	HMM-265	4/24/67	20	Cumberland, Rhode Island
Dulude, Daniel D LCpl	2186420	HMM-265	4/25/67	20	Cumberland, Rhode Island

248

Name	Service Number	Unit	Date	Age	Hometown
Dunbar, Charles L SSgt					
Duncan, Billy R LtCol		CO-2-1	5/19/68		
Dunham, Richard F Cpl	2077038	K-3-4	3/23/67	22	Rochester, New York
Dunn, John F 1stLt	096578	POW	8/19/69	35	Providence, Rhode Island
Dunn, John H LtCol			12/65-10/66		
Dunn, Vincent Cpl	1924381	L-3-4	7/15/66		
Dunning, Clifford R Capt	082152	Advisor	11/18/67	29	Berkeley, California
Duphiney, Randall W Maj		HMM-361	10/28/65		
Durand, Hershal D Cpl		H-2-7	8/22/66		
Durham, Larry W Cpl					
Durham, Thomas W Pfc	2486190	E-2-5	3/27/69*	19	Richmond, Virginia
Dustin, Charles R Sgt		B-1-5	4/20/68		
Duvall, Doyle W SSgt		F-2-7	12/18/65		
Dye, Andrew T SSgt		USNMP	8/27/67		
Early, Richard J 2dLt			10/12/68		
Easter, Boyce E Pfc			3/18/68		
Eaton, Robert F LCpl			6/23/68		
Eberhardt, Edward V Sgt					
Ector, Jerry Pfc	2406562		7/5/68*	20	Cincinnati, Ohio
Edgar, Gene E Pfc	2337757	B-1-26	3/30/68		
Edwards, Daniel L Pfc	2291073		8/10/68*	18	Ceredo, West Virginia
Edwards, Michael J Pfc			2/2/68		
Edwards, Ted W 2dLt	0100215		2/2/68*	23	Charlotte, North Carolina
Edwards, Thomas B III 1stLt					
Egger, Charles H F Maj	063656	HMM-165	9/10/67		West Palm Beach, Florida
Eggers, Michael A Cpl			5/17/68		
Eisenbach, Charles R II 2dLt	0101622	D-1-Recon	7/4/68		
Eisenson, Henry L Maj			10/12/67		
Elder, William F Cpl			9/9/65		
Elkins, Roger L Pfc	2387144		2/17/69*	23	Fort Gibson, Oklahoma
Ellefson, David J LCpl	542600326		4/22/70*	19	North Bend, Oregon
Eller, Franklin P Jr Capt	067808	Advisor	12/31/64		
Eller, John A LCpl	2351913		8/23/68*	24	Norfolk, Virginia
Ellis, Frank B Maj	084468	HMM-265	1/14/67		
Ellis, Gerald L Maj					
Emberger, George J SSgt					
Emerick, George A Sgt	1863789	I-3-3	4/18/65		
Emerson, William Capt	093908		2/3/68*	26	Concord, Massachusetts
Emery, Lawrence W Cpl			6/29/65		
Emmons, Michael A Pfc					
Emrick, Ervin J SSgt	1889464	I-3-3	5/11/69*	29	St. Louis, Missouri
Enedy, Robert J Sgt	2151824		4/30/68*	22	San Diego, California
Engel, Donald F Capt	092342	HMS-16	11/26/67		Springfield, Ohio
Englade, Bertly V Jr Cpl					
Epps, Robbie L LCpl			2/6/68		
Eriksen, Darrell G Sgt	2348367	C-3-Recon	3/5/69	25	Los Angeles, California
Ericksen, Erik C Sgt		E-2-9	9/9/68		
Erickson, Roger A 1stLt			9/17/68		
Eron, John R LCpl	2277659	M-3-3	3/16/68		
Erpelding, Wayne C LCpl	2143564		2/9/68		
Eshelman, William P Maj	077473	Advisor	2/2/68	30	Silver Spring, Maryland
Esmond, Donald V 1stLt	095503	HMM-364	11/17/69		
Espenes, Olav J 2dLt			8/18/68		
Espinola, Robert J Cpl			1/27/68		
Esslinger, Dean E LtCol	045012		4/21/67	41	Sheffield, Iowa
Estes, Edward S LCpl	2329731	C-1-5	2/13/68*	23	Dallas, Texas
Eubank, Gareth D Pfc					

Name	Service No.	Unit	Date	Age	Hometown
Eustis, Michael S 1stLt			5/15/75		
Evans, Eddie L Cpl					
Evans, Gary G Pfc					
Everett, Lucious L Sgt	2106822		12/9/66*	20	Detroit, Michigan
Everett, Michael T LCpl	2372400	HMM-165	4/15/69	19	Meridian, Mississippi
Ewers, Norman G LtCol	028152	HMM-163	3/31/65	41	Tujungai, California
Fales, William E SgtMaj					
Falk, Frederick J Jr LCpl	2322062		1/26/68*	19	Torrington, Connecticutt
Farley, James C Jr Cpl	1937825	HMM-163	3/31/65	21	Tucson, Arizona
Farlow, Gary A LCpl	2263163		5/12/67*	19	North Olmstead, Ohio
Fassett, Randolph D Sgt	1963302	I-3-4	7/20/66	24	Sacramento, California
Fedorowicz, John M Sgt			4/16/68		
Feille, William B 1stLt			12/18/65		
Fellers, Robert M 2dLt			2/28/68		
Fenton, Larry W Capt			6/7-11/69		
Ferracane, Louis J Jr Capt	090153	VMA-224	5/29/72	30	Braintree, Massachusetts
Festa, Donald Capt		A-1-9	3/3/67		
Fiala, Joseph B Cpl	2231752	I-AAmphib	3/01/68	23	Great Falls, Montana
Fields, Joseph P Cpl			12/19/66		
Figueroa, Dennis C LCpl					
Fillon, William LCpl			2/2/67		
Finkel, Charles LCpl	2282715		9/4/67*	19	New York, New York
Fisch, David A LCpl	2197161		5/16/67*	20	Remsen, Iowa
Fisher, J R LtCol			8/18-24/65		
Fisher, Jeffrey M 1stLt		G-2-4	9/21/67		
Fisher, Larry P SSgt					
Fisher, Thomas F LCpl	2143355	F-2-9	7/5/67		
Fitch, William H LtCol	055351	VMA-513	2/21/68	38	Fort Meade, Florida
Fite, William C III 1stLt	094694	Advisor	2/17-24/68	25	Clearwater, Florida
Fitzgerald, Arthur L GySgt					
Flanagan, Lawrence J Maj			5/10/67		
Fleischer, Charles W Jr 1stLt			3/6/70		
Fleming, William B LtCol			12/2/66		
Flood, Denis W Pfc		M-3-5	5/13-14/67		
Floren, Jimmy E Cpl	2325565		11/6/67	21	Klamath Falls, Oregon
Flores, Librado SSgt					
Floyd, David A LCpl	2259076		3/1/69*	20	Minden, Louisiana
Floyd, Donald Cpl	2269120	A-1-1	2/9/68		
Foley, Gifford T Cpl					
Fontaine, Edward L SSgt			7/2/68		
Ford, Vernon J LCpl		M-3-5	7/22/66		
Forgea, Bernard LCpl			8/30/67		
Forness, Richard W LCpl			6/16/68		
Forte, Ollie SSgt	1803556		6/11/68*	30	Raleigh, North Carolina
Foster, Douglas G Cpl	2221643		9/14/68*	21	Beaver, Washington
Foster, Jerome C LCpl	2145219		3/30/68		
Foster, Larry E Pfc	2376944		12/26/68*	18	Lenoir City, Tennessee
Fox, George C LtCol			1/22-3/18/69		
Fox, Thomas L Pfc			5/10/67		
Foy, Thomas L Pfc	2277787		5/10/67*	20	Coolidge, Georgia
France, Phillip S LCpl	2294742		10/14/67*	20	Baltimore, Maryland
Francis, Glen A Pfc			9/7/67		
Francis, Larry J LCpl			7/1/70		
Frank, Harvey E Sgt			8/2/68		
Franks, Michael D LCpl					
Frash, Wilford E Cpl					
Frasier, Ronald R Pfc					

Frazier, Jerry R Pfc	2457855		2/26/69*	18	Des Moines, Iowa
Frazier, Melvin D Pfc	2366536	B-1-26	3/30/68		
Frederick, John W Jr CWO	333240838	POW	5/66-4/67	48	Manito, Illinois
Frenier, David E LCpl	2517744	CAP-1-2-3	5/8/70	20	Langhorne, Pennsylvania
Fretwell, John B 1stLt					
Frey, Kevin J LCpl					
Fricker, Jerrell T Capt			9/19/68		
Friel, Joseph A Pfc	2209039		9/21/66*	21	West Roxbury, Mass.
Friese, Laurence V Capt			2/11/68		
Frisina, JohnT 1stLt					
Frost, Carlton A Pfc	2261252		5/19/68*	20	Winslow, Maine
Fryman, Roy A GySgt	1356690	Advisor	8/24/69	36	Paris, Kentucky
Fulford, CarltonW Jr 2dLt		D-1-5	9/4/67		
Fullerton, Donald G Sgt	1532460	H-2-4	12/26/65		
Fults, Lawrence A Jr Pfc	2198691		3/13/68*	20	Tucson, Arizona
Furman, James T 1stLt					
Gaboury, Laurence R Capt			8/14/66		
Gaffney, Kenneth M Cpl					
Gaffney, Kenneth M Cpl			1/29/67		
Gaffney, Michael F. LCpl	2323201		7/29/67*	20	Chicago, Illinois
Gagnet, Ronald Pfc					
Gaines, Byron A Jr Pfc	2308724		12/28/67*	20	Jacksonville, Florida
Galiana, Rudolph S Pfc	2297083		4/21/67*	20	Los Angeles, California
Galindo, Benjamin L Cpl					
Galindo, Herman Cpl			4/19/68		
Gallegos, Carlos E Cpl			3/7-20/66		
Galyardt, Robert G GySgt	1409591	H&S-1-1	1/31/68	32	Russell, Kansas
Gammack, Gregg L Capt		HMM-361	5/10/67		
Gandy, William G SSgt			5/24/68		
Garber, Charles P 1stLt			2/25/69		
Garcia, Richard Pfc	2251755		1/30/67*	19	Galveston, Texas
Gardner, Donald R Capt	079807	C-3-Recon	8/18/66	28	Memphis, Tennessee
Garner, Cecil A Sgt	1306811	HMM-163	3/31/65		
Garner, Rickey D Pfc	2139942		3/5/66*	18	Dallas, Texas
Garrett, Charles SSgt		HMM-165	12/8/66		
Garringer, David F 2dLt	0104040		8/22/68*	22	San Francisco, California
Gartman, Jerald B Capt			3/6/68		
Garvey, Vaughn D Pfc			1/30/66		
Gates, Phillip R Cpl	2326768	HMM-361	8/10/69	20	Georgetown, Ohio
Gatlin, Thomas Pfc			7/12/65		
Gaugush, Jeffrey A 2dLt			9/5/66		
Gawlinski, Stanley A Jr Pfc			8/24/68		
Gayer, Kenneth E Sgt	2248157		1/25/69*	22	Fresno, California
Gelinas, Timothy K. Cpl	2163569		11/10/68	19	Woonsocket, Rhode Island
Gentile, Wayne M Cpl			3/4/68		
Gentry, George H Jr Maj	053634	XO-2-7	12/18/65	36	Baytown, Texas
Gibbons, Donald R GySgt			12/9/67		
Gibbs, Joseph W III Capt			8/17/67		
Gibson, Peter Cpl	2366795		5/10/69*	19	Orlando, Florida
Gibson, Richard LCpl			3/16/69		
Giddens, Lavon Cpl	2288707		3/3/68*	20	Detroit, Michigan
Giguere, John P Capt					
Giles, Jerrald E Capt		K-3-9			
Gilley, William B Sgt	2090023	F-2-9	5/20/67		
Gillis, James E Maj	058243	VMO-2	12/8/65	35	Long Beach, California
Giordano, Andrew M LCpl	2206251		9/4/67*	19	Smithtown, New York
Giretti, Anthony A 2dLt	0106806		3/19/69*	22	Baldwin, New York

Name	Service No.	Unit	Date	Age	Hometown
Glaenzer, George W Sgt					
Glass, Billy W LCpl	415826675		4/19/70*	21	Covington, Tennessee
Glawe, Thomas D Pfc	2130228	C-1-Recon	6/16/66*	18	Rockford, Illinois
Gleason, Robert J Sgt	1525006		3/21/66	28	Santa Rosa, California
Glenn, Clifford D LCpl			6/20/66		
Glover, Bobby Sgt			2/28/66		
Glover, Leo P 1stLt		K-3-4	7/18/66		
Goble, Woodruff C 1stLt	095262	HMM-262	8/24/68	25	Livingston, New Jersey
Godwin, Solomon H CWO2	432525883		1/31/68*	33	Hot Springs, Arkansas
Golub, Richard M Sgt					
Gomez, Harold Cpl	2178660		2/21/67*	20	East Chicago, Illinois
Gonzales, David Cpl			12/18/68		
Gonzales, Edwardo J LCpl	2227946		5/3/67*	20	Sinton, Texas
Goodman, Edward M Sgt					
Goodrum, Lance A Capt					
Goodwin, Forrest 1stLt	091778		3/2/67*	25	Tylertown, Mississippi
Goodwin, Paul B Capt	086261	K-3-3	6/11/69	31	Portsmouth, Virginia
Goodwyn, Ben R 1stLt			3/28/66		
Gordon, James T Maj	069896	HMM-362	2/19/67	34	Odell, Illinois
Gorney, Jerry E 1stLt	093926		3/3/67*	24	Hudson, Ohio
Gorton, Ralph S III 2dLt	0103511		12/28/67-5/27/68*	25	Boise, Idaho
Gosch, Thomas C 1stLt	096807		2/21/68*	34	Oceanside, California
Gose, Elvin W Pfc	2357960		3/18/68*	19	Cumberland, Indiana
Goss, Jeffery A LCpl	2261627		2/7/68*	19	Orem, Utah
Grace, Robert L. Cpl					
Grammar, William M 1stLt	091923		5/20/67*	25	Oklahoma City, Oklahoma
Grantham, James T Sgt	1951293	L-3-4	2/23/67		
Graves, Floyd A Cpl	2115496		8/26/66		
Graves, Joel E Cpl			5/3/69		
Graves, Paul L LCpl	2448323	I-3-26			
Gray, Alfred M Maj			5/14/67		
Gray, Andrew D Cpl			5/7/68		
Gray, Danny R Pfc			2/10/69		
Gray, Gary G Pfc	184368782		8/26/69*	22	Rimersburg, Pennsylvania
Gray, Ruzell Pfc	2384529		5/31/68*	20	Crockett, Texas
Green, Terry R LCpl			12/20/66		
Green, William F 2dLt			6/29/68		
Greenberg, Gerald Cpl			9/6/67		
Greenberg, Leroy F Jr Pfc			4/16/66		
Greene, Bruce A Maj					
Greer, Jesse R Maj	065804	HMM-361	4/3/67	36	Pearl, Mississippi
Greer, Matthew E Cpl	2142211		5/5/68*	21	East Palatka, Florida
Greer, Vasco R III 1stLt					
Gregory, Simon H 1stLt			3/5/66		
Gress, Howard K Jr Maj		HMM-265	6/8/69		
Griego, Cresenciano Jr Pfc			5/28/68		
Griffin, Albert Sgt			10/30/65		
Griffin, Walter J L Pfc	2450222		6/18/69*	20	Hawkins, Texas
Grignon, Andrew L Cpl			2/23/68		
Grim, Thomas M SSgt					
Grimes, Michael B LCpl	2242452		3/22/67*	20	North Hollywood, California
Grinalds, John S Capt			9/2-4/66		
Grist, William A LCpl	2337813		5/28/68*	19	Bessemer, Pennsylvania
Griswold, Gary C Pfc	2289655		10/14/67*	20	Bethel, Connecticutt
Gross, Wayne W 2dLt	0105109		8/19/68*	27	Carroll, Iowa
Gross, William H E Jr GySgt	1152829	K-3-9	9/5/66		
Grove, Robert W GySgt	306455		2/16/65*	47	Casper, Wyoming

Name	Service No.	Unit	Date	Age	Hometown
Grover, Lewis Pfc					
Groves, Donald D LCpl					
Gruerman, Gary R Pfc			12/17/66		
Grunewald, Bruce W LCpl	2286472	3-Recon	10/21/66	19	Springfield, Illinois
Grunewald, Bruce W Cpl	2286472	3-Recon	3/8/68*	20	Springfield, Illinois
Gudjonsson, Gunnar Capt	093148	Advisor	6/25-27/71	29	Perrysburg, Ohio
Guinee, Vincent J Maj	064735	HMM-261	7/9-10/66	34	New York, New York
Guinee, Vincent J Maj	064735	HMM-261	8/10/66	35	New York, New York
Gulash, David J Sgt	1898797		9/12/67*	25	Flint, Michigan
Gull, Rawlin C Sgt		HMM-161	1/1/66		
Gum, William E SSgt			4/18/69		
Gump, Jackie A Pfc		G-2-9	1/13/66		
Gundlach, Richard M LCpl					
Gunning, Roger O 1stLt			12/13/67		
Gurrola, Michael A Capt					
Gustafson, Gordon A Pfc					
Gutzwiler, Norman P Cpl			9/24/68		
Guy, John W Maj			2/25/69		
Haaland, John D 1stLt			9/10/67		
Haar, Raymond L T Jr Sgt			11/30/67		
Hackett, David S 1stLt	092088		4/30/67*	23	Ligonier, Pennsylvania
Hackett, William R LCpl	2250676		10/27/67*	21	Chicago, Illinois
Hadnot, Otha N SSgt			9/5/66		
Hadsock, William A Pfc	2334155		8/18/68*	19	Tarpon Springs, Florida
Haga, Gene H 2dLt	0108674	A-1-7	5/29/69	28	Jacksonville Beach, Florida
Hagan, John R 2dLt	257666152	G-2-9	4/19/68	22	Savannah, Georgia
Hagemann, Richard L Cpl					
Hagen, Jerome T LtCol			2/27/71		
Hagerty, Roy H 1stLt	094171	HMM-263	3/19/69	24	Greenville, North Carolina
Haggerty, Ancer L 1stLt			9/11/68		
Hainsworth, John J Capt			2/1-2/68		
Hair, John C III Sgt			9/10/68		
Haley, Harrison L Capt	080836		5/26/68*	31	Martinez, California
Haley, William J Jr Cpl					
Hall, Edward M Pfc			8/18/68		
Hall, Rickey W LCpl	308547327		8/10/69*	20	Indianapolis, Indiana
Hamblett, Robert B LCpl	2486513	D-1-7	11/12/69*	19	Roanoke, Virginia
Hamilton, David A Pfc	2326751		10/14/67*	19	Springfield, Ohio
Hamilton, Don E 1stLt	082187	HMM-163	3/31/65	25	Eastchester, New York
Hamilton, Robert E Capt			7/30-31/67		
Hamm, John R Pfc			5/31/68		
Hammel, Alfred A SSgt					
Hammonds, Roy LCpl	458827840		1/4/70*	21	Waxahachie, Texas
Hammons, Herbert D LCpl	2332783	D-1-5	2/15/68*	20	Pocasset, Oklahoma
Hancock, David Capt			3/7/68		
Hanifin, Robert T Jr LtCol			2/27/66		
Hanley, Patrick J LCpl			6/7/69		
Hanna, Rocky W Pfc	2486550		1/11/69*	18	Addy, Washington
Hannah, Samuel J 2dLt	0101288		6/7/68*	25	Reily, Ohio
Harbin, David D LCpl	2238359	H-2-5	2/4/68		
Hardin, Richard P 1stLt	094172	HMM-364			
Hardy, Warren Jr Cpl	2171504		6/15/67*	23	Montgomery, Alabama
Harrell, Roger P Capt	263542237		10/31/66*	28	Jacksonville Beach, Florida
Harrington, Myron C Jr Capt	081869	D-1-5	2/15/68	27	Georgia
Harris, Charles E LCpl	2312798		1/14/68*	20	Norfolk, Virginta
Harris, John A SSgt	1518077	D-1-1	7/23/66	30	Birmingham, Alabama
Harrison, Bruce W Cpl			2/24/69		

Name	Service No.	Unit	Date	Age	Hometown
Harrison, Clyde L LCpl			8/25/68		
Harrison, James R Cpl	2349898		3/9/69	18	Reseda, California
Harshman, Richard L 1stLt	091599	G-2-4	9/21/67	25	Denver, Colorado
Hart, James W Jr Cpl			5/16/67		
Hart, Michael K Pfc	2512333	D-3-Recon	5/16/69	19	Louisville, Kentucky
Hartley, William L Capt	087550		8/23/66*	27	Memphis, Tennessee
Hartney, Alan H Capt					
Harvey, Michael A Pvt	2366216	H&S-2-4	2/25/69*	18	Milwaukee, Wisconsin
Harville, Lawrence GySgt	1640020		5/9/68*	30	Princewick, West Virginia
Haskell, William C 2dLt	0106577	K-3-3			
Hatfield, John C GySgt		K-3-9	7/4/67	36	West Virginia
Hathcock, Carlos II Sgt			9/16/69	27	Little Rock, Arkansas
Hatzfield,William G LCpl					
Hausrath, Donald A Jr 2dLt	0103550	F-2-5	2/3-4/68*	22	Villa Park, California
Hawley, Jack E Capt			2/18/68		
Hayden, Thomas R LCpl			5/18/68		
Hayes, Fred J SSgt	1822754		4/13/68*	25	Walnut Creek, California
Hayes, Ivey J Cpl	2236650	K-3-3	4/4/69*	19	Jesup, Georgia
Hayes, James M 2dLt	094769	B-1-11	4/21/67		Wauwatosa, Wisconsin
Hayes, Leonard C 1stLt			7/17/65		
Hayes, Ray A Sgt	1942851		9/17/68*	24	Knoxville, Tennessee
Hayes, William A Pfc	2359755		6/6/68*	19	Chicago, Illinois
Haynes, John L 2dLt			9/2/66		
Hazelwood, John E Cpl	2268715		5/28/68*	24	Gypsum, Kansas
Hazen, Donald L LCpl			1/19/68		
Head, Glen R Pfc					
Head, William H Jr SSgt	1973115	B-1-3	8/17/67	25	San Marcos, California
Heald, Ronald E Maj	073991	VMO-6	2/8/67	31	Adams, New York
Heeter, James R Pfc	2374329		8/18/68*	19	Spencer, West Virginia
Helton, John K Sgt	2046079		7/6/67*	24	Griffin, Georgia
Helton, Michael P Cpl			2/4/68		
Hembrough, John A Pfc	2465384	H&S-2-4	2/25/69	20	Jacksonville, Illinois
Hemingway, Joseph E Sgt			11/16/66		
Hemp, Stuart F Pfc	225741571		8/22/69*	19	Richmond, Virginia
Henderson, Earl W 1stLt			4/6/68		
Henderson, Jim A Jr Cpl			6/2/67		
Henderson, William B SSgt	1588608	F-2-5	3/24/67	27	Memphis, Tennessee
Henderson, William T 2dLt	089766	A-3-Recon	7/12/65	23	Princeton, New Jersey
Hendricks, Robert LCpl			2/24/68		
Henebury, Joseph D LCpl	2114415		12/9/65	21	Belmont, Massachusette
Hengevelt, William G Cpl					
Henning, Thomas L Sgt	2264035	C-3-Recon	6/1/69	20	Canton, Ohio
Henricks, Charles D 1stLt	0102443	HMM-161	3/23/69*	26	Solana Beach, California
Henry, Clark G Maj		XO-3-4	7/18/66		
Henry, Howard B Maj	218285097		11/12/69*	36	Baltimore, Maryland
Henry, Richard H 1stLt					
Henry, Walter M Pfc	2388813		8/23/68*	19	Seattle, Washington
Henson, Clark L Jr Sgt	2063752		6/7/68*	21	Joplin, Missouri
Henson, Fred B Jr Cpl					
Herlihy, Patrick E Pfc			8/29/68		
Herman, Charles W Cpl			5/17/69		
Herman, Steven G Cpl			5/8/67		
Hernandez, Jose F Cpl		1-Anglico	7/11-16/72		
Hernandez, Leonardo Sgt					
Herrera, Manuel Pfc	2106574		3/21/66*	22	Pueblo, Colorado
Herrera, Phillip A LCpl	2140517	G-2-4	9/8/66*	21	Selma, California
Herring, Charles L Cpl			1/30/66		

Herringer, Charles L SSgt			1/17/66		
Herrington, Richard L 1stLt	0103562	HML-167	12/31/69	23	San Leandro, California
Herrod, Randell D Pfc	2503459	K-3-3	7/28/69	20	Calvin, Oklahoma
Herron, Mark P LCpl			2/23/68		
Hertberg, Edward C LtCol	064604	HMM-164	5/11/72	42	New York, New York
Hescock, Donald W Pfc					
Hesser, Peter M 1stLt	526462823	G-2-3	2/6/68	24	Benson, Arizona
Hester, James A Cpl					
Hester, Michael P LCpl			2/22/69		
Hester, William W Pfc	2399347		7/1/68*	19	Philadelphia, Pennsylvania
Hettinger, John R Pfc	2323783	A-1-1	9/25/67		
Hewitt, John R 2dLt			2/6/68		
Heyward, Robert LCpl			9/1/68		
Hickey, Lloyd R Cpl			2/8/69		
Hicks, Larry D Pfc			2/22/67		
Higgins, Jerome Pfc	2457197	D-1-7	11/12/69*	19	Springfield, Ohio
Higgins, John F LCpl	2420162		12/8/68*	19	Lincoln Park, New York
Higgins, Martin C Capt					
Hignight, Daniel J Cpl			8/9/68		
Hildreth, Raymond S LCpl	2147409	C-1-Recon	6/16/66		
Hilgartner, Peter L LtCol	051942	CO-1-5	9/4-6/67		
Hill, Byron E 1stLt					
Hill, John M Sgt	407626238		8/22/69*	23	Middletown, Kentucky
Hill, Thomas K Sgt			3/18/68		
Hill, Twyman R LtCol	045538	1-MPB	1/30/68	38	Denton, Texas
Hilliard, George S Jr LCpl			7/18/68		
Hiltbrunner, Donnal E Capt	080851	VMA-533	10/29/67	29	Bushton, Kansas
Hilton, Judson D Jr 1stLt	095616	HMM-463	5/1/68	23	St. Paul, Minnesota
Hinkle, Dennis A 2dLt			6/11/67		
Hinkle, Thomas F Capt	086682	M-3-9	2/9/69	28	Wilmington, Delaware
Hinojosa, Juan N Jr LCpl			9/26/65		
Hinson, Alan W Capt					
Hinson, Amos B 1stLt	086290	K-3-3	8/18/65	26	Montgomery, Alabama
Hinson, Don Pfc	2466761		12/22/68*	20	New York, New York
Hinson, Donald SSgt			3/11/66		
Hitzelberger, Daniel A Capt			2/5/69	29	Glassboro, New Jersey
Hoare, Thomas J Jr 2dLt	095789		1/7/68*	23	Bellerose, New York
Hoban, John J Cpl			7/4/66		
Hobbs, Thomas A 1stLt			4/7/69		
Hoch, Larry D LCpl	2438147	G-2-1	5/3/69*	21	Topton, Pennsylvania
Hodges, Homer L Jr LCpl	2094758		9/9/68*	22	Mineral Wells, Texas
Hodges, Richard P Cpl	2172138		2/22/69*	20	Atlanta, Georgia
Hoeck, Richard J LCpl	1960766	H-2-4	8/18/65		
Hoff, John R Jr 2dLt			3/26/70		
Hoffert, Duwayne W Maj			2/6/68		
Hoffman, Richard C 1stLt	0105132	K-3-3			
Holden, Thomas J 1stLt	0849419		8/23/66	25	Hasbrouck Heights, New Jersey
Holden, Thomas J 1stLt	0849419		10/22/66*	25	Hasbrouck Heights, New Jersey
Holler, Donald D SSgt			2/2/68		
Holloway, James O Jr LCpl	2355107		4/4/68*	25	Newark, New Jersey
Hollowell, Leon R Pvt			6/4/65		
Holmes, Walter C Sgt			12/27/65		
Holmgreen, John C Jr 2dLt			3/17/67		
Holt, Robert N GySgt			8/21/67		
Holtzclaw, Gary E 1stLt	0101637		4/10/69	24	Corbin, Kentucky
Holycross, Richard L CWO			9/7/67		
Holzmann, James C Cpl	2479199		8/4/70	22	North Olmstead, Ohio

Name	Service No.	Unit	Date	Age	Hometown
Honeycutt, James Q LCpl			10/22/66		
Honsinger, Arthur W Pvt	2300745	G-2-5	2/7/68		
Hooton, Richard J Jr Capt	088161	HMM-363	2/22/69	27	Pensacola, Florida
Hoover, Ronald E 1stLt	096988				
Hopkins, John I Capt		Advisor	2/22/66	31	Brooklyn, New York
Hopkins, Julius B SSgt					
Horak, Frank J Jr Capt			3/3-6/67		
Horcajo, Robert A Pfc	2425989		2/23/69*	19	Milpitas, California
Horn, James M 1stLt	0104465	G-2-9	4/21/69	24	Stillwater, Oklahoma
Horner, Richard L 2dLt			2/1/68		
Horton, Charles R GySgt			5/8/67		
Hoskins, Sheldon D Cpl	2261445		10/7/68*	20	Blackfoot, Idaho
Houghton, John P LCpl			1/10/67		
Houghton, Kenneth J Col			4/25/67		
House, Charles A LtCol			3/10/66		
Houze, Benjamin C Jr LCpl			8/19/69		
Hovanesian, Daniel G 1stLt	0106803	AO-11	12/31/70	24	Watertown, Massachusetts
Howard, Ralph Pfc			2/6/68		
Howe, Leroy C Cpl	2153778		5/13/67*	19	Holland Patent, New York
Hoyez, James K Pfc	2352555		9/11/68*	19	Albany, Oregon
Huchison, Joseph F LCpl			6/2/69		
Huckins, Raymond L LCpl			4/25/67		
Huckstep, Gordon W LCpl					
Hudson, Thomson J Jr 1stLt			10/20/70		
Huebner, Anthony C Capt			10/10/66		
Huff, Edwin L Capt			9/12/66		
Huffman, Donald R Maj			2/23/69		
Huffman, James W Capt			4/21/69		
Huffman, James W Capt					
Hughes, David M LCpl					
Hughes, Robert C 1stLt	091695	HMM-163	3/5/67	27	Camp Hill, Pennsylvania
Humphrey, Gilbert W Jr 1stLt			9/19/68		
Humphries, Claude Jr Cpl			9/24/66		
Hundley, David D 1stLt	0101583	HMM-165	12/8/68		
Hunt, Homer S SSgt					
Hunt, William H 2dLt	0106804		2/25/69*	22	Merritt Island, Florida
Hurtado, Albert S LCpl	2072324		9/19/66*	20	National City, California
Huskey, James H Sgt			4/4-6/68		
Hutchins, Normand I LCpl			8/21/68		
Hutchinson, Edward L Jr Capt	090290	C-1-9	7/2/67	26	Merritt Island, Florida
Hutchinson, Franklin G Jr Maj			3/16/69		
Hutchinson, Kenneth P Jr LCpl	2290977		6/5/68*	18	Huntington, West Virginia
Hutchison, Joseph F LCpl					
Hutton, William R Cpl	2141953	K-3-4	9/28/66	19	Canoga Park, California
Hynes, Michael M 1stLt			6/7/67		
Inks, Earl L LCpl			3/21/66		
Inman, Linwood J LCpl			8/26/66		
Inscore, Roger V Cpl	2234781		5/26/67*	21	Huntington Beach, California
Irvin, Stephen L Cpl	2305659	H-2-5	9/10/67*	20	Columbia, Missouri
Irwin, David L Cpl			6/11/70		
Jackson, Curtis R LCpl	2010458	G-2-3	6/4/65		
Jackson, Kenneth E Pfc	2441265		2/5/69*	19	Beckley, West Virginia
Jackson, Marlin W Cpl		H&S-3-7	5/18/68		Moriarty, New Mexico
Jackson, Richard D Capt	080223	M-3-4	1/29-2/22/67	30	Huntington, West Virginia
Jackson, Terry K LCpl	2400904	K-3-9	2/13/69	21	Hawkinsville, Georgia
Jacobs, Quiles R Cpl	2235586	B-1-26	6/5/68	22	Compton, California
Jacques, Raymond J Jr Sgt		B-1-9	5/12/66		

Jadlow, Robert L 1stLt		B-1-9	5/12/66		
Jakovac, Donald L Pfc		D-1-4	2/2/68		
Jakubowski, Walter P Sgt	640095	C-3-Eng.	5/29/66		
James, Buddy L Sgt	1579538	I-3-4	7/20/66		
James, Danny D SSgt	1178515	E-2-3	8/22/65	33	Chester, Illinois
James, Lee R GySgt		Advisor	9/5/65		
James, Richard D Cpl	2382319	L-3-26	12/8/66*	20	Shelbyville, Virginia
Jandik, Frank Jr Sgt	2132892	D-1-5	2/15/68		
Jarboe, Bernard K Pfc		L-3-7	3/21/66		
Jarrell, Eugene E Pfc					
Jasinski, Daniel Sgt		CADA	2/2/68		
Jenkins, Carl E LCpl	2091760	C-1-7	9/8/65		
Jenkins, Charles E Sgt	2116407	D-1-5	9/4/67	21	Pittsburgh, Pennsylvania
Jenkins, Homer K 1stLt	085550	H-2-4	8/18/65		
Jenkins, James A Cpl	2339189	C-1-3	5/20/69*	18	Marion, North Carolina
Jenkins, Robert M SSgt					
Jensen, Duane S Maj		HMM-364	11/8/70		
Jensen, Paul A 1stLt	095672	VMO-6	2/16/68*	23	Asheville. North Carolina
Jensen, Robert R SSgt		A-1-9	2/22/69		
Jesperson, Marshall W Sgt					
Jessup, Daniel G Sgt		I-3-26	1/20/68		
Jester, Herbert A Pfc	2369954	K-3-27	5/24/68		
Jette, Peter L Cpl		D-1-4	5/8/67		
Jinkerson, Victor Cpl	2286460	K-3-3	2/7/68		
Joeckel, Charles E Cpl		A-1-7	1/23/68		
Johann, John C Sgt	1132242	E-2-7	5/12/68	32	Greenwich, Connecticut
John, Richard H Pfc	2142092	A-3-MTB	3/21/66		
Johnson, Charles H Sgt	2062309	D-3-Recon	6/13/69*	25	Baldwin Park, California
Johnson, Dennis G LCpl	2406779	F-2-9	3/28/69*	20	Cincinnati, Ohio
Johnson, James R SSgt	1859910	D-3-Recon	9/2/68	27	Highland Falls, New York
Johnson, James T Cpl					
Johnson, Joe V Cpl					
Johnson, Julius C Cpl		C-1-26	9/24/66		
Johnson, Ken H Capt					
Johnson, Larry A Sgt	2232731	A-1-Recon	9/20/68*	21	Varna, Illinois
Johnson, Michael J Cpl		G-2-4	3/19/69		
Johnson, Robert F II Sgt		K-3-5	9/6/67		
Johnson, Terry W Sgt		Advisor	2/23/69		
Johnson, Thomas A Sgt					
Johnson, Timothy P Cpl					
Johnson, William D Jr Cpl	2357895	B-1-Recon	7/3/68*	20	Kokomo, Indiana
Johnson, William M Sgt					
Johnson, William S Cpl		E-2-26	12/5/68		
Jones, Andrew L Pfc		1-Recon	4/23/69		
Jones, Barry T 1stLt	0103599	F-2-27	8/23/68	22	Mentor, Ohio
Jones, Charles D 1stLt	088170	C-1-7	12/5/65		
Jones, Clarence W SSgt		3-Tanks	8/26/66		
Jones, David R 1stLt	0101182	E-2-4	5/1/68	24	Silver Spring, Maryland
Jones, Douglas A 1stLt		Anglico	9/23/65		
Jones, Edward R Cpl	2253584	G-2-5	7/30/68	20	Fairlawn, New Jersey
Jones, James H LCpl	2366047	E-1-Recon	8/1/68*	21	Beltsville, Maryland
Jones, James L Jr 2dLt		G-2-3	5/27/68	24	Kansas City, Missouri
Jones, James L Jr Cpl					
Jones, Jesse Jr Pfc					
Jones, Joe N Sgt		H-2-4	5/2/68		
Jones, John H Sgt	2152507	C-1-3	8/16/67*	19	Nashville, Tennessee
Jones, John J LCpl		HMM-164	11/7/68		

Name	Service No.	Unit	Date	Age	Hometown
Jones, Joseph J Sgt	2147920		7/3/68*	21	Scotland Neck, N C
Jones, Larry G Sgt		I-3-9	7/6/68		
Jones, Otis R Cpl	401722637	B-1-7	6/26/70*	20	Donerail, Kentucky
Jones, Robert L GySgt					
Jones, Wayne E GySgt		M-3-26	3/4/67		
Jordan, Charles F Cpl		F-2-7	4/12/69		
Jordan, Kenneth D Capt	461580434	3-Recon	1/13-16/67	29	Houston, Texas
Jordet, Ronald G LCpl	2156757	K-3-4	9/26/66*	21	Reedpoint, Montana
Joyce, Michael J Jr Cpl					
Judkins, Paul G. Maj					
Judson, Donald H SSgt					
Julian, Paul M Pfc		B-1-3	8/17/67		
Justis, Donald E SSgt		L-3-5	6/11/68		
Juul, John F Capt		D-1-4	5/8/67		
Kabeller, George R Cpl	2043283	H-2-7	3/4/66		
Kahabka, James G Cpl					
Kalm, Raymond W Capt					
Kappmeyer, Paul J Sgt	2013858	M-3-9	8/20/66*	22	Indianapolis, Indiana
Karkos, Norman F Sgt					
Kasson, Leonard C Cpl	2118060	K-3-4	9/28/66	20	Cincinnatus, New York
Kaus, Harry L Jr Pfc	2077042	H-2-4	8/18/65*	18	Dunkirk, New York
Kaylor, James N LCpl		E-2-26	6/7/68		
Kean, Billie O SSgt	1851628		3/16/68*	25	Alexandria, Ohio
Keaveney, John P Cpl		A-1-Amphib	1/20/68		
Keaveney, Paul S LCpl		Recon	2/7/70	27	New Smyrna Beach, Florida
Keckler, Richard C Capt	093224	HMM-364	1/11/69	26	New York, New York
Keddy, Michael L Sgt		D-1-Recon	5/6/68		
Keefe, Floyd M GySgt	1332594	1-5	3/19/69*	35	Montgomery, Alabama
Kegel, John C 1stLt					
Kegley, Walter M Sgt		CAC-2-3	8/6/68		
Keif, David J Pfc		F-2-5	2/4/68		
Keilty, Kevin P LCpl		M-3-9	2/19/69		
Keister, Roger P Cpl		E-1-Recon	8/1/68		
Keith, Archibald Pfc	2241203	K-3-4	9/27-28/66*	23	Bainbridge, New York
Keleher, Michael K Sgt					
Kellams, Glennis R Sgt	1858569		4/13/68*	25	New Albany, Indiana
Kelleher, Richard A SSgt	1556718		4/30/68		
Keller, Albert W Maj		Advisor	9/15/66		
Keller, D.W.		3-Recon	9/15/66		
Kelley, Paul X LtCol	050603	CO-2-4	3/21/66	37	Boston, Massachusetts
Kelly, John A 1stLt	088887	I-3-3	8/18/65		
Kelly, John A Capt	088887				
Kelly, Ronald J Cpl		7-Eng.	9/4/67		
Kelly, Vincent J Jr SSgt		F-2-7	2/25/66		
Kelly, Vincent J Jr GySgt					
Kendall, George P Jr GySgt	1103292	Intel.	1/31-2/4/68*	37	Missoula, Montana
Kendley, Patrick D Capt	095388		8/13/66	32	Boothbay, Maine
Kennedy, Bruce T Pfc	2430740	L-3-3	8/26/68*	19	Canada,XC
Kennedy, Robert R Jr LCpl					
Kennedy, Thomas J Jr Capt	069955	Advisor	6/12/66*	36	Erie, Pennsylvania
Keppen, Thomas R 1stLt	0103608	B-1-3	7/6/68*	22	Evansville, Indiana
Kerrigan, Thomas G 2dLt	0106816	L-3-1	5/5/69	23	Newark, New Jersey
Keshner, Keo J Pfc	2481163	A-1-5	6/8/69*	21	New Florence, Missouri
Kettering, Alvah J Capt	067506	HMM-263	12/9/65		
Keys, William M Capt		D-1-9	3/5/67		
Kiely, Denis J Maj		VMA-235	3/16/68		
Killian, Mark A Sgt					

Kim, Yung G GySgt					
Kimener, Robert P 2dLt	0110642	B-1-7	6/26/70		
Kines, Charles G 2dLt					
King, Charles W 2dLt		L-3-26	4/14/68		
King, Cleveland Jr Cpl		C-1-4	3/1/69		
King, George R Jr Cpl					
King, Samuel L LCpl	2184066	B-1-1	2/19/67		
Kinnaman, George M Sgt	1986364	G-2-3	10/22/66	22	Springfield, Oregon
Kirk, Alexander Capt	089986	HMM-164	8/3/67	24	Keansburg,,New Jersey
Kisala, Walter Pfc	2079832	Recon	2/13/66*	18	Chicago, Illinois
Klages, Robert J 1stLt	094840	B-3-Amphib	8/1/67*	23	St. Louis, Missouri
Kline, Garry D Sgt		A-1-Recon	5/26/69		
Kline, Robert J LCpl	2288879	L-3-7	4/10/68*	20	Bay City, Michigan
Knapp, William F Jr LCpl		B-7-MTB	3/26/69		
Knight, Jerome G Pfc					
Knight, John E Jr Capt					
Knight, Terry W Cpl					
Knight, William A Capt		HMM-362	9/26/68		
Koehler, David J Pfc	2537986	I-3-3	6/4/69*	20	Clarence Center, N. Y.
Kolakowski, Henry Jr Capt	081631	1-3-5	1/30/68	29	Farmington, Michigan
Kolter, Bruce 2dLt	0107436	M-3-3	6/17/69*	23	Wapakoneta, Ohio
Konn, Raymond LCpl					
Konrady, Lester W Cpl	2124523	L-3-5	7/18/66	20	West Palm Beach, Florida
Kopka, John R 1stLt	090184		10/22/66	26	Auburn, Massachusetts
Kosoglow, Joseph J Pfc	2074108	C-1-Recon	6/16/66	20	
Krages, Bert W. Maj					
Kreh, Gary H Cpl	2175644	A-1-4	5/8/67*	19	Flint, Michigan
Kretzschmar, William Capt	082939	VMA-533	10/29/67	29	Brooklyn, New York
Krogh, Richard O Cpl	2266195	L-3-3	8/26/68*	21	Mercer Island, Wash.
Kruger, Earl A Capt		Advisor	4/28-30/72		
Krulak, Charles C		L-3-3	6/3/69	27	Quantico, Virginia
Kubik, Kenneth A 2dLt	266669896	C-1-Recon	10/22/69*	25	Hollywood, Florida
Kuci, Richard A Maj	058735	HMM-361	8/18/66	35	Coraopolis, Pennsylvania
Kuci, Richard A Maj	058735	HMM-361	10/12/66	35	Coraopolis, Pennsylvania
Kuehlmann, Werner G LCpl		K-3-5	11/24/68		
Kufeldt, Edward Capt	089361	VMO-6	2/7/68	27	Homestead, Florida
Kupcho, Thomas G Pfc					
Kupec, Keith L Pfc	2113873	E-2-1			
Kurtz, Normand F Cpl		D-1-7	12/20/67		
Kuske, Gregory W Sgt		HMM-165	3/6/68		
Kustaborder, Thomas W Cpl	2421708	K-3-9	2/14/69*	22	Altoona, Pennsylvania
Lacey, Fred E Jr Maj	064297	HMM-364	10/17/68	38	Monroe, Louisiana
Lackey, Ira E Sgt		E-2-4	7/8/67		
Lagrone, Leonard Jr LCpl		G-2-9			
Laine, Elliot R LtCol		CO-3-9	1/25-3/15/69		
Lake, Bruce R 1stLt	0101584	HMM-265	12/6/68	21	Harrisville, New Ham.
Lala, Nolan J Pfc		C-1-MTB	1/31/68	19	Denver, Colorado
Lamb, Allan W Capt	065948	RLT-7	8/18/-24/65	37	Ellensburg, Washington
Lambrecht, Donald M Sgt	1931632	L-3-4	9/25/66		
Lamontagne, Edward J LtCol		3-MarDiv	1/31/68		
Lampo, Stephen F 1stLt		Advisor	1/31/68		
Landes, Burrell H Jr Capt	079715	B-1-3	7/6/67	28	Topeka, Kansas
Landreth, Alfred F Jr LCpl					
Landry, Daniel J Cpl	2098154	C-1-Recon			
Landry, Eddie L LCpl	2035493	H-2-4	8/18/65*	20	Gonzales, Louisiana
Langdon, Howard W Jr 1stLt	0102068	C-1-Recon			
Langevin, George Pfc	2290384	C-1-Recon	10/14/67		

Name	Service No.	Unit	Date	Age	Hometown
Langley, David F Sgt	2130678	D-1-1	7/5/68*	23	Washington, D.C.
Langley, William D Cpl					
Lanham, Daniel L LCpl		D-1-5	8/29/68		
Lanham, Daniel Sgt	2379976				
Lantry, Merrill L Cpl	1993291	1-7	9/2/65*	22	Detroit, Michigan
Laramy, Robert E Capt		TAC	2/22/68		
Larson, Edward D Pfc	2138412	D-1-26	9/19/66	21	St. Louis Park, Minnesota
Larson, Stephen P 1stLt					
Lasseter, Lee T Maj					
Latting, Charles W Capt	077176	M-3-1	3/5/66		
Lau, James 1stLt	085372	2-7	3/4/66		
Lawrence, Gearie E Pfc		D-1-7	4/16/69		
Lawrence, John F LCpl	2455299	F-1-7	4/30/69*	21	Norfolk, Virginia
Lawrence, Larry E LCpl	2307915	H&S-RLT-26	6/6/67*	19	Brunswick, Georgia
Lawrence, Michael J Pfc	054401671	H-2-7	8/23/69*	19	Maplewood, New Jersey
Laws, Billy W Pfc	2156134	K-3-4	9/26/66*	23	Kansas City, Missouri
Lawson, Archie H LCpl		E-2-4	3/18/68		
Lawson, Charles A Sgt	1912373	E-2-1			
Lawson, Curtis G Maj		VMA-533	7/25/68		
Leaf, Stephen D Cpl		A-1-1	3/7/69		
Lebaugh, Christopher M LCpl					
LeBlanc, Ross A LCpl		I-3-3	9/7/67		
Lee, Alex Capt	070686	F-2-7	3/4/66	32	Hemet, California
Lee, Cleo E 1stSgt	1023518				
Lee, Douglas W Cpl	2112997	C-1-4	3/26/67*	20	Winston-Salem, N C
Lee, Fielding J Cpl					
Lee, George N Jr Cp		H-2-1	5/17/68		
Lee, Gregory W Capt		HMM-362	8/10/66		
Lee, Johnnie P Sgt					
Lee, Vincent B 2dLt	019340263	I-3-5	11/23/69*	24	Lawrence, Massachustts
Lefefe, Anthony T Sgt		C-1-9	7/6/67		
Leftwich, William G LtCol	413465361	CO-2-1	8/4/70	39	Germantown, Tennessee
Legas, David S 1stLt	0104263	HMM-364	6/1/70	27	Ogden, Utah
Legaux, Merlin P Cpl	2144012	K-3-4	7/18/66	19	New Orleans, Louisiana
Lehoullier, Paul R LCpl	2336494	I-3-1	4/5/69*	21	Somersworth, New Hampshire
Lenna, Frank Sgt		E-2-5	8/17/67		
LeNoue, Bruce V Cpl	2162858	A-1-1	3/26/67*	20	Anoka, Minnesota
Leon, Mario R Pfc	2398690	F-2-9	3/29/69*	18	Milwaukee, Wisconsin
Leonard, William Cpl	030384103	F-2-7	1/14/70*	21	Marlborough, Massachusetts
Leshow, William F Cpl					
Lewin, Lanny K Cpl					
Lewis, Frederick E Maj					
Lewis, Willie R Pfc		C-1-4	6/6/68		
Libutti, Frank 2dLt	0100427	C-1-9	7/2/67		
Lifred, Hubert M LCpl		L-3-9	9/15/68		
Limones, Jesus M Pvt	2256502	D-1-4	5/8/67*	19	Del Rio, Texas
Linde, Richard V Pfc	2218294	C-1-1	12/21/66*	26	Miamitown, Ohio
Lindsay, Paul T 2dLt		F-2-7	11/12/68		
Lindsey, Henry J LCpl		D-1-1	6/28/68		
Linkous, Noah R Pfc	2238101	C-1-7	11/2/69		
Linn, Orie O LCpl			4/30/67		
Linn, Robert A II 2dLt					
Lipscomb, Roger D Sgt		K-3-1	1/15/67		
Little, James J SSgt	1410063	E-2-1	12/16/65		
Lively, Stephen G LCpl		9-Amphib	7/11/72		
Livingston, Alastair J Cpl	2133814	C-1-Recon	10/10/66		
Livingston, Bruce B LCpl	2263489	I-3-4	9/2/678	18	Lorain, Ohio

260

Livingston, James E Capt		E-2-4	3/18/68	28	Telfair, Georgia
Livingston, Lawrence H Capt		Advisor	4/12/72		
Livingston, Thomas E Sgt	2094261	C-1-1	2/7/68		
Lloyd, Edward J 1stLt	088909	G-2-7	2/22/66		
Lloyd, Lowell R LCpl	2265956		5/26/67*	20	Woodlawn, Illinois
Lochridge, Willard F 2dLt		B-3-Tanks	9/5/66		
Lockwood, Bryce F SSgt			6/8/67		
Lockwood, Robert H Maj	069751	H&MS-36	1/28/67	33	Greenwich, Connecticut
Lofink, Walter F GySgt	563664	F-2-7	3/16/67	41	Staten Island, New York
Logan, Thomas E Pfc					
Logan, Westley R 1stLt	0100436	VMO-2	12/18/68	25	Fulton, Missouri
Lomen, William W Cpl	2315005	C-1-1	7/7/68		
Long, Donald E Pfc	2222600	G-2-5	2/5/68		
Looney, Kenneth LCpl	2213785	B-1-1	12/15/67		
Looney, Paul T Capt	089775	HMM-164	5/10/67*	25	Shelburne Falls, Massachusetts
Loop, James S Maj	071973	HMM-161	2/23/69	29	San Marino, California
Lopez, Adrian S Pfc	2375936	3-Recon	2/16/68*	19	San Martin, California
Lopez, David LCpl	2341710	L-3-7	9/14/68	19	Austin, Texas
Lopez, Felix R Sgt		B-1-4	3/20/66		
Lopez, Joseph P Cpl	2135326	E-2-7	9/19/68*	23	Denver, Colorado
Lopez, Joseph Pfc	2344087	C-1-5	2/13/68		
Lopiano, Richard C LCpl		E-2-4	2/9/68		
Lopinto, Frank T LCpl	2253402	B-1-9	4/27/67	19	Lyndhurst, New Jersey
Loucks, Burdett W GySgt					
Lough, Robert M Jr SSgt	1881709	H&S-1MarDiv	2/23/69*	27	Moundsville, West Virginia
Loughrey, Wayne F 1stLt	089856	E-2-9	3/25/66		
Lounsbury, Theodore W Jr LCpl					
Love, Clarence L LCpl	2383315	L-3-5	12/1/68*	19	Tyler, Texas
Love, Donald E Capt		MAG-16	12/25/67		
Lowder, Charles L 1stLt		1-Recon	8/10/69	24	Sullivan, Illinois
Loweranitis, John L Cpl	2052170	I-3-9	9/3/66*	22	Du Bois, Pennsylvania
Lozano, Samuel H Pvt		B-1-27	6/17/68		
Lucas, Robert D Pfc					
Lucus, Gary A Sgt	1859141	HMM-265	7/15/66	25	Cody, Wyoming
Lund, Craig L Pfc		M-3-9	5/1/68		
Lund, Dean T SSgt					
Lunsford, Glen T Sgt	2101197		2/6/68*	20	Danville, Virginia
Lunsford, Robert L SSgt		A-1-1	2/13/66		
Lyle, Charles R LCpl		CAP 1-3-5	6/26/68		
Lynch, Eugene A Capt					
Lyon, John W 1stLt	0875797	H&S- 2-1	12/10/65		
Lyon, Thomas H GySgt		H-2-7	9/21/68		
Lyons, Joseph W Cpl	2315470	1-Recon	6/5/68*	22	Phoenix, Arizona
Lyons, Paul C Sgt					
Lyons, Roger G Pfc	2369478	E-2-4	2/9/68*	19	Amelia, Ohio
Lyons, Walter J 2dLt	0100447	E-2-7	6/15/67*	21	Jacksonville, Arkansas
Maas, Bertram A LtCol	061155	VMO-6	8/19/68	37	St. Paul, Minnesota
MacCormack, Dana F 1stLt		C-1-7	2/15/68		
Machulda, Thomas E Sgt		1-Recon	2/7/68		
MacKenna, James J GySgt	1356083	E-1-2	5/29/66*	37	Denver, Colorado
Madden, Ernest J Cpl	2137377	D-1-5	5/12/67*	20	Wellsville, Ohio
Maddox, Richard G Capt	095664	D-1-7	9/2/68	32	Cupertino, California
Maggi, David R Cpl					
Mahoney, John M Capt	076396	K-3-4	3/17/67	34	Brooklyn, New York
Main, Stanley W 1stLt					
Maki, Roger L LCpl		L-3-3	1/12/69		
Maldonado, Robert P Pfc		I-3-7	1/30/67		

Name	Service Number	Unit	Date	Age	Hometown
Mallette, Robert D LCpl		H-3-3	11/28/67		
Mallobox, Jesse A Pfc	2297064	D-2-12	5/13/69	21	El Centro, California
Malnar, John M SgtMaj	528234	2-4	4/30/68	41	Sawyerville, Illinois
Malnar, John M SgtMaj	528234	2-4	5/2/68*	41	Sawyerville, Illinois
Maloney, William R LtCol		VMO-6	2/1/67		
Manac, Don Pfc	259805632	H-2-7	8/20/70	20	Fargo, Georgia
Manfra, Howard T Jr Sgt		M-3-5	9/4/67		
Mangrum, Richard G LCpl	2213707	L-3-4	1/7/68*	19	Lynn Haven, Florida
Mangual, Jose M Pfc	119407620		1/14/70*	20	New York, New York
Mara, Donald E Sgt		M-3-3	11/11/68		
Marcantel, William E Capt	083491	Advisor	6/22/66	25	Iowa, Louisiana
Marcombe, Stephen G LCpl	2303802	M-3-5	6/2/67*	20	Westwego, Louisiana
Marengo, Anthony H SSgt					
Maresco, Richard E Capt		K-3-5	1/26/67		
Marino, Jack Jr SSgt	991615	A-1-Amphib	8/18/65		
Marinos, Nicholas SSgt		F-2-5	8/6/68		
Markham, Joel M LCpl					
Marks, David C Sgt	2044624	B-1-5	6/9/69	28	Venice, California
Marks, David E Capt	283493	F-2-1	2/28/68		
Marsden, Robert P Cpl	012404784	K-3-5	1/20/71*	19	Randolph, Massachusetts
Marsh, James W LtCol	050763	CO-3-3	3/6/68		
Marsh, William C SSgt	1637431	A-1-ATanks	2/24/68*	27	Amarillo, Texas
Marshall, Billy G SSgt		A-1-4	2/26/66		
Martin, Emerson Pfc	2475620	A-1-7	5/29/69*	21	Church Rock, New Mexico
Martin, Ervin P Jr 2dLt		D-1-5	8/29/68		
Martin, John A Maj		VMA-242	10/27/67		
Martin, Justin M II 2dLt	0103097	F-2-3	8/15/68	23	Alexandria, Louisiana
Martin, Laurence A SSgt	517200	D-1-3	6/29/65		
Martin, Robert J Maj		Advisor	3/19-25/71		
Martin, Rodney J Pfc		D-1-5	10/26/68		
Martin, "W" "L" 1stSgt					
Martinez, Donacano F GySgt		G-2-26	5/16/67		
Martinez, Jorge Pfc	2341584	M-3-7	7/28/68*	19	San Antonio, Texas
Martinez, Manuel O Maj	067305	HMM-161	9/18/65		
Martinez, Robert LCpl	2083073	C-1-Recon	6/16/66		
Marvel, Jerry W LtCol		POW	2/68-8/69		
Mascarenas, Alcadio N LCpl	2129236	C-1-Recon	6/16/66*	22	Sapello, New Mexico
Mastrion, Robert J Capt		G-2-4	3/30/68		
Matern, Robert S Sgt	2131996	L-3-9	6/1/67*	25	Worcester, Massachusetts
Matheny, Roy W LCpl		L-3-4	6/15/68		
Mathews, Robert A Capt	080639	H&MS-16	3/13-14/67	29	Lake Villa, Illinois
Mathews, Vincent M LCpl		B-1-4	10/27/67		
Mathis, Jack D Sgt		C-3-Recon	5/22-23/66		
Mattern, Larry A Pvt		D-1-1	7/23/66		
Matthews, Gordon B 1stLt	097328	B-1-1	2/7/68*	36	Bloomfield, Iowa
Matthews, Harry E Pfc	2321080	I-3-3	2/16/68*	19	New York, New York
Mattie, John G Jr Sgt	1982986	H-2-9	4/16/66		
Mattingly, Robert E 2dLt		H&S-3-Tanks	8/5/66		
Maxim, Robert J Cpl		B-1-9	8/24/67		
Maxson, Leonard W Pfc		1-SPB	3/13-26/68		
May, Dennis P LCpl		M-3-1	1/10/67		
Mayfield, Leonard Pfc		A-2-5	4/25/68		
McAllister, Robert A Pfc	2359816		8/18/68*	20	Tinley Park, Illinois
McCall, Gerald A SSgt	1592696		7/13/68*	28	Atlantic City, New Jersey
McCallum, Daniel P LCpl		D-1-1	9/24/66		
McCardell, Raymond J Cpl	2148831	C-1-Recon	2/29/68		
McCart, Daniel P 2dLt		K-3-4	3/17/67		

Name	Service No.	Unit	Date	Age	Hometown
McCart, Daniel P 2dLt					
McCarter, James W Jr Capt	085448		10/14/67*	27	New Orleans, Louisiana
McCarthy, Brian S 1stLt					
McCarthy, Peter R Capt		Advisor	7/30-31/67		
McCarty, James A Capt	069975	AOO-2-4	3/10/65		
McCauley, Bertram W Maj	058997	HMM-263	9/17/66		New Albany, Indiana
McClain, David L Pfc		H-2-9	12/18/65		
McClain, William D Sgt	2024794		5/16/68*	22	Waco, Texas
McClary, Patrick C III 2dLt		A-1-Recon	3/5/68	26	Pawleys Island, South Carolina
McClintock, Ted E SgtMaj	338430	3-3	1/15/69*	47	Seattle, Washington
McCluey, Harry H Pfc					
McConnell, Paul R 1stLt		E-2-5	4/22/68		
McCord, William C Cpl		B-2-7	8/10/68		
McCormick, Charles M Cpl	2290978	H-2-5	9/29/68		
McCormick, James P LCpl		G-2-26	4/7/68		
McCourt, Edward F 2dLt		I-3-3	11/28/66		
McCoy, James H SSgt		F-2-5	2/4/68		
McCusker, Thomas M.	2039010	A-3-Recon	1/21/67	20	Elizabeth City, N C
McCracken, Jack H Capt		HMM-165	6/3/67		
McDonald, Alan V Cpl		H-2-5	2/5/68		
McDonald, Guy T Sgt			2/30/68		
McDonnell, John "M" Pfc					
McElroy, J R Jr Maj					
McElroy, J. R. Jr. Maj					
McGee, Stephen D LCpl	2231850	M-3-26	5/9/68*	18	Mishawaka, Indiana
McGinley, Gerald G LCpl	2424469	A-3-Recon	12/5/68	20	Concord, California
McGrath, Thomas H LCpl	2381139	G-3-12	2/25/69*	18	Homewood, Illinois
McInturff, David L 1stLt	091629	H&S-1-5			
McKee, Thomas E LCpl	2066048		7/6/67*	20	Palm Springs, California
McKeon, Joseph T Jr 2dLt	094899	B-1-3	5/10/67*	23	Chicago, Illinois
McKim, Edward A Sgt	2058209	D-3-MP	1/31/68*	23	Dallas, Texas
McKinny, James O Pfc	2055426	C-1-Recon	6/16/66*	18	Monroe, Louisiana
McLaughlin, Thomas H LCpl		C-1-26	9/21/66		
McLean, Ronald W 1stLt	0105587	A-3-Recon	6/8/69*	24	Beverly Hills, California
McMahon, Daniel K Jr 1stLt		D-1-4	9/16-19/66		
McMillin, Donnell D Sgt	1813597	F-2-7	3/4/66*	25	Mena, Arkansas
McMullin, Robert LCpl		L-3-5	5/12/69		
McMurray, Daniel D 2dLt	0102572	B-1-7	8/10/68	22	Toledo, Ohio
McNalley, Ronald Sgt		C-1-7	1/31/68		
McNally, Paul A LCpl		D-1-5	5/12/67		
McQuerry, Thomas O Sgt		A-1-4	3/6/68		
McQuown, Max LtCol		CO-1-3	2/2/68		
McVey, Lavoy D Capt	521448976	C-1-Recon	3/2/70*	32	Lamar, Colorado
McWilliams, James P Maj					
Mead, James M Maj	073315		4/22/68	32	Somerville, Massachusetts
Meade, Joseph L Pfc	2450534	M-3-26	1/25/69*	19	Kingsport, Tennessee
Meadows, Charles L Maj	083834	G-2-5	2/6/68	29	Beaverton, Oregon
Mees, William L SSgt	2077837	G-2-1	5/5/69		
Meester, Harold W Pfc		G-2-9	6/14/66		
Meier, Terrance L SSgt	1999759	M-3-3	4/30/67*	22	Portland, Oregon
Meilinger, John J Cpl		I-3-1	11/12/66		
Melim, Patrick R F K Sgt		C-1- Recon	5/28/67		
Melson, Wilton E Jr Cpl		D-3-Recon	5/15/69		
Melton, Walter W Jr GySgt	1434949	G-2-3	6/1/69		
Melton, William R 2dLt		F-2-5	9/30/68		
Melvin, James L Cpl	2182214	A-1-1	11/26/67*	20	East Boxford, Massachusetts
Menagh, Philip S 2dLt		F-2-7	3/22/68		

Mendenhall, William E Sgt					
Mendoza, Albert R Cpl					
Menzies, Alexander J N LCpl	2133773	B-1-3	4/2/66*	20	Walworth, New York
Meskan, Donald J Maj	076109	HMM-262	9/15/69	34	Minneapolis, Minnesota
Messer, James M 2dLt		L-3-3	9/13/69		
Meydag, Richard H Maj		VMO-6	4/24/69		
Meyer, Ronald W 2dLt	091945	C-1-5	6/16/66*	23	Dubuque, Iowa
Michalowski, Raymond J LCpl	2323809	K-3-5	2/2/68*	18	Chicago, Illinois
Michalski, James Pfc	2471622	I-3-3	6/4/69*	21	La Porte, Indiana
Mickelson, Dennis E LCpl	2394453	A-3-Recon	12/5/68*	19	Eugene, Oregon
Mihalovich, John M Cpl	2108819	G-2-27	3/15/68*	22	Milwaukee, Wisconsin
Mikaele, Puni Sgt		I-3-9	6/27/69		
Miller, Allen P Sgt	1985062	D-3-Recon	12/19/66*	24	Midwest City, Oklahoma
Miller, Dana L Cpl	2263958	D-2-12	5/13/69*	20	Akron, Ohio
Miller, Donald E P Maj		VMO-2	4/23/69		
Miller, Edwin D Sgt	1805091	Advisor	2/17/71	31	Fenton, Missouri
Miller, Floyd E Cpl	2190910	F-2-1			
Miller, Fredrick W Cpl	2012460	M-3-7	4/21/66*	22	Berlin, Ohio
Miller, James E LCpl	210385830		10/27/70*	18	Lancaster, Pennsylvania
Miller, Richard E 1stLt		1-Recon	4/12/69		
Miller, Roger Cpl					
Miller, Russell P Pfc	2322957	D-1-3	5/10/67*	19	South Bend, Indiana
Miller, William LCpl		M-3-4	3/14/69		
Miller, Willie E LCpl	2343048	CAP-1-3-3	8/2/68		
Mills, Michael T Pfc		G-2-3	4/30/67		
Millsap, William C Pfc	2135609	F-2-1	2/28/66		
Minehart, Russell E Sgt	1522495	B-1-9	7/12/65		
Mitchell, Curtis Pfc	2300587	B-1-5	9/4/67*	19	Jacksonville, Florida
Mitchell, Mack E Capt	057303	HMM-262	11/27/68	42	Mishawaka, Indiana
Mitchell, Paul H Jr LCpl	2103805	M-3-4	10/5/66*	20	Mentor, Ohio
Mitchell, Thomas E Jr Sgt	2247666	D-1-5	5/24/68	22	Sacramento, California
Mixon, Michael J Sgt		B-1-5	9/4/67		
Mixon, William H Cpl	1906658	E-2-3	8/22/65		
Moguel, Albert Pfc		B-1-26	3/30/68		
Mollett, Chester A Sgt	2356833268	F-2-3	8/7/69*	26	Peytona, West Virginia
Monday, Alvin LCpl	2156748	K-3-9	9/9/68*	23	Eunice, Louisiana
Mondragon, James W Pvt		A-1-Amphib	3/7/68		
Montague, Paul J Capt		HMM-165	3/29/68		
Montague, Paul J Maj		POW	6/70-3/73		
Montez, Frank J Cpl	549788812	A-1-Recon	9/20/69*	19	Salinas, California
Montjoy, Norris D SSgt		F-2-1	5/19/68		
Moody, Jimmy D Pfc	2273558	H&S-3-3	3/24/67*	20	Kennett, Missouri
Mooney, Clifford D 1stSgt	1045500	C-3-Recon	3/16/67	36	Shawnee, Oklahoma
Moore, Brian D Capt	072242	E-2-4	2/9/66		
Moore, Dan Pfc		H-3-12	8/25-26/66		
Moore, Kenneth W 1stLt					
Moore, Kenneth W 2dLt					
Moore, Phillip A Pvt	2269400	A-1-7	4/22/67*	20	Marengo, Ohio
Moore, Willard T LCpl		A-1-11	4/16/66		
Moore, William R LCpl	2060008	1-Recon	12/16/65*	20	Richmond, California
Moores, Kenneth F Pfc	2422372	B-1-4	10/8/68*	19	Waltham, Massachusette
Morey, Alfred W Sgt		HMM-463	6/28/70		
Morgan, Dennis J LCpl		M-3-7	9/16/68		
Morgan, Edward E LCpl		D-1-9	2/18/69		
Morgan, Henry L Sgt	2034970	E-2-3	12/28/67*	22	Benson, North Carolina
Morgan, Michael R LCpl	2243845	M-3-3	4/30/67*	21	Bethpage, New York
Morgan, Wilkes R 1stLt		MAG-18	2/23/69		

Moriarty, William S Capt		Advisor	7/30-31/67		
Moro, Michael E Pfc		A-1-4	5/8/67		
Morris, Daniel M Cpl		G-2-5	2/7/68		
Morris, Phillip W Sgt		F-2-4	9/21/67		
Morris, Richard A Cpl	2172310	D-1-5	2/22/68		
Morris, Ronald D SSgt	1954054	K-3-7	8/23/68		
Morrison, Gary L Pfc					
Morrison, Lonnie W Pfc	2338568	B-1-26	3/30/68		
Morrison, Michael K 1stLt		HMM-161	6/9/70		
Morrison, Robert S 1stLt	087345	H-2-4	8/18/65		
Morrison, Ronald C 1stLt		A-1-Tank	2/15/68		
Morrissey, John T.		3-Recon	8/17/67		
Morrissey, John T Jr Cpl		HMM-161	8/12/67		
Morrow, Alfred J Jr LCpl	2171423	HMM-161	3/23/69		
Morrow, Harold E GySgt	1136878	M-3-26	7/21/67*	36	Valencia, Pennsylvania
Moser, Keith M II Pfc	2250629	F-2-5	6/2/67*	20	Lowell, Michigan
Moss, Richard A GySgt					
Mower, Kenneth T Jr Sgt	1938716	M-3-5			
Moy, William K III Cpl			9/4/67		
Moyle, Wesley A Pfc	2336949	B-1-1	12/15/67*	20	Duquesne, Pennsylvania
Much, Gary W LCpl	2082695	L-3-27	5/18/68		Marlon, Wisconsin
Mueller, Charles E LtCol	1096342	CO-2-7	5/4/68		
Mugler, Charles R LCpl					
Mulhearn, James J Jr 1stLt		CAC-1-3	9/13/69		
Mullen, James R 2dLt		I-3-7	11/19/67		
Mullen, Richard W 2dLt	093384	K-3-4	9/28/66		
Mullins, James R LCpl	2128488	B-1-26	5/29/68*	20	Franklin Furnace, Ohio
Mulvihill, Daniel K LCpl	2102047	C-1-Recon	6/16/66		
Munson, Stephen A 2dLt		L-3-3	3/3/68		
Munter, Weldon R Capt	059909	VMO-3	2/23/68	27	Portland, Oregon
Muraca, Patrick J LCpl	2418335	H-2-9	2/17/69	20	Dalton, Massachusetts
Murphy, Dennis G Pfc	2467070	1-Recon	6/18/69*	18	Copiague, New York
Murphy, Edmond J Maj		HMM-363	9/4/67		
Murphy, Edward T Cpl	2030755		5/21/67*	23	Levittown, New York
Murphy, James K 1stLt			3/18/69		
Murphy, Kenneth R Sgt			2/3/68		
Murphy, Kevin J 1stLt	0105995	G-2-5	5/15/69	23	Beverly, Massachusetts
Murphy, Michael A Sgt					
Murphy, Thomas E SSgt			4/20/68		
Murphy, Thomas H Jr Pfc			7/31/68		
Murphy, Walter M Maj	075028	H&S-1-1	1/31/68*	31	New York, New York
Murray, David R Cpl			2/18/69		
Murray, Freddie L LCpl	2065527	A-3-Recon	7/12/65	18	Weirsdale, Florida
Murray, Grover 2dLt					
Mutschler, John L Pfc	363522764		8/10/69*	20	Clarksville, Michigan
Myatt, James M 1stLt			3/20/66		
Myers, Dale S LCpl	2349067	M-3-3			
Myers, Donald F Sgt		C-1-9	2/13/69		
Myers, Donald F Sgt					
Myers, Leo B 1stLt			2/11/68		
Nachtrieb, Mallery O LCpl					
Nail, James D LCpl					
Nappi, Patrick 2dLt					
Naugle, Russell W LCpl	2336710	C-1-7	2/15/68*	18	Republic, Pennsylvania
Navadel, George D Capt	075389	M-3-9	6/1/67	30	Buffalo, New York
Neal, Earnest LCplD-1-9			4/29/68		
Neal, Hiahwhanah R Cpl	2168567	M-3-27	5/24/68		Talihina, Oklahoma

Neal, Richard I 1stLt		I-3-9	3/30-31/67		
Neal, Richard I Capt Advisor			5/22/70		
Neblett, Lynell LCpl	2351619	F-2-7	9/29/67*	20	Blackstone, Virginia
Negron, William P Capt		C-1-4	6/5/68		
Nelson, Gregory H 1stLt		VMO-6	6/17/69		
Nelson, Jacob GySgt		G-2-4			
Nelson, Jacob GySgt		G-2-4			
Nesmith, Joseph Q Jr Capt	1930148	HMM-165			Santa Ana, California
Neu, Melvin P SSgt	1871047	I-3-3			
Neuss, William H Capt	092447	C-1-3	10/11/67*	24	Yaphank, New York
Nevarez-Oliveras, Jose A Sgt					
Neville, George G Jr Cpl	2098958	A-3-Recon	9/23/66	20	Rockville, Maryland
Newby, Thomas J Pfc	2293178	CAP-2-1-5	2/23/69		
Newman, Michael E 2dLt		G-2-5	3/28/69		
Newton, Leonard L Pfc	2387353	I-3-26	1/19/68*	19	Stockton, California
Nichols, Daniel C 1stLt	0104295	D-2-12	2/17/69	25	Westfield, New Jersey
Nichols, Daniel C 1stLt	0104295	D-2-12	5/13/69*	26	Westfield, New Jersey
Nickerson, Michael K 1stLt	0100556	HMM-364	4/14/69*	25	Indianapolis, Indiana
Niedopytalski, John N Jr Cpl					
Nielsen, Howard B Capt		M-3-5	9/11/68		
Niesen, Paul W LtCol	051752	HMM-161	7/17/68		
Ninojosa, Juan N Jr LCpl					
Niotis, John D Capt		L-3-5	2/22/68		
Nolan, James M Capt			12/18/65		
Normand, Paul D Pfc		E-2-12	6/5/69		
North, Donald R Jr Cpl		D-1-3	11/11/67		
North, Oliver L 2dLt	0106162	K-3-3		26	Philmont, New York
Northington, William C LCpl	2407330	A-1-9	2/22/69	20	Prattville, Alabama
Northrop, Thomas E Cpl	2332091	B-1-1	5/31/68		
Norton, Chandois M LCpl		HMM-262	5/18/68		
Norton, John E Cpl	260720316		12/29/70*	19	Fort Oglethorpe, Georgia
Nowak, Laurance S 1stLt					
Noyes, David W 2dLt	0102079	M-3-7	11/2/67		Birmingham, Michigan
Nulty, Thomas G 1stLt		K-3-26	11/24/68		
Nunez, Larry B Cpl			9/4/67		
Nye, Lindsey H Cpl	2148825		5/14/67	20	Carver, Massachusetts
Nyulassy, Arnold C 1stLt		K-3-7	8/28/69		
O'Bannon, Robert III Sgt	2002103	E-2-4	3/13/68*	22	San Bernardino, California
O'Brien, Joseph J Maj		G-2-3	7/22/67		
O'Connell, George J Jr 1stLt	090982	HMM-163	3/5/67	25	Highland Park, Illinois
O'Connell, John P 2dLt		E-2-4	8/12/69		
O'Connor, Brian R 2dLt	094002	H-2-1	1/29/67*	27	Andover, Massachusetts
O'Connor, Martin E Maj		Advisor	11/5/69		
O'Donnell, John W Maj		Advisor	8/6-7/66		
O'Leary, Patrick C LCpl					
Ogden, Howard Jr LCpl	2312138	G-2-7	10/18/67*	19	Omaha, Nebraska
Ohanesian, Victor LtCol	050708	CO-2-3	2/28-3/1/67*	40	New York, New York
Okada, Danny G Cpl		HMM-164	11/5/68		
Olenski, Paul F Pfc	2181660	C-1-Recon	7/26/68		
Olsen, Spencer F SSgt	1951058	E-2-9	3/16/67	24	Fowler, Colorado
Olson, Bruce G Sgt					
Orlett, Paul J SSgt	1458705	K-3-5	5/12/67	32	Portsmouth, Ohio
Orsburn, Lyndell M Capt	076293	H&S-3-3			
Ortiz, Jose A LCpl	450866149	I-3-26	8/24/69*	21	Corpus Christi, Texas
Ortiz, Melecio Cpl	2164601	I-3-5	5/13/67*	22	Crystal City, Texas
Osgood, William H Capt		C-1-3	1/19/68		
Ott, Theodore A Sgt		1-Recon	6/18/69		

266

Name	Service No.	Unit	Date	Age	Hometown
Otto, Charles E 1stSgt		E-2-4	3/13/68		
Owens, Bennett H Jr Sgt	1499308	M-3-9	3/21/66	26	Jacksonville, Florida
Owens, Mackubin Jr 2dLt		B-1-4	5/25/69		
Pace, David C Pfc					
Pace, Simone J 2dLt	091989	A-1-9	5/21/66		
Pacello, Francis D Capt	082483	M-3-5	8/26/68	28	Wilmington, Delaware
Pacheco, Eugenio Cpl					
Pacholke, Norman L SSgt	1648557	B-1-7	10/10/68	28	Manilla, Iowa
Padilla, Jose M GySgt		M-3-9	4/30/68		
Padilla, Rodney J A LCpl		I-3-7	2/7/68		
Page, Douglas B Capt	090578	FAC-1-4	3/20/69	30	Susanville, California
Page, James E Capt	068990	F-2-1	12/10/65	37	Tulsa, Oklahoma
Palacios, Benjamin Jr SSgt		F-2-5	5/22/68		
Paladino, Robert J LCpl		L-3-4	2/26/69		
Palembas, Richard A Sgt					
Palmason, Stephen T 1stLt	095621	VMO-6	11/25/68	25	Salem, Oregon
Palmer, David E Cpl		A-1-Recon	6/11/70		
Palmer, Leonard J Jr LCpl	2447708	K-3-7	3/11/69	19	Berkeley, Illinois
Palumbo, Charles F Cpl					
Pannell, Horace L Pfc					
Parker, Milton SSgt	1548859	A-1-1	2/5/68		
Parker, Paul D II 1stLt	0102654	HMM-263	1/31/70		
Parks, Gordon E LCpl					
Parlett, Phillip G Cpl		M-3-4	3/14/69		
Parmelee, Bruce C Pfc	2249008	I-3-1	4/21/67*	20	Reading, Massachusetts
Parr, William T Cpl		C-1-9			
Parrish, Daniel I Cpl		CAP-L-5	3/15/68		
Parrish, Joseph P Cpl		1-Recon	4/25/69		
Parrish, Robert E 2dLt					
Parry, Dale T GySgt	1072827	HMM-165	3/29/68	36	Ogden, Utah
Parsons, James R Maj		HMM-364	2/4/68		
Parton, Floyd E LCpl	2388524	B-1-4	10/8/68*	19	Asheville, North Carolina
Parton, John E Cpl	520502260	Advisor	6/30/72	24	Douglas, Arizona
Pasieka, Stanley J Cpl					
Pate, Gerald S Maj	060342	HMM-261	66	33	Murfreesboro, Tennessee
Patrinos, Charles 1stSgt		E-2-3	5/1/67		
Patten, David D Sgt					
Patterson, Eldridge Jr Cpl		L-3-26	4/14/68		
Patterson, Robert L Pfc					
Patton, Donald R Cpl					
Patton, Jack L Cpl		M-3-4	1/25/68		
Patton, Robert F CWO-3			6/5/64	36	San Antonio, Texas
Paul, James R Sgt	2043910	H-2-4	2/5/67*	20	Huntington, Indiana
Paulin, John T LCpl	2487685	C-1-26	6/7/69*	20	Owensboro, Kentucky
Pavey, Chester R 1stSgt	642952	I-3-3	3/25/67*	36	Anderson, Indiana
Payne, Darnell M Pfc	2474947	E-2-9	4/23/69*	20	Falls Church, Virginia
Payne, Jack S SSgt		I-3-4	7-1-68		
Pearce, Donald L SSgt		K-3-4	6/17/69		
Pearson, Millard L LCpl		C-3-Eng	4/13/66		
Peatross, Oscar F Col	07196	CO-7	8/18-24/65	49	Frogmore, South Carolina
Peavler, Lawrence A Cpl		B-1-1	5-13-67		
Peck, Garrette W III LCpl	2180320	H-2-9	8/2/66	24	Washington, D.C.
Peko, Lolesio Pfc		G-1-5	8-10-66		
Pembleton, Elias S SSgt					
Pennington, Kenneth E 1stLt	240686098	VMO-2	4/21/69*	26	Durham, North Carolina
Perez, Ernesto Pfc	2370282	B-1-11	2/15/67*	19	Rake, Iowa
Perez, Jesus R Pfc	2389862	F-2-5	6/23/68*	21	Kingsville, Texas

Perez-Padin, Juan R LCpl	583281953	E-2-7	8/26/69*	21	Quebradillas, Puerto Rico
Perino, Anthony Cpl		H-2-9	7/29/67		
Perinotto, Ernest D Pfc	2438154	B-1-7	11/17/68*	20	Allentown, Pennsylvania
Perriguey, Charles D Jr 1stLt	0111588	HMM-367	12/8/69	24	San Gabriel, California
Perry, Henry SSgt					
Perry, Larry E 1stLt	0102206	C-1-1	6/5/68		
Perry, Richard W Sgt	19811901	E-2-7	9/19/66*	24	Marion, Arkansas
Perryman, James M Capt	067837	VMO-6	6/16/66	33	Washington, D.C.
Persky, Donald N 1stLt		HMM-463	9/11/70		
Person, Barnett G GySgt					
Persons, Henry H 1stLt	0101378	Wps-1-5	2/1/68*	24	Fort Wayne, Indiana
Peters, Anthony J Sgt	1948609	K-3-9	7/4/66	22	Oxford, Pennsylvania
Peters, James P Pfc		D-1-5	9/11/68		
Peters, William J Jr 2dLt		1-Recon	4/12/69*		
Peters, William L Jr 1stLt	0102208		6/21/69	26	Fort Dodge, Iowa
Petersen, John W III Cpl	2295074	G-2-1	3/4/68		
Peterson, Dennis J Cpl					
Peterson, Michael I 1stLt					
Peterson, Robert V LCpl	2242658	I-3-5	1/30/68*	20	Canton, Mississippi
Petit, Matthew M LCpl		D-1-5	12/20/67		
Petrone, Louis G Jr LCpl	2355206	L-3-4	1/7/68*	22	Morristown, New Jersey
Petrunio, Darryl J Cpl		I-3-9	5/31/68		
Pettengill, Harold D Maj		L-3-5	5/26/67		
Petteys, David M Capt	086421	HMM-265	6/30/67	25	San Diego, California
Pettigrew, William M III Capt					
Pfeltz, Albert R III 1stLt	091971	B-3-Recon	8/24/67	22	Pittsburgh, Pennsylvania
Philips, Ralph F Jr Sgt		B-1-Amphib	1/14/66		
Phillips, Jack W Capt	077504		10/14/67*	32	Mission, Kansas
Phipps, Daniel R 2dLt	335365593		5/17/67	22	San Diego, California
Phipps, Lanny W LCpl	2255099	A-1-7	12/7/68*	23	Rutherford, New Jersey
Piatt, Joseph M Jr Capt					
Picciano, Terrance A LCpl	2366238	E-2-26	6/6/68*	19	Baraga, Michigan
Pierce, Daniel P LCpl	2162927	A-1-1	9/25/66	20	Pine Island, Minnesota
Pilson, Darwin R Sgt		B-1-5	9/10/66		
Pina, Ronald C Cpl	2466510	CAP-1-2-3	5/8/70	22	Boston, Massachusetts
Pineiro, Ismael LCpl		C-1-26 9	/24/68		
Pinkard, Robert E SSgt		H-2-5	2/5/68		
Pinkerton, Robert N Cpl		C-1-7	3/1/67		
Piotrowski, Daniel J LCpl	2122153	B-1-3	4/2/66*	20	Jackson, Michigan
Pipes, Kenneth W Capt	081285	B-1-26	3/30/68	30	Fresno, California
Pitman, Charles H Maj		HMM-265	4/8/67		
Planchon, Randall T II Cpl	2296855	M-3-4	5/16/68*	20	Long Beach, California
Platt, Jonas M BGen	06644	CG-TFD	12/20/65		
Pless, Stephen W Capt		VMO-6	6/2-4/67	27	Decatur, Georgia
Pohlman, Lyn W Cpl	2033359	A-1-1	10/30/65		Cincinnati, Ohio
Poniktera, Stanley F Jr LCpl	2374602	F-2-3	5/28/68*	18	Bethlehem, Pennsylvania
Pontius, John J Cpl		1-Eng	2/16/67		
Poole, Henry J Capt	094013	G-2-5	8/18/68	25	Portland, Oregon
Porrello, Richard D 2dLt		C-1-4	2/28/69		
Porrello, Richard D 2dLt		C-1-4	3/1/69		
Porter, Mervin B Col		MAG-36	3/5/66		
Porter, Richard L 2dLt		H&S-3-12	8/26/66		
Porterfield, Charles W Capt	082117	VMA-3-11	3/24/68*	28	Portland, Oregon
Porteur, Kraig M Cpl					
Post, Gary L Capt		VMA-235	3/16/68		
Potocki, Robert A Cpl		A-1-4	2/2/68		
Powell, Raymond L Cpl	1975645		11/12/66*	22	Kansas City, Missouri

Name	Service #	Unit	Date	Age	Hometown
Powers, Mark F LCpl	2428638	K-3-9	2/14/69*	20	St. Petersburg, Florida
Powles, Thomas G Pfc	2140524	C-1-Recon	6/16/66		
Prather, Ronald R JR Sgt	2177783	A-1-Tanks	2/7/68*	23	Cave Junction, Oregon
Prescott, Alexander F IV 1stLt		H-2-4	3/18/68		
Prescott, Alexander F IV 1stLt		H-2-4	4/30/68		
Prewitt, Robert C Capt		B-1-7	3/5/66		
Price, Donald L Maj		Advisor	4/16/72		
Price, Thomas H Cpl		B-1-9	3/2/67		
Prichard, John L Capt	081650	I-3-4	1/27/68*	29	Oklahoma City, Oklahoma
Prince, Phillip E Sgt	1531289	CAP-P-2-7-4	5/11/67	25	Delray Beach, Florida
Proctor, James P LCpl	2124481	H-2-9	7/29/67*	21	Tampa, Florida
Prommersberger, James E Sgt	2012082	C-3-Eng	4/16/66*	21	Youngstown, Ohio
Puliafico, Frederick GySgt		H-2-5	8/22/69		
Puller, Lewis B Jr 2dLt	2398118	G-2-1	10/11/68	22	Saluda, Virginia
Pupuhi, Rodney H Sgt		D-1-Recon	2/19/68		
Purnell, Richard M 1stLt	085430	I-3-3	8/18/65		
Purvis, Bernard G LCpl	2391296	A-1-3	1/29/69*	20	Norfolk, New York
Quinlan, Maurice J 1stLt	0100607	HMM-364			
Quinn, Francis X LtCol		CO-3-7	2/23-28/69		
Quinter, Robert H Jr 1stLt	010221	HMM-161	6/11/70	23	Reading, Pennsylvania
Rachon, Charles J Pfc	232078	M-3-1	4/21/68*	22	White Plains, New York
Rackhaus, John P LCpl	326443107	A-1-7	5/29/69	20	Marshall, Illinois
Radcliffe, Henry J M Capt		A-1-9	2/8/68		
Radcliffe, Henry J M Capt					
Radics, Emil J Col		CO-1	2/12/67		
Radish, Danny L Sgt	2454292	HMM-262	2/12/70	20	Eureka, Montana
Ragsdale, Gary W LCpl	562762164	E-1-Recon	6/14/70*	19	Kernan, California
Rainey, Larry L Pfc	2494868	K-3-9	2/27/69*	18	Heyworth, Illinois
Rait, Donald M J Jr 1stLt	0102223	M-3-4	5/16/68	23	Fullerton, California
Ralston, Arthur N LCpl					
Ralston, David J 2dLt		C-3-Tanks	4/19/68		
Ramirez, Efrain A LCpl					
Ramos, Roberto LCpl	2396857	H-2-26	1/15/69*	18	Hartford, Connecticutt
Rangel, Antonio Sgt		L-3-3	5/14-19/65		
Raper, Charles D 2dLt		L-3-4	5/15/68		
Raper, Robert J Pfc					
Ratcliffe, Edward K Cpl	2136993	C-1-5	2/19/67	19	Cranston, Rhode Island
Ratliff, Arch Jr Capt	089061	HMM-363	10/22/67	25	Abilene, Texas
Ratliff, Fred A Sgt	2015147	A-1-7	12/7/68*	23	Denver, Colorado
Rau, Arnold B Pfc					
Rawson, William A 2dLt	0100614	I-3-5	6/2/67*	25	Lake Forest, Illinois
Ray, Ronald D Capt		Advisor	6/31/67		
Ray, Ronald D Capt		Advisor	7/12/67		
Ray, Ronald J LCpl	389501974	B-1-7	8/12/69*	20	Greenleaf, Wisconsin
Rayo, Joseph A Sgt		E-2-1	9/9/66		
Reali, James W Cpl					
Rebelo, Joaquim V LCpl	2254243	B-1-1	1/29/67*	20	Newark, New Jersey
Reed, Louis J SSgt	1383118	G-2-3	10/22/66*	30	White Plains, New York
Reed, Paul M Cpl	2039088	E-2-4	8/23/66	20	Roanoke, Virginia
Reed, Van S Maj	066952	HMM-165	12/8/68	36	Gainesville, Florida
Reek, Donald L LCpl					
Reese, Clifford E LtCol	063327	HMM-367	3/23/71	44	Greensboro, North Carolina
Reese, Clifford E LtCol	063327	HMM-367	3/28/71	44	Greensboro, North Carolina
Reese, Merle W GySgt					
Reeves, Daniel M LCpl		A-1-Amphib	1/20/68		
Reeves, Edward R LCpl					
Reeves, James A Sgt		C-1-7	3/28/66		

Name	Service #	Unit	Date	Age	Hometown
Register, Kenneth L Pfc		A-1-7	5/1768		
Reid, Sandy R Cpl		B-3-Recon	12/11/68		
Reilly, Donald J Maj	061230	VMO-2	11/18/65	36	St. Louis, Missouri
Reisinger, Richard F Cpl					
Renegar, Edwin J 2dLt					
Renteria, Joe M LCpl	2270433	M-3-9			
Resnick, Robert A LCpl	2375393	I-3-4	7/1/68*	19	Upper Darby, Pennsylvania
Restivo, Anthony Jr Pfc	2030200		5/21/66		
Retrask, John R LCpl					
Reynolds, Charles A Maj		VMO-3	5/10/67		
Reynolds, John R Cpl		E-2-27	8/26/68		
Reynolds, Paul R Sgt	2090099	G-2-3	2/6/68		
Rhodes, John E 1stLt	0103759	HMM-367	9/21/69	25	Glendora, California
Rhodes, John E 1stLt	0103759	HMM-367	11/14/69	25	Glendora, California
Ribillia, Mariano Jr Pfc	2388352	K-3-5	1/21/69*	19	Puunene, Hawaii
Rice, Gary A LCpl					
Rice, Johnny B LCpl					
Rice, Ronald R Capt		Advisor	6/13/71		
Rich, Robert C Cpl	2224376	VMO-6	3/24/68		
Richards, Chester C GySgt	1417087	D-1-7			
Richards, John H Jr LCpl		A-1-3	1/22/69		
Richardson, Benjamin Cpl	2245536	L-3-5	5/26/67*	23	Detroit, Michigan
Richardson, Jerry W Cpl					
Richwine, David A 2dLt	091490	K-3-4	7/16/66	22	Overland Park, Kansas
Rickman, William J Pfc	2237378	L-3-7	2/21/67*	18	Altoona, Pennsylvania
Rider, James W Capt	077451	VMO-2	3/10/66	30	West Seneca, New York
Rider, James W Capt	077451	VMO-2	5/21/66	30	West Seneca, New York
Riely, Daniel L Cpl					
Riggs, William W 1stLt					
Riley, Dennis H LCpl	306561331	CAP-1-4-4	12/31/69*	19	Tell City, Indiana
Riley, Edward F Capt					
Riley, James C Pfc	2278227	B-1-3	5/10/67*	19	Pleasant Hill, California
Riley, James T Capt	095179	HMM-463	2/22/68*	32	Zeigler, Illinois
Rilk, Harlen C Cpl	2254415	3-Amphib	9/16/67*	21	Dover, New Jersey
Rimpson, Robert L. Pfc	2036627	I-3-3	8/18/65		Kansas City, Missouri
Rindfleisch, Jon A Maj		Advisor	12/31/67		
Rinehart, Benny D Capt	072921	HMM-36	8/18/65	29	Vandalia, Illinois
Ring, Edwin R GySgt		C-1-4	3/1/69		
Ringler, Robert L Jr Cpl	2099691	I-3-7	12/17/66*	20	Brackenridge, Pennsylvania
Riordan, James P 2dLt					
Riordan, Patrick C Pfc	2359732	F-2-1	5/19/68*	18	Des Plaines, Illinois
Rios, Henry A LCpl	2190833	F-2-7			
Ripley, John W Capt		L-3-3	8/21/67	27	Radford, Virginia
Rismiller, Larry J Sgt		L-3-4	2/17/69		
Risner, Richard F Maj		MAG-12	4/26/68		
Rivera, Antonio G Cpl					
Rivera, Virgilion LCpl		B-1-4	5/22/68		
Rivers, Frederick M Jr Capt		HMM-163	8/22/68		
Rivers, Robert R 1stLt					
Roark, Bruce G LCpl					
Roath, Louis P III 1stLt					
Roberson, James J 2dLt					
Roberts, Derold E SSgt	1659087	B-1-1	12/15/67		
Roberts, Harley R Sgt	2077470	H-2-3	7/7/68*	21	Richville, New York
Robertson, J W P LtCol		CO-3-26	11/20-12/9/68		
Robertson, Merle E LCpl	2388054		9/10/68*	19	Campbell, California
Robinette, Randall S 1stLt		HMM-161	6/9/70		

Robinson, Andrew R Cpl		E-2-3	8/10/69		
Robinson, Jimmie L LCpl					
Robinson, John C II LCpl	2236557	B-1-7	8/10/68*	21	Savannah, Georgia
Robinson, Robert GySgt		A-1-3	3/7/68		
Robson, Jon R Maj	069499	VMO-2	9/15/66	32	Tucson, Arizona
Rock, George B Sgt		1-Amp-11	2/21/68		
Rockey, William K LtCol	050776	CO-3-5	1/30/68	40	Washington, D.C.
Rodger, Donald W 1stLt		I-3-9	3/31/68		
Rodgers, Larry J Pfc	2353911	D-1-7	3/17/68*	20	Ranger, Texas
Rodrigues, David E Cpl		E-2-1	3/21/68		
Rogers, Harry W 1stLt	932445		5/14/65	40	Portland, Maine
Rohweller, Robert T 1stLt	0100638	K-3-9	2/16/69	25	Jacksonville, Florida
Rollings, Wayne E 1stLt		1-Recon	4/11/69		
Roman, Joseph G Capt	083648	HMM-265			
Romero, Robert W Capt	093402		4/28/68*	26	San Diego, California
Romig, David J LCpl		H&S-2-5	3/15/70		
Rood, Gary A Pfc	2122346	F-2-7	3/4/66	19	Toledo, Ohio
Rosolie, Walter W Cpl	2282831	A-1-5	2/13/68*	19	Rosedale, New York
Ross, Bruce J 1stLt		VMO-6			
Ross, Frank M Jr SSgt	1117022	Sniper-1-1	3/18/68*	35	Memphis, Tennessee
Ross, Michael R Capt	088020	D-2-12	5/13/69*	29	Lubbock, Texas
Ross, Reid R Jr Cpl	2395408	I-3-26	12/4/68*	19	Flinton, Pennsylvania
Ross, Ronald J Cpl	2177979	H&S-5	2/7/68		
Rosser, James E LCpl		D-1-7	4/6/68		
Rosser, Richard C Jr Capt	093408	HMM-164	7/18/68	27	North Hollywood, California
Rosser, Richard C Jr Capt	093408	HMM-164	8/1/68	27	North Hollywood, California
Rostad, Theodore W Cpl	1876996	HMM-163			
Roth, Harold B Jr Maj	054026	HMM-364	6/29/68	37	Minneapolis, Minnesota
Roth, Raymond A Jr Sgt		Inter	3/12/71		
Roundtree, Louis GySgt	662089				
Rousseau, Joel Sgt		I-3-5			
Rowden, John W Pfc	2352892	G-2-5	2/9/68*	21	Jacksonville, Oregon
Rowe, Larry E Pfc		B-1-5	6/9/69		
Rowe, Michael M LCpl					
Rowling, Lamont Sgt		E-2-4	5/25/68		
Royster, Douglas LCpl	2097047	G-2-1	6/26/66*	19	Philadelphia, Pennsylvania
Royston, Joseph E Cpl					
Rozanski, Edward C LCpl	2250985		9/4/67*	20	Chicago, Illinois
Rozumniak, David S Cpl					
Rubin, Roy G LCpl	2293045	F-2-9	3/28/69*	19	New York, New York
Ruddick, Morris E Jr 1stLt	093410	F-3-Recon	6/14/67	24	Mahwah, New Jersey
Rudisill, Thomas R Cpl					
Ruffer, Jack A Capt					
Ruiz, Jose Cpl	2282540	C-1-9	4/16/68*	24	New York, New York
Runyen, Thomas G 1stLt					
Runyon, Marvin T III 2dLt		E-2-7	2/23/69		
Rushing, James M 2dLt	0104763	K-3-7	12/16/68*	23	Pensacola, Florida
Rusnak, Robert J Cpl	2337996	K-3-9	9/9/68*	19	Johnstown, Pennsylvania
Russell, Glenn W Jr Capt		HMM-362	1/22/68		
Russell, Richard L 2dLt					
Russell, Verner R Cpl		CAP-0-1	1/21/68		
Ryan, Richard W LCpl					
Ryan, William F 1stLt	0104333	C-1-3	5/24/69	24	Buffalo, New York
Sabo, Roy T SSgt					
Sachtleben, George W Capt		H-2-9	6/5/69		
Sakowski, Eugene J LCpl					
Salles, Daniel L Cpl					

Salmon, Christopher B Capt	088969	HMM-361	9/21/67	26	MCAS El Toro, California
Salter, Martin E Jr Maj	062172	HMM-363	12/21/67	40	Greenville, Mississippi
Salvati, Ralph J Maj	07108	XO-2-5	2/4/68	34	Russellton, Pennsylvania
Sampietro, Scott B LCpl					
Sampsei, John D Pfc					
Sanchez, Jimmy P Cpl	2072279	L-3-1	3/5/66*	23	Los Angeles, California
Sanchez, Manuel Cpl					
Sanders, James M 1stLt		AO	2/8/68		
Sanders, Samuel C LCpl		CAP-2-7-1	6/17/70		
Sankey, David H Pfc		A-1-9	7/6/67		
Santos, Ruben SSgt					
Sarti, Lawrence E Sgt					
Sasek, Richard J Capt	081030		7/6/67*	30	Topeka, Kansas
Sasser, John R Sgt		E-2-9	3/24-25/66		
Sausau, Eli SSgt					
Sawyer, Kenneth V Cpl		HMM-364	10/21/69		
Saxon, Clyde E LCpl	2461616	G-2-7	3/18/69*	19	Waynesboro, Georgia
Scafidi, Vincent A Pfc		H-2-4	5/2/68		
Scalici, Dennis F LCpl		L-3-3	5/8/68		
Scalici, Dennis F Cpl		L-3-3	8/26/68		
Scanlon, Michael J Cpl	2136902	3-Recon	1/17/67*	21	Norwalk, Connecticutt
Schaefer, Charles H 1stLt	352363120	H-1-1	8/24/69*	24	Streator, Illinois
Schaper, John P Sgt		HMM-164	8/14/69		
Schatz, Robert A Sgt					
Schermerhorn, James 1stLt					
Schley, Harold B Jr SSgt		A-3-Tanks	7/28/69		
Schmidt, Joseph A Jr Cpl					
Schneider, Gerard B Cpl		D-1-5	9/10/68*		
Schneider, Harry W Cpl	2201049	VMO-5	2/16/68*	20	Janesville, Wisconsin
Schrader, Peter A Cpl	2265855	M-3-5	11/7/67	20	University City, Missouri
Schreiner, Andrew M Jr Sgt					
Schultz, Daniel R Cpl					
Schulze, Richard C LtCol	083080	CO-3-3	6/16/69		
Schwanda, Rudy T 1stLt	095386		2/23/68	24	Haddon Heights, N J
Scipio, Robert A LCpl					
Scott, Fred A LCpl					
Scriven, Woodrow Sgt		G-2-4	5/2/68		
Scully, Patrick R Jr 1stLt	0101464	K-3-9	7/17/68*	23	Chicago, Illinois
Scuras, James B 2dLt					
Sekne, Sylvester LCpl	2367097	E-2-7	4/12/69*	19	Cleveland, Ohio
Sellers, Donald T Sgt		D-1-4	2/2/68		
Sellers, Wiley J Maj	428543970	HMM-262	3/6/70		Brooklyn, Mississippi
Semenuk, JohnM Pfc					
Seminara, Charles B SSgt	121264398	E-2-3	8/10/69*	33	Syracuse, New York
Serna, Marshall J Jr Pfc		E-2-4	5/2/68		
Serrano, Francisco C LCpl		F-2-1	9/24/68		
Serrano, John R Cpl	2320960		7/28/68*	19	New York, New York
Setser, Robert 1stLt					
Sexton, Raymond D LCpl	2305797	D-1-5	2/15/68	18	Ullin, Illinois
Seybold, Gerald C 2dLt	279263320		4/28/71*	36	Concord, New Hampshire
Shafer, Eric D Sgt					
Shafer, Francis L Jr Capt	083900		3/30/68*	29	Newkirk, Oklahoma
Shafer, Leslie H Pfc	2407202	K-3-3	2/22/69*	18	Dayton, Ohio
Shainline, Thomas E Pfc	2399720	C-3-Recon	12/12/68	20	Collegeville, Pennsylvania
Shainline, Thomas E Cpl	2399720	C-3-Recon	6/1/69	21	Collegeville, Pennsylvania
Shalkosky, Marion S Jr Sgt					
Shankey, Hugh R GySgt		HMM-167	3/28/71		

Sharp, Oliver R LCpl					
Sharpe, Thomas E Pfc	2377204	L-3-27	5/18/68*	19	Emmett, Michigan
Shaver, Carl A Maj	082539	L-3-7	5/19/68	30	Plattsburg, Missouri
Shaw, James A SSgt		F-2-9	1/8/66		
Shaw, James G LCpl					
Shear, James L Pfc					
Sheehan, James P Capt					
Sheehan, John J Capt	085321	Advisor	9/14-17/68	28	Somerville, Massachusetts
Shehan, Timothy Cpl		MAG-18	2/23/69		
Shellem, Robert P LCpl	2347256	B-1-7	4/28/68*	19	Atlantic City, New Jersey
Sheridan, Robert F Maj					
Sherin, Duane V 2dLt	0100672	H-2-5			
Sherman, Edward J 1stLt		C-1-26	6/7/69		
Sherrill, Richard W LCpl	429982413	CAP-1-3-9	9/13/69*	18	Hartman, Arkansas
Sherrod, Edward H Pfc	446460283	K-3-7	9/28/6920*		Oklahoma City, Oklahoma
Shibley, Kamille K 1stLt					
Shields, John M Capt		VMO-6	6/16/66		
Shiffler, George M Jr Maj					
Shipley, Jack R Jr Cpl		A-1-Eng	3/15/68		
Shivers, Stephen L GySgt					
Shoemaker, David H Sgt	2040598	M-3-7	11/2/67*	21	San Jose, California
Shore, Samuel E 2dLt	0103795	B-1-26	6/15/68	25	Maryville, Tennessee
Shreve, Ernest L Cpl		B-5-SPB	6/30/68		
Shubert, Ronald G LCpl					
Sibilly, John R Sgt	2205959	I-3-3	9/7/67*	21	Richmond Hills, New York
Sieloff, Richard J LCpl					
Siler, Jerry E 2dLt	097889	3-Recon	1/1/67	33	Omaha, Nebraska
Silvear, Thomas A Capt					
Simmons, Herolin T SSgt	1900256	E-2-1	5/29/66	24	Ahoskie, North Carolina
Simmons, Jack E Capt		VMA-242	10/31/67		
Simmons, William N Maj	079498	HMM-161	11/25/68		
Simms, James W 2dLt	0106294	D-1-9	2/11/69	24	Carrollton, Missouri
Simms, James W 2dLt	0106294	D-1-9	2/26/69*	24	Carrollton, Missouri
Simon, Jerry W LCpl	2012697	A-1-9	5/21/66		
Simpson, Jerry I Capt		Advisor	7/30-31/67		
Simpson, Willie L LCpl		C-2-5	1/26/71		
Sims, John D LCpl		D-1-5	8/29/68		
Singer, Michael E Pfc	2367488	D-1-1	7/5/68*	19	Canton, Ohio
Sisson, Ronald P LCpl	2089489	1-Recon	12/16/65*	23	Hulberton, New York
Sites, David T Maj					
Siva, Thurlo J SSgt					
Sivak, David M LCpl			6/16/68		
Skalba, John J Cpl	2042737	D-1-1	1/5/66*	20	Detroit, Michigan
Skinner, Robert E Sgt	2316143	B-3-Recon	7/7/68	21	Winchester, Indiana
Skogland, Dale E Cpl					
Skweres, Steven W Cpl	2318296	HMM-165			
Slack, Paul D Capt	067841	Advisor	2/7/66	34	Des Moines, Iowa
Slater, Albert C Jr Capt	084435		5/13/67	26	Venice, California
Sleeper, John A Sgt	2249559	C-1-Recon			
Slocum, Danny M Cpl		3-Recon	2/16/68		
Small, Richard C Sgt	2080326	F-2-7			
Smith, Charles L Pfc	2456090	A-1-9	3/4/69*	18	Oklahoma City, Oklahoma
Smith, Clifton B LCpl	2287748	H-2-9	11/30/67*	21	Midland City, Alabama
Smith, Clyde D Maj		VMA-224	4/9/72		
Smith, Coy E LCpl		G-2-9	2/5/69		
Smith, Dennis A LCpl		D-2-12	2/8/68		
Smith, Frederick W 1stLt		K-3-5	5/27/68		

Name	Service No.	Unit	Date	Age	Hometown
Smith, George W LtCol		CO-1-9	3/18/69		
Smith, Gilbert E 2dLt					
Smith, James L Pfc	2457759	M-3-4	3/13/69*	18	Washington, Illinois
Smith, Joseph N Capt	064240	Advisor	10/27/63-4/25/64	33	Austin, Texas
Smith, Michael S Sgt		K-4-12	11/10/66		
Smith, Ralph E Cpl	2121251	D-1-5	5/12/67*	21	Conyngham, Pennsylvania
Smith, Ray L 2dLt	0102290	A-1-1	2/4/68	21	Shidler ,Oklahoma
Smith, Ray L 1stLt	0102290	A-1-1	7/7/68	22	Shidler, Oklahoma
Smith, Robert W Capt					
Smith, Ronald S LCpl		G-2-4	3/19/69		
Smith, Stanley D Sgt					
Smith, Terry L Cpl	2306818	M-3-26	2/20/68*	20	Nashville, Tennessee
Smith, Timothy J Pfc	2381891	I-3-3	9/9/68*	20	Lake Geneva, Wisconsin
Smith, William N Cpl					
Smith, William R Capt	084181	F-2-3	3/14/68	27	New Rochelle, New York
Snyder, Robert A Cpl					
Soard, Charles LCpl	2128430	C-1-5	1/29/70	22	Portsmouth, Ohio
Soderling, Jerry M SSgt					
Soldner, Dennis M Cpl	2282431	C-3-Recon	6/1/69	19	Woodside, New York
Sooter, Gary E Pfc	2133934	B-1-7	3/5/66*	19	Independence, Missouri
Southworth, Ronald H Cpl	2102784	H&S-2-2	3/31/67*	21	Massena, New York
Spahn, Jordan A SSgt					
Spainhour, Walter J Jr 1stLt	085876	A-5-Recon	9/15/66*	26	Lenoir, North Carolina
Spare, Wayne J Sgt	2312160	M-3-7	2/13/68*	20	Baltimore, Maryland
Sparks, Herbert C LCpl					
Spawn, Stanley I SSgt		VMA-223	3/29/69		
Spencer, James L Jr LCpl		F-2-5	2/6/68		
Spencer, John B Pvt					
Spencer, Thomas E Cpl		D-1-4	4/26/68		
Squires, Robert J Capt	088986	K-3-7	8/23/68		
Staggs, Daniel A Pfc		E-2-26	6/6/68		
Stamps, Oliver C SSgt	351300508	G-2-7	1/7/70*	31	Baltimore, Maryland
Stanford, Charles R 1stLt		D-2-5	12/9/70		
Stankiewicz, Kenneth D LCpl	2063870	H-2-4	8/18/65*	19	Buffalo, New York
Stansell, Breck S LCpl					
Staples, Thomas H 2dLt	0103818	H-3-7	1/29/68*	23	Petersburg, Michigan
Starbuck, Robert F Sgt	1939063	A-1-Recon	2/3/67*	25	Montgomery, New York
Starick, Michael G 2dLt		A-1-7	5/6/70		
Steadman, Henry W Maj	059087	HMM-361	11/18/65	40	Cascilla, Mississippi
Steadman, Henry W LtCol	059087	HMM-364	12/19/70	45	Cascilla, Mississippi
Steele, David L Maj	079444	HMM-263		31	Jupiter, Florida
Steinbach, Thomas R LCpl	2384229	B-1-Recon	11/29/68*	21	Texas City, Texas
Steiner, Donald E Cpl		E-2-7	8/18/68		
Stensland, William C Capt	079569	A-1-1	12/15/67	29	San Antonio, Texas
Stern, George E 1stLt					
Stevens, Ernest A Pfc	2115400	K-3-4	7/18/66		
Stevens, Michael J 1stLt					
Stevens, Walter T Cpl					
Stewart, David T LCpl		F-2-9	8/31/68		
Stewart, Marvin R LCpl					
Stick, Michael O 2dLt		D-1-4	2/2/68		
Stickel, James L Sgt					
Stinson, David T SSgt					
Stokes, Alvin Pfc	2228293	A-3-Recon	9/23/66	19	Bellville, Georgia
Stokes, Colben B Pfc	2101657	H&S-1-MPB	1/30/68*	21	Laurel, Mississippi
Stokes, Thomas A Pfc					
Stokes, Thomas M Maj	064904		2/18-22/67	35	Charles Town, West Virginia

274

Stoppa, Michael D Cpl	2122149	M-3-27	5/24/68		
Storm, Dennis M 2dLt					
Storm, Ralph D. Jr. Cpl	522527158		7/27/69*	27	Union City, California
Strahm, Robert E Pfc	2263104	F-2-9	11/17/66*	18	Kenton, Ohio
Strange, John B 1stLt		G-2-4	3/11/69		
Strange, Richard L Sgt	2039191	G-2-1	6/25/66*	24	Richmond, Virginia
Strassburg, Terry A Sgt	2345236	A-1-1			
Strehle, Ernest W Cpl	2022568	F-2-4	6/25/66*	20	Mundelein, Illinois
Strickland, Charles E SSgt		I-3-5	6/19/69		
Strickland, James M 1stLt		F-2-9	8/31/68		
Stroud, Roger L Cpl	2341655	C-1-1	7/7/68*	18	Corpus Christi, Texas
Suarez, John Pfc		I-3-4	11/25/68		
Sugg, Robert B LCpl					
Sullivan, Brian R 1stLt					
Sullivan, David O LCpl	2378304	I-3-9	2/14/69*	20	Quincy, Massachusetts
Sullivan, Hugh J Jr Sgt	1915920	C-1-3	6/5/65*	23	Allentown, Pennsylvania
Sullivan, Joseph H SSgt	1851528	C-1-7	9/15/66*	24	Dillon, South Carolina
Sullivan, Thomas J 1stLt	0102448	HMM-364	2/7/69	21	Tappan, New York
Sumner, Norman B Sgt					
Sutherland, Reginald J Cpl	102400718	CAP-1-4-6	11/10/69	21	Hartsdale, New York
Swindle, Orson G III LtCol		POW	7/7-30/69		
Swindle, Orson G III LtCol		POW	8/21-23/67		
Szymanski, John S 2dLt	1824342	C-1-4	3/23/67*	26	Trenton, New Jersey
Taber, Edward A III 1stLt		A-3-Amphib	6/18/67		
Talone, James R 1stLt		B-1-9	8/22/68		
Tatum, Harold D GySgt	1102779	B-3-Tanks	9/10/67*	35	Sandy Springs, Georgia
Taufi, Aouliolitau F LCpl	586220978	D-1-1	4/5/69*	23	Los Angeles, California
Taylor, Bayard V 2dLt		H-2-4	4/30-5/2/68		
Taylor, Billy J Cpl	2311662	CAP-1-3-3	8/2/68*	20	Wyandotte, Michigan
Taylor, James B Jr LCpl		A-3-Recon	3/20/69		
Taylor, James C Sgt					
Taylor, John S Pfc	2369008	C-1-3	5/20/69*	21	Granby, Connecticutt
Taylor, Kenneth T Capt		Advisor	7/31/66		
Taylor, Michael L Cpl		HMM-364	12/19/70		
Taylor, Richard B Capt	0700569	Advisor	10/31/63	31	Boston, Massachusetts
Taylor, Richard H Maj	076381	E-2-4	9/21/67		
Taylor, Terry W LCpl					
Taylor, William E Pfc	517606196		3/23/70*	19	Billings, Montana
Taylor, William E Pfc		F-2-9	11/30/67		
Teiken, Dennis M Cpl					
Telles, Jose A SSgt					
Tennant, Byron L 2dLt	0106684	L-3-4	2/28/69*	24	Farmville, Virginia
Tenney, Joseph R Capt	079574	K-3-5	9/6/67		Cape Cod, Massachusetts
Ter Haar, Raymond L Jr Sgt					
Terhorst, Bernard R Maj	068004	HMM-263	2/23/69	37	St. Paul, Minnesota
Terhorst, Bernard R Maj	068004	HMM-263	4/19/69*	37	St. Paul, Minnesota
Terrain, Clyde J Pfc					
Terry, Hunter M LCpl	2448732	I-3-26			
Tersteege, Paul F SSgt	1532700	D-1-1	1/24/69*	33	Tuscon, Arizona
Tharp, John J Maj		HMM-165	1/28/68		
Theer, Richard E Capt	077292	E-2-7	12/10/65	29	Davenport, Iowa
Theiss, William L Sgt					
Theriault, David G Cpl		F-2-5	2/2/68		
Thiewes, Ronald C 2dLt					
Thomas, Daniel G Cpl		A-3-Amphib	1/25/68		
Thomas, Velpeau C 2dLt		I-3-7			
Thome, Richard J LCpl					

Name	Service #	Unit	Date	Age	Hometown
Thompson, David B Sgt		1-Recon	1/11/69		
Thompson, Harvey E LCpl	2077393	D-1-5	1/5/68		
Thompson, John R Cpl					
Thompson, Leslie D Sgt	2366588	M-3-5	3/3/69*	18	Tampa, Florida
Thompson, Robert B Cpl	2275075	B-1-5	4/20/68*	22	Grants Pass, Oregon
Thompson, Stephen M LCpl	2390565	D-2-12	5/13/69*	18	Baltimore, Maryland
Thompson, Wayne W SSgt		Advisor	2/27/68		
Thoms, Robert L SSgt		D-1-5	2/15/68		
Thomson, Robert B Cpl	2190293	3-Recon	2/16/68*	20	Colorado Springs, Colorado
Thuesen, Thomas R LCpl	2375951	M-3-27	5/18/68		
Tigue, Thomas M 2dLt					
Tilghman, Richard K LCpl					
Till, Willard H Jr Pfc	2339848	E-2-9	4/23/69*	20	Raleigh, North Carolina
Tillery, Jerry T Pfc	2174609	H-2-5	2/3/68*	22	Philadelphia, Pennsylvania
Tilley, Robert O 1stLt	091071	K-3-5	9/6/67	29	San Diego, California
Timmons, Durward E Jr Cpl		I-3-5	9/10/68		
Tines, Robert W Pfc					
Tinker, John G LCpl	2295077	F-2-7	10/28/67*	19	New Boston, Illinois
Tiscia, Joseph R Jr Cpl		H&S-2-5	2/7/68		
Todd, Gary G 2dLt		D-1-5	6/24/69		
Todd, George G Cpl		G-2-7	5/7/68		
Todd, Horace B Cpl		CAP-1-3-3	8/2/68		
Todd, Larry D Cpl		11-Eng	2/2/68		
Tokarz, Anthony P 1stLt	089467	K-3-7	3/21/66	23	Fairmont, West Virginia
Tolan, Paul D Cpl					
Tolbert, Roosevelt Jr Pfc		C-1-7	12/8/68		
Tolleson, Frederic L Maj	067844	Advisor	3/19-25/71	39	Sisterdale, Texas
Tolliver, Jimmy E SSgt	1813850	VMO-6	2/16/68*	28	Cromona, Kentucky
Tonkin, Terry L		FAC-2-9			
Tonucci, Richard L Cpl	2011754	H-2-4	8/18/65	21	Derby, Connecticut
Torres, Felipe Cpl	2320197	I-3-26	12/8/68		
Torrey, Phillip Capt		A-1-5	6/9/69		
Toth, William Jr Pfc					
Townes, Raymond M LCpl		E-2-26	8/16/69		
Townsend, Gary R LCpl	2424290	F-2-5	9/30/68*	21	Orchard Park, New York
Trautwein, Henry J Jr Capt					
Trautwein, Henry J Jr Capt		C-1-1	7/7/68		
Traylor, Corey S LCpl		9-Eng	2/26/69		
Trevino, Elias Sgt					
Trivette, Marion C Jr Pvt		VMO-6	3/24/68		
Trujillo, Gilardo J Sgt		C-11-Eng	2/2/68		
Tubbs, James L Jr Cpl			1/22/68		
Tuckwiller, Frank W Capt	234601968	B-1-3	9/9/68	29	Lewisburg, West Virginia
Tully, James M Maj		Advisor	6/20-21/72		
Tully, Lester A Cpl	2221284	G-2-5	1/31/68	21	Woodville, Florida
Turner, David J 1stLt		D-2-11	3/19/69		
Turner, Earl J Pfc		E-2-4	5/17/68		
Turner, Lindsay C Pfc	248885140	E-2-3	8/10/69*	20	Edgemore, South Carolina
Turner, Willis S LCpl		D-1-9	5/27/68		
Twardowski, John M Sgt					
Tweten, Ray G LCpl					
Twilling, Henry M III LCpl	2140441	K-3-27	5/24/68		
Twohey, Richard B LtCol	577327		9/2/68		
Tyler, James H Cpl	2347958	HMM-165			
Tyler, James Sgt					
Tyson, Stuart H Cpl	2412740	M-3-5	6/7/69*	22	Norfolk, Virginia
Uhl, Thomas F Cpl	2244036		10/27/67	18	New York, New York

Name	Service No.	Unit	Date	Age	Hometown
Underhill, Herbert SSgt		C-1-7	3/28/68		
Underwood, Billy L Pfc	2340074	M-3-7	2/23/69*	20	Asheboro, North Carolina
Ungar, Thomas D Capt		VMA-121	3/30/68		
Ungerer, William P Sgt		A-1-7	2/6/68		
Upshaw, Charles R Capt	079074	HMM-364	5/0/67	34	Blythe, California
Utter, Leon N LtCol	049824	CO-2-7	12/18/65	41	Miami, Oklahoma
Utter, Leon N LtCol	049824	CO-2-7	3/4/66	41	Miami, Oklahoma
Vacca, William P 2dLt	095128	H&S-1-5			
Valadez, Robert S Pfc					
Valdez, John B Sgt	523688647	I-3-5	6/19/69*	21	Rocky Ford, Colorado
Valle, Guillermo, Cpl	084322559		9/6/70*	26	New York, New York
Vallerand, Larkin O LCpl	2113431	F-2-4	6/25/66*	21	Tracy, California
Valuzzi, Rocco F Maj	079796	HMM-463	3/31/71	33	Brooklyn, New York
Valvik, Robert A Cpl	2076561	A-1-1	2/1/68		
VanAntwerp, William M Jr Capt	075400	B-3-Amphib	9/16/67*	30	Albany, New York
Van Dyke, Gilbert E LCpl		E-2-5	5/8/66		
Vanderveer, James A 2dLt					
Van Meter, Johnny L LCpl					
Vanriper, James K Capt	089000	Advisor	8/13/66	28	Brownsville, Penn
VanRiper, Paul K Capt		M-3-7	2/23/69		
VanRiper, Paul K Capt		M-3-7	2/7/66		
Vanvalkenburgh, Edward J Jr GySgt		F-2-5	2/7/68		
Vanzandt, Ray L Cpl		D-1-5	6/2/67*		
Varelas, Alfred R LCpl	2186264	D-1-26	6/22/67		Springfield, Mass
Vargas, Manuel S Jr Capt		G-2-4	3/18/68	29	Winslow, Arizona
Vargas, Pedro R LCpl					
Varney, Ronald T LCpl	2374153	H&S-3-9	2/24/69*	21	Belfry, Kentucky
Vasel, Ralph W LCpl		CAP-1-2-4	4/12/70		
Vasquez, Jesus R Sgt	2126694		1/30/68*	20	El Paso, Texas
Vasterling, Allan C 1stLt	089002	HMM-361	8/19/66	26	Ironton, Missouri
Vaughn, Edward L Cpl	1946372	H-2-4			
Vaughn, Joe E Pfc					
Vega, Michael C LCpl					
Veitz, Scott O LCpl					
Vercauteren, Richard F 1stLt	0104377	H-2-9	2/17/69	22	Manchester, New Hampshire
Vermass, Dwight A LCpl		F-2-3	8/7/69		
Victor, Ralph G LCpl	2131887	C-1-Recon	6/16/66		
Viera, Marion SgtMaj		1-2	7/3/69		
Villalobos, Arthur G Pfc	2413041	E-2-5	5/15/69*	19	Compton, California
Vivilacqua, Theodore R 2dLt	0106177	H-2-5	5/11/69	22	Long Beach, California
Vogel, Peter J Capt	079164	HMM-163	3/31/65		
Vogelgesang, Donald A 2dLt	092012	H-2-5	10/7/66	28	Canton, Ohio
Vojtisek, James R Pfc		B-1-27	6/17/68		
VonHarten, William R LtCol		XO-1-9	3/4-5/67		
Voyles, Jerry D 1stLt					
Wade, Billy F Cpl	2061433	H-2-1	6/25/66		
Wade, Howard W LCpl		C-1-26	10/6/66		
Wade, Nicholas M Pfc		H-2-5	2/5/68		
Wade, William G LCpl	2012781	L-3-7	3/21/66*	20	Berea, Ohio
Wadley, Harold E Sgt	1192794	H-2-5	9/10/67	33	Stanley, Idaho
Waggoner, Michael G Pfc					
Wagner, John M Capt		VMA-242	10/25/67		
Wahlsten, Bruce R Cpl		B-1-Tanks	2/21/69		
Waitulavich, George J Jr Sgt					
Waldrop, Roy E Pfc		G-2-7	5/7/68		
Walker, Arthur G GySgt					
Walker, David E 1stLt	088592	HMM-161	4/21/66	25	Abington, Pennsylvania

Name	Service No.	Unit	Date	Age	Hometown
Walker, Gary W LCpl					
Walker, Victor R LCpl	2287163	L-3-9	4/30/68		
Walkley, Robert M LCpl	2365067	B-3-Tanks	3/24/69*	21	Ionia, Michigan
Wallace, Marvin C LCpl					
Wallace, Paul H 1stLt		A-1-9	4/4/68		
Wallace, Robert L LCpl		L-3-9	4/30/68		
Walls, Robert L Pfc	2340399	C-1-7	12/21/67*	18	New Orleans, Louisiana
Walsh, Robert T SSgt	1399730	HMM-361	8/10/66*	30	La Crosse, Wisconsin
Walters, Charles Cpl					
Walters, Joseph E 2dLt		M-3-5	8/9/68		
Walton, Grover W SSgt	1574776	E-2-1	5/17/68		
Wandro, James M Pfc	2482623	C-1-5	6/11/69*	19	San Mateo, California
Ward, Harold T Jr Maj	257505432	Advisor	9/16-17/63		
Ward, James R Pfc					
Ward, Joel D Capt		E-2-9	1/20-3/69		
Ward, Robert J SSgt		H-2-4	4/30/68		
Ward, Robert O SSgt					
Warmbrodt, Jon F 2dLt	0107564	L-3-26	1/25/69*	22	Santa Monica, California
Warner, James H Capt		POW	10/67-6/69		
Warshaw, Joel M Capt		VMA-242	10/31/67		
Washut, Walter J Cpl	2156755	D-3-9	5/20/67*	19	Sheridan, Wyoming
Wasko, Michael J Jr Maj		HMM-463	2/23/71		
Watington, Ralph H Jr Cpl	2104550	D-1-4	5/8/67*	21	New York, New York
Watkins, David C Maj		HMM-167	1/5/69		
Watson, Albert C Jr LCpl	2260334	F-2-26	10/15/67*	20	Mauston, Wisconsin
Watson, Michael O Cpl		G-2-7	3/24/68		
Watters, Kenneth L Cpl					
Wayand, Frederick E Cpl	2206553	HMM-165	10/10/68		Greenwich, Connecticut
Weatherholtz, Donald A SSgt		D-1-4	4/26/68		
Weaver, Dale L LCpl	2264241	K-3-9	7/17/68*	18	Honey Brook, California
Weaver, Larry H LCpl	2162182		5/3/67	18	Evening Shade, Arkansas
Webb, James H Jr 1stLt		D-1-5	5/9/69	23	St. Joseph, Missouri
Webber, Brian L 1stLt	095696	I-3-26	12/8/68*	24	Albuquerque, New Mexico
Webster, Robert E 2dLt					
Weede, Richard D Capt		D-1-4	4/26/68		
Weeks, Robert W Capt					
Wegener, Joseph B II LCpl	1930274	HMM-165	10/10/68	25	Phoenix, Arizona
Weh, Allen E 2dLt		A-3-Recon	8/4/67		
Weigand, Phillip S Capt					
Weise, William LCol	057704	CO-2-9	3/18/68	39	Philadelphia, Pennsylvania
Weiss, Peter W 2dLt	0103881	B-1-26	3/30/68		
Weldon, Bucko W Cpl		G-2-7	3/20/68		
Wells, Mashall R Capt		Advisor	4/8/72		
Wells, Robert LCpl		B-1-5	6/9/69		
Welman, Dennis W LCpl	2162886	E-2-4	8/23/66*	21	Hanska, Minnesota
Wenger, Howard W SSgt					
West, Alfred M 1stLt		HMM-362	11/4/68		
Westbrook, Emmett D Pfc					
Wetendorf, Gerald C Capt		VMA-533	10/25/67		
Whalen, Garland G Cpl	2287396	C-1-3	1/31/69*	20	Denver, Colorado
Wheeler, John B III LCpl					
Wheeler, Kenneth W Cpl	2303494	HMM-262	5/10/69*	23	Brownwood, Texas
Whipple, Oliver M Jr Maj	076023	F-2-9	3/16/67		
Whisenhunt, James H LCpl	2247981	M-3-3	4/30/67*	23	Crescent City, California
White, Bobby R Cpl		H-2-9	2/2/68		
White, David L Capt	088184	HMM-262	5/25/69	28	Memphis, Tennessee
White, David L Capt	088184	HMM-262	6/7-10/69	28	Memphis, Tennessee

Name	Service No.	Unit	Date	Age	Hometown
White, Gregory A Cpl					
White, Harry Cpl					
White, John C III 1stLt	0103886	H-2-5	11/1/68*	24	Dayton, Ohio
White, Johnel N Pfc		B-1-26	6/16/68		
White, Owen Jr Pfc	2439631	M-3-5	9/11/68*	20	Chicago, Illinois
Whitfield, Douglas W Pfc					
Whitmer, Maurice P Cpl	2157170	D-1-5	2/15/68	20	Spring Valley, California
Whitted, George L WO	099531	AO	5/5/68	37	Salem, Oregon
Whittingham, Joseph M Pfc		H-2-3	5/14/68		
Whoolery, Tracy L SSgt	1920881	C-1-1	11/1/67*	26	Baltimore, Maryland
Whorton, William S Capt	090258	Advisor	7/25/68	26	Junction City, Kansas
Whyte, Charles J Sgt	2108109	I-3-27	5/28/68*	24	Olympia, Washington
Wicks, James G Cpl		E-2-7	8/18/68		
Wickwire, Peter A LtCol	051969		7/4/67	39	Mountain Lakes, New Jersey
Wiedhahn, Warren H Jr Maj					
Wielebski, John T Cpl	2201169	A-1-26	5/23/68	20	Milwaukee, Wisconsin
Wigg, Jerry R Cpl	1694359	C-1-7	12/17/68	29	Portland, Oregon
Wiggins, Paul D Pfc					
Wildprett, William R Capt					
Wiley, Joseph F Pfc		M-3-4	3/13/69		
Wilhelm, Charles E Capt	090259	Advisor	5/5/69		
Wilke, Edward S Cpl					
Wilkerson, Steven D LCpl	2376520	M-3-7	12/26/68*	20	Wakefield, Nebraska
Wilkins, Robert J LCpl	2100350	H-2-9	12/18/65*	20	St. Charles, Missouri
Willcox, Clair E LtCol		CO-1-4	3/21-4/3/69		
Williams, Charles E Cpl		D-1-7	2/16/69		
Williams, Dempsey H III 1stLt	082159	Advisor	3/9/65*	25	Fayetteville, North Carolina
Williams, Freddy R SSgt	1433034	G-2-5	8/18/68*	32	Plains, Georgia
Williams, Gary D Pfc		F-2-9	2/28/66		Lovelock, Nevada
Williams, Howard C LCpl	2384892	A-1-1	7/8/68*	20	Gueydan, Louisiana
Williams, James L Capt		H-2-4	3/18/68		
Williams, James L Capt		H-2-4	4/30/68		
Williams, James Sgt	2088210		8/4/67*	20	Oklahoma City, Oklahoma
Williams, Johnny B Pfc	2427993	D-1-5	8/29/68*	24	Nacogdoches, Texas
Williams, Ken B Cpl					
Williams, Kenneth J Cpl					
Williams, Robert B Capt		B-1-1	12/23/69		
Williams, Terry E Cpl	2325376	C-1-1	3/18/68		
Williams, Theodore J LCpl	2266152		1/2/68	22	St. Louis, Missouri
Williams, Thomas E Jr 1stLt	0100873	HMM-262	3/5/69	25	Pensacola, Florida
Williamson, Curtis C Cpl		L-3-7	10/17/66		
Williamson, Frederick C Jr 1sLt	090498	E-2-4	3/21/66		
Williamson, Robert M Jr LCpl		B-3-Tanks	8/17/66		
Willis, Robert T 2dLt					
Willis, Theodore J LtCol		CO-1-4	4/12/68		
Willoughby, David H 2dLt	090371	F-2-9	7/29/67		
Willson, Gordon R 1stLt		B-3-Recon	3/15/66		
Wilson, Dale E Sgt		D-1-5	11/17/69	19	Troutman, North Carolina
Wilson, Donald D Maj					
Wilson, Douglas E CWO		VMA-242	10/27/67		
Wilson, Frederick J III Capt	090444	VMA-164	7/4/67	26	Wakefield, Rhode Island
Wilson, Henry L LCpl	2359352	B-1-1	5/31/68		
Wilson, Lyndol R Pfc		H-2-5	2/3/68		
Winebar, Francis E SSgt		A-1-4	8/26/66		
Winebar, Francis E GySgt		A-1-4	3/20/66		
Winecoff, David F Capt	085492		2/21/68	29	Everett, Washington
Winfrey, James A Cpl	497527494	F-2-3	8/7/69*	23	Webster Groves, Missouri

Name	Number	Unit	Date	Age	Hometown
Winston, Herbert T Maj		Advisor	6/5/69		
Winston, William O Cpl	2208724	C-1-5	5/10/67	20	Atlanta, Georgia
Withers, Charles A LCpl		B-1-7	8/12/69		
Withey, Robert R Cpl	2026895	D-1-3	7/17/65		
Witt, James P 2dLt	0106078	D-1-7	2/14/69*	21	Fairview Park, Ohio
Wojcik, Michael F Sgt		3-Amphib	5/21-22/66		
Womble, William T Jr LCpl	2168383	E-2-3	5/3/67*	18	Norfolk, Virginia
Wood, David R Sgt					
Wood, Lester E Sgt					
Wood, Walter J 1stLt	0105408	F-2-9	4/28/69	22	Chester, Pennsylvania
Woodall, John B 1stLt	093518	K-3-9	4/30/67*	23	East Alton, Illinois
Woodham, Tullis J Jr LtCol	053444	CO-3-27	5/13/68	39	Jacksonville, Florida
Woodring, Willard J Jr Maj	059686	CO-3-9	7/10/67	40	Springfield, Missouri
Woods, Sterling S Cpl	2101086	B-1-3	5/10/67*	21	Virginia Beach, Virginia
Woods, Theodore Cpl		B-1-5	6/9/69		
Worley, Thomas J Jr LCpl	2386080	G-2-9	4/21/68*	20	Detroit, Michigan
Worrel, Thomas D LCpl	311565545	A-1-Recon	4/23/70*	20	Roanoke, Indiana
Wray, Robert B Sgt	2098565	CAP-1-3-9	9/13/69	22	Winston Salem, N C
Wright, Edward R LCpl		D-1-9	2/11/69		
Wright, William F Cpl		F-2-4	8/23-24/66		
Wunsch, Michael C Capt	201349278	A-3-Tanks	7/27/69	25	Feasterville, Pennsylvania
Xavier, Augusto M 1stLt	088544	VMA-311	3/10/66	24	San Jose, California
Yale, Richard S GySgt			2/23/69		
Yates, John C Sgt		A-1-Amphib	7/14/67		
Yates, Thurman B LCpl		3-3	3/24/67		
Yeddo, Larry J Cpl	2133031	A-1-Amphi	12/5/66	21	North Bangor, New York
Yeoman, Richard J 2dLt					
Ynacay, Robert S GySgt		B-1-7	6/4/68		
Ynda, Benjamin Jr Cpl		G-2-7	9/8/70		
York, Hillous Sgt					
Young, Floyd W Cpl					
Young, Gerald V Sgt		A-1-1	10/17/67		
Young, James R LtCol		CO-3-1	3/4/66		
Yunck, Michael R Col		TAC-1-MAW	12/10/65		
Zahn, Leland D SSgt	1084924	C-1-9	4/5/67*	37	Harris, Iowa
Zaptin, Edward R 2dLt					
Zende, Floyd W LCpl		M-3-1	9/18/67		
Zeno, Stanward Jr LCpl	2147012	H-2-4	8/17/66		
Zimmerman, Edward "C" LCpl					
Zimmerman, Robert E 1stLt		L-3-5	2/22/68		
Zwicker, Ralph M III Sgt		L-3-7	6/30/66		
Zwirchitz, Dennis J Pfc	2381896		3/16/68*	20	Abbotsford, Wisconsin

NOTE:

Clyde Bonnelcyke earned two additional Silver Stars as a member of Company D, 2nd Battalion (Airmobile), 8th Army on 8/26/69 and 4/4/70.

NAVY CORPSMAN

Name	Number	Unit	Date	Age	Hometown
Bardwell, Robert J HMC		A-1-3	7/17/65		
Bates, Gilyard H HM3		BC-1-5	1/7/68		
Bollinger, Lawrence C		A-1-9	5/21/66		
Bradford, Richard			3/5/69		
Brown, Bruce E HN3	B811996		6/3/69*	22	San Francisco, California
Byrne, Conal J Jr HM3	7887094		9/21/67*	23	Drexel Hill, Pennsylvania
Campion, Charles G HM3					

Name	Service No.	Unit	Date	Age	Hometown
Cole, Alonzo P HN3					
Cooper, David					Winipeg, Ontario
Crawford, Charles H HM3	6874759		5/29/67*	26	Batavia, Ohio
Cress, Kenneth E HM3					
Davis, Blakely I Jr HM3	B304575		7/29/67*	20	Bradenton, Florida
Gibbs, Michael G HM3	7959992		4/25/67*	21	Del Rio, Tennessee
Gray, William R HN3	1383786		1/28/69*	22	Fulton, New York
Groshong, Allen E HM3	B204557		4/8/68*	20	Newport News, Virginia
Hunting, Neil HM2					
Keller, Allen N HM1					
Kirkham, Donald A HM3					
Kulas, Robert W. HM3		H&S-3-5			
Loy, James R HN	B506923		1/11/68*	20	Green Bay, Wisconsin
Luttrell, Lloyd I HN3	B202273		1/24/69*	22	Lexington, Kentucky
Machmer, James A HM3					
Mariskanish, Edward HN3	B416918		5/9/68*	19	Barnesboro, Pennsylvania
Morris, Shane A HM3	7933529	A-1-9	5/21/66	19	Carmichael, Pennsylvania
Muller, Daniel S HN3	B586711		6/4/69*	25	Pittsburg, Kansas
Peterson, Richard A HM2					
Phelps, Huger L HN3	B504280		2/10/69*	22	Greenfield, Indiana
Rackow, Andrew C HM2	B407475		8/6/68*	20	University Park, Penn
Rion, Donald J HM3	7747310	M-3-3	12/10/66*	24	Northbrook, Illinois
Schindeler, Theodoor K HN					
Schon, John E HM2	9149203		5/26/67*	20	Portland, Oregon
Smith, Robert L HM3					
Stone, Douglas D HM3		I-3-3	2/9/69		Colorado Springs, Colorado
Strunk, William L HM3	9150696		2/24/67*	32	Denver, Colorado
Tarrance, James A HN	B317129		12/4/68*	20	Jacksonville, Florida
Teague, Michael A HM3	9193333		5/2/68*	23	Brownwood, Texas
Thirkettle, Michael A HM3	6766414		11/26/67*	20	Whittier, California
Thompson, Stephen R HM3		3rd Force	2/16/68		
Trescott, Charles R HM3	5980445		5/3/66*	19	Dearborn, Michigan
Wallace, Clarence E HMC		A-1-3	11/14/68		
Watson, Donald P HM3					
Whinery, Roger L HN	B605148		6/1/67*	22	Fredonia, Kansas
Willeford, Alton W HM3					
Williamson, Michael L					

To add names and/or information to any of the medals lists a person may contact the author at 183 Steiner Road #117, Lafayette, Louisiana 70508-6000 or e-mail <redoubt@bellsouth.net>

GLOSSARY

A-gunner: assistant gunner.

AK-47 or AK: standard 7.62mm communist rifle.

Amtrac: armored amphibious troop carrier.

APC: armored personnel carrier.

Artie: slang for artillery support.

ARVN: Army of the Republic of Vietnam; a South Vietnamese unit or soldier.

Arizona Territory: hostile region southwest of An Hoa near the Que Son Mountains.

Autorotation: a rapid descending glide without engine power in a helicopter.

B-40: standard, shoulder-fired communist rocket.

B-52: a long-range heavy bomber.

BAS: battalion aid station.

Basecamp: a unit's home base.

Beaucoup: French for 'many.'

Below: downstairs.

Bird: any aircraft.

Blooper: slang for an M-79 grenade launcher. Derived from the sound it made.

BLT: Battalion Landing Team.

Blown Away: to be killed.

Body Bag: a plastic zipper bag for corpses.

Boot: a Marine recruit who is taught the rudiments by DI's.

Bouncing Betty: a mine designed to pop up and explode at waist level.

Bulkhead: a wall.

Bush: any place outside a base where contact with the enemy is a real prospect.

C-130: large cargo plane.

CAC: combined action company.

CAP: combined action platoon; joint American Marine / South Vietnamese militia units set up to protect specific villages.

Cav: cavalry; specifically, the 1st Air Cavalry Division, U.S. Army.

Charles, Charlie, Mr. Charles, Victor Charlie: slang name for the Viet Cong.

Chicom: a Chinese manufacturer.

Chieu Hoi: expression of surrender.

Chopper: helicopter.

Chow: food.

Claymore: standard, fan-shaped, antipersonnel U.S. mine.

CO: commanding officer.

Concertina: barbed wire.

Corpsman: Navy medic.

CP: command post.

C rations, or C-rats, or Cs, or rats: combat field meals packed in metal cans.

Cruise: tour of duty.

CS: nonlethal tear gas.

C-4: high explosive putty-like material.

C-130: a cargo-transport airplane.

Deck: Marine term for the floor or ground.

DI: Marine drill instructors who train boots to be effective Marines.

DMZ: demilitarized zone, dividing line between North and South Vietnam at the 17th parallel.

D.O.A.: dead on arrival.

Doc: common Marine nickname for their Navy corpsmen.

Dud: an explosive that has failed to detonate.

Duster: Army light tank of WWII vintage mounting twin 40mm Bofors air defense guns. Deployed as part of the Duster organization were quad .50 caliber machine guns mounted on trucks or directly to the ground.

Dust Off: medical evacuation

E-8: tear gas launcher.

.45: standard U.S. pistol.5

FAC: forward air controller.

Fast movers: slang for jets.

Field: any place outside a base where contact with the enemy is a real prospect.

Field of fire: an area a weapon can effectively cover.

Firebase: artillery support base.

Firefight: exchange of fire with the enemy.

Fire-mission: requested artillery support.

Fix, a: location

Flak jacket: sleeveless armored vest designed to stop shell or grenade fragments.

Flechette: canister rounds containing small steel darts.

FO: forward observer; man who directs artillery fire.

Frags: slang for fragmentation grenades.

Get it on: to fight.

Gook: derisive, common American nickname for the Vietnamese.

Greased: slang expression for 'killed'.

Grid Square: specific area on a map.

Grunt: popular nickname for the Marine combat infantrymen.

Gung Ho, Gungey: a professional, enthusiastic

Gunny: Marine gunnery sergeant.

Gunship: a heavily armed helicopter.

Halazone tablets: water purification tablets.

Hatch: Marine term for door or window.

H.E.: High Explosives.

Head: bathroom.

Helicopter Valley: the Song Ngan River Valley in northwest Quang Tri Province.

HMH: Marine Corps heavy helicopter squadron.

HMM: Marine Corps medium helicopter squadron.

H&I: Harassment & Interdiction fire.

Ho Chi Minh Sandals: crude sandals made from rubber tires.

Ho Chi Minh Trail: main NVA supply route.

Hootch: any small building; specifically, the straw huts of the peasants.

Hot LZ: enemy on landing zone.

Hot: dangerous

Huey: nickname for the UH-1D helicopter.

Humping: slang for marching with a heavy load through the bush.

H-34: an older helicopter used by the Marines.

H&S: headquarters & service unit.

HQ: headquarters.

Illumination: night fire.

Incoming: incoming artillery or mortar fire.

In-country: to be in Vietnam.

Indian Country: enemy territory.

JP-4: jet fuel.

K-Bar: Marine Corps knife

Klick: kilometer.

KIA: killed in action.

Kit Carson Scout: former Communist who defected to the allies, was retrained, and volunteered to fight alongside the Americans; usually one was assigned to each infantry platoon as a scout and interpreter.

LAAW: light assault weapon; standard, shoulder-fired U.S. rocket.

Ladder: stairs.

LCU: landing craft, utility.

Leatherneck Square: a bloody killing ground in northern Quang Tri Province.

LP: listening post

LZ: landing zone.

M-16: standard 5.56mm U.S. rifle.

M-60: standard 7.62mm U.S. machine gun.

M-79: grenade launcher.

MACV: Military Assistance Command Vietnam, overall U.S. command in Vietnam.

MAG: Marine air group.

Mechanical Mule: small, flat-bed, four-wheel vehicle.

Medevac: a medical evacuation helicopter; to evacuate casualties.

MIA: missing in action.

MOS: military occupational specialty.

MTB: motor transport battalion.

Mustang: an up-from-the-ranks officer.

Mutteris Ridge: the Nui Cay Tri Ridge in northern Quang Tri Province.

Nam: nickname for Vietnam.

Napalm: Jellied gas bombs dropped from aircraft.

NCO: noncommissioned officer.

NET: radio network.

No Sweat: no problem, easy.

Number One: first class, the best.

Number Ten: the worst.

NVA: North Vietnamese Army; a North Vietnamese soldier.

OD: olive drab.

Ontos: small tracked vehicle mounted with six 106mm recoilless rifles.

Payback: Marine term for revenge.

Phantom: F-4 fighter jet.

Piastre: Vietnamese currency.

Pogue: a Marine assigned to a rear area.

Point, Pointman: the lead man in a patrol.

Police: Marine term for 'cleaning up.'

PRC-25: radio

Puke, a: a worthless individual

Punji Stakes: sharpened bamboo stakes.

Purple Heart: a medal awarded to those wounded by hostile fire.

R&R: Rest and Relaxation, a trip out of Vietnam that every serviceman was supposed to get once during his one-year tour.

Racks: beds.

Recon: reconnaissance.

Retrograde: a night withdrawal movement.

Rock-and-Roll: slang for fully automatic fire.

Rockpile, the: a strategic 700 foot high granite outcropping in Quang Tri Province.

R.P.G.: rocket propelled grenade.

Saddle Up: an order to put on your packs and move out.

Sapper: enemy infiltrator whose job was to destroy Marine defensive positions.

Satchel Charge: explosive packaged in a canvas bag with handle.

Scuttlebutt: Marine term for 'rumors.'

Silver Star: our nation's third highest award for valor.

Seabees: Navy construction battalions.

Sea Knight: nickname for the Marine/Navy version of the CH-46 helicopter.

Short, Short-timer: soldier whose tour of duty in Vietnam was almost finished.

Short Round: an accidental delivery of ordinance on our own forces, friendly fire.

Sky Pilot: the chaplain.

Slope Head: an oriental.

Sparrowhawk: a small reaction force of Marine infantrymen.

Spider hole: nickname for enemy foxhole.

Spooky: nickname for plane mounted with rapid fire mini-guns.

Squared away: organized.

Tail-end-Charlie: the last man who covers the rear end of a column.

TAOR: tactical area of responsibility.

Tet: the Vietnamese lunar new year; specifically, the massive communist offensive launched during the 1968 Tet celebrations.

TOC: tactical operations center.

Tracer: a bullet with illumination.

Triage: the process of sorting out the wounded according to the seriousness of their wounds.

III MAF: Third Marine Amphibious Force; overall Marine command in Vietnam.

USAF: United States Air Force.

USMC: United States Marine Corps.

VC: Viet Cong; a South Vietnamese guerilla.

VMA: Marine Corps fixed-wing attack squadron.

VMF: Marine Corps fixed-wing fighter squadron.

VMO: Marine Corps observation squadron.

WIA: wounded in action.

Willie-Peter, W.P.: white phosphorous.

World, the: anyplace but Vietnam.

XO: executive officer.

BIBLIOGRAPHY

BOOKS:

Anderson, Charles R. *The Grunts*. San Rafael, CA: Presidio Press, 1976.

Anderson, Charles R. *Vietnam: The Other War*. Novato, CA: Presidio Press, 1982.

Ball, Phil. *Ghosts and Shadows:* A Marine in Vietnam, 1968-1969. Jefferson, NC: McFarland & Company, Inc., 1998.

Bartlett, Tom. *Ambassadors in Green*. Washington, D.C.: Leatherneck Association, Inc., 1971.

Baxter, Gordon. *13/13: Vietnam: Search & Destroy*. Cleveland, Ohio: The World Publishing Company, 1967.

Blakeney, Jane. *Heroes: U.S. Marine Corps, 1861-1955*. Washington, D.C.: Jane Blakeney, 1957.

Bergsma, Herbert L. *Chaplains with Marines in Vietnam, 1962-1971*. U.S. Marine Corps, 1985.

Burkett, B.G. and Glenna Whitley. *Stolen Valor*. Dallas, Texas: Verity Press, Inc., 1989.

Brandon, P.E. *Gunny*. McMinnville, Oregon: P.E. Brandon, 1995.

Camp, R.D. *Lima-6*. New York, NY: Berkley Books, 1985.

Caputo, Philip. *A Rumor of War*. New York, NY: Holt, Rinehart and Winston, 1977.

Clark, Johnnie M. *Guns Up!* New York, NY: Ballantine Books, 1984.

Conroy, Michael R. *Don't Tell America*. Red Bluff, CA: Eagle Publishing, 1992.

Corson, William R. *The Betrayal*. New York, NY: W.W. Norton & Company, 1968.

Cortesi, Lawrence. *The Magnificent Bastards of Chu Lai*. New York, NY: Zebra Books, 1986.

Cosmas, Graham A. and Lieutenant Colonel Terrance P. Murray. *U.S. Marines in Vietman: Vietnamization and Redeployment, 1970-1971*. U.S. Marine Corps, 1986.

Culbertson, John J. *A Sniper in the Arizona; 2nd Battalion, 5th Marines, in the Arizona Territory, 1967*. New York, NY: Ivy Books, 1999.

Culbertson, John J. *Operation Tuscaloosa: 2nd Battalion, 5th Marines at An Hoa, 1967*. New York, NY: Ballantine Books, 1997.

Cummings, Delano. *Moon Wash Warrior*. Rockbridge Baths, VA: Signal Tree Publications, 1989.

Ehrhart, W.D. *In the Shadow of Vietnam: Essays, 1977-1991*. Jefferson, NC: McFarland & Company, Inc., 1991.

Ehrhart, W.D. *Ordinary Lives*. Philadelphia, PA: Temple University Press, 1999.

Eilert, Rick. *For Self and Country*. New York, NY: William Morrow and Company, Inc., 1983.

Estes, Jack. *A Field of Innocence*. New York, NY: Warner Books, 1987.

Fails, William R. *Marines and Helicopters, 1962-1973*. U.S. Marine Corps, 1978.

French, Albert. *Patches of Fire*. New York, NY: Anchor Books, 1997.

Guidry, Richard A. *The War in I Corps*. New York, NY: Ivy Books, 1998.

Hammel, Eric. *Ambush Valley*. Novato, CA: Presidio Press, 1990.

Hammel, Eric. *The Assault on Khe Sanh: An Oral History*. New York, NY: Warner Books, 1989.

Hammel, Eric. *Fire in the Streets: The Battle for Hue, Tet 1968*. Chicago, IL: Contemporary Books, 1991.

Hammel, Eric *The Seige of Khe Sahn: An Oral History*. New York, NY: Warner Books,

1989.

Hax, John H. *Life of Pops*. Trumbull, CT: Unpublished, 1998.

Helms, E. Michael. *The Proud Bastards*. Carmichael Press, 1990.

Henderson, Charles W. *Marine Sniper*. New York, NY: Berkley Books, 1986.

Henderson, Charles W. *Marshalling the Faithful*. New York, NY: Berkley Books, 1993.

Hendrickson, Paul. *The Living and the Dead*. New York, NY: Vintage Books, 1997.

Herr, Michael. *Dispatches*. New York, NY: Alfred A. Knopf, Inc., 1968.

Herrod, Randy. *Blues Bastards*. Washington, D.C.: Regnery Gateway, 1989.

Hodgins, Michael C. *Reluctant Warrior*. New York, NY: Fawcett Columbine, 1996.

Jaunal, Jack W. *Vietnam '68 Jack's Journal*. San Fransico, CA: Denson Press, 1981.

Jordan, Kenneth N. Sr. *Men of Honor*. Atglen, PA: Schiffer Military History, 1997.

Kelly, Jeff. *DMZ Diary: A Combat Marine's Memoir*. Jefferson, NC: McFarland & Company, Inc., 1991.

Kimball, William R. and Roger L Helle. *Pointman*. Colfax, Iowa: Roger Helle, 1991.

Klein, Joe. *Payback*. New York, NY: Alfred A Knopf, 1984.

Kovic, Ron. *Born on the Fourth of July*. New York, NY: McGraw-Hill, 1976.

Krulak, Victor H. *First to Fight: An Inside View of the U.S. Marine Corps*. Annapolis, MD: Naval Institute Press, 1984.

Lake, Bruce R. *1500 Feet Over Vietnam*. Haverhill, NH: Almine Library, 1990.

Layne, MacAvoy. *How Audie Murphy Died in Vietnam*. Anchor Books, 1973.

Lee, Alex. *Force Recon Command*. New York, NY: Ivy Books, 1995.

Lehrack, Otto J. *No Shining Armor: The Marines at War in Vietnam*. Lawrence, KS: University Press of Kansas, 1992.

Lippard, Karl C. *The Warriors*. Lancaster, TX: Vietnam Marine Publications, 1983.

Marks, Richard E. *The Letters of Pfc. Richard E. Marks, USMC*. Philadelphia, PA: J.B. Lippincott Company, 1967.

McClary, Clebe. *Living Proof*. Atlanta, GA: Cross Road Books, 1978.

McGlone, Randall K. *Guts & Glory*. New York, NY: Pocket Books, 1992.

Miller, John G. *The Bridge*. Annapolis, MD: Naval Institute Press, 1989.

Millett, Allan R. *Semper Fidelis: The History of the United States Marine Corps*. New York, NY: The Free Press, 1991.

Melson, Charles D. *US MARINE in Vietnam 1965-73*. London: Osprey, 1998.

Meskan, Donald J. *Stranger in Two Lands: A Vietnam Diary*. Pellingham, WA: Unpublished, 1998.

Moskin, J. Robert. *The U.S. Marine Corps Story*. New York, NY: McGraw-Hill, 1977.

Murphy, Edward F. *Semper Fi Vietnam*. Novato, CA: Presidio Press, 1997.

Murtha, Gary D. *Timefighter: A Marine in Vietnam*. Kansas City, MO: GDM Publications, 1985

Nofi, Albert A. *Marine Corps Book of Lists*. Conshohocken, PA: Combined Publishing, 1997.

Nolan, Keith W. *Battle for Hue: Tet, 1968*. Novato, CA: Presidio Press, 1983.

Nolan, Keith W. *Death Valley: The Summer Offensive, I Corps 1969*. Novato, CA: Presidio Press, 1987.

Nolan, Keith W. *Operation Buffalo: USMC Fight for the DMZ*. Novato, CA: Presidio Press, 1991.

Norman, Michael. *These Good Men*. New York, NY: Crown Publishers, Inc., 1989.

Norton, Bruce H. *Force Recon Diary, 1969-1970*. New York, NY: Ballantine Books, 1992.

Novak, David and Marian. *We Remember*. Rockbridge Baths, VA: Leatherneck Cottage

Press, 1993.

O'Connor, John J. *A Chaplain Looks at Vietnam.* Cleveland, OH: The World Publishing Company, 1968.

Petteys, David M. *"Marine Helo".* Vicenza, Italy: Egida, 1995.

Puller, Lewis B. Jr. *Fortunate Son.* New York, NY: Grove Press, 1991.

Prados, John and Ray W. Stubbe. *Valley of Decision.* New York, NY: Dell Publishing, 1991.

Rhodes, John R. *Rejoice or Cry.* Danbury, CT: John R. Rhodes, 1996.

Russell, Richard A. *Hell in a Helmet.* Milford, MI: Richard A Russell, 1989.

Sasser, Charles W. and Craig Roberts. *One Shot - One Kill.* New York, NY: Pocket Books, 1990.

Shore, Moyers S. II. *The Battle of Khe Sanh.* Washington, D.C.: Historical Division, HQMC, 1969.

Shulimson, Jack. *U.S. Marines in Vietnam: An Expanding War, 1966.* Washington, D.C.: (History and Museums Division, HQMC, 1984).

Simonsen, Robert A. *Every Marine: An Oral History of a Marine Battalion in 1968 Vietnam.* Riverside, CA: Unpublished, 1996.

Simmons, Edwin H. *The Marines in Vietnam, 1954-1973.* U.S. Marine Corps.

Simmons, Edwin H. *The United States Marines.* New York, NY: The Viking Press, Inc., 1976.

Sinke, Ralph E.G. Jr. *Don't Cry For Us.* Kingsport, TN: REGS Enterprises, 1984.

Smith, Charles R. *U.S. Marines in Vietnam: High Mobility and Standdown, 1969.* U.S. Marine Corps, 1988.

Smith, S.E. *The United States Marine Corps in WWII.* New York, NY: Random House, 1969.

Solis, Gary D. *Marines and Military Law in Vietnam: Trial by Fire.* U.S. Marine Corps, 1989.

Solis, Gary D. *Son Thang: An American War Crime.* Annapolis, MD: Naval Institute Press, 1997.

Spainhour, Jud. *Carolina Marine.* Lenoir, NC: Walter J. Spainhour, 1967.

Spencer, Ernest. *Welcome to Vietnam, Macho Man.* Corps Press, 1987.

Spiller, Harry. *Death Angel.* Jefferson, NC: McFarland & Company, Inc., 1992.

Stevens, Paul D. *Navy Cross Vietnam.* Forest Ranch, CA: Sharp & Dunnigan, 1987.

Stoffey, Bob. *Cleared Hot: A Marine Combat Pilot's Vietnam Diary.* New York, NY: St. Martin's Press, 1992.

Stubbe, Ray W. *Khe Sanh: The Final Formation.* Wauwatosa, WI: A Special Edition of the Khe Sanh Veteran Magazine, 1995.

Sturkey, Marion F. *Bonnie Sue: A Marine Corps Helicopter Squadron in Vietnam.* Plum Branch, SC: Heritage Press International, 1996.

Telfer, Gary L. *U.S. Marines in Vietnam: Fighting the North Vietnamese, 1967.* U.S. Marine Corps, 1984.

Timburg, Robert. *The Nightingale's Song.* New York, NY: Simon & Schuster, 1995.

Trotti, John. *Phantom Over Vietnam.* Novato, CA: Presidio Press, 1984.

Vetter, Lawrence C. Jr. *Never Without Heroes.* New York, NY: Ivy Books, 1996.

Ward, Joseph T. *Dear Mom: A Sniper's Vietnam.* New York, NY: Ivy Books, 1991.

Warr, Nicholas. *Phase Line Green.* Annapolis, MD: Naval Institute Press, 1997

West, Francis J. Jr. *Small Unit Action in Vietnam: Summer, 1966.* Washington, D.C.: U.S. Marine Corps, 1977.

West, Francis J. Jr. *The Village*. New York, NY: Harper & Row, 1972.
Winter, Ronald. *Masters of the Art*. New York, NY: Carlton Press, 1989.

MAGAZINE ARTICLES:

Bartlett, Tom. "In the Highest Tradition." *Leatherneck,* 1965, 1999
de Borchgraves, Arnaud. "The Battle for Hill 400." *Newsweek,* Oct. 10, 1966, pp. 46-48.
Burrows, Larry. "One Ride with Yankee Papa 13." *Life,* April 16, 1965, pp. 24-unk.
Christy, Howard A. "Patrolling Hill 55: Hard Lessons in Retrospect." *Marine Corps
    Gazette*, pp. 77-80
McNiff, John. "Operation Hastings Offensive." *Vietnam,* February 1998, pp. 34-40.

FICTION:

Amos, James. *The Memorial*. New York, NY: Avon Books, 1989.
Anderson, Robert A. *Cooks & Bakers*. New York, NY: Avon Books, 1982.
Anderson, Robert A. *Service for the Dead*. New York, NY: Avon Books, 1986.
Baviello, Paul M. *Corpsman Up*. Salt Lake City, UT: Northwest Publishing, 1994.
Buonanno, C. *Beyond the Flag*. New York, NY: Tower Books, 1981.
Crew, Randolph E. *A Killing Shadow*. Greenville, SC: Artec Publishing, 1996.
Dye, Dale A. *Run Between the Raindrops*. New York, NY: Avon Books, 1985.
Gazzaniga, Donald A. *A Few Good Men*. San Diego, CA: A.J. Books, 1988.
Gillis, Gerald L. *Bent, But Not Broken*. Orangeburg, SC: Sandlapper Publishing, Inc.,
    1986.
Glick, Allen. *The Winter Marines*. New York, NY: Bantam Books, 1987.
Gorsky, K.W. Jr. *Thirteen Months*. New York, NY: Vantage Press, Inc., 1989.
Hasford, Gustav. *The Short-Timers*. New York, NY: Harper & Row, 1979.
Hiler, Craig. *Monkey Mountain*. New York, NY: Leisure Books, 1983.
Huggett, William T. *Body Count*. New York, NY: G.P. Putnam's Sons, 1973.
Rodriguez, Michael W. *Humidity Moon: Short Stories of the Vietnam War*. San Antonio,
    TX: Pecan Grove Press, 1998.
Roth, Robert. *Sand in the Wind*. Boston, MA: Little, Brown & Company, 1973.
Sasser, Charles W. *The 100th Kill*. New York, NY: Pocket Books, 1992.
Webb, James. *Fields of Fire*. Englewoods Cliffs, NJ: Prentice-Hall, Inc., 1978.

NAME INDEX